P9-CMY-042

WITHDRAWN

WITHDRAWN

The Provo Experiment

The Provo Experiment

Evaluating Community Control of Delinquency

LaMar T. Empey
University of Southern California

Maynard L. Erickson
University of Arizona

Lexington Books
D.C. Heath and Company
Lexington, Massachusetts
Toronto   London

Library of Congress Cataloging in Publication Data

Empey, LaMar T. and Erickson, Maynard L.
The Provo Experiment.
Mass.   Lexington Books
Sept. 1972   5-1-72   72-3547

Copyright © 1972 by D.C. Heath and Company.

All rights reserved. No part of this publication may be reproduced or transmitted in any form or by any means, electronic or mechanical, including photocopy, recording, or any information storage or retrieval system, without permission in writing from the publisher.

Published simultaneously in Canada.

Printed in the United States of America.

International Standard Book Number: 0-669-83857-8

Library of Congress Catalog Card Number: 72-3547

365.979
E55p

To
Monroe Paxman and Max Scott—

Two men without guile;
One, a judge of wisdom and foresight;
The other, a colleague of integrity and dedication.

30135

30132

Contents

List of Figures

List of Tables

Preface

When a description of the Provo Experiment in Delinquency Rehabilitation first appeared in the literature, it was greeted with mixed reviews. On one hand, there was favorable comment because the Experiment was one of the first attempts to provide a community alternative to incarceration for persistent delinquent offenders. Further, it was built upon a series of assumptions that were sharply at odds with most of those which had guided correctional efforts in the past. The emphasis of the Experiment upon the sociological factors associated with delinquency; its use of group techniques in which delinquents were both contributors to, and recipients of, group decisions; its emphasis upon the alteration of community institutions and its use of an experimental design attracted wide and often favorable attention.

On the other hand, the very features which were greeted with favor by some were greeted with disfavor by others. Many professionals and behavioral scientists objected to what they considered an excessive and polemical attack on the importance of psychological and personal factors. Questions were raised regarding the use of group techniques and the possibility that they were similar to those used by the Chinese in Korea. Members of the judiciary and legal profession objected to the participation of the local juvenile court in the assignment of subjects to experimental and control groups; they saw it as a serious infringement of judicial rights and privileges. And some local politicians and bureaucrats looked with disfavor on the changes in financial and operational procedures which the Experiment required.

Since that time, of course, significant and general changes, many of which lend credence to ideas suggested by the Experiment, have occurred. Because of a growing awareness of the importance of societal institutions, both in the causes and treatment of delinquency, community programs have become much more common. The legal and helping professions are inclined, increasingly, to support the need for more research and experimentation. And the use of group techniques has become such a fad that it may fall of its own weight before the strengths and weaknesses of such techniques can be appropriately evaluated.

Yet, with all these changes, two things about the ultimate fate of the Experiment are significant. First, the experimental program is dead. Despite preliminary information that its effects were salutory, and that community models were being used increasingly, local political and bureaucratic support was withdrawn even before the study was completed. Opposition from different quarters, overt and covert, was such that the program could not be continued once the experimental phase was completed.

Second, the results of the Experiment have never been published. Its long-range impact on serious offenders has never been made known. This is a significant omission which this work attempts to correct.

Specifically, it will seek to accomplish three things: (1) to make explicit the underlying assumptions and operational guidelines of the Experiment; (2) to provide a detailed accounting of the impact of the experimental program on offenders, made possible by the use of an experimental design; and (3) to provide a process description of experimental operation. This operational description will include (1) organizational characteristics and problems; (2) delinquent consumers' perceptions of the program; (3) the nature of the community response; and (4) the kinds of political opposition that were generated. It is hoped that the information generated by this study will reveal the relative merits of community programs for serious offenders and will contribute to contemporary theory and its application to field research.

Acknowledgment

This book, small compensation though it is, provides the opportunity for us to acknowledge our debts to a long list of people and organizations:

... to Judge Monroe J. Paxman, currently Executive Director of the National Council of Juvenile Court Judges, without whose courage and sustaining leadership the Provo Experiment would never have been completed, or even started; ... to the staff members of the Experiment whose remarkable dedication and lasting friendships can never be forgotten:

Max Scott, the program director, whose integrity, desire to improve, and selfless concern for others was an inspiration to all; Steve Lubeck, who devoted years of his unusual research talents to the formulation, collection and analysis of data; Jerry Rabow, who helped to conceptualize the Experiment and to give it substance and stability when it was first beginning; Ferrell Brown, who, along with Scott, was a bulwark in maintaining the operational side of the study; and Mervin White and William Yee, who assisted with the conduct of the research; ... to the funding agencies that made the research possible: the Ford Foundation, and its representatives who have since become lifelong friends, David Hunter, Mary Kohler, and Dyke Brown; the Public Health Service, Research Grant No. 14397, and Saleem Shah and George Weber of the Center for the Study of Crime and Delinquency, National Institute of Mental Health; the National Institute of Law Enforcement and Criminal Justice, Grant No. NI-050; Biomedical Sciences Support Grant, RR-07012-50, National Institutes of Health; and Charles G. Mayo, Dean of the Graduate School at USC;

... to the Utah State Juvenile Court Judges Council, the Utah State Industrial School, and the Utah State Bureau of Criminal Identification, whose unusual and wholehearted cooperation made possible the long-term follow-up of boys in this study; to the members of the Citizens' Advisory Council in Provo, and to Joan Geyer, who, in the face of long odds, worked so hard to make Pinehills a reality; ... to the young men who contributed so much in their own ways to Pinehills and to the welfare of other young men like themselves; ... to all of our university associates, especially Richard F. Curtis at the University of Arizona, and Solomon F. Kobrin and Malcolm W. Klein at USC who provided advice and counsel; ... to the Computer Sciences Laboratories at USC and the University of Arizona, the Health Sciences Computing Facility at UCLA (sponsored by National Institutes of Health Grant FR-3) for assistance and facilities; and to the Department of Sociology at Arizona for secretarial help and resources; ... and, finally, to Elaine Corry, one of those gifted and indispensable persons who makes an art out of the conduct of research and the preparation of a manuscript.

We express our gratitude to these people.

The Provo Experiment

1

Theoretical and Operational Guidelines

This chapter is devoted to a description of the Provo Experiment in Delinquency Rehabilitation as it was first set forth in the *American Sociological Review* (Empey and Rabow, 1961) over ten years ago. A resurrection of this statement is important for several reasons.

Most important is the fact that if the Experiment is to be fully understood and evaluated, the early thinking that went into it—with all its weaknesses as well as its strengths—must be fully represented. A description of the original design must not now be colored by that which has been learned in the decade since the study first began. But beyond the obvious necessity for candor, the resurrected statement can serve other functions as well.

The Provo Experiment was one of the first attempts to establish and evaluate a community alternative to incarceration for serious offenders. Community programs have since become common, reflecting significant changes in political and social, even scientific, attitudes. This description of the Experiment as it was originally conceived can now be used as a kind of benchmark against which some of the implications of a decade of change can be judged.

First of all, the Experiment illustrates some of the hazards of conducting a long-term study. During the ten or eleven years it took to actually operate the experimental program, to collect long-term follow-up data, and to analyze and to publish the findings, some momentous political and social upheavals occurred. It might be anticipated, therefore, that quite aside from the scientific merits of the study, it will be evaluated in terms of nonscientific values and standards that may differ markedly from those that prevailed when the Experiment first began. In the light of significant social change, for example, a program that itself appeared radical at its inception may appear conservative, even punitive and archaic, today. Indeed, the investigator may find, as we have found, that our own nonscientific values have changed. Hence, if we were setting up another program today, it would be different from that described below, not necessarily because we have proven alternatives, but because our own sentiments regarding the offender and his problems have changed. The point is that social, political, and scientific considerations weigh heavily in evaluations of the Experiment and greatly influence its ultimate impact.

On the other hand, it is useful to consider, while reviewing a description of the Experiment, whether significant increments have been added in the past decade to the knowledge base upon which improved correctional programs might be constructed: What new advances have been made in delinquency and

1

correctional theory? Given the trend toward community programs, what new models have been devised? What evidence is there that community programs are effective—both in terms of their help to the offender and their ability to protect the community?

Since changes have occurred in the sentiments by which the Provo Experiment will be evaluated, it will be useful to consider whether a model of its type may still be useful, or whether there are viable alternatives. Thus, an analysis of the contrasts between current demands for change and the availability of the necessary knowledge and tools by which to implement them, provides one means for considering the current state of the art.

In the remaining sections of this chapter the original theoretical and operational guidelines for the Provo Experiment will be presented. Some minor editorial changes have been made. The experimental program, for example, is described in the past rather than present tense since it no longer exists. And since the original research design was brief, it has been expanded and treated separately in following chapters.

Sociological Theory and Correctional Programs*

Despite the importance of sociological contributions to the understanding of delinquent behavior, relatively few of these contributions have been systematically utilized for purposes of rehabilitation (Cressey, 1955:116). The reason is at least partially inherent in the sociological tradition, which views sociology primarily as a research discipline. As a consequence, the rehabilitation of delinquents has been left, by default, to people who have been relatively unaware of sociological theory and its implications for treatment.

This situation has produced or perpetuated problems along two dimensions. On one dimension are the problems engendered in reformatories where authorities find themselves bound, not only by the norms of their own official system, but by the inmate system as well. They are unable to work out an effective program because (1) the goals of the two systems are incompatible; and (2) no one knows much about the structure and function of the inmate system and how it might be dealt with for purposes of rehabilitation[1] (Glaser, 1958:697; Sykes and Messinger, 1960; McCorkle and Korn, 1954). Furthermore, the crux of any treatment program has ultimately to do with the decision-making process utilized by delinquents in the community, *not* in the reformatory. Yet, the decisions which lead to success in "doing time" in the reformatory are not of the same type needed for successful community adjustment. Existing conditions

*The reproduction of the original article by LaMar T. Empey and Jerome Rabow, "The Provo Experiment in Delinquency Rehabilitation," *American Sociological Review* 26 (October 1961): 679-695, is made by permission of the American Sociological Association and the authors. Grateful acknowledgment is expressed to both.

may actually be more effective in cementing ties to the delinquent system than in destroying them (Sykes and Messinger, 1960:12-13; McCleery, 1957; Cloward, 1960; Wheeler, 1961).

The second dimension of the problem has to do with the traditional emphasis on "individualized treatment" (Cressey, 1955:116). This emphasis stems from two sources: (1) a humanistic concern for the importance of human dignity and the need for sympathetic understanding (Milner, 1959:4); and (2) a widespread belief that delinquency reflects some kind of personal pathology (Hakeem, 1958; Glaser, 1956:435). If, however, sociologists are even partially correct regarding the causes for delinquency, these two points of view overlook the possibility that most persistent delinquents do have the support of a meaningful reference group and are not, therefore, without the emotional support and normative orientation which such a group can provide. In fact, a complete dedication to an individualistic approach poses an impasse: How can an individual who acquired delinquency from a group with which he identifies strongly be treated individually without regard to the persons or norms of the system from whom he acquired it (Cressey, 1955:117)?

A successful program for such a person would require techniques not normally included in the individualized approach. Adamson and Dunham (1956) even implied that the clinical approach could not work successfully with habitual offenders. It should no more be expected that dedicated delinquents can be converted to conventionality by such means than that devout Pentecostals can be converted to Catholicism by the same means. Instead, different techniques are required for dealing with the normative orientation of the delinquent's system, replacing it with new values, beliefs, and rationalizations and developing means by which he can realize conventional satisfactions, especially with respect to successful employment.

This does not suggest, of course, that such traditional means as probation for dealing with the first offender or psychotherapy for dealing with the disturbed offender can be discarded. But it does suggest the need for experimental programs more consistent with sociological theory, and more consistent with the sociological premise that most *persistent* and *habitual* offenders are active members of a delinquent social system (McCorkle, Elias, et al., 1958: Weeks, 1958; Elias and Rabow, 1960).

Theoretical Orientation

With regard to causation, the Provo Experiment turned to a growing body of evidence which suggested two important conclusions: (1) that the greater part of delinquent behavior is not that of individuals engaging in highly secretive deviations, but is a group phenomenon—a shared deviation which is the product of differential group experience in a particular subculture (Cloward and Ohlin,

1960; Cohen, 1955; Cohen and Short, 1958:20-37; Kobrin, 1951; Merton, 1957; Miller, 1958; Shaw, 1929; Shaw, McKay, et al., 1931; Sutherland, 1947; Tannenbaum, 1938; Thrasher, 1936; Whyte, 1943); and (2) that because most delinquents tend to be concentrated in slums or to be the children of lower-class parents, their lives are characterized by learning situations which limit their access to success goals (Cloward, 1959; Cloward and Ohlin, 1960; Merton, 1955, 1957, 1959).

Attention to these two conclusions does not mean that emotional problems (Erikson, 1955) or "bad" homes (Toby, 1957; Nye, 1958) can be ignored. But only occasionally do these variables lead by themselves to delinquency. In most cases where older delinquents are involved, other intervening variables must operate, the most important of which is the presence of a delinquent system—one which supplies status and recognition not normally obtainable elsewhere. Whether they are members of a tight-knit gang or the amorphous structure of the "parent" delinquent subculture (Cohen and Short, 1958), habitual delinquents tend to look affectively both to their peers and to the norms of their system for meaning and orientation. Thus, although a "bad" home may have been instrumental at some early phase in the genesis of a boy's delinquency, it must be recognized that it is now other delinquent boys, not his parents, who are current sources of support and identification. Any attempts to change him, therefore, would have to view him as more than an unstable isolate without a meaningful reference group. And, instead of concentrating on changing his parental relationships, they would have to recognize the intrinsic nature of his membership in the delinquent system and direct treatment to him as a part of that system.

There was another theoretical problem. An emphasis on the importance of the delinquent system raised some questions regarding the extent to which delinquents are without any positive feeling for conventional standards. Vold (1951:460) has said that one approach to explaining delinquency ". . . operates from the basic, implicit assumption that in a delinquency area, delinquency is the normal response of the normal individual—that the nondelinquent is really the 'problem case,' the nonconformist whose behavior needs to be accounted for." This is a deterministic point of view suggesting the possibility that delinquents view conventional people as "foreigners" and conventional norms and beliefs as anathema. It implies that delinquents have been socialized entirely in a criminal system and have never internalized or encountered the blandishments of conventional society (Glaser, 1958).[2]

Actually, sociological literature suggests otherwise. It emphasizes, in general, that the subparts of complex society are intimately tied up with the whole (Bordua, 1960:8; Williams, 1955),[3] and, specifically, that delinquents are very much aware of conventional standards; that they have been socialized in an environment dominated by middle-class morality (Cohen, 1955:133); that they have internalized the American success ideal to such a degree that they turn to illegitimate means in an effort to be successful (Merton, 1957) or, failing in that, engage in malicious or retreatist activities (Cloward, 1959; Cloward and Ohlin, 1960; Dubin, 1959); that they are profoundly ambivalent about their delinquent behavior (Cohen, 1955:133; Cohen and Short, 1958:21; Kitsuse and Dietrick, 1959:311); and that in order to cope with the claims of respectable norms upon them, they maintain a whole series of intricate rationalizations by which to "neutralize" their delinquent behavior (Sykes and Matza, 1957).

This suggests that delinquents are aware of conventional structure and its expectations. In many conventional settings they can, and usually do, behave conventionally. But it also suggests that, like other people, they are motivated by the normative expectations of their own subsystem. Consequently, when in the company of other delinquent boys, they may not only feel that they have to live up to minimal delinquent expectations but to appear more delinquent than they actually are, just as people in church often feel they have to appear more holy than they actually are.

If this is the case, the problem of rehabilitation is probably not akin to converting delinquents to ways of behavior and points of view about which they are unaware and which they have never seriously considered as realistic alternatives. Instead, their feeling of ambivalence might be an element which could be used in rehabilitation.

An important sociological hypothesis based on this assumption would be that the ambivalence of most habitual delinquents is not primarily the result of personality conflicts developed in such social *microcosms* as the family but is inherent in the structure of the societal *macrocosm*. A delinquent subsystem simply represents an alternative means for acquiring, or attempting to acquire, social and economic goals idealized by the societal system which are acquired by other people through conventional means.

If this hypothesis is accurate, delinquent ambivalence might actually be used in effecting change. A rehabilitation program might seek (1) to make conventional and delinquent alternatives clear; (2) to lead delinquents to question the ultimate utility of delinquent alternatives; and (3) to help conventional alternatives assume some positive valence for them. It might then reduce the affective identification which they feel for the delinquent subsystem and tip the scales in the opposite direction.

Major Assumptions for Treatment

In order to relate such theoretical premises to the specific needs of treatment, the Provo Experiment adopted a series of major assumptions. They are as follows:

1. Delinquent behavior is primarily a group product and demands an

approach to treatment far different from that which sees it as characteristic of a "sick," or "well-meaning" but "misguided," person.

2. An effective program must recognize the intrinsic nature of a delinquent's membership in a delinquent system and therefore must direct treatment to him as a part of that system.

3. Most habitual delinquents are affectively and ideologically dedicated to the delinquent system. Before they can be made amenable to change, they must be made anxious about the ultimate utility of that system for them.

4. Delinquents must be forced to deal with the conflicts which the demands of conventional and delinquent systems place upon them. The resolution of such conflicts, either for or against further law violations, must ultimately involve a community decision. For that reason, a treatment program can be most effective if it permits continued participation in the community as well as in the treatment process in order to force realistic decision-making.

5. Delinquent ambivalence for purposes of rehabilitation can be utilized only in a setting conducive to the free expression of feelings—both delinquent and conventional. This means that the protection and rewards provided by the treatment system for *candor* must exceed those provided either by delinquents for adherence to delinquent roles or by officials for adherence to custodial demands for "good behavior." Only in this way can delinquent individuals become aware of the extent to which other delinquents share conventional as well as delinquent aspirations and only in this way can they be encouraged to examine the ultimate utility of each.

6. An effective program must develop a unified and cohesive social system in which delinquents and authorities alike are devoted to one task—overcoming lawbreaking. In order to accomplish this, the program must avoid two pitfalls: (1) it must avoid establishing authorities as "rejectors" and making inevitable the creation of two social systems within the program; and (2) it must avoid the institutionalization of means by which skilled offenders can evade norms and escape sanctions (McCorkle and Korn, 1954). The occasional imposition of negative sanctions is as necessary in this type of system as in any other system.

7. A treatment system will be most effective if the delinquent peer group is used as the means of perpetuating the norms and imposing the sanctions of the system. The peer group should be seen by delinquents as the primary source of help and support. The traditional psychotherapeutic emphasis on transference relationships is not considered the most vital factor in effecting change.

8. A program based on sociological theory may tend to exclude lectures, sermons, films, individual counseling, analytic psychotherapy, organized

athletics, academic education, and vocational training as primary treatment techniques. It will have to concentrate, instead, on other matters: changing reference group and normative orientations; utilizing ambivalent feelings resulting from the conflict of conventional and delinquent standards; and providing opportunities for recognition and achievement in conventional pursuits.

9. An effective treatment system must include rewards that seem realistic and credible to delinquents. They would include such things as peer acceptance for law-abiding behavior or the opportunity for gainful employment rather than badges, movies, or furlough privileges, which are designed primarily to facilitate institutional control. Rewards, therefore, must only be given for realistic and lasting changes, not for conformance to norms which concentrate on effective custody as an end in itself.

10. Finally, in summary, a successful program must be viewed by delinquents as possessing four important characteristics: (1) a social climate in which delinquents are given the opportunity to examine and experience alternatives related to a realistic choice between delinquent or nondelinquent behavior; (2) the opportunity to declare publicly to peers and authorities a belief or disbelief that they can benefit from a change in values; (3) a type of social structure which will permit them to examine the role and legitimacy (for their purposes) of authorities in the treatment system; and (4) a type of treatment interaction which, because it places major responsibilities on peer group decision-making, grants status and recognition to individuals, not only for their own successful participation in the treatment interaction, but for their willingness to involve others.[4]

Program Characteristics

The Provo Program, consistent with these basic assumptions, resided in the community and did not involve permanent incarceration. Boys assigned to it were repeat rather than first-time offenders, ages 14-18 years. In fact, many were candidates for a reformatory. Nevertheless, all of them lived at home and spent only a part of each day at Pinehills (the program center). Otherwise, they were free in the community.

Community and Official Support

The experimental program was begun with the blessing and guidance of the judge of the local juvenile court. Without his influence, in fact, it could not have existed. The judge and the program were also supported by a volunteer group of professional and lay people known as the Citizens' Advisory Council to the Juvenile Court. The operational and research costs of the Experiment were financed by county funds and a grant from the Ford Foundation.

Relations with welfare agencies and the community were informal but cooperative. This was due to three things: the extreme good will and guiding influence of the judge; the efforts of the Citizens' Advisory Council to generate community support; and the willingness of city and county officials, at least initially, to lend support to an experimental program of this type.

Community cooperation was probably enhanced by strong Mormon traditions. However, Utah County was in a period of rapid transition which began in the early days of World War II with the introduction of a large steel plant, allied industries, and an influx of non-Mormons. This trend, both in industry and population, continued throughout the life of the study. The treatment program was located in the city of Provo, but drew boys from all major communities in the county—many of which bordered on each other, ranging in size from four to forty thousand. The total population from which it drew its assignees was about 110,000.

Delinquent Population

Despite the fact that Utah County is not a highly urbanized area the concept of a parent delinquent subculture had real meaning for it. While there were no clear-cut gangs, it was surprising to find that delinquent boys from the entire county who had never met knew each other by reputation, went with the same girls, used the same language, or sought each other out when they changed high schools. About half of them were permanently out of school, did not participate in any regular institutional activities, and were reliant almost entirely upon the delinquent system for social acceptance and participation.

In the absence of public facilities, the delinquents assigned to the program were transported to and from home each day in automobiles driven by university students. Their offenses ran the usual gamut: vandalism, trouble in school, shoplifting, car theft, burglary, forgery and so forth. Highly disturbed and psychotic boys were not assigned. The presentence investigation was used to exclude these people. They constituted an extremely small minority.

Number in Attendance. No more than twenty boys were assigned to the program at any one time. A large number would have hindered attempts to establish and maintain a unified, cohesive system. This group of twenty was broken into two smaller groups, each of which operated as a separate discussion unit. When an older boy was released from one of these units, a new boy was added. This was an important feature because it served as the means by which the culture of the system was perpetuated.

Length of Attendance. No length of stay was specified. It was intimately tied to the group and its processes because a boy's release depended not only upon his own behavior, but upon the maturation processes through which his group went. Release usually came somewhere between four and seven months.

Nature of the Program. The program did not utilize any testing, gathering of case histories, or clinical diagnosis. One of its key tools, peer group interaction, was believed to provide a considerably richer source of information about boys and delinquency than clinical methods.

The program was divided into two phases. Phase I was an intensive group program, utilizing work and the delinquent peer group as the principal instruments for change. During the winter, those boys who were still in school continued to attend. Those who were not in school were employed in a paid city work program. On Saturdays, all boys worked. Late in the afternoon of each day boys left school or work, came to Pinehills, and attended a group meeting. After the meetings were completed, they returned to their own homes. During the summer every boy attended an all-day program which involved work and group discussions. On rare occasions a boy might work apart from the others if he had a full-time job.

Phase II was designed to aid a boy after release from the intensive activities of Phase I. It involved two things: (1) an attempt to maintain some reference group support for a boy; and (2) community action to help him find employment.

Phase I: Intensive Treatment

Every attempt was made in Phase I to create a social system in which social structure, peer members, and authorities were oriented to the one task of instituting change. It was felt the more relevant to this task the system was, the greater would be its influence.

Social Structure. There was little formal structure in the Provo Experiment. Patterns were abhorred which might have made boys think that their release depended on refraining from swearing, engaging in open quarrels, or doing such "positive" things as saying, "yes sir" or "no sir." Such criteria as these would play into their hands. They soon learn to manipulate them in developing techniques for beating the system. Consequently, other than requiring boys to appear each day, and working hard on the job, there were no formal demands. The only other daily activities were the group discussions at which attendance was optional.

It was theorized that the absence of formal structure would help to do more than avoid artificial criteria for release. It might also have the positive effect of making boys more amenable to treatment. In the absence of formal structure, for example, they would be uneasy and not quite sure of themselves. Thus, the lack of clear-cut definitions for behavior could help to accomplish three important things: (1) to produce anxiety and turn boys toward the group as a method of resolving their anxiety; (2) to leave boys free to define situations for themselves—leaders begin to lead, followers begin to follow, and manipulators begin to manipulate—behavior that must be seen and analyzed if change is to take place; and (3) to bind neither authorities nor the peer group to prescribed courses of action. Each would be free to do whatever was needed to suit the needs of particular boys, groups, or situations.

On the other hand, the absence of formal structure obviously did not mean that there was no structure. But that which did exist was informal and emphasized ways of thinking and behaving which were not traditional. Perhaps the greatest difference lay in the fact that a considerable amount of power was vested in the delinquent peer group. It was the instrument by which norms were perpetuated and through which many important decisions were made. It was the primary source of pressure for change.

The Peer Group. Attempts were made to involve a boy with the peer group the moment he arrived. Instead of meeting with and receiving an orientation lecture from authorities, he received no formal instructions. He was always full of such questions as "What do I have to do to get out of this place?" or "How long do I have to stay?", but such questions were never answered. They were turned aside with "I don't know," or "Why don't you find out?" Adults would not orient him in the ways he had grown to expect, nor would they answer any of his questions. He was forced to turn to his peers. Usually, he knew someone in the program, either personally or by reputation. As he began to associate with other boys, he discovered that important informal norms did exist, the most important of which made *inconsistency* rather than *consistency* the rule. That which was appropriate for one situation, boy, or group may not have been appropriate for another. Each merited a decision as it arose.

Other norms centered most heavily about the daily group discussion sessions. These sessions were patterned after the technique of guided group interaction, which was developed at Fort Knox during World War II and at Highfields (Bixby, McCorkle, 1951; McCorkle, Elias, et al., 1958; Abrahams and McCorkle, 1946). Guided group interaction emphasizes the idea that only through a group and its processes can a boy work out his problems. From a peer point of view, it has three main goals: (1) to question the utility of a life devoted to delinquency; (2) to suggest alternative behavior; and (3) to provide recognition for a boy's personal reformation and his willingness to reform others.

Guided group interaction grants to the peer group a great deal of power, including that of helping to decide when each boy is ready to be released. This involves "retroflexive reformation" (Cressey, 1955:119). If a delinquent is serious in his attempts to reform others, he must automatically accept the common purpose of the reformation process, identify himself closely with others engaged in it, and grant prestige to those who succeed in it. In so doing he becomes a genuine member of the reformation group and in the process may be alienated from his previous, prodelinquent groups.[5] Such is the ideal and long-term goal. Before it can be realized for any individual, he must become heavily involved with the treatment system. Such involvement does not come easy and the system must include techniques which will impel him to involvement. Efforts to avoid the development of formal structure have already been described as one technique. Group processes constitute a second technique.

Before a group would help a boy "solve his problems," it usually demanded that he review his total delinquent history. This produced anxiety, because while he was still relatively free, it was almost inevitable that he had much more to reveal than was already known by the police or the court. But any reluctance on his part to be honest was not taken lightly. Norms dictated that no one in the group could be released until everyone was honest and until every boy helped to solve problems. A refusal to be candid showed a lack of trust in the group and slowed down the problem-solving process. Therefore any recalcitrant boy was faced with a real dilemma. He could either choose involvement or risk attack by his peers. Once a boy did involve himself, however, he learned that some of his fears were unwarranted. What went on in the group meeting was sacred and was not to be revealed elsewhere.

A second process for involvement lay in the use of the peer group to perpetuate the norms of the treatment system. One of the most important norms suggested that most boys in the program were candidates for a reformatory. This was shocking to them because even habitual delinquents do not ordinarily see themselves as serious offenders. Delinquents, like most others, think the worst can never happen to them. Yet the tradition was clear: most failures at Pinehills were sent to the Utah State Industrial School. Therefore each boy had a major decision to make: either he made serious attempts to change or he was sent away.

The third process of involvement could only occur in a community program. Each boy had the tremendous problem of choosing between the demands of his delinquent peers outside the program and the demands of those within it. The usual reaction was to test the situation by continuing to identify with the former. Efforts to do this, however, and to keep out of serious trouble were usually unsuccessful. The group was a collective board on delinquency; it usually included a member who knew the individual personally or by reputation; and it could rely on the meeting to discover many things. Thus the group was able to use actual behavior in the community to judge the extent to which a boy was involved with the program and to judge his readiness for release. The crucial criterion for the program was not what an individual did while in it, but what he did while he was *not* in it.

The fourth process involved a number of important sanctions which the group could impose if a boy refused to become involved. It could employ familiar techniques such as ostracism or derision, or it could deny him the status and recognition which come with change. Furthermore, it could use sanctions arising out of the treatment system. For example, while authorities could impose restrictions on boys in the form of extra work or temporary detention, the group was encouraged to explore reasons for the action and to help decide what future actions should be taken. A boy might have been placed in detention over the weekend and told that he would be returned there each weekend until his group decided to release him. It was not uncommon for the group, after thorough discussion, to return him one or more weekends despite his protestations. Such an occurrence would be less likely in an ordinary reformatory because of the need for inmates to maintain solidarity against the official system. But it was possible in the Pinehills setting because boys were granted the power to make important decisions affecting their entire lives. Rather than having other people do things to them, they were doing things to themselves.

The ultimate sanction of the group was refusal to release a boy from the program. Such a sanction had great power because it was normative to expect that no individual would be tolerated in the program indefinitely. Pinehills was not a place where boys "did time."

Authorities. The third source of pressure toward change rested in the hands of authorities. The role of an authority in a treatment system of this type is difficult. On one hand, he cannot be seen as a person whom skillful delinquents or groups can manipulate. On the other hand, he cannot be perceived permanently as a "rejector." He must do everything possible, therefore, to create an adult image which is new and different.

Initially, authorities were probably seen as rejectors. It will be recalled that they did not go out of their way to engage in regular social amenities, to put boys at ease, or to establish one-to-one relationships with boys. Adult behavior of this type was consistent with the treatment philosophy. It attempted to have boys focus on the peer group, not adults, as the vehicle by which questions and problems were resolved.

Second, boys learned that authorities would strongly uphold the norm which said that Pinehills was not a place for boys to do time. If, therefore, a boy did not become involved and the group was unwilling or unable to take action, authorities would. Such action varied. He might have been required to work all day without pay, occasionally be placed in detention, or be put in a situation in which he had no role whatsoever. In the last case, he was free to wander around the Center all day but was neither allowed to work nor given the satisfaction of answers to his questions regarding his future status.

Boys were seldom told why they were in trouble or, if they were told, solutions were not suggested. To have done so would have provided them structure by which to rationalize their behavior, hide other things they had been doing, and escape the need to change. Consequently, they were left on their own to figure out why authorities were doing what they were doing and what they must do to get out of trouble.

Situations of this type precipitate crises. But whatever happened the boy's status remained amorphous until he could come up with a solution to his dilemma. This dilemma, however, was not easily resolved.

There was no individual counseling since this would have reflected heavily on the integrity of the peer group. Consequently, a boy could not resolve his problems by counseling with or pleasing adults. His only recourse was to the group. But since the group waited for him to bring up his troubles, he had to involve himself with it or he could not resolve them. Once he did, it was necessary for him to reveal why he was in trouble, what he had been doing to get into trouble, or how he had been abusing the program. If he refused to become involved, he could be returned to court by authorities. This latter alternative occurred rarely, since adults have more time than boys. While they can afford to wait, boys find it very difficult to "sweat out" a situation. They feel the need to resolve it.

As a result of such experiences, boys were often confused and hostile. Such feelings might be cause for alarm elsewhere but they were welcomed at Pinehills. They were taken as a sign that a boy was not in command of the situation and was therefore amenable to change. Nevertheless, the treatment system did not leave him without an outlet for his feelings. The meeting was a place where his anger and hostility could be vented—not only against the program, but against the adults who ran it. But when he expressed his confusion and hostility, it became possible for the group to analyze, not only his own behavior, but that of adults, and to determine where the behavior of all was leading. Initial perceptions of adults which were confusing and provoking could then be seen in a new way. The treatment system placed responsibility upon a boy and his peers, not adults, for changing delinquent behavior. Thus, adult behavior which was initially seen as rejecting could be seen as consistent with this expectation. Boys had to look to their own resources for problem solutions. In this way, they were denied social-psychological support for "rejecting the rejectors," or for rejecting decisions demanded by the group. Furthermore, as a result of the new adult image which was pressed upon them, boys were led to examine their perceptions regarding other authorities, and, thereby, learned to see those with whom they had previously had difficulties in a new, nonstereotyped fashion.

Work and Other Activities

Any use of athletics, handicrafts, or remedial schooling involves a definition of rehabilitation goals. Are these activities actually important in changing delinquents? In the Provo Experiment they were not thought to have inherent value in developing nondelinquent behavior. In fact they were viewed as detrimental because participation in them often became criteria for release. At the same time, work habits were considered vitally important. Previous research suggested that employment is one of the most important means of changing reference from delinquent to law-abiding groups (Glaser, 1958). But, such findings simply pose the important question: How can boys be best prepared to find and hold employment?

Sociologists have noted the lack of opportunity structure for delinquents, but attention to a modification of the structure (assuming that it can be modified) as the sole approach to rehabilitation overlooks the need to prepare delinquents to utilize employment possibilities. One alternative for doing this is an education program with all its complications. The other is an immediate attack on delinquent values and work habits. The Provo Experiment chose the latter. It hypothesized that an immediate attack on delinquent values, previous careers, and nocturnal habits would be more effective than an educational program. Sophisticated delinquents, who are otherwise very skillful in convincing peers and authorities of their good intentions, are often unable to work consistently. They have for too long believed that only suckers work. Thus, concentration was upon work habits. Boys were employed by the city and county in parks, streets, and recreation areas. Their work habits became one focus of group discussion and an important criterion for change. After release, they were encouraged to attend academic and vocational schools. A discussion of the work program—how it was set up, how well it worked, and whether it seemed to accomplish the objectives set for it—may be found in Chapter 7.

The Starter Mechanism: Putting the System in Motion

There are both theoretical and practical considerations relative to the purposeful creation of the social structure at Pinehills and the process by which it was developed. The foregoing discussion described some of the structural elements involved and by inference suggested the means by which they were introduced. However, the following is presented as a means of further clarification.

The first consideration involved the necessity to establish a structure that could pose realistically and clearly the alternatives open to habitually delinquent boys. What are these alternatives? They can continue to be delinquent and expect, in most cases, to end up in prison; or they can learn to operate sufficiently within the law to avoid being locked up. Acceptance of the second alternative by delinquents would not mean that they would have to change their entire style of living, but it does mean that most would have to find employment and be willing to disregard delinquent behavior in favor of the drudgery of everyday living.

Until these alternatives are posed for them in a meaningful way, delinquents will not be able to make the necessary decisions. The need, therefore, was for the type of structure at Pinehills which could pose these alternatives initially without equivocation and thus force boys to consider involvement in the rehabilitative process as a realistic alternative.

By the time delinquents reached Pinehills, they had been cajoled, threatened, lectured, and exhorted—all by a variety of people in a variety of settings: parents, teachers, police, religious leaders, and court officials. Most had developed a set of manipulative techniques which enabled them to neutralize verbal admonitions by appearing to comply with them, yet refraining all the while from any real adherence. For that reason, it was concluded that *deeds*, not *words*, would be the chief means for posing clearly the structural alternatives open to them.

Upon arrival, the first delinquents assigned to Pinehills had every reason to believe that this was another community agency for which they possessed the necessary "techniques of neutralization." It was housed in an ordinary two-story home; authorities spent little time giving instructions or posing threats. It must have seemed, therefore, that Pinehills would not constitute a serious obstacle; they could find some means to avoid involvement.

After attending only one day, a rather sophisticated boy was not at home to be picked up for his second day. Instead, he left a note on his front door saying he was at the hospital visiting a sick sister. Official reaction was immediate and almost entirely opposite to what he expected. No one made any efforts to contact him. Instead, a detention order was issued by the court to the police, who arrested the boy later that evening and placed him in detention. When he was eventually returned to Pinehills, no one said anything to him about his absence. No one had to; he did not miss again. Furthermore, he had been instrumental in initiating the norm which said that the principal alternative to Pinehills was incarceration.

A second incident established this norm even more clearly. After having been at Pinehills for two months and refusing to yield to the pressures of his group, a boy asked for a rehearing in court, apparently feeling that he could manipulate the judge more successfully than he could the people at Pinehills. His request was acted upon immediately. He was taken to jail that afternoon and a hearing was arranged for the following morning. The judge committed him to the state reformatory.[6] After that, there was never a request for a rehearing. In a similar way, especially during the first year, boys who continued to get in serious trouble while at Pinehills were recalled by the court for another hearing and assigned to the reformatory. These cases became legendary examples to later boys. Adults never had to call attention to them; they were passed on in the peer socialization process.

Once such traditions were established, they could be used in another way. They became devices by which to produce the type of uncertainty characteristic of social settings in which negative sanctions should be forthcoming but do not appear. The individual is left wondering why. For example, not all boys who missed a day or two at Pinehills were punished. In some cases, nothing was said to the individual in question. He was left, instead, to wonder when and if he would be punished. Likewise, other boys who had been in serious trouble in the community were not always sent to the state reformatory but were subjected to the same kind of waiting and uncertainty. Efforts were made, however, to make it impossible for boys to predict in advance what would happen in any particular case. Even adults could not predict this, relying on the circumstances inherent in each case. Thus, both rigidity and inconsistency were present in the system at the same time.

The same sort of structural alternatives were posed regarding work. Boys who did not work consistently on their city jobs, where they were being paid, were returned to Pinehills to work for nothing. At Pinehills, they were usually alone and had to perform such onerous tasks as scrubbing floors, washing windows, mowing the lawn, or cutting weeds. They might be left on a job for hours or weeks. The problem of being returned to work with the other boys for pay was left to them for their own resolution, usually in the group. So long as they said nothing, nothing was said to them except to assign them more work.

This type of structure poses stark but, in our opinion, realistic alternatives. It was stark and realistic because boys were still living in the community, but for the first time could sense the possibility of permanent incarceration. However, another type of structure, less stringent, was needed by which boys could realistically resolve problems and make choices. Since, as has been mentioned, peer group decision-making was chosen as the means for problem resolution, attention was focused on the daily group meetings as the primary source of information. It became the focal point of the whole treatment system.

The first group, not having any standards to guide it (except those which suggested resistance to official pressures), spent great portions of entire meetings without speaking. However, consistent with the idea that deeds, not words, count, and that a group has to resolve its own problems, the group leader refused to break the silence except at the very end of each meeting. At that time, he began standardizing one common meeting practice: he summarized what had been accomplished. Of silent meetings, he simply said that nothing had been accomplished. He did point out, however, that he would be back the next day—that, in fact, he would be there a year from that day. Where would they be? The problem was theirs.

When some boys could stand the silence no longer, they asked the group leader what they might talk about. Rather than make it easy for them he suggested something that could only involve them further: he suggested that someone might recite all the things he had done to get in trouble. Boys responded by reciting only those things they had been caught for. In his summary, the leader noted this fact and suggested that whoever spoke the next time might desire to be more honest by telling all. Boys were reluctant to do this but, partly because it was an opportunity to enhance reputations and partly because they did not know what else to do, some gave honest recitations. When no official action was taken against them, two new and important norms were introduced: (1) the idea that what is said in the meeting is sacred to the meeting; and (2) that boys can afford to be candid—that, in fact, candor pays.

The subsequent recitals of delinquent activities ultimately led to a growing awareness of the ambivalence which many delinquents feel regarding their activities. In the social climate provided by the meeting, some boys began to express feelings and receive support for behavior which the delinquent system, with its emphasis on ideal-typical role behavior, could not permit.

Eventually, the meeting reached a stage where it began to discuss the many things which occurred daily, at Pinehills and elsewhere in the community. These happenings, rather than impersonal, easily speculated-about material, were urged as the most productive subject matter. For example, many boys had reached the stage of trying devious rather than direct methods of missing sessions at Pinehills. They came with requests to be excused for normally laudatory activities: school functions, family outings, and even religious services. But, again adults refused to take the traditional course of assuming responsibility and making decisions for boys. Boys were directed to the meeting instead. This not only shifted the responsibility to them, but provided the opportunity to develop five important norms: (1) those having to do with absences; (2) the idea that the place for problem-solving is in the meeting; (3) that everyone, not just adults, should be involved in the process; (4) that if a boy wants the meeting to talk about his problems, he has to justify them as being more important than someone else's; and (5) that any request or point of view has to be substantiated both by evidence and some relevance to the solution of delinquent problems.

It became obvious that even simple requests could be complicated. Boys found themselves using their own rationalizations on each other, often providing humorous and eye-opening experiences. The climate became increasingly resistant to superficial requests and more conducive to the examination of pressing problems. Boys who chose to fight the system found themselves fighting peers. A stubborn boy could be a thorn in the side of the whole group.

The daily meeting summaries took on increased importance as the leader helped the group: (1) to examine what had happened each day; (2) to examine to what ends various efforts were leading—that is, to examine what various boys were doing, or not doing, and what relevance this had for themselves and the group; (3) to suggest areas of discussion which had been neglected, ignored, or purposely hidden by group members; and (4) to describe the goals of the treatment system in such a way that boys could come to recognize the meaning of group discussions as a realistic source of problem resolution.

The structural lines associated with the meeting eventually began to define not only the type of subject matter most relevant to change, but the general means for dealing with this subject matter. However, such structure was extremely flexible, permitting a wide latitude of behavior. Great care was taken to avoid the institutionalization of clear-cut steps by which boys could escape Pinehills. Problem-solving was viewed as a process—a process not easily understood in advance, but something which develops uniquely for each new boy and each new group.

Finally, in summary, the Pinehills system, like many social systems, had some rigid prerequisites for continued membership. The broad structural outlines carefully defined the limits beyond which members should not go. However, unlike most extreme authoritarian systems, there was an inner structure, associated with the meeting, which did not demand rigid conformity and which instead permitted those deviations which were an honest expression of feelings.

The admission of deviation within the structural confines of the meeting helped to lower the barriers which prevent a realistic examination of their implications for the broader authoritarian structure, either at Pinehills or in society at large. Boys were able to make more realistic decisions as to which roles, conventional or delinquent, would seem to have the most utility for them.

Phase II: Community Adjustment

Phase II involved an effort to maintain reference group support and employment for a boy after intensive treatment in Phase I. After his release from Phase I, he continued to meet periodically for discussions with his old group. The goal was to utilize this group in accomplishing three things: (1) acting as a check on a boy's current behavior; (2) serving as a law-abiding reference group; and (3) aiding in the solution of new problems. It sought to continue treatment in a different and perhaps more intensive way than such traditional practices as probation or parole.

Efforts to find employment for boys were made by the Citizens' Advisory Council. If employment was found, a boy was simply informed that an employer needed someone. No efforts were made by some well-meaning but pretentious adult to manipulate the boy's life.

These steps, along with the idea that delinquents should be permitted to make important decisions during the rehabilitative process, are consistent with structural-functional analysis, which suggests that in order to eliminate existing structure, or identification with it, one must provide the necessary functional alternatives (Schur, 1957:304).

Appropriateness of Techniques

Many persons disapproved of what they considered a harsh and punitive system at Pinehills. If, however, alternatives are not great for habitual delinquents, a program that suggests otherwise is not being honest with them. Delinquents are aware that society seldom provides honors for *not* being delinquent; that, in fact, conventional alternatives for them have not always promised significantly more than delinquent alternatives.[7] Therefore, expectations associated with the adaption of conventional alternatives should not be unrealistic.

On the other hand, it should be remembered that every effort was made at Pinehills to include as many positive experiences as possible in terms familiar to delinquents. The following are some which seemed to function:

1. Peers examined problems which were common to all.
2. There was a recurring opportunity for each individual to be the focal point of attention among peers in which his behavior and problems became the most important concern of the moment.
3. Delinquent peers articulated in front of conventional adults without constraint with regard to topic, language, or feeling.
4. Delinquents had the opportunity, for the first time in an institutional setting, to make crucial decisions about their own lives. This in itself was a change in the opportunity structure and was a means of obligating them to the treatment system. In a reformatory, a boy cannot help but see the official system as doing things to him in which he has no say: locking him up, testing him, feeding him, making his decisions. Why should he feel obligated? But when some important decision-making is turned over to him, he no longer has so many grounds for rejecting the system. Rejection in a reformatory might be functional in relating him to his peers, but in the Pinehills system, it was not so functional.
5. Delinquents participated in a treatment system that granted status in three ways: (1) for age and experience in the treatment process—old boys had the responsibility of teaching new boys the norms of the system; (2) for the exhibition of law-abiding behavior, not only in a minimal sense, but for actual qualitative changes in specific role behavior at Pinehills, home or with friends; and (3) for the willingness to confront other boys, in a group setting, with their delinquent behavior. (In a reformatory where he has to contend with the inmate system, a boy can gain little and lose much for his willingness to be candid in front of adults about peers, but at Pinehills it was a primary source of prestige.) The ability to confront others often reflects more about the *confronter* than it does about the *confronted*. It is an indication of the extent to which he has accepted the reformation process and identified himself with it.[8]
6. Boys can find encouragement in a program which poses the possibility of relatively short restriction and the avoidance of incarceration.
7. The peer group is a potential source of reference group support for law-abiding behavior. Boys commonly refer to the fact that their group knows more about them than parents or friends.

Summary and Implications

This statement has described an attempt to apply sociological theory to the treatment of delinquents. It concentrated not only upon treatment techniques, but the type of social system in which these techniques had to operate. The overall treatment system it described was like all other social systems in the sense that it specified generalized requirements for continued membership in the system. At the same time, it legitimized the existence of a subsystem within it—the meeting—which permitted the discussion and evaluation of happenings and feelings which may or may not have supported the overall normative structure of the larger system.

The purposeful creation of this subsystem simply recognized what seemed to be two obvious facts: (1) that the existence of contrary normative expectations among delinquent and official members of the overall system would ultimately result in the creation of such a subsystem anyway; and (2) that such a system, not officially recognized, would pose a greater threat, and would inhibit to a greater degree, the realization of the overall rehabilitative goals of the major system than would its use as a rehabilitative tool.

This subsystem received not only official sanction but granted considerable power and freedom to delinquent members. By permitting open expressions of anger, frustration, and opposition, it removed social-psychological support for complete resistance to a realistic examination of the ultimate utility of delinquent versus conventional norms. At the same time, the freedom it granted was relative. So long as opposition to the demands of the larger system was contained in the meeting subsystem, such opposition was respected. But continued deviancy outside the meeting could not be tolerated indefinitely. It had to be seen as dysfunctional because the requirements of the overall treatment system were identified with those of the total society and those requirements would ultimately predominate.

At the same time, the overall treatment system included elements designed to encourage and support the adoption of conventional roles. The roles it encouraged and the rewards it granted, however, were oriented to the peer-group and concentrated mainly on the normative expectations of the social strata from which most delinquents come: working-class rather than middle-class. This was done on the premise that a rehabilitation program is more realistic if it attempts to change normative orientations toward lawbreaking rather than attempting (or hoping) to change an individual's entire way of life. It suggested, for example, that a change in attitudes and values toward work pure and simple was more important than attempting to create an interest in the educational, occupational, and recreational goals of the middle class.

The differences posed by this treatment system, as contrasted to many existing approaches to rehabilitation, are great. Means should be sought, therefore, whereby the techniques and orientation of this project could be treated as hypotheses and verified, modified, or rejected.

In the next two chapters, the research component of the Experiment is set forth. Chapter 2 is devoted to a description of the experimental design, and to the selection of experimental and control groups. In Chapter 3, a framework is sketched for analyzing the experiment in organizational terms. By combining these two types of analyses, it will be possible to assess the outcome of the Experiment and to determine in what way the experimental organization may have contributed to that outcome.

2 The Experimental Design

The contemporary trend in corrections is away from imprisonment and toward the use of community alternatives for law violators. Yet, at a time that is marked by the importance of scientific study in other areas, the number of true experiments in corrections could almost be counted on the fingers of one hand (Wheeler and Cottrell, 1966:44). What is revealed, as a result, is the large gap between humanitarian proclivities favoring innovation and change, on one hand, and a fundamental lack of evidence, on the other, as to whether that change has achieved desired objectives. This conclusion may be underscored by the fact that what few experiments have been conducted have produced inconclusive results (Berelman and Steinburn, 1968; Empey, 1969; Empey and Lubeck, 1971). It is clear, as a consequence, that the scientific credibility of the Provo Experiment, as well as its utility in a practical sense, depends on the adequacy of its experimental design, and whether it can be shown that its effects were any more desirable than traditional approaches.

This chapter is devoted to a presentation of the experimental design that was adopted. It is broken into four major sections: (1) a presentation of the criteria that were used for selecting delinquents for inclusion in the study; (2) a description of the methods used to assign them to experimental and control groups; (3) an assessment of the comparability of experimental and control groups; and (4) a presentation of the methods that will be used to assess experimental effects both in the short- and long-run.

Selection Criteria

One consideration overrode all others in deciding which delinquents should be included in the study: the experimental program was designed to work with the more serious delinquent offender. A number of different studies had reported success rates for regular probation which varied between 60 and 90 per cent, with the modal rate at about 75 per cent (see summaries by Grunhut, 1948; and England, 1957). What was lacking, therefore, was some approach that would be more successful with those who failed on probation, and as a result were often incarcerated.

Since this particular delinquent population, universally, is of great concern to everyone, it was not difficult to obtain agreement from local officials that it should become the object of study. To be more specific, the following selection criteria were used:

1. Only repeat offenders would be chosen, except in that rare instance where a boy's first referral to court was because of multiple and serious offenses.
2. The target population would largely be 14 to 18 year-olds. Only in rare circumstances would anyone younger be chosen.
3. Overtly psychotic and severely retarded boys would not be included.
4. Boys with a record of capital offense or assaultive sexual behavior would not be included.

Once these criteria were applied, it turned out that they were applicable to a population of only about 15 per cent of all the cases coming before the Provo juvenile court during the 5 years of the study from 1959 through 1964. The remainder were either too young or did not have a history of delinquency that warranted inclusion. Further, the latter two criteria—those having to do with psychosis and serious assault—did not turn out to have much relevance since they were interpreted broadly. The presentence report was used as the basis for identifying these characteristics, and few if any boys had been defined as psychotic. Likewise, while several boys had records of sexual offenses or fighting, these were not deemed serious enough to warrant exclusion. Thus, the subjects chosen constituted a virtual enumeration of all serious offenders from Utah County for the years 1959-1964.

Once having defined the offender population, a second design problem had to do with the fact that all members of this population were not treated uniformly by officials. Some delinquents, although they had been in court before, were placed for a second, third, or even fourth time on probation. Others, because their acts were deemed more habitual or serious, were incarcerated. Provision had to be made in the design by which to account for these variations in legal response.

This was done by treating probationers and incarcerated offenders as separate correctional populations, and selecting from each of them an experimental and control group. That is, all boys assigned to probation were treated as a distinct population from which a probation experimental and probation control group were chosen. The same was true for that population ordinarily incarcerated.

Although there were obvious practical grounds for distinguishing, as we did, between the probation and incarceration populations, we did not know for certain whether the two actually differed with respect to official delinquency, either in volume or seriousness. While it is usually assumed that the incarceration population is the more delinquent, and thus the more difficult to work with, those assumptions were not tested prior to selection. Consequently, one objective of this research will be to examine them. If there were no empirical grounds for separating the two populations, then any such findings would have numerous ramifications.

In any event, the practical consequences of separation were the selection of two sets of experimental and control groups, one set for probation and one for incarceration. And, although programming would be the same for both experimental groups, it would be different for the two control groups. Moreover, when it came time to assess program effectiveness, the most relevant comparisons would be between each individual set of groups, not among all four. That is, probation experimentals would be compared with probation controls, and incarceration experimentals with incarceration controls.

Selection of Experimental and Control Groups

The following steps were taken, first, to distinguish probation and incarceration populations and, then, to select experimental and control groups from each of them. First, the research staff, along with the chief probation officer, went over the record of each delinquent coming before the court. This was done in order to determine whether he met the criteria listed above. The case file of each boy who did so was tagged so that the judge, upon reviewing the case prior to hearing, would know that the boy was a potential subject.

Second, the court hearing was held. If a potential subject was adjudged guilty, the selection process continued.

Third, the judge was then faced with a placement decision. He was asked to make this decision as though the Experiment did not exist. Where would he ordinarily place the boy? Would he continue him on probation, or incarcerate him in the state training school?

Fourth, it was after the court had made this decision that the random selection procedure came into play. The judge was provided by the research staff with two series of numbered envelopes. One series was for selecting individuals, either for the probation experimental or the probation control groups, while the second was used for the incarceration experimental or incarceration control groups.

Each set of envelopes contained randomly selected slips of paper on which were written either *experimental group* or *control group*. Assuming, for example, that the judge had decided he would ordinarily incarcerate a boy, he would then open the top envelope in the incarceration series. Depending on what was written on the slip in the envelope, he would announce his decision to the boy. If it said *experimental* group, the boy would be placed in the experimental program; if it said *control* group, he would be incarcerated. The whole process is diagrammed in Figure 2-1.

In ideal terms, this procedure was set up so that it would not interfere with the judicial process regarding the alternatives previously available to the judge. However, once that process had run its regular course, the experimental alternative became possible only through random selection. If successfully implemented, the addition of this selection device would not only permit comparison of the relative effectiveness of the new program with both of the

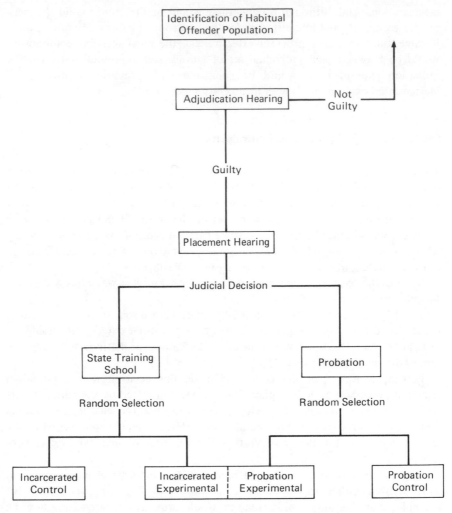

Figure 2-1. Selection of Experimental and Control Groups.

traditional alternatives, but would encourage an assessment of the impact of a range of correctional controls ranging from minimum to maximum. Thus, the judge was willing to participate in the Experiment because he felt that, in the long run, his contributions to research would far outweigh the problems associated with his participation. Although there were obvious ethical, if not legal, problems associated with the random selection of offenders, existing alternatives were probably worse, especially where incarceration was being used without assessment of its relative effectiveness. As McCorkle and Korn

(1954:94-95) point out, we have equated humanitarianism with effectiveness and failed to recognize that the humane care of offenders is not necessarily the same thing as helping them or preventing new delinquency. This study might make a contribution by evaluating the effectiveness both of a new and traditional approach.

Problems of Implementation

As is nearly always the case, emergent problems interfered with an ideal implementation of the complete experimental design just described. The reasons were twofold: first, as mentioned previously, the population of offenders who met the criteria for inclusion in the Experiment constituted only 15 percent of all cases coming before the juvenile court in Utah County, and since the court was small, this proportion was not always adequate to fill one experimental and two control groups. More important, however, was the fact that the judge had always been disinclined to commit boys to the State Industrial School.[1] That was one of the reasons he was participating in the study in the first place; he was anxious to find other alternatives for both effectiveness and economic reasons. Consequently, while those two problems did not interfere with an adequate filling of the probation experimental and control groups, the two incarceration groups were not adequately filled. The judge tended most frequently to choose the probation alternative, even for the more serious offenders, leaving the two incarceration groups without adequate numbers for comparison purposes.

By early 1962, it was clear that unless we abandoned our original randomization procedure for the incarceration experimental and control groups, the Experiment would suffer. Consequently, we did two things. First, we accepted all boys in the experimental program who would otherwise have been incarcerated, adding them to the few who had already been randomly assigned. Secondly, we took steps to choose a comparison group from the Utah State Industrial School, a group comprised of offenders from the entire state rather than the Provo court only.

An intensive analysis of the characteristics of these boys during the four preceding years (1959 through 1962) suggested that approximately 40 of them, meeting the criteria of the Experiment, were being assigned to the State Industrial School annually. Therefore, if data were gathered on this population throughout the remaining years of the Experiment, something over a hundred boys could be used to supplement the incarceration control group.[2]

Although we had no alternative but to take this step, we recognized full well that it would raise critical questions regarding this part of the experimental design. Inherent in abandoning the randomization procedure was the necessity to provide empirical evidence regarding the extent to which valid comparisons could be made between the incarcerated experimental and control groups.

Comparability of Experimental and Control Groups

In order to assess sample comparability, it was necessary to ask two major questions. The first is whether there were sufficient grounds, other than judicial decision, for separating the total population of repeat offenders into two subpopulations, one comprised of probationers and the other of incarceration offenders. Although it was hypothesized that the two subpopulations would differ significantly, evidence is needed regarding the accuracy of that hypothesis. If the hypothesis is not confirmed, then the selection of two separate sets of experimental and control groups was not appropriate, and some other basis will have to be found upon which to make comparisons.

The second question is based on answers to the first. If it can be shown that the two subpopulations did differ, it is still necessary to indicate whether the experimental and control groups selected from each subpopulation can be compared with some confidence. The hypothesis in this case is that experimental and control groups from each subpopulation *did not* differ; that is, *probation* experimentals and controls will be sufficiently similar to warrant being compared, while the same will be true for the *incarceration* experimentals and controls. The extent to which confidence can be placed in the results of the Experiment depends upon a test of this hypothesis for each subpopulation.

These two questions were examined carefully, looking not only at the offense histories of the delinquents involved but at their ages and socioeconomic statuses as well. The detailed results of that analysis, including tables and detailed statistical data, may be found in Appendix A. Only a summary of the findings is provided here.

Comparison of Probation and Incarceration Subpopulations

The detailed findings shown in Appendix A provide support for the hypothesis that the probation and incarceration subpopulations did differ. The average number of offenses per boy in the incarceration subpopulation was 7.27, as contrasted to a mean of only 4.96 offenses for the probation subpopulation. Hence, there was a large difference of 2.31 offenses between the two. Moreover, when offenses were divided into categories of seriousness, the incarceration subpopulation had committed more offenses of a high serious nature (15 vs. 13 per cent), more of a medium serious nature (64 vs. 58 per cent), and fewer of a low serious nature (21 vs. 29 per cent).[3] There were other findings which also indicated that boys who would have been, or were incarcerated, had longer and more serious histories of delinquency than probationers. Hence, based on court decision, their separation into two subpopulations for the purpose of selecting two different sets of experimental and control groups seems to have been reasonable.

Comparability of Experimental and Control Groups

The comparability of experimental and control groups was assessed first in terms of offense *frequency*. When sample means were compared, it was found that neither the probation nor the incarceration groups differed significantly (z = 1.47 and z = 1.80, respectively). However, since z scores approached significance, a test for homogeneity of variance was run. And while it was not significant for the two randomly selected probation groups ($P >$ .05), it was significant for the two incarceration groups ($P <$ .002). This finding indicated the necessity to determine whether the lack of homogeneity for the latter two groups was due to large overall differences or to the excesses of a few individuals.

An analysis of offense frequency distributions revealed that the latter explanation was the correct one. A minority of the most delinquent controls had been more delinquent than a minority of the most delinquent experimentals. Even so, tests of significance of difference between proportions at all points along the distribution from low to high rates of delinquency indicated that none of the differences was beyond the .05 level. Thus, although a great deal of caution would have to be exercised in making comparisons between the two incarceration groups, such comparisons did not seem to be ruled out entirely by these findings. Meanwhile, the two probation groups were very much alike at all points along the distribution, attesting to their comparability.

When comparability was assessed in terms of offense *seriousness*, two things were found. First, the two probation groups were virtually identical, no matter whether low, medium, or high serious offenses were being considered. The use of random selection had clearly served its purpose. Second, the two incarceration groups, where random selection had broken down, were not as much alike. Yet, it was found that, when the effects of a few extreme cases were controlled, the two groups were more alike than different. In only two of eighteen comparisons were differences beyond the .05 level. Hence, the findings again seemed to argue in favor of making cautious and conservative comparisons between the two, rather than rejecting all comparisons entirely.

There has been considerable documentation of the fact that *age* is inversely related to delinquency (cf. Glaser, 1964:36; Wilkins, 1969:54-56; Bernard, 1957:421, 444; McCord, McCord and Zola, 1959:21; Dunham and Knauer, 1954:490-96). The law violations of most young people tend to diminish as they move into adulthood. Hence, it seemed wise to make comparisons on this variable.

The mean age for all samples was about 16½. A comparison of the two sets of experimental and control groups shows that the controls in both cases were about five months older than the experimentals. Although these differences were small in substantive terms, they were significant in statistical terms ($P <$ .05). A search for the sources of these differences revealed that there were more

17-year-olds in each control group. Otherwise, differences in sample proportions at each age level were not statistically significant, nor were the rates of delinquency at each age level. Nevertheless, the findings warrant careful consideration.

If there is anything to the notion of maturational reform (Matza, 1964:22-26), the slightly older ages of the controls may tend to favor them when recidivism rates are compared; that is, they could have slightly lower delinquency rates due to the independent effects of age. Hence, steps will be taken to control for age differentials when overall experimental effects are assessed.

The final comparison involved *socioeconomic status*. A host of theorists (Cohen, 1955; Lemert, 1951; Wilson, 1970 and others) have suggested that it might have an overriding effect on correctional practices and their outcomes. Hence, the various groups were compared with respect to this variable.

The analysis revealed that the status levels of the four groups were remarkably similar. All of them were concentrated toward the lower-middle segment or upper-lower segment of the status scale, and all were highly comparable.

In conclusion, the findings provided greater support for the hypothesis of comparability for the two probation groups than it did for the two incarceration groups. It is our feeling, however, that rather than fully accepting or fully rejecting that hypothesis for the latter two groups, it should be treated as questionable, with subsequent analyses taking that categorization into account. Thus, rather than fully aborting or fully accepting any further comparisons, the procedure that would be most consistent with the data would be that of presenting comparative follow-up findings, but treating them conservatively and with reservation. If that were done, it seems to us, the advantages of comparing the two incarceration, as well as the two probation groups, would outweigh the disadvantages of omitting them entirely from the analysis.

Assessment of Experimental Effects

It would seem that where serious offenders are involved in community programs, the effects of these programs on delinquent behavior might best be assessed in two ways: (1) in the short run, while they are under direct supervision; and (2) in the long run, after they have been released from supervision. As will be seen in the next chapter, there are many theoretical reasons for this conclusion, from the standpoint of the offender as well as from the standpoint of the community. Consequently, steps have been taken to assess effectiveness in both ways.

Original plans made provision for the analysis of delinquency rates, both during and for one year after release from supervision. However, in early 1969, cooperation was obtained from all juvenile court judges in Utah, the Utah State

Industrial School, and the Utah State Bureau of Criminal Identification by which complete offense histories on all subjects to that date, both juvenile and adult, could be acquired. In addition to assessing short-run effectiveness, this enabled us to conduct a long-term follow-up study of at least four years on all boys who were released in the early years of the study. The acquisition of these longitudinal data has added immeasurably to the evaluation of the experimental program, indeed to the other forms of correctional intervention represented by the probation and incarceration control groups.

The follow-up data gathered in 1969, linked with other data we had already collected, provided us with the entire delinquency histories of subjects from their first to their last recorded offense. Remarkably few cases were lost. As indicated in Table 2-1, 341 boys were originally selected for inclusion in the study, and, of this group, only 15 boys, or 4 per cent of the total, could not be included in the follow-up.[4] Thus, the attrition rate was so small that the results should not be seriously affected.

In later analyses, both inprogram and postprogram effectiveness will be assessed in terms of recidivism rates. But, as the next chapter will indicate, recidivism rates are not the only criteria that are important. Another criterion has to do with the organizational character of the experimental program and, from the standpoint of the offender as well as the conventional person, it seemed a credible one—a program that could address some of the operational inadequacies of prior correctional endeavors. The overall effectiveness of the Experiment will be much better understood if, in fact, the two kinds of analyses are intertwined.

Table 2-1
Attrition Rates of Experimental and Control Subjects

Group	Number Selected	Number in Analyses	Percent Lost
Probation Experimental	75	71	5.3
Probation Control	80	79	1.3
Incarcerated Experimental	48	44	8.3
Incarcerated Control	138	132	4.4
Total	341	326	4.4

3 A Framework for Organizational Assessment

Chapter 1 was devoted to describing the theoretical underpinnings for the Provo Experiment and the ways they were operationalized for the purposes of intervention. It was suggested that, if delinquency is primarily a group phenomenon and if delinquents lack access to conventional successes and satisfactions, a program comprised of two main building blocks might be most successful.

The first block would be built around group techniques, designed to counteract the group forces that were hypothesized to have led to delinquency in the first place. If delinquent behavior and the rationalizations that support it are group properties, then it was suggested that groups should become both the target and the medium of change.

The second block emphasized the importance of removing some of the obstructions to legitimate achievement for delinquents. Any inclination by the delinquent to want to change as a result of his experience in the group part of the program would be met by some opportunity for him to do so in the community. In fact, the program should be a part of, not separate from, the community.

Considerable attention was also devoted to the systemic or organizational character of the new program, but neither that part of the description nor the analysis of its underlying theory was adequate. If the reader is to gain a better understanding of the Experiment, therefore, he needs a framework by which he can better contrast its character with that of earlier, more traditional, correctional organizations. The reason is that the facts about any program—what goes on in them, what fundamental problems are encountered, or even what their success and failure rates are—do not speak for themselves. Facts must always be interpreted, and the interpretation depends upon the presence of some kind of explanatory framework.

Compliance and Organizational Type

Etzioni (1961) suggests that there are three major organizational types whose contrasting characteristics might be useful in constructing such a framework. These types are *coercive, normative,* and *utilitarian* organizations.

Coercive organizations are those—prisons, custodial mental hospitals, prisoner-of-war camps—whose primary goal is the maintenance of order, and whose means of securing compliance are force and coercion. Such organizations may vary in the extent to which coercion is used, but basic to the operation of all of them has been the assumption that strong controls are a necessity. Unless an organization can immobilize offenders, usually by physical restraint and caste-like relations between them and staff members, it will not be able to realize other important objectives.

As Etzioni (1961:72-3) suggests, these goals and means are negative. Such organizations are concerned primarily with preventing the reoccurrence of certain events rather than producing an object or service. All are predominantly order-oriented.

Normative organizations, in contrast, are organizations in which normative power is the major source of control. Compliance rests primarily on the internalization of rules that most participants see as legitimate, and to which, as a result, they are willing to make a personal commitment. The techniques for control rest on learning and socialization, on the quality of leadership, on acceptance of an ideology, and on the manipulation of the symbols of social prestige more than on coercion and force (Etzioni, 1961:40).

The goals of normative organizations are what Etzioni (1961:73) calls "culture goals"; that is, they are concerned (1) with the transmission or creation of culture through the sciences and arts; (2) with applying existing knowledge for the purposes of social betterment; or (3) with meeting the needs of people for affiliation with groups of their own choosing. As examples of normative organizations, universities are concerned with education and the generation of new knowledge; hospitals are concerned with curing the sick; and churches are concerned with maintaining and transmitting the moral and social orders. A therapeutic mental hospital, or an innovative correctional organization, might even be defined as a normative organization to the extent that it is concerned with applying new knowledge to the task of restoring the mental patient or deviant to a legitimate role in society. The classification of such an organization as normative, however, would depend on its primary goals and upon the techniques it uses to resocialize the individual.

The third type of organization—the *utilitarian* organization—has economic goals. It is concerned with the production of goods and services for pay. Thus, its major means of social control come through remunerative power such as the manipulation of wages, fringe benefits, working conditions, and similar rewards (Etzioni, 1961:31-2). While involvement in such organizations may vary from mild alienation to mild commitment, it is a kind of calculative or rational involvement in which the primary concern is with financial reward. Manufacturing industries, banks, insurance companies, restaurants, and even such governmental organizations as the Post Office, are all utilitarian organizations.

Obviously, there is considerable overlap among these three organizational types and the methods they use to exercise social control. For example, Etzioni (1961:32) points out that in utilitarian organizations, remunerative power—wages and benefits—are presumably the major means by which order is maintained. Yet much of the work done by such people as teachers, nurses, or scientists takes place in normative organizations, where, in addition to financial rewards, there are satisfactions inherent in the nature of the work roles themselves. Moreover, such people as students or patients are usually members of these organizations even though they do not receive pay for their participation. Instead, they seek organizational services and other benefits which are found for the most part only in normative organizations. Thus, because organizations are often mixed rather than pure types, any classification of them as totally coercive, normative, or utilitarian is not wholly accurate. Nevertheless, such a classification does possess considerable potential for our concern with characterizing the nature of the Provo organization and assessing its impact.

The Experiment and Social Order

The first benefit has to do with the relationship of the Experiment to the maintenance of social order. Although any number of euphemistic terms are used to describe the purposes for which correctional organizations exist, and the methods they use, all of them are concerned, in the last analysis, with the problem of securing the compliance of offenders with organizational and societal rules. In the case of the Provo Experiment, for example, outside observers often expressed initial interest in the innovative aspects of the program but in the end usually returned to this one overriding issue. Some observers did not think the experimental organization was coercive enough. They saw it as an invitation to disaster because it had sacrificed physical or residential controls and because offenders exercised considerable power in it. The organization was more likely to produce chaos, they thought, than order. Other observers felt that the program was too coercive, too concerned with order. Rather than fostering new roles and prospects for offenders, it had only substituted new, and even sinister, methods for controlling them.

These polar points of view often seemed to imply that the main issue was one of no order at all versus an excessively high degree of order. But that was not really the main issue; the terms were too simple. Etzioni's analysis (1961) suggests that it is not the presence of social rules that seems to be the primary issue in distinguishing among organizational types; social order of some kind is present in every organization—coercive, normative, or utilitarian. Rather, it is the goals for which any social order exists and the relatively different ways it is maintained, that seem to be of crucial importance.

In coercive organizations, for example, order is an end in itself; it is the primary reason for which such organizations exist. In normative and utilitarian organizations, by contrast, social order is a means to other ends—the production of services or objects. To be sure, such organizations are often rigid and unresponsive to need, but, in a relative sense, they are much more concerned with the ways in which rules can be used to achieve other objectives than coercive organizations. Moreover, the pursuit of these other objectives seems far more successful in facilitating the socialization of members and in ensuring their commitments to the social order, than do coercive organizations.

The fact that normative organizations are concerned with the creation of new ideas, with learning, or with the alleviation of human ills, not only seems to meet obvious social needs, but is inherently more satisfying to members. In a similar way, utilitarian organizations, with all their problems, not only perform important economic functions but provide more rewards than do coercive organizations for compliance to rules.

Given these considerations, it is clear that observers of the Experiment were right in implying the need to examine the organizational character of the new program. But in order to do so, more than a superficial analysis would be required. It would be necessary to sort out the extent to which coercive, normative, and even utilitarian features were incorporated into its structure, how it was seen by delinquents, and whether it was more functional than traditional organizations in bringing about offender and community change. Until such an evaluation is made, in fact, excessive concern over recidivism rates may be misplaced. Until one can understand the nature of a correctional organization, an analysis of its impact can have very little meaning. Hence, our later examination of recidivism rates will be intertwined with an examination of the organizational character of the Experiment itself.

Organizational Goals

One clue as to the character of the experimental organization can be gleaned from its announced objectives. The first was traditional. The Experiment was designed to reduce delinquency. Thus, in a formal sense, this order goal was not different from that of any other correctional organization. However, the location of the Experiment in the community, its nonresidential character, and its lack of physical controls automatically precluded total reliance on coercion as a means of achieving it. Hence, if the formal objective of delinquency reduction were to be realized, it is clear that the pursuit of order could not be an end in itself. Other kinds of goals would have to be sought.

One of these was normative in character. By using group techniques, by seeking to reduce the social distance between staff and offenders, and by granting the power to offenders to be involved in making important decisions, an attempt was made to increase the normative power of the organization. Through increased participation by delinquents in the program, it was hoped that they would be more inclined to legitimate and internalize organizational and societal rules, and to make a personal commitment to them.

Another goal was utilitarian. By having a city work program, by paying wages for it, and by seeking employment for boys after they left the program, some remunerative rewards were provided. Hypothetically, these rewards and the utilitarian work activities associated with them would also enhance the noncoercive power of the organization, and perhaps help to develop a more willing commitment to conventional rather than delinquent behavior.

The major question as to whether these latter goals could be achieved, however, is the fact that the organization on occasion was coercive. In order to secure compliance to a few basic rules, some use of negative sanctions was made. Hence, the organization was, at best, a mixed one—possessing characteristics that were at times normative, at times utilitarian, and at times coercive. There is no question that it was much different from traditional places of incarceration where coercion is more in evidence, but whether it was more successful in terms of delinquency reduction, and more desirable in terms of the welfare of delinquents themselves, is another matter.

Rules of the Game

In more specific terms, another set of questions has to do with the rules of the new correctional game that was played at Provo. What rationale lay behind their use? What were they like? And how well did they foster socialization and organizational solidarity as well as predictability and order?

In terms of a rationale, it was hypothesized that, if adequate substitutes for the force and physical restraints of the coercive organization were to be found, greater attention would have to be devoted to the development of social and psychological alternatives—to the cultivation of internalized normative constraints. Although some forms of coercion might be necessary to control extreme behavior, the correctional experience would have a more lasting effect if it were based on the internalization of rules that most members of the organization saw as legitimate.

This was a large order to fill. Given the fact that the Provo Experiment represented a radical departure from correctional tradition, there were few guidelines and precious little theory upon which to rely in trying to develop new kinds of organizational rules. Moreover, the assumptions underlying the Experiment were highly ambitious in the sense that they indicated that delinquents should be active participants in the development of many of these rules. In a sense, an attempt was being made to start a small social movement in which community, as well as organizational, change might be the result, and in which delinquents along with staff would be key members. This explains why it was not mere compliance to a long list of formal rules that was sought, but the development of, and commitment to, an ideology that might portend a more functional way for dealing with the problems of youthful deviance.

While he failed to provide specific guidelines, Cohen (1955:61) has outlined

the conditions that seem to give rise to new and collective forms of adjustment—
conditions that seem to parallel very closely those that prevailed when the Provo
Experiment was set up. Said Cohen:

The crucial condition for the emergence, of new cultural forms is the existence,
in effective interaction with one another, of a number of actors with similar
problems of adjustment. These may be the entire membership of a group or only
certain members, similarly circumstanced, within the group. Among the conceiv-
able solutions to their problems may be one which is not yet embodied in action
and which does not, therefore, exist as a cultural model. . . .

. . . For the actor with problems of adjustment which cannot be resolved within
the frame of reference of the established culture, each response of the other to
what the actor says and does is a clue to the directions in which change may
proceed further in a way congenial to the other and to the the direction in which
change will lack social support. And if the probing gesture is motivated by
tensions common to other participants, it is likely to initiate a process of mutual
exploration and joint elaboration of a new solution. . . .

. . . We may think of this process as one of mutual conversion. The important
thing to remember is that we do not first convert ourselves and then others. The
acceptability of an idea to oneself depends upon its acceptability to others.
Converting the other is part of the process of converting oneself.

According to Cohen, then, the experimental program might well be engaged in
developing a new correctional model, a model not then in existence, but one
which might be more successful than previous ones in achieving correctional
goals. There were two major problems, however, that had to be faced in trying
to develop any such model.

The first had to do with the fact that delinquents would be assigned
involuntarily, not voluntarily, to membership in the organization. As a result,
the organization would be in a double bind. Given a choice, few delinquents
would elect membership; even less likely would they subject themselves to the
pains and time associated with serious involvement. On the other hand, there
was the expectation by legal authorities, if not the larger community, that
participation by delinquents would be mandatory, especially since it was often
in lieu of incarceration for many of them. Some means for dealing with this
problem had to be found.

A second problem had to do with the efforts that were made to develop the
normative character of the organization. Even though it was felt that delinquents
should play a participatory role, their abilities to do so would be hampered by
the fact that their membership in the organization would be of short duration.
The only permanent members would be the staff.

The problem was analogous to that faced by many universities and other
normative organizations today where transitory members such as students play
an increasingly important role. While such persons have legitimate reasons for

exercising greater amounts of power and influence, their capacity to contribute is often hampered by an inadequate knowledge of, and prior experience in, these organizations. As a result, they often make changes and put new practices into motion with which they do not have to live later on. Because they are concerned with the immediate future, they sometimes fail to recognize the long-range implications of their acts and decisions. In other words, while it was clearly desirable to have delinquents play a participatory role in the Provo Experiment, it was also necessary to establish means by which organizational stability and continuity could be maintained.

The Ground Rules

When working with delinquents, attempts to reconcile these two demands are like walking a tightrope. While one is always well advised to leave as much latitude as possible for individual variation and for meeting unique problems, one is forced to recognize that organizational needs are also important. An organization, like an individual, needs sustenance. At times, in fact, organizational and individual needs are in direct conflict. If, as Cohen (1966:4-5) implies, a group of delinquents (and staff) is asked to commit itself to the pursuit of difficult and trying goals, it must have confidence in the rules which govern that pursuit and must be reassured that others will play by the same set of rules. Otherwise trust is undermined and the organization is weakened. As a consequence, steps were taken to define a short list of three basic ground rules that would serve as boundary-maintaining norms. These norms were essentially proscriptive in character, indicating those kinds of behavior that would be required for continued membership in the organization.

The first norm reflected the legal position of the delinquent. As ordered by the court, he would be required to attend the program regularly. Very few excuses for nonattendance would be accepted.

The second specified that no physical violence would be tolerated. Not only is physical aggression, or the threat of aggression, quite common among delinquent boys, but it is especially likely to occur in a program where the free expression of feelings and opinions was to be encouraged.

It is also true that in most correctional programs a few strong and aggressive boys attempt to dominate others through physical force. Hence, steps had to be taken, not only to prevent these acts within the program, but to prevent their occurrence in the community. The whole experimental endeavor might be endangered by a very few individuals if some limits on violent behavior were not set.

The third, and final, ground rule was more amorphous. It specified that, over time, a decrease in delinquent behavior would be required. On one hand, it seemed unrealistic to expect that boys who had been in a lot of trouble would immediately cease being delinquent merely because they had been assigned to the program, especially in terms of such juvenile status activities as drinking, being "ungovernable" at home, or "incorrigible" in school. Since the purpose of the program was to find ways for reducing these problems and, more important, to prevent boys from becoming adult criminals, it could not be assumed that all such difficult behavior would cease immediately. Rather, any changes would be the result of a developmental process.

On the other hand, it was felt that the Experiment could not be a haven for boys simply "to do time"; that is, to adopt a cynical stance in which their only intent was to appear to conform without actually doing so. If that were to occur, confidence and trust would indeed be undermined, and the organization weakened, especially for those boys who were seriously trying to make some changes.

In terms of categorizing the nature of these *pro*scriptive rules, therefore, it is clear that their primary function was the maintenance of order and stability and that, on occasion, some coercion would be necessary to reinforce them, especially in the early days of the program before some normative constraints could be developed.

While it was hoped that coercion could be held to a minimum, its use would not be without any redeeming features. Foremost among these was the fact that the Experiment was designed to *retain* boys in the community, and to act as a deterrent to their being permanently incarcerated. Paradoxically, therefore, the occasional imposition of temporary controls might actually be more successful in achieving that objective than if boys were left totally unrestrained, even though they were continuing to get into trouble. The temporary reinforcement of ground rules could serve as a means of avoiding incarceration and could dramatize the importance of becoming involved in the program. In this way, the omnipresent threat of permanent incarceration might be avoided.

Prescriptive Guidelines

Since the ground rules were essentially *pro*scriptive in character, ways had to be found by which the rules of the new correctional game would make provision for the involvement of delinquents in solving problems and sharing in important decisions. Chapter 1 stressed the importance of turning to the delinquent peer group as a resource rather than a liability. That was done because the task of increasing the normative power of the experimental organization, and of managing tensions in the open community, could not depend solely on the reinforcement of *pro*scriptive rules by a small group of staff members. It was necessary to develop *pre*scriptive norms as well by which delinquents could share in the exercise of power, and through which a sense of organizational solidarity and trust might be cultivated.

Organizational solidarity is based upon a sense of community and a belief that the organization is committed to the welfare of *all* of its members, delinquents as well as staff. Closely related is the concept of *organizational trust*. Ordinarily, trust is defined in personal terms, in terms of the confidence one person has in another, and in his readiness to be influenced by that other. This is an important kind of trust, especially where the relationship between a correctional staff member and an offender is involved.

Organizational trust refers to the confidence members have in the organization itself, in its goals, its rules, and its methods. If they have a sense of organizational distrust, even unfounded, the organization is weakened because motivation is undermined. To distrust the organization ". . . is to see one's own efforts as pointless, wasted, and foolish, and the future as hazardous and uncertain" (Cohen, 1966:5).

It is not hard to see why it has been so difficult to cultivate a sense of solidarity and trust in correctional organizations. As Parsons (1970:3) implies, the staff-offender relationship in them is analogous to the merchant-consumer relationship in commercial organizations. It is a one-way relationship in which the consumer (i.e., offender) can either take the product or leave it. In such an organization, therefore, anything resembling full membership for the consumer is meaningless because he is powerless to affect the services delivered to him.

In some organizational contexts, this state of affairs is reasonably acceptable. In a hospital, for example, a person who is seriously ill does not have the knowledge to diagnose and treat his illness. He relies on the medical staff for that kind of expertise. And while he may be unhappy with the service at times, it is difficult for him to deny his pressing personal need for the product.

The problems that face the offender in a correctional organization, however, do not fit the medical model. One crucial difference has to do with the fact that, unlike the sick person, the offender is not a willing and voluntary consumer. Were it not for the fact that he is required by legal action to be a "consumer," he would not even consider buying the correctional product. But even then— even if he overcomes his initial resistance to its purchase—he is unsure of its quality and whether it will do him any good. Hence, while there is some assurance that treatment in a hospital will help cure physical illness, there is much less assurance that the correctional experience will "cure" the offender's delinquency. From his perspective, in other words, correctional programs lack credibility for two reasons.

The first has to do with the stigma associated with being an offender. While there are elaborate rites of passage that induct the offender into an undesirable, deviant status, there are no equivalent rites for inducting him back out of it (Erikson, 1964:16). Once he is labeled, it is difficult for him to discard the degrading effects of that label, either in a social or personal sense.

These problems are often compounded by a stigmatizing role in a correctional setting. The delinquent's pervading sense of inadequacy, originally generated in the community, is carried over and made worse. Consequently, there seems to be a pressing need for him to develop greater personal competence and a better self-image through participation in a correctional program in which he plays a more active role in determining his own destiny.

Although it is logical to assume that correctional organizations should perform these functions, they have found it difficult. Even if treatment-oriented, they tend to be organized in such a way that the degrading effects of being an offender are perpetuated, not reduced. The reason is that correctional officials, even those in a treatment role, have a subtle and paradoxical symbiotic relationship with offenders. The status of the official, his helping or custodial role, is structured in such a way that the offender must forever occupy a subordinate position in the organization. This is indicated by the dichotomous positions with which we are used to describing staff and offender relationships: "guard-inmate," "client-caseworker," or "patient-therapist." There are simply no gradient roles in between (cf. Empey and Lubeck, 1971:61-8).

In our present ways of thinking, these organizational positions are mutually exclusive categories, designating permanent positions filled by either offenders or staff members. Little or no effort has been devoted to ways by which an offender might be moved, step by step, into new roles—roles that connote change in some desired direction, roles that carry with them new expectations and rewards for conventional behavior, roles that decrease the stigma associated with an offender or inmate status, and roles that decrease the social distance between staff and inmate groups. So long as these conditions remain, it is not difficult to see why the "consumer" role for the offender is a difficult one, and why it is so hard for him to discard the delinquent label.

A second reason correctional organizations lack credibility is because they have had so little impact upon the community institutions, the neighborhoods, or the networks of conventional young people that must be altered if the socially inclined delinquent is to take his place once more as a welcome and acceptable person. Although the need for community and institutional change is well recognized, very little success has been achieved in bringing about this change. Instead, the burden for change still rests primarily on the offender. To be sure, the offender is a legitimate target for change, but in the last analysis it is the pattern of interaction between him and the community that will have to be the ultimate target. In order to capture the trust of the offender, therefore, it is clear why new and more effective program prescriptions are needed—guidelines that indicate what new things should be done, not just what offenders should *not* do.

At Provo, the first *pre*scription involved the simple expedient of keeping the program small and nonresidential, and making it of short duration. It was anticipated that many of the institutional problems just mentioned could be avoided if the conditions that produce them were discarded totally. In the absence of the degrading effects of captivity, for example, a strong inmate system, organized around inmate leaders, would be less likely to develop.

The second was to locate the program in the community. By doing so, and by establishing a community work program, the community itself would have to make some changes. A focus by delinquents and staff upon daily life in one's own town, rather than upon daily life under confinement, would automatically make the program somewhat more credible.

The third main prescription involved the use of group techniques. By including offenders in problem-solving and decision-making roles, it was anticipated that power could be shared on a collective basis, and exercised in a group setting. This approach, it was assumed, would not only bring staff and offenders together to deal with shared problems, but would greatly alter their roles.

The major problem associated with trying to define prescriptive guidelines had to do with the participatory role that offenders were to play. Unless they were involved in giving substance to many specific norms, their confidence and trust could not be secured. All norms and expectations, either for staff or boys, could not be defined in advance if offender points of view were not honored. Hence, in place of trying to define all prescriptive norms in advance, the best that could be done for staff was to provide some suggestive guidelines by which they might structure their own behavior when interacting with delinquents. Many of these guidelines were implied in Chapter 1.

Staff members should avoid playing the traditional role of authority wherever possible. Except for the need to reinforce the three ground rules mentioned earlier, they should not assume that they know the answers to all questions; they should not accept sole responsibility for trying to resolve difficult problems; and they should reinforce the overriding importance of a collective approach to all these matters in the daily group meeting. About the only matters on which there was complete certainty were that the group meeting would be the main cog around which the overall program would revolve, and that this meeting would be a privileged sanctuary in which any topic could be discussed, or any feeling expressed. Under no circumstances, unless the whole group decided otherwise, would action be taken on a subject that was revealed in the meeting. In other words, openness and candor were considered virtues for which all possible supports should be cultivated.

In the interest of building trust and commitment, it would be the group leader's task to perform a training function designed to decrease his own power and participation, and to increase those of the delinquent members of the group. His job was to facilitate and guide group interaction rather than to try always to dictate the course that it should follow. Wherever possible, he should also attempt to support and praise candor, trying to reward problem-solution and to avoid responding in a negative way to deviant behavior.

From an early stage of development in which there was considerable resistance and testing, it was hoped that the overall process would work toward a stage in which delinquents would carry increasingly heavy responsibilities: analyzing problems, making plans, preventing difficulties, making decisions, and sharing with staff the rewards, as well as the pains of the reformation endeavor.

In other words, the staff member would be involved in trying to train his own replacements by increasing the competence of offenders to deal with their own problems.

In trying to enhance the normative character of the program, an attempt was made to develop a new reference group for the individual delinquent whose influence would be felt, not only within the confines of the program itself, but in the community as well. In some cases, a new, prosocial reference group might act as a deterrent to further delinquency; in others, it might be a source of identification and help; and in others, it might be a means of acquainting members of the community with the values and norms of the new program. Moreover, this approach would change radically the way in which staff and offender competence would be judged.

By placing greater emphasis upon the functional as well as control aspects of the staff role, the criteria for evaluating staff behavior would become more like that for evaluating offender behavior than traditionally had been the case. The fact that staff members participated in daily group meetings meant that their responses to others, and to day-to-day problems, could be subject to the same scrutiny as offender responses. If their actions were questionable, if someone objected to them, they might receive immediate attention; conversely, if they seemed to be helpful, that could be noted also. But no matter what the responses were, information would be quickly and widely shared. Under such circumstances, therefore, it would be possible to use a somewhat similar, rather than double, standard for judging the contributions of everyone to the collective welfare. This particular approach, it was hoped, would lead to an increase in organizational solidarity and trust, and to an extension of the license of the program to deal with delinquency in new ways.

Obviously, attempts to implement difficult and ambiguous guidelines of this type were not without their problems—problems about which others will want to be informed. Hence, Chapter 6 will be devoted to a discussion of the group developmental process, and to some of the things that were learned from it. For now, the main thing to be recognized is that a few ground rules provided only the general framework within which everyone had to work. Beyond that, it was anticipated that prescriptive norms—norms concerned more with problem-solution and organizational solidarity—would have to emerge from the process of daily group interaction in which both staff and delinquents engaged. To the extent that these norms emerged and were internalized by the members of the organization, the organization would succeed. To the extent that they did not emerge, it would fail.

Sanctions

The successful development of new rules depended very much on the kinds of sanctions—the rewards and punishments—that were used to reinforce them. "All rules," as Cohen (1966:4) points out, impose a certain discipline and effort, a subordination of impulse and self-interest to the common understandings. In no human enterprise, whether it be marriage, business, or politics [or corrections], can one take for granted that, if he plays by the rules, things will go his way. He may get bored. The costs may be disproportionate to the rewards. There may be quicker or easier means of getting what he wants out of the game than are permitted by the rules. . . . There are always temptations, therefore, to quit, to give to the activity less of himself than is expected of him, to cut corners, or otherwise to violate understandings.

In other words, no matter what rules were adopted at Provo, no matter how functional they might have been for some, they would create a potentiality for deviance in others. A fundamental question, therefore, was in knowing how to respond to deviance, especially in light of the complexity of trying to reconcile personal and organizational needs.

As explained in the original description, it was suggested that this task should be attacked in two ways. First, steps should be taken immediately to dramatize and to reinforce the basic ground rules of the program. This burden, especially in the early stages, should fall upon staff members. Since boys would be new to group participation, they would be in no position, either by inclination or experience, to assume responsibility for so difficult a role. The sanctions that might have to be used initially, and from time to time after that, would often be coercive—i.e., special work detail or even temporary detention. The underlying idea was that from the very outset, attempts should be made to establish firm traditions regarding the importance of attendance, of nonviolence, and of using the program as a means for decreasing delinquent behavior. Once these traditions were established, deviance would be less common and both boys and staff could then move on to more important matters. Though undesirable, the occasional use of temporary controls as a means of keeping boys in the community would be preferable to the usual practice of incarcerating them.

In many ways, it was felt that the application of negative sanctions for the violation of ground rules, or the giving of support for candor, would be the easiest parts of the sanctioning task. Far more difficult would be the task of developing positive sanctions in which delinquents as well as staff might become the sanctioners. It was theorized that there would be some reward for delinquents inherent in being left in the community in lieu of incarceration, in gaining some reference group support from peers for making changes, in being able to be candid with adults and having their points of view considered, and in being able to make crucial decisions about their own lives. But these are rather abstract rewards that might or might not be adequate with delinquent boys. Except for the pay that the boys would receive in the work program, there would be no physical means within the organization for symbolizing progress and change in remunerative terms.

It was anticipated that boys would participate in deciding when any individual was ready to leave the program. Although this was a method of symbolizing the rite of passage to nondeviant status, it would scarcely be equivalent to the arrest and trial that had brought the boy to the program in the first place. Hence, a basic question for later consideration is not merely whether these sanctions were appropriate to the task of building organizational solidarity and socializing delinquents, but whether the ground rules and the prescriptive guidelines were appropriately defined and developed. Would the organization be an effective one? If so, what problems might have to be addressed in trying to improve it? If not, what other alternatives might be tried?

Organizational Scope

The final organizational element to which attention is required has to do with the size of the experimental organization, its location in the community, and its concern with effecting community change. Etzioni (1961:160-1) uses the term *scope* to refer to the element being considered. In his terms, scope refers to "... the extent to which the activities of the participants of an organization are limited to other participants in the same organization. ... Organizations whose participants share many activities are *broad* in scope." Thus, in Goffman's (1961) terms, a total institution such as a prison would be an example of an organization with a *broad* scope, one that tries to make provision for all aspects of an offender's life—food, shelter, work, recreation, education and even sex. It would be one in which the interaction and interdependence of members with outsiders would be extremely small.

By contrast, an organization like the Provo Experiment was *narrow* in scope, since it made formal provision for the sharing of only a few activities for its members, such as work and daily group meetings. Even though many of the boys spent time informally with each other outside the confines of the program, their interaction with nonparticipants was extensive, involving daily contacts with families, schools, friends, city workers, and others who had no direct relationship to the program itself. Out of each 24-hour day, boys spent only a few hours in the program. Thus, while the creation of a narrow organization for the experiment was consistent with the notion that new correctional forms are needed, it did not automatically follow that better results would be forthcoming. A narrow organization automatically sacrifices some of the means for involvement and control that are inherent in broader, coercive organizations.

Relative to this matter, Etzioni (1961:166) points out that the scope of any organization is related to two major variables that directly affect the participation and compliance of its members: *saliency* and *level of tension.*

Saliency refers to the personal significance of participation in one type of organization as contrasted to another. The broader the scope of an organization, he argues (1961:162), the greater its saliency. "When the scope is broad, actors have fewer alternative opportunities for emotional investment; hence whatever their lot in the organization, it acquires great significance." When organizational scope is narrow, by contrast, salience may decline drastically because of the involvement of members in activities outside the organization. One might expect it to have much less impact on their total lives. Hence, while the salience of a broad, coercive organization may be oppressive and negative to its members, as the prison literature suggests, the reverse could easily be true in a narrow community organization. It may simply have too little, rather than too much, influence, suggesting that if the affective involvement of the offender, his sense of trust and commitment to it are important, then one risks their loss the more narrow the organization becomes.

This was a matter of considerable significance at Provo. How could a short nonresidential program be expected to develop enough normative power or utilitarian rewards to seriously affect all the forces that impinge upon delinquents' lives? There were many reasons for considering it desirable to do so, not just for the purposes of control, but for other reasons as well. There is considerable complaint, for example, about the impersonal and segmentalized character of modern organizations, and their failure to involve members, especially delinquents, on any kind of total basis. If the Experiment were to realize its objectives, therefore, it simply could not be just another replica of these organizations. Moreover, any appearance of an inability to control dangerous or delinquent behavior could jeopardize the Experiment in the eyes of the ordinary citizen. From many different standpoints, therefore, the narrow scope of the new program raised questions.

From another perspective, however, it could be argued that an organization of narrow scope might be in a better position to claim the loyalties and trusts of its members if it could be shown that it would not jeopardize their interests in other organizations. Moreover, its presence in the community was a way of involving outsiders—ordinary citizens, politicians, school officials—and confronting them with the problems of change.

Clearly, the assumption was that if offenders could be encouraged to maintain conventional ties, the Experiment would be more salient in the long run than a broad, total organization where all such ties were lost. Yet, these assumptions must be treated as hypotheses, not as axioms. Delinquents, especially those who have been through court procedures several times, are rarely motivated to participate in any program on any basis other than a superficial one. If they can avoid involvement, they will do so. Thus, an examination of program saliency is certainly one issue that merits a careful presentation of data.

A second dimension of organizational scope that can affect member participation is *level of tension*. Every organization precipitates strains that must be managed yet released productively (Etzioni, 1961:162). The greater the scope of the organization, the more it will have to be concerned with tension management. In a prison or mental hospital, for example, there is no other place for the release of tension other than within the organization itself. Hence, the less successful it is in managing tension, the more disruption will be likely to occur.

In contrast, Etzioni (1961:162-63) argues that narrow organizations can rely on *natural* ventilation. The interaction of members with nonmembers allows for tension release in other ways and in other pursuits. Consequently, there is less need within the organization to assume full responsibility for tension management. Again, however, this is a conclusion that may need serious qualification when applied to a community correctional program. There are at least two problems with which it must be concerned.

First, any community program must be concerned with its own integrity, as seen from the perspective of the delinquent. Continued and flagrant delinquent behavior is a threat, not only to the community, but to the trust and solidarity of the organization itself. It signifies to those boys who are serious about trying to stay out of trouble that the organization is incapable of addressing the very problem for which it was set up.

Second, a program must be concerned with public expectations that tensions will be managed and the community protected. Hence, if the ventilation of tensions is done in a reasonably conventional way, there will be no problem. But if they are ventilated in a way that results in serious delinquency, the freedom of the delinquent and the program is endangered.

The reason that these two problems are so difficult to deal with, as Etzioni (1961:164) points out, is because the norms of society have always tended to pervade correctional organizations, not the reverse. Criminal and delinquent populations have low status, and neither they nor the people who process them have ever been in much of a position to make changes. The result is that correctional organizations, traditionally, have been in a position of followership, not leadership. Citizens are not used to having the needs of correctional organizations imposed on them.

Etzioni (1961:163-4) does imply that tensions can be managed and salience increased to the extent that a narrow community program can make its norms and values "outwardly pervasive" to the extent that it can exercise some normative constraints over the delinquent and his community. This is what normative organizations of many types—churches, hospitals, or civic organizations—try to do—to affect individual behavior and social policy. But since their efforts are far from completely successful, it is evident how difficult the task is. In fact, public reactions to this problem reflect ambivalence, even bewilderment.

In a recent national survey, the Joint Commission on Correctional Manpower and Training (1968:1) discovered that people were highly conflicted regarding the administration of justice and unable to recognize the contradictions inherent in their own opinions. "One must conclude," says the report, ". . . that the public feels that the corrections system is currently inadequate. At the same time, the public is not eager to bring about change. . . ." If community programs are to survive, they will have to reverse past trends and make their own norms outwardly pervasive.

In addition to its intraorganizational activities, an effort was made to accomplish this feat in the Provo Experiment by seeking both governmental and citizen support. On a governmental level, some funding, although small, was obtained from county government. This was a significant step in light of the fact that all probation services in Utah are the responsibility of the state. Although many of the delinquents who attended the program might have been incarcerated otherwise, the fact that they remained in the community meant that they were still technically on probation. Hence, the support of local county government was extraordinary.

In a similar way, a work program was funded by the city of Provo and a neighboring community. Again, the cost of this endeavor was not great, but the symbolic gesture was important. Ways had to be found to overcome child labor laws and the resistance of many city employees and citizens to any effort to employ delinquents.

On a citizen level, two special groups were appointed. The first was a special advisory council to assist in the consideration of policy questions; to seek citizen support; and to respond to any political, bureaucratic, or lay resistances that might develop. The second was an employment committee to find work for boys after they had been released from the program.

Given the nature of all these preparations, therefore, an important goal of later analyses will be to determine to what extent the narrow experimental organization had two kinds of normative impact: whether it was a salient one to delinquents in terms of reducing their delinquent acts and enhancing their involvement in conventional pursuits; and (2) whether it was successful in establishing and maintaining a supportive environment in the community itself.

Summary and Implications

The analysis has suggested that the experimental organization at Provo was at times coercive, at times normative, and at times utilitarian. Although it differed markedly from the overwhelming coercive nature of traditional correctional organizations, a significant question is whether it could be more successful in achieving its announced objectives.

To assist in answering that question, it was suggested that the following organizational elements should be considered.

Basic Ground Rules. The Provo Experiment attempted to alter the rules by which the whole correctional game was played. But in order to maintain organizational stability, it selected a few ground rules to indicate the outer limits within which the game would be played. One important question, therefore, is whether, in fact, stability was achieved.

Prescriptive Norms. The task of making the experimental organization a credible one to delinquents depended upon the development of a sense of solidarity and trust. This required a sharing of power and the use of group techniques to solve everyday problems. It was hoped that new rules would emerge as a result of a process of interaction between staff and offenders. Consequently, it would be important to learn more about (1) the developmental process that was used to build solidarity and to share power; and (2) how well this process helped to socialize delinquents and to bring about the necessary changes on their side of the delinquent-community interactional spectrum.

Sanctions. The successful use of both proscriptive and prescriptive norms depends very much upon the kinds of sanctions, both positive and negative, that are used to reinforce them. It becomes very important, therefore, to learn what the impact of various sanctions were, and whether they helped to achieve desired objectives.

Organizational Scope. The Provo organization was *narrow* rather than broad in scope. This placed special burdens upon it, not always characteristic of the closely controlled, coercive organization. Therefore, one would want to know (1) whether the organization was a *salient* one to delinquents; (2) in what way *tensions* among delinquents were ventilated in the open community; (3) whether the organization successfully managed tensions by extending its normative influence outward; and (4) whether the organization had a normative impact upon the community as well as upon offenders.

All of the foregoing concepts and elements overlap. Proscriptive and prescriptive norms are obviously crucial to determine how well tensions were managed. Likewise, attempts to develop organizational solidarity and trust are related to the long-term salience of the program and whether, beside the immediate effects, it had an impact on delinquents. Subsequent chapters will take these overlapping characteristics into account. The analysis of organizational issues will be intertwined with an analysis of delinquency and recidivism rates. In that way, it may be possible to gain a better understanding of the relationship between the two.

4

Rules of the Game: The Consumer's View

This chapter is directed to an examination of the way delinquents saw the rules of the game at Provo. It presents their subjective reactions to the basic ground rules, to the efforts that were made to involve them, and to the way sanctions were used. These reactions provide useful reflections on the theoretical assumptions of the Experiment and indicate whether, from the viewpoint of the consumer, the experimental organization was credible.

The Ground Rules

It will be recalled that the three ground rules—required attendance, no physical violence, and no perpetual "doing of time"—were designed to perform two major functions. The first was to ensure at least a minimum of organizational stability. If both offenders and staff were to commit themselves to the goals of the enterprise, to forego other alternatives, and to make an investment in the future, they would have to have some confidence that others would share the same feeling and would play by a common set of rules.

Second, the systematic reinforcement of ground rules might help to dramatize the narrowing range of alternatives open to serious delinquents. Tannenbaum (1938) once noted that, while a community may become annoyed with some of its youth and label them delinquents, these same boys often fail to apply the label to themselves, especially before any catastrophic social response such as jail. Boys may see their behavior as being a little out of line, but they do not see it as delinquent. For them to internalize the delinquent label would be to accept the customary (but probably mistaken) notion that they are by nature criminal.

Our experience with delinquents has been in the same vein. While police, judges, teachers, probation officers, and even parents often become increasingly impatient with the repeat offender, he rarely accepts their definition of him, certainly he does not see himself as being criminally inclined. Thus, despite repeated signs that he is in serious trouble—arrests, warnings, and appearances in court—he rarely takes seriously the idea that his continued freedom is in jeopardy. Jail, like car wrecks, always happens to other people.

While this unwillingness of delinquents to view themselves as criminally inclined may be a positive sign, it does not mean that they necessarily see themselves as *non*delinquent either. Instead, as Matza (1964:27-30) suggests, they tend to be "drifters" who, because their ties to basic societal institutions are tenuous, tend to be disaffiliated and vascillating persons. Committed neither to delinquency nor nondelinquency, they are much more subject to peer influence and situational pressures than are those adolescents whose institutional ties are stronger. Hence, the first step in the correctional process may not be that of trying to change young people who are firmly committed to a delinquent self-image. Rather, it might be to help them to recognize their tendencies to drift, their uncertain social status, and the kinds of difficulties that could be associated with both. Unless some changes are made, the more serious delinquent runs the immediate risk of losing his freedom, and the long-range risk of failing to find himself.

In implementing the Provo Experiment, efforts to develop both organizational stability and to dramatize alternatives were intertwined. There was little about its format or staff remarks on the day that delinquents first arrived that might have indicated to them that the Experiment had to be taken seriously. On the surface, it did not appear much different from other court-imposed programs. As early as the second day, one boy simply stayed away. When it was learned from his mother that he had no legitimate excuse, staff did not ignore him or try to locate, cajole, or threaten him. Rather, they appeared before the juvenile judge, obtained a court order, and placed him in temporary detention. Another boy, whose menacing and abusive behavior with city work supervisors threatened to end that tenuous part of the program before it got started, was arbitrarily removed from his paid job and returned to Pinehills where he had to work for nothing—sweeping floors, washing windows and caring for the lawn.

In neither case were other boys consulted regarding these first, arbitrary impositions of sanctions. That was to come later. For the present, staff assumed the responsibility, trying to dramatize the limits within which everyone could interact and to build some organizational traditions.

This policy did not end with the imposition of each sanction. An effort was made to maximize its implications for other boys, for the organization itself, and for the particular individual in question. The art of sanctioning someone would have little value either as a deterrent or as a device for learning if it remained entirely impersonal and intangible.

As a consequence, the boy who was placed in detention was not detained permanently. He continued to attend the group meeting each day so that his interaction with others would not be cut off. In most cases, he also continued to attend school or to participate in the work program, returning to detention only at night. It was anticipated that neither he nor his problem could be ignored. It was hoped that, in addition to underscoring the importance of basic expectations, three major benefits might result.

The first would be inherent in the chance to draw a dramatic contrast between freedom and the loss of freedom. When a person is permanently incarcerated, his chances to exercise a new option are lost, and there is no opportunity for his peers to learn from his experience. At Provo, that was not the case; both issues were public and could be explored.

Second, the imposition of a negative sanction indicated to the individual that he, above all, should do something. Staff members did nothing directly to ameliorate the problem until the boy sought some resolution himself, then it was suggested that the issue might be one that the group should consider.

Finally, this emphasis upon group problem-solving was a means of underscoring the importance of the daily meeting and its role in the program. Once traditions had been established, increased participation by delinquents would enhance the normative powers of the organization, and the need for coercive sanctions would decrease. But while it was hypothesized that these kinds of benefits might result, the more basic issue is whether delinquents saw programmatic activities in this light.

Offender Perceptions

A study of the reactions of the boys to these matters reveals an interesting trend, beginning with an almost totally negative reaction to the methods that were used, followed by a softening of attitude toward, and some support for them. Speaking of his early reactions, one boy summarized a virtually unanimous opinion. "Right from the start," he said, "I thought I was being shit on. I didn't think a place like this would help nobody."

Then, reflecting somewhat more deeply upon the issues, he gave a rather strong statement in favor of developing and supporting a basic set of expectations. Said he, "I think that one of the things you do when you first come here is to feel everyone out to see how far you can go. An' even though I hated their guts at first when I couldn't beat their time, I think it is a good thing when they put you in your place right away an' let you know you can't get away with nothin'—that you can't bullshit them along."

While not all the boys agreed with this statement, most of their comments were ambivalent. They expressed extreme resentment toward the setting of limits, followed by rather candid admissions that a definitive expression of expectation was useful. One boy said that, "When I first come to Pinehills I never thought of problems the way they do around here. The result was I wasted a lotta time. If they hadda been rougher on me, I would of seen my problem a lot quicker and maybe did something about them faster."

These kinds of responses allude to the difficult role that staff was asked to play, and the awkward position in which it put delinquents as well as staff. On one hand, staff members were expected, especially in the early days, to establish the normative boundaries of the program and to dramatize alternatives—efforts that often required that they behave in an authoritarian way. On the other hand, they were to avoid shouldering all the responsibility for the solution of problems and the exercise of controls. Their behavior must often have seemed contradictory in the extreme.

Over and over, the reactions of boys to the staff role reflected its contradictory character. On one hand, they said, "I like Mr. _____ and Mr. _____ even though they don't act themselves. They act different to us so we don't shit on them. At least I don't have anything against them. The way they act, or acted—it kept me in line."

On the other hand, the staff role was confusing. "I tried to do two things when I first come to Pinehills—act the big man around the other guys, and brown nose the staff. None of 'em worked. I found out I was low man on the totem pole in the group meetings, an' when brown nosin' the staff didn't work I got all confused. What I ended up doin' was arguin; for the sake of arguin'."

These comments summarized the opinion that the imposition of some coercive sanctions, accompanied by the uncustomary behavior of staff, were perceived as having a controlling and stabilizing effect. But did these actions also help to dramatize the importance of making choices and resolving problems?

As might be anticipated, most opinions implied that choices had been well dramatized:

"I thought when I first come that, the staff members, and everybody, acted like a bunch of pricks—like God Almighty. Now I see it is really a lot different. There is even some human in them. They more or less had to do what they did because it goes right along with their job. I think the one thing that really helped the boys is to let them know how serious they are in trouble, and what it can really do to them."

Opinions as to whether boys actually experienced long-range benefits from this experience, however, were somewhat divided. There was the rather surprising finding that most of the boys who had actually been detained temporarily considered that experience to be the single most important event in their entire stay.

"What was the most important thing that happened to you here?"
"Going to jail. It helped me change."
"How did that help you change?"
"Made me think. I was so close to Ogden (the State Reformatory) that it wasn't funny. When I was in jail I decided to tell the truth, and start doin' somethin' about it."

There is the very real question as to whether the detention experience that led to this rather typical comment did, in fact, start a series of events that led to different patterns of adjustment. Jailhouse repentance is a common phenomenon. Under the duress of some trying experience, most people resolve to make changes which they fail to make.

One boy illustrated a rather good insight into this problem:

"What things did you dislike the most about Pinehills?"
"I used to hate kids gettin' put on work detail or goin' to jail at night. I used to think it was real chickenshit."
"Why do you think people like Mr._____or Mr._____do that to kids?"

"I think they do it to help them learn. If they learn or not, I don't know."
"Did you get locked up while you were at Pinehills?"
"Yes."
"Did you learn anything?"
"Yes, one main thing. I learned I couldn't get by with nothin'. Even though I hated it, it done me good to get caught for some of the things I was doin'."

While the imposition of a sanction apparently had a deterrent effect on this boy, he was not certain whether the experience, either for himself or others, would help him "learn." His was a fair and objective appraisal. One cannot build an entire program on the exercise of coercive sanctions by staff. Less than a fifth of all boys were even detained, and even then for a period of no longer than a few days. And, though some kinds of sanctions were levied on a larger proportion of the boys by staff (or more often by the group), not all boys were sanctioned. For everyone to benefit, means had to be found to make optimal use of the issues the sanctions symbolized.

Use of the Group

There were two lines of theory that provided the rationale for a collective group approach. First, in reflecting much current thinking in social science, Cressey (1965:90) has argued that any person is seen as a part of the kinds of social relationships and values in which he participates.

He obtains his essence from participation in rituals, values, norms, roles, schedules, customs and regulations of various kinds which surround him. The person (personality) is not separable from the social relationships in which he lives.

Second, this frame of reference may well apply to crime and delinquency as well.

This is to say that criminal behavior is, like other behaviors, attitudes, beliefs and values which a person exhibits, the *property* of *groups*, not of individuals. Criminal and delinquent behaviors are not just *products* of an individual's contacts with certain groups; they are in a very real sense "owned" by groups rather than by individuals, just as the French or English language is owned by a collectivity rather than by any individual (Cressey, 1965:90).

If these assumptions are correct, it would seem that change would be most likely to occur if it were a group rather than a private property, if it were a mutual rather than a private conversion. If delinquent behavior and the rationalizations that support it are group properties, and if the person and the group are two facets of the same thing, it follows that groups might become both the target *and* the medium of change. The acceptability of prosocial behavior to the individual would depend upon its acceptability to a group of significant others. If these others changed, the individual would be more likely to change.

Further, as Cressey (1965:95) has suggested, delinquents working with other delinquents might be able to accomplish something that nondelinquents could not. A group-oriented program in which delinquents played by rules

... ought to be effective to the degree that the criminal-as-an-agent-of-change prevents criminals from using the techniques of neutralization—the verbalizations—which he, himself, used in perpetrating offenses, and to the degree that new anticriminal verbalizations are substituted ... Theoretically, at least, the degree of rapport is increased if these 'persons with socially acceptable standards of conduct' are themselves criminals-turned-reformers such as social workers and prison guards. Just as men are relatively unaffected by radio and television dramatizations, they are unaffected by verbalizations presented by men they cannot understand and do not respect.

Cressey (1955:119) felt that the involvement of delinquents in this way would result in what he called "retroflexive reformation." If a delinquent were serious in his attempts to reform others, he would be more inclined to accept the common purpose of the reformation process and identify himself closely with it. He would become a genuine member of the reformation group and would be alienated from his previous prodelinquent groups. This participation would be consonant with the notion of attempting to build a normative organization in which the internalization of prosocial norms and the building of reference group controls and supports would serve long-range objectives.

A fundamental question that this theory does not answer is how the first delinquent-turned-reformers are to be cultivated, how either an individual or a group can be encouraged to reach a stage in which "retroflexive reformation" is likely to occur. Actually, the task might not be so difficult as it first appears.

Despite the fact that delinquents are highly susceptible to peer influence—probably more susceptible than nondelinquents (Empey and Lubeck, 1968)—this does not mean that they are unaware of conventional values and expectations. Despite their tendencies to drift and, on occasion to be delinquent, they are not, as pointed out in Chapter 1, like strangers from Mars. Having been socialized in an environment dominated by middle-class morality (Cloward and Ohlin, 1960), they may have internalized the American success ideal to such a degree that they are ambivalent about their own delinquent behavior (Cohen, 1955:133).[1] That may be why, as Sykes and Matza (1957:664-70) suggest, they maintain a whole series of intricate rationalizations by which to explain away their delinquent behavior.

If that is true, the feelings of ambivalence could be used to encourage the consideration of nondelinquent alternatives. This experiment might also convince delinquents that they did have serious problems, and that they should weigh more carefully the choices available to them. Their analyses of these possibilities might reduce their identification with the delinquent system and tip the scales in the opposite direction.

In seeking to determine whether these theoretical assumptions had merit, at least from the perspective of the delinquent, it is important to consider several issues: (1) whether delinquents appeared to recognize any connection between the efforts that were made to dramatize problems and the use of the group meeting as a device for solving those problems; (2) whether, in contrast to staff, they felt their own participatory role was of special significance; (3) whether they exhibited any tendency to exercise a normative influence; and (4) whether their participation seemed to enhance a sense of trust in the program. Responses to these issues may help to indicate whether theory favoring an active role for offenders has any merit.

The Group Function

It will be recalled that many boys seemed to feel that the reinforcement of ground rules had made a strong impression on them. But did they see any connection between this kind of pressure and the problem-solving function the group was supposed to perform? There were many indications that they did:

"I mentioned that being locked up won't help a guy out of trouble. Understanding why you got there might, but the jail itself won't. You have to get the understanding, an' that comes in the group meeting."

"Looking back, did the boys in your group do anything that helped you?"

"They helped me most when they put me in jail for not showin' up. When I got out, I said I wanted to get drunk that night an' the meeting talked to me about it."

"How did that help?"

"Well, for one thing, I didn't go out an' get drunk. They talked to me quite a bit. They pointed out to me I was playing a tough role, an' that going on a blast now was the same ol' thing with me."

"So what happened?"

"I can't say I was a goodie-goodie right off, but one thing that stuck with me was when they showed me that how I was acting was the way I was talking and treating my mother and my girl. I was being an ass. I thought a lot of my girl an' I saw I was only makin' things worse not better. Her ol' man don't like me anyhow, an' what I wanted to do wouldn't help."

While these comments are supportive of the notion that both the constraining and deliberate capacities of the group may have been helpful, it would be a mistake to take them at face value. The reason is that a great deal of socialization must have taken place in the program in which boys *learned* that the group was *supposed* to help them. Consequently, they would be inclined to be supportive even if they had not received as much help as they believed they had. Nevertheless, they held strong opinions regarding its utility, and their remarks were at times quite candid and objective, sometimes refreshingly so.

One sentiment that was especially pronounced was the idea that peers were of greater help than staff:

"Boys know more about themselves than grownups do. The first couple months don't do any good. Then you find out that the meetin' knows you better than you know yourself. They can tell when you're lyin'. They can tell you things about yourself, an' find out what your problems are."

While one might wish to debate whether boys know more about themselves, and their problems, than "grownups" do, that is not the point. The point is that most boys believe that to be the case; help from other boys was the most important element.

One boy whose ego was strong, and who was a leader, described his progressive involvement in the program.

"When I first come here, I thought I was screwed. I didn't know nothin', so I joined the "nonsquealers" club.

(He did not "join" the nonsquealer's club; he started it. It was comprised of a small group of boys who decided that they would go through the motions of involvement, but would actually make no changes. Although they managed for a few weeks to keep their outside delinquent activities quiet, their downfall came because they were exploiting and manipulating other boys in the program. Under the protections provided by the group meeting, and because they resented what was happening, these boys revealed the whole operation.)

"When the cover come off that little operation, I started to tell the truth 'cause it seemed like the meeting was tryin' to help me. I was surprised because of what I'd done. They were tryin' to help me all the time, but I just realized it. So I started tryin'."

"Everybody has a responsibility up here; the meetin' has most of the say so. I like that."

"I like Mr. _____ and the sad secretary, but what I really like is the guys makin' their own decisions."

With very few exceptions, then, the comments in release interviews favored the notion that boys had much to offer, and that their participation was preferred. In fact, as some organizational traditions began to develop, the group began to take over some of the control functions formerly exercised solely by staff. One of these functions had to do with the issue of attendance, and whether some boys should be excused from the program. Although the use of coercive sanctions early in the program tended to deter overt kinds of resistance and manipulation, that did not mean that they disappeared. Instead, they became much more subtle and difficult to deal with.

One boy, for example, who had never been known for his deep religiosity suddenly turned up with a letter written by his minister asking if he could be excused from further involvement in the program so he could attend daily religious instruction in its place. Another boy had an even better excuse. He wanted to go to work full time so he could support his widowed mother.

While such overtures had a distinct manipulative and devious ring about them, it was hard for staff not to take them seriously. To deny the importance of one boy attending church and the other going to work, would be to deny a host of common-sense and theoretical beliefs that both were important. But when staff, to whom these requests were directed, made all the decisions, they were almost always bad decisions.

Trying to do what they thought was best for boys, staff made exceptions and allowed some individuals to be excused from the program. But not only did these boys soon drop out of the "rehabilitative" and laudatory activities for which they were excused, they got into trouble again. Moreover, whenever any exception was made, especially for a new boy, it only invited requests for more exceptions. Hence, the organizational norms that had been so painfully constructed began to erode.

As a result, staff did what their theory said they should have been doing all the time anyway—sharing these problems with their groups and asking for a collective decision. When that was done, it was surprising how often a supplicant's rationale withered under the group's scrutiny. A great deal of support was given to Cressey's belief that delinquents often understand the motives and rationalizations of other delinquents better than staff members do. Yet, even the group proved fallible on occasion.

Consider, for example, the following excerpt from a group meeting in which it was discovered that a boy who had supposedly had a serious operation had actually fabricated the need for the operation, and had even described the whole hospitalization process in order to avoid the program. What was most surprising to everyone was the fact that this boy had not only been successful in deceiving the group, but his best friend as well. The "best friend," Johnny, was incredulous. He is the one who keeps persistently asking why his long-time buddy had lied to him.

Johnny: I've been around Dave all his life, but I believe he lied to me.
Sam: He lied to everybody. He just let it slip that he ain't had no operation.
George: You actually figured all the angles didn't you, Dave?
Johnny: Why'd you lie to me . . . to everybody?
Dave: I was just figurin' on how I could get out of Pinehills, so I come up with this excuse—sayin' I had to go to the doctor an' have an operation.
Roy: Did you really see a doctor?

Johnny: But, Dave, I asked you a question. Why'd you lie to me?
Dave: I saw a doctor. He just said I had a bone bent out of place—or somethin'—but I didn't need no operation.
Johnny: Well, what about me? What did you think I'd do, rat on you or somethin'?
Dave: I don't know. I thought you was startin' to change, an' I wasn't sure I could trust you.
George: You got in trouble for lyin' once before, didn't you Dave?
Dave: Yah.
Johnny: How'd you feel about lyin' to all of us, Dave—puttin' things over on us?
Dave: "I felt pretty clever at first. I guess I still do now. Uh, that's a problem I'm goin' to have to work on.
Sam: You got a bullshittin' problem, all right.

Obviously, Dave was a boy of not inconsiderable talent and imagination. One has to admire his skills. But he also had some serious problems. He had been in and out of trouble since he was ten years old, and his latest offense was for burglary. He was a member of a small group of delinquent boys whose exploits were impressive.

The results of involving group members in these kinds of problems were twofold. First, when devious behavior of this kind was discovered by a boy's peers and they as well as staff were being manipulated, the reactions tended to enhance the normative power of the organization and to dramatize the need for alternatives.

Second, it was decided collectively that no one would be excused from the usual routine until the group got to know him better, and until he had demonstrated that he merited being made an exception. Later on, some boys were excused to take a full-time job but, even then, a way was usually found for them to participate in group meetings until everyone felt confident that they should be released completely from the program. This created some conflicts with parents, and even with the wives of two boys who were married, but its results were much less disastrous, organizationally and personally, than when staff made all of the decisions. This conclusion, in fact, raises an interesting question. How were staff perceived?

Perceptions of Staff

With respect to group function, delinquents seemed to feel that it was the teaching and interpretive capacities of a group counselor, not his advice or an overly active role, that were of greatest importance. Speaking of the teaching role, one boy said, "Mr.   taught me to help other kids. I think when you do that you help yourself. His job was important in letting me know when I was out of line, but it was the other guys that had to help me do somethin' else."

Another boy expressed much the same sentiment, except that he may have placed even less emphasis on the direct benefits of staff counseling.

"What can the group leader do that helps the most?"

"To shut up an' let the boys figure things out' "

"Mr.   suggested a lot of things that helped, like we should check each other out when we're workin'! An' he made an overall summary so that you got the main thing of what the meetin' was about. But I jus' don't like to listen to adults lecturing . . . it is boring as hell."

"All the help I got, I got from other guys in the meetin'—nine other guys instead of one stupid adult talkin' to you. I felt they done the same things I done, an' know exactly how I feel, an' why I do them things."

Not all boys felt quite this strongly, but the theme was a persistent one. It was the capacity to listen, to understand, and to suggest plausible courses of action and interpretations, therefore, that boys best liked from group leaders.

"My most important meeting was the one I found out what was behind me—you know, to get it out front. Mr.   summed it up in one sentence. He said, 'I think the reason you are doing these things is that you think that you are really bad, an' that the only way you can prove it to yourself is to go out an' do these things.' "

"This is important to me 'cause I don't think nobody has ever understood me. Once somebody knew what I was really like, I felt like I could really change."

Besides suggesting that this boy had benefited from the group leader's interpretation, whether correct or not, his comments implied that he may have liked the leader as well. Actually, it was not that simple. Given the coercive as well as the functional aspects of the staff role, boys tended to be ambivalent when it came to the matter of interpersonal affection. Their personal feelings for the group leader were somewhat conflicted.

"I didn't like Mr.   ,   at first, an' when I heard what the other guys said about him, I disliked him even more. The way he approaches things, he won't come right out an' ask you. He wants *you* to figure it out. At first, I didn't understand why he did this—it pissed me off. But then I started to understand and like him. When the other guys said I liked him, that kinda shook me. I didn't want to admit it. Most of the other guys hated him as far as I know. Even so, there's a lot of people I hate and still respect. I think even if I would have hated him, I would have respected him."

The possibility that most boys were ambivalent about staff is further suggested by the distinctions they drew between the staff member who was the leader of the group of which they were a member, and other staff members in general. If they liked anyone, it was their group leader, but this liking was rarely generalized to anyone else. Expressions of respect for staff were far more common overall than were expressions of affection.

This may be due in part to the fact that many delinquents find it difficult to express overt affection for any male. It also implies that the deliberate efforts of staff to crystallize issues, then sit back and expect boys to figure out what to do about them, probably hindered the development of close interpersonal ties. Whether this was helpful or harmful is difficult to judge. While the finding is not especially surprising, there are those who would argue that counseling staff should not be expected to set limits, even to use coercive methods, and be successful group leaders as well.

Earlier in this chapter, for example, we saw that when delinquents first entered Pinehills and demands were made that they adhere to basic ground rules, they were more likely to react with feelings of anger and resentment than with feelings of trust. As one boy said, "I didn't think this place would help nobody." One basic issue, therefore, is whether boys trusted the program enough to be candid about some of the more sensitive problems they sometimes had—problems such as homosexuality or window-peeping. Not only might they be unwilling to discuss such problems because of the kind of role that staff played, but because the behaviors they imply run counter to the masculine image that delinquents usually try to project.

Candor and Trust

The excerpt that follows speaks directly to these issues. In it, a boy expresses his reactions to the discussion of sensitive matters.

"When the guys would talk about personal problems, it would hit me—like window-peeping and then sitting there jacking off. I did stuff like that."

"I would always worry that these things would come up about me because it was on my record, an' I would hate to bullshit the meeting if it did come up."

"Finally, one day I felt I had to get it off my chest so I brought it up. I was ashamed; I never thought nobody else would do somethin' like that. I thought them other kids would laugh at you."

"They took it more adult; not one guy giggled except Rocky, but I expected that from him. The other guys was serious."

"I was surprised when I found out the other guys did it just as often as me. 'So what was the problem?,' they said. It was just my way of thinkin' that was so bad. I more or less thought I was one in a million, but I wasn't. It was a relief."

Aside from the possibility that this boy may have been helped personally, these comments implied that norms had developed which were supportive of the idea that one could, with some assurance and trust, talk about almost any topic. This seemed to be an important development for two reasons: first, because delinquents rarely have a close group of associates with whom they can reveal and discuss sensitive subjects and, second, because the cultivation of trust and candor in this organization was an important objective. Correctional programs have been noteworthy for their absence of both of these elements. But here, the organizational context did not seem to preclude their development. Perhaps it was because boys played such a central role in the group aspects of the program.

"When you try to explain something to someone else, it helps you. An' when another boy tells why he steals, you might start thinkin' about it, an' think it was the same reasons you done something."

"Then, when you look at that problem, an' how to solve it, it helps every boy. Every meetin' helps every boy."

These comments run counter to the generally accepted notion that boys will not talk about sensitive matters, especially those that are the property of others, because to do so would be to make them a rat or a fink. Boys were understandably reluctant to talk about others, if not themselves. How, then, did boys become more willing to speak openly, and to trust some of their most difficult problems to the deliberations of the group?

Perhaps the most significant force was the zealous effort made, first by staff and later by delinquents, to adhere to the norm that whatever topic was discussed in a group meeting was sacred to that meeting. It would not be revealed elsewhere, and no sanctions would be imposed for any revelation. The person who broke this norm outside the meeting, not the one who talked openly in the meeting, was the deviant. This meant that staff members had to resist the pressures of legal authorities to reveal privileged material, and the delinquents had to resist the pressures of their peers. It was a problem for everyone, not just offenders.

This privilege extended even to the discussion of heretofore undiscovered and often serious delinquent acts. Such acts could not be ignored, but rather than being sanctioned, they were discussed with the group in an effort to determine what course of action should be taken. If, after a collective decision had been made, it proved necessary to include others in on the problem, that would be done, but not until the decision was made.

One boy, for example, revealed in a group meeting that just prior to his being assigned to the program, he had participated in a burglary of a supermarket in which he and another boy had stolen several hundred dollars. He was fearful that his part in the burglary would be discovered, and that he would be returned to court. The problem was further complicated by the fact that his associate in the burglary was not in the program, and might be resistant to any effort to rectify the act.

The problem was the subject of discussion for a long time. Eventually, the group and the boy decided that he would speak to his associate, and both sets of parents, to see if all would agree to hold a meeting with the manager of the supermarket regarding the burglary. If these family groups would agree to take that step, the staff of the experiment would speak to the police and other legal authorities to see if they would be willing to let the boys, the parents, and the maanger work out a joint agreement for dealing with the burglary in a nonofficial way.

To make a long story short, that course of action was followed. The parents and the boys talked to the store manager and he agreed not to prosecute providing that the boys would work regularly at the market to pay off the debt. Once this was agreed upon, the police chief then required that the boys meet with him to give their assurances that they would follow this plan. Fortunately, everyone was faithful to his word: an unsolved burglary case was cleared by the police, and the boys worked off their debt. But perhaps more important, this event provided at least one dramatic instance in which candor paid off.

There were other problems associated with the group meeting as a privileged sanctuary, however. The major one had to do with the individual who continued to get into trouble, but who was unwilling to reveal or deal with this fact. In other words, he was in violation of the norm that the experiment was not a place to do time. When that occurred, one of two things tended to result. First, he might be arrested by the police, in which event no effort was made by people at the experiment to interfere with the regular, legal course of events. If he was tried in court, a staff member might be called upon to testify regarding his progress in the experiment, but the judge made the decision as to whether he would be left in the program or given a new placement. When that happened, it was clear to most boys that this was not the most desirable alternative.

Second, if the individual's behavior was not a matter of official record, but was eventually revealed in the meeting, not by himself, but by someone else—a staff member or another boy—the group had to figure out what course of action should be followed. In some cases, he might be sanctioned by the group in some way because of his own unwillingness to deal with the problem. In others, group problem-solving was the only reaction. The point is, however, that if the individual was not willing to try to make changes himself and was not open with the meeting, the group did not have to adhere to its norm favoring no sanctions for the revelation of information. Protection extended only to those who were willing to try to resolve their problems.

Interestingly, group members were often more concerned with the tendency for other boys to talk about sensitive information outside the meeting than they were about staff tendencies to do so. Some boys liked to gossip about the things they heard in the meeting. Soon the norm favoring the sacredness of meeting material became a matter for group, not just staff, concern. Once boys could see that confidentiality had some utility, they tended to support it.

Another reason boys were willing to be candid was self-interest, plain and simple. Said one boy, "I didn't want the other guys to know everything about me, but I could see I wasn't goin' to get out unless I told the truth. It seems like you could go to the meetin' and talk about anything you want, an' not be considered a fink. If I woulda been tellin' the truth all along, I would of been out of here a long time ago."

A second reason seemed to stem from the feelings of ambivalence which boys felt. On one hand, there were the obvious constraints on candid behavior, both personal and social. "At first, when I was a new boy, I hated to go to the meetin'. I was scared shitless. I thought them other guys were crazy for tellin' the truth."

On the other hand, there were several indications that the opportunity to break through some of the stereotyped ways boys have of dealing with each other was satisfying. Several investigators have alluded to the aggression that seems to characterize interaction in delinquent groups. Matza (1964:42-43) uses the term "sounding" to refer to the incessant plumbing, often through insult, by which delinquent boys test one another's commitment to delinquency or conventionality. Miller (1958:519) speaks of the focal concerns of such groups as toughness, smartness, and excitement. Whatever the terms, delinquent groups do not seem to be groups in which boys feel especially secure and able to relax. They are under constant pressure to protect a status to which they have only a partial and often uncertain commitment. The group sessions at Provo seemed to provide some relief from these tensions and to permit some insight into the personal and not always desirable motivations that are associated with the desire to behave in a delinquent way.

"The reason I think I can stay out of trouble now is 'cause I think I can face it. I don't think I have to steal or drink like a fish just to get kids to like me. If they don't like me for what I am, why should I put all my effort into tryin' to bullshit them into thinkin' I'm somethin' I ain't."

"At first I thought it was kinda neat to brag about the things you done. Now when somebody tells me how drunk he got last night, I think, 'You dumb bastard.' "

Other boys seemed to gain some satisfaction out of reversing their usual roles, and trying to help others.

"To tell the truth, I like to do it—I like to help other guys. For the first four months here, I was in trouble every night. But the thing I like best about Pinehills is the chance of talkin' serious to other kids. That's what grabbed me."

Closely related was the notion that the capacity to operate openly may have been a source of status. Certainly, that was one of the objectives in trying to use groups as a medium of change in which, as group norms changed, the symbols of social status would change as well.

"Telling the truth about myself was awful hard for me, but rattin' on other guys was even harder. What really changed my opinion though was when I saw other people looked up to you when you could tell the truth. They bullshit to everybody themselves, but respect you when you don't bullshit. This is a thing that is hard to learn. It gave me more peace of mind."

Finally, there were comments suggesting that "telling the truth" was functional.

"The first boy that goes in the meeting an' tells the truth is the one that helps the most. I feel that really started it for me. They never did correct me before; if they would have corrected me before it would have helped sooner."

"I admit I sound stupid because I started out feelin' the whole thing was the biggest bunch of horseshit. But in the group meeting we really dug into everything an' tried to understand why. That is why lots of kids get into trouble, 'cause they don't understand why. This is what I liked, talkin' about anything you want, an' tryin' to understand."

Summary and Implications

This chapter has been devoted to the way the delinquent consumer in the Provo Experiment perceived the rules of the game that were played there. Almost unanimously, they disliked and resented the coercive methods that were used to reinforce the ground rules. Yet, they also admitted that such methods had not only helped to maintain organizational stability, but had caused them to reflect seriously upon the problems facing them. Many, in fact, considered the imposition of some sanction as the major turning point in their experiences at Pinehills.

Delinquents felt that the greatest long-range benefits were derived from their active participation in a problem-solving, decision-making role. While the sanctioning of deviant behavior had made them cautious, and even reflective, and while staff members could teach, guide, and interpret, it was help provided by one's peers that was of greatest value.

In some ways, these findings are not particularly surprising. Boys hated and feared punishment, and gained satisfaction from those activities in which they shared some power and authority. Yet, there are other ways in which the findings pose some difficult issues.

Sanctions and Deterrence

Perhaps the most troublesome issue is whether the benefits gained from the exercise of negative sanctions were adequate to counterbalance their more harmful aspects. On one hand, research and theoretical speculation has suggested generally that negative sanctions are of little use in ensuring conformity to norms (cf. Tannenbaum, 1938:478; Ball, 1955; Tappan, 1960:243-55; Reckless, 1967:508). Studies of the relation of capital punishment to murder or incarceration to recidivism suggest that punishment does not deter the punished person or deter others. As a consequence, recent trends, both in a philosophical and legal sense, have been in the direction of protecting the rights of offenders, especially juveniles, against the excessive use of coercive controls.

On the other hand, the delinquents in this study were virtually unanimous in their opinion that negative sanctions "had kept them in line," and that their use had virtually pushed many boys into a greater involvement in the more constructive aspects of the experimental program. According to their comments, deliberate efforts to dramatize alternatives and to encourage a new mode of adjustment had had the desired effect.

Even though this result runs counter to the literature, it was not without support from a number of other sources. Not only have many social scientists called attention to a series of empirical and logical weaknesses in older studies of the deterrent effects of punishment (Walker, 1965:241-260; Glaser, 1964; Wilkins, 1969; Zimring, 1971), but more recent studies in laboratory settings, somewhat closer in character to the Provo Experiment, have suggested that negative sanctions may indeed have a deterrent effect. Under some circumstances, the use of negative reinforcement is both effective and efficient for the person involved (Bandura and Walters, 1963; Bandura, 1969:118-216). Moreover, there is some indication that the fear of punishment, as well as the anticipation of reward, has a strong influence on human behavior (Bandura, 1969:118-216). Even when punishment is considered in the abstract, a belief that the probability of punishment is high may directly affect the likelihood of deviant behavior (Jensen, 1969). These and a number of other studies suggest that punishment may deter, especially when it is personalized in some way, and when it is believed that punishment is a probability.

Such findings were not totally unlike the Provo Experiment where, although not all boys were negatively sanctioned, the experience of seeing or hearing about one's peers being sanctioned was reported to have a deterrent effect. A key question is whether the violation rates of delinquents in this study actually decreased. If, as the boys suggested, they were kept in line by real or threatened sanctions, an immediate drop in official delinquent behavior should have occurred. If, on the other hand, the older literature is correct, official rates will not have changed. This question can, and will, be examined in the next chapter. By having empirical data, we can shed more light on these issues.

Humanitarian and Practical Issues

Even though real or threatened punishment might actually deter delinquent behavior, the humanitarian character of the current trend away from punishment may be the most desirable in the long run. Unfortunately, however, this trend sometimes overlooks the need to draw some subtle distinctions. In seeking what most people would consider to be a desirable goal, the trend may actually be incorporating some harmful features into legal practices and decision-making.

In the case of the serious offender, for example, there is a need to be careful about the difference between total and prolonged incarceration which is likely to be harmful, and the use of a variety of transitory controls in the community which may be helpful. When that distinction is not drawn, authorities are placed in the difficult, if not dangerous, position of having to choose between the two extremes—either total incarceration or total freedom. No middle ground is left open to them, such as that used at Pinehills where the occasional imposition of sanctions was made a part of, not separated from, an integrated form of community intervention. Some deviant acts could be deterred merely because boys were aware that punishment could be a reality.

It is simply not true that some controls are never needed, or that all boys will respond to a program voluntarily. For example, one boy showed up at the Provo Experiment on his first day carrying a loaded pistol. It was only by chance that the pistol was discovered and taken from him. In another case, two brothers, along with a third, exconvict brother, were planning an armed battle with a second group in which their weapons included chains, brass knuckles, and a sawed-off shotgun. Gang rumbles occur in small towns as well as urban centers. Who would argue that something should not be done to control them—something that would be in the interest of the protagonists as well as the community?

As it turned out, neither of these events resulted in the imposition of coercive controls. Because each was discovered in the group meeting, and because peers reacted negatively, the controls were largely normative. But had not some traditions been built up in the program which made punishment a possibility, it is questionable whether normative constraints would have been adequate. It is probably significant that negative feedback was given immediately to potential deviants before they could get into further trouble, not after. When they and others can see that trouble is being presented, not just punished after the fact, it has more meaning.

In the ordinary community, by contrast, there are few resources by which to deal directly with such problems. Not only are normative controls lacking, but official controls are usually so impersonal and so far removed from the everyday lives of delinquent boys that they have little deterrent effect. Hence, the basic issue is not that of deciding for or against the total removal of all controls, but that of finding the most effective and humane way by which to make use of them.

The opinions of adult exoffenders on these very issues are revealing. In most cases, they are far more restrictive and demanding when they participate as reformers than we were. In one program with which we are familiar in Los Angeles, where a group of exoffenders are operating their own prevention and correctional programs, these men argue strenuously against any tendency to weaken basic demands. It is their opinion that unless deviance is immediately sanctioned or prevented, their organization will become a place in which some persons will shoot dope, stash needles, or hide contraband, simply because it is safer to do so there than on the streets. In another case, in a community halfway house, a parolee was stabbed to death because he had been pushing dope and had apparently failed to live up to his part of a bargain. The killer was never discovered. Thus, exoffenders are adamant that steps are necessary to prevent such happenings.

In a similar way, Synanon (cf. Yablonsky, 1965) is very demanding. On one hand, Synanon has received a great deal of favorable attention because it is a nonpublic organization which has pioneered unique ways for working with addicts and alcoholics. Yet, on the other hand, it is willing to accept new persons as members only under a rigid set of expectations. Unless a person is willing to adhere to them, he is unceremoniously booted out with little chance to return.

The exercise of this kind of sanction by Synanon reflects the obvious fact that no single program can be successful with everyone. Yet, a distressing thing about it is its irretrievable character. Once exercised, its effects are hard to undo. In a way, it is an ultimate sanction. In the Provo Experiment, by contrast, an attempt was made to use temporary sanctions, not to *eliminate* people but to *retain* them—to keep them as a part of the program and community, not to leave them to some other fate. This is a crucial distinction.

Since public agencies, unlike Synanon, must deal with every offender, their only recourse, when they decide to exclude someone, is usually to incarcerate him. This is precisely the alternative that should be avoided. But, in order to avoid it, it would seem that some provision must be made in community programs for the introduction and use of temporary controls, both normative and coercive. If this were done, it would mean that one could not view community programs and the use of some controls as polar opposites—the way jail and probation are viewed as opposites. Rather, the main distinction would be among types of control.

When the word "control" is used, it need not always refer to physical control, such as detention. Rather, the search must continue for more effective normative means in which the client population plays a more important role. One lesson that was learned in the Provo Experiment, perhaps too late, was how effective symbolic and informal controls could be. On some occasions, a group would decide that an individual should stay home temporarily at night, refrain from seeing certain friends, or stop drinking if these things were continuing to get him into trouble. Staff were understandably skeptical that such methods could be successful, but when boys participated in their determination, they made it their business to see that their methods worked.

On many occasions, they knew with considerable certainty whether an individual had fulfilled the group's expectations. They could recite where he had been the night before, with whom he had been, and what he had done. Their network of information was much greater than that of staff. The impact of the program was more pervasive than it would have been had staff attempted to exercise all prerogatives themselves. Had that been done, most boys would have been inclined to thwart not support correctional goals.

Positive Sanctions

Undoubtedly, the reason many boys thought so highly of their participation in the program was because it was rewarding to them. In seeking to find better answers to correctional problems, one cannot be concerned solely with negative sanctions. Positive reinforcement is also vital—and difficult to achieve.

When one works with delinquents, one is often overwhelmed by the difficulties of locating any familiar, accessible, and culturally sanctioned means for rewarding boys. Despite the somewhat euphoric way that boys in this study reacted to their role in the program, there are reasons to question whether its capacities to provide rewards were adequate.

It was not uncommon to find that while any staff member or delinquent could readily suggest various forms for punishing or controlling behavior, few could suggest means for rewarding it. Such means were simply not a part of their cultural repertoires. This seemed to be reflected in the fact that, when delinquents were asked in their release interviews what could be done to make Pinehills a better place, they either had little to suggest of a positive nature, or indicated that the program should be made tougher, not easier.

"I think it is better if boys don't like this place. Adults shouldn't be friends with them, and the work supervisors should be tougher. Be stricter."

In other words, few boys alluded consciously to the need for such powerful rewards as respect, sympathetic understanding, or acceptance. These things were not a part of their cultural repertoires when they came, and apparently the program did not do enough to develop them. One boy, however, alluded to the problems of change, and why interpersonal support is such an important part of it.

"I think it is one of the hardest things to do to change. There are so many things to overcome. I think a person has to live Pinehills, and live changing day and night. What is discouraging though is when you are changing and no one knows you are changing."

It would be inaccurate to suggest that boys were totally unaware of the progress of others at Pinehills. Relations were too intimate for that. Nevertheless, this boy's poignant comments describe a problem likely to be present in correctional settings where offenders and staff tend to be defensive and distrustful of each other. Each not only tends to respond to the other in rigid and stereotyped ways, but relations among delinquents themselves tend to be stereotyped. Their constant need to protect status or to exhibit toughness is not conducive to a sympathetic understanding of the frailties of the human personality.

The problem is further complicated by the inevitable contrasts and conflicts that appear when some boys in a program are attempting to change while others are not. There is a definite need on the parts of the reformer group for some kind of protection against excessive deviancy by a few. Psychologically, it seems difficult for them to maintain their own acceptance of prosocial norms, their own changes in role, or their own abilities to help others unless there is a program climate that is strong and supportive.

It is not that offender-reformers are totally committed to punishment or that they are unwilling to help others. But their senses of personal security and social solidarity seem to require obvious limits on the ranges of behavior that can be tolerated. "I think," said one boy in the Silverlake Experiment (Empey and Lubeck, 1971:233), "that it is discouraging when a guy is changing and there are a few pricks around who are doing just the opposite. It gums the whole works up and the group spends all its time putting fires out."

In a similar way, Bullington, Mann and Geis (1969:456-63) report that exaddicts who had been hired to work with practicing addicts experienced considerable role conflict between their new-found inclination to adopt conventional behavior, and the job demands placed upon them as street workers. Their relationships with practicing addicts were such a forceful reminder of what they had been, and could again become, that it seemed necessary for them "to put distance between themselves and their clients in order to secure a firm middle-class footing." Punishment, of course, is one method reformers can use to accomplish this. Not only does it serve to put distance between them and the deviant, but it is less costly in personal and organizational terms—in terms of the rebuffs any reformer is likely to receive, and in terms of the patience and respect he must exhibit if he is to win the confidence and cooperation of the deviant. The task of finding rewards is even more complicated.

5

Program Salience and the Short-Run Control of Delinquency

This chapter is concerned with the relative capacity of the experimental program to control delinquent behavior during the intervention period. There are some compelling reasons for presenting data on this particular issue.

In Chapter 3, it was suggested that community correctional organizations, which by necessity are narrow in scope, must automatically sacrifice some of the means for involvement and control that are inherent in broader, coercive organizations. When scope is narrow, the salience of the organization to the offender may not be especially great. This is why arguments are often made by the police and a frightened public that society is not well protected by community programs, and that other potential lawbreakers are not deterred. A key question, therefore, is whether narrow correctional organizations can successfully manage the tensions of offenders in the open community while they are undergoing the intervention experience.

A second major reason for examining this question has to do with the group nature of the program, and the deliberate attempts that were made to make the delinquent group both the target and medium of change. Rather than encouraging the adoption of prosocial norms, the efforts that were made to enhance collective solidarity and cohesion among delinquents might have had the opposite effect. These efforts might have encouraged the perpetuation of delinquent perspectives rather than reducing or eliminating them.

While there was relatively little evidence regarding this issue when the Provo Experiment first began, the results of a number of gang studies since then have suggested that the consequences of the group approach could have been undesirable. Among other things, detached workers with street gangs have attempted to contact, to establish relations with, and to make those gangs, rather than the individuals within them, the target of change. Gang workers have sought to substitute organized meetings, athletic pursuits, and other seemingly interesting group activities for the usual activities of street gangs. Hopefully, gang members would coalesce around the detached worker, the gangs would be converted into prosocial clubs, and delinquency would be reduced. Yet, there is virtually no evidence that this particular kind of group work has been particularly successful (cf. Miller, 1962; Berelman and Steinburn, 1968; Klein, 1971).

According to Klein (1971), the problem is not that street workers are unable to contact and to enhance a sense of solidarity among gang members and between themselves and the gang, but that these results do not bring about a

73

reduction in delinquent behavior. He found that gangs often did meet more often under the sponsorship of a worker, and that there was an increase of cohesion in them. But, ironically, increased cohesion in the gangs was accompanied by an *increase*, not a decrease, in delinquency. Klein (1971:239) concluded, therefore, that adult sponsorship of a group approach may only serve to reinforce deviant values and behaviors not to dissipate them.

In support of his belief that efforts should not be made to use the group as a medium of change, Klein (1971:225-264) presents some rather impressive evidence that programs might be more successful if they attempted to dissolve delinquent groups and peer influence by providing boys with viable alternatives on an individual basis—one-to-one adult sponsorship, employment, tutoring, counseling and so on. Under ordinary circumstances, delinquent groups are held together more by the external pressures of an antagonistic community than by the force of internal relationships that are inherently rewarding. Nothing should be done, therefore, to make them more cohesive.

While the Provo program can scarcely be equated with street work, the questions that Klein raises are serious ones. Although delinquents reported that the techniques used in the Provo Experiment had had a controlling influence on their behavior, at least during the intervention period, one can not take their subjective assessments at face value. Some empirical evidence is needed. Hence, the short-run effectiveness of the experimental program will be assessed in two ways: (1) by comparing the dropout rates for the two sets of experimental groups with the rates for the two control groups; and (2) by comparing the official delinquency rates for these same groups.

Dropout Rates

The analysis of dropout rates is important for both practical and research reasons. In practical terms, it is important to obtain some general measure of the extent to which correctional programs, especially those in the community, are able to retain and work with serious offenders. In this Experiment, an important objective was to keep delinquents in the program and in the community. Thus, evidence relative to the success of that endeavor is important.

This interest is paradoxical in light of Lerman's (1970:321-2) finding that many correctional organizations do not include dropouts in their assessments of outcome. In some cases, they may even take steps to obscure their existence. Consider his summary analysis of the problem:

One private residential center in New York state studied by the author controls its population to the extent of rejecting seventeen boys for every one accepted for residential treatment. This institution (hereafter referred to as "Boysville") considers many nonpsychological factors in exercising discretion at intake; that is, age, previous record, ethnicity, space in the cottages. Having exercised this population control at intake, Boysville then proceeds to use its freedom to reject boys who "resist treatment." An unpublished study by the author of Boysville found that 31 per cent (51 out of 164) of the boys in the sample released from the institution were classified as not completing treatment. Most of these boys (40) were sent to state training schools. The average length of their stay at the private institution was sixteen months, far exceeding the customary remand period of ninety days. Had these boys been sent to nearby "Statesville" at intake, their average stay would have been only nine months.

Nor is this problem unique to private, nonsectarian organizations in New York state; it is just more acute at Boysville. A study of Highfields . . . reveals that 18 per cent of the population released did not complete treatment. A study of another special program in Michigan reveals a rate of 18 per cent. An unpublished study of a sectarian residential treatment center in New York State disclosed a rate of 25 per cent. Street, Vinter and Perrow comment that in one institution, "many boys were screened out in the first three months." . . .

Lerman (1970:322) goes on to point out that such organizations cannot reasonably take credit only for those who successfully complete treatment and then avoid becoming delinquent after release. Instead, they should take credit for "internal" failures as well, those who become dropouts in the course of treatment. Otherwise, the result may not only be misleading, but obscure the importance of avoiding the imposition of even more severe sanctions upon the young person.

In research terms, it is just as important to determine what the effects on delinquents are of partial, as well as full exposure to program stimuli. Paradoxically, there is a real possibility that dropouts, so-called program failures, may do as well after only partial exposure to treatment as those who receive full exposure, especially if there are harmful as well as beneficial effects in the treatment experience.

As it turned out in this study, dropout rates did not pose an overwhelmingly serious problem in either practical or research terms. As may be seen in Table 5-1, almost nine out of ten boys in the probation experimental and control groups completed their respective programs. The incarceration experimental group lost a slightly higher proportion (16 per cent) but, given the fact that this group would have been incarcerated had not the experimental program been in existence, this loss was not excessively high. Finally, there were no dropouts from the incarceration control group, something that might have been anticipated since they were confined in a rather secure, total institution.

In a general sense, these findings suggest that it may be possible to retain and work with serious offenders in the community. At least in this case, only 26 boys, or 13 per cent of the 194 assigned to the three community samples, failed to complete their respective programs. The low dropout rates suggest that the majority were not sufficiently delinquent to warrant incarceration during their periods of supervision.

Since, overall, only 26 of 326 subjects (8 percent) became dropouts, it will be

Table 5-1
Percentage of Dropouts from Experimental and Control Groups

Sample	Number Assigned	Dropouts Number	Percent
Probation Experimental	71	9	13
Probation Control	79	10	13
Incarceration Experimental	44	7	16
Incarceration Control	132	0	0
Totals	326	26	8

possible to determine with some confidence the long-term influence on delin-quents of experiencing the total effects of experimental and control stimuli. While it will be necessary later on to make sure the various samples are comparable after losing some subjects, the fact that 92 per cent are available is certainly helpful.

Assessment of Program Effectiveness

The second concern is the relative effectiveness of the various programs in controlling delinquency while subjects were under supervision. As Vasoli (1970:378-379) points out, however, any assessment of program effectiveness depends not only upon the behaviors of offenders, but upon the way effective-ness is defined and measured. Consequently, effectiveness criteria had to be set before rates could be compared.

In his study of the subject, Vasoli (1970) found that although all of a population of 622 adult federal probationers were officially counted as successes *during* their probationary periods, about one-quarter of them (155) had committed one or more felonies, to say nothing of misdemeanors. These felonies, moreover, included 1 case of homicide, 2 cases of rape, 31 cases of burglary, 33 cases of larceny, 34 cases of auto theft, 26 cases of embezzlement and many others.

"How could this be?," asked Vasoli. In the main, it was an artifact of record-keeping. When a federal probationer committed a new offense, it usually came under state rather than federal jurisdiction. Therefore, the federal officer terminated probation, relinquished jurisdiction, and cleared the federal record. On paper, the probationer was a "success" because he was not guilty of committing another federal offense. Although this practice has now been ended, it illustrates only one of the problems of providing valid data.

A second set of problems is inherent in the fact that any correctional program has multiple rather than a single goal. It is concerned with many kinds of offender adjustment—familial, educational, vocational and interpersonal—not just with law-violating behavior. If success is being achieved in terms of these other objectives, that success may provide grounds for overlooking some law violations (cf. Cressey, 1958 for a discussion of the issues). Moreover, correctional programs should be concerned with degrees, as well as absolute measures, of offender change. It may be a serious mistake to consider an offender a failure on the basis of one additional violation when, in terms of his prior record, he committed offenses with great frequency. A diminution of offense rate, especially if no offenses were serious, may be evidence of desirable change.

Finally, a third set of measurement problems is associated with the kinds of delinquency-related criteria that can be used in evaluating program effectiveness while offenders are under supervision. They can be divided into two general types: those that concern themselves with violation rates, and those that have to do with the way cases are officially disposed. Each of these, in turn, can be calculated in several different ways.

Violation rates can be determined by:

1. Arrests: How many offenders are arrested and charged with a new offense?

2. "Technical" Violations: How many offenders are described as failing to live up to the conditions of their probationary or other status—failing to pay a fine, to go to school, or to refrain from associating with other delinquents?

3. Petitions Filed: How many new petitions are filed with the court listing new arrests, technical or other violations?

4. Adjudication: How many offenders are found guilty of a new violation as the result of formal or informal court action?

One might establish violation rates by obtaining data from one or more of these different points in the legal process. However, it is apparent that different violation rates will be observed, depending upon the measure used. In general, the further one moves from the arrest toward the adjudication criterion, the lower the rate will be.

Program effectiveness can also be determined by the way in which cases are disposed. Rather than pay attention to offense behavior, this method implies the importance of the way the offender is treated.

Change in Status. How many offenders, even after a violation of some kind, experience no change in supervisory status? Presumably, one might evaluate effectiveness in terms of the number of cases in which there is no change in supervisory status vs. those in which a more severe sanction is imposed; i.e., removal from probation and confined. The imposition of a more stringent sanction would be recorded as "failure"; retention on the same status would be defined as a "success."

Time under Supervision. What are the relative times two groups of offenders are kept under supervision? In one study of parole (Adams, 1962), effectiveness was determined, not by the number of parolees found guilty of new offenses or the number reconfined, but by the *amount of time* they were reconfined. Effectiveness was a function of the time (and effort) necessary to work with the offender before he was again returned to the community.

The use of methods such as these implies judgments on the parts of someone that some cases are less serious than others, or that, given all the circumstances, variations in response are required. Presumably, any program resulting in less severe dispositions would be judged the more effective. However, any person who has ever carefully examined court records soon discovers that many boys, when returned to court for another disposition hearing, may have committed a long list of new offenses. Unless some attention is paid to them, therefore, a great deal of important information is lost which the new disposition only obscures. Equivalent dispositions are often given to two different boys, although one is charged with only one offense while the other has several. Given these and other problems, arrest rather than dispositional data seemed most appropriate for the assessment of inprogram effectiveness.

In the first place, the public is more concerned with reductions in the numbers and seriousness of delinquent acts than with the ways they are disposed. It is the capacity of community programs to reduce such acts that must be demonstrated if they are to receive public support. Although there is some merit in the argument that correctional programs cannot possibly be held responsible for the factors that can influence offender behavior (Reckless, 1955:26-42), correctional people cannot have it both ways. They cannot take credit for their successes while, at the same time, discounting responsibility for their failures. As Glaser (1970:535-536) points out, increasing pressure is being exerted on correctional agencies to provide better justifications for their expenditures of huge sums of money and costly intrusions into people's lives than mere headcounts and subjective testimonials regarding correctional effectiveness. Little can be gained in the long run by using effectiveness measures that obscure rather than reveal the most basic kinds of information.

Another consideration had to do with the fact that, about the only single outside criterion of effectiveness common to the different programs under study—probation, experimental intervention, and incarceration—was delinquent behavior. While it might have been desirable to assess the realization of other goals—education, improved family relations, changes in peer relations, or work skills—these goals were not uniformly shared by all the programs involved. Consequently, an examination of their capacities to reduce delinquent behavior seemed to be the fairest to all.

Exhaustive tabulations of arrest data, including referrals to the court by all officials, not just police, were made. Such data were obtained from every juvenile court in Utah, from the Utah State Industrial School, and from the Utah State Bureau of Criminal Identification.

Since we were concerned exclusively with offenses committed in the community, all behaviors of the incarceration control group that constituted a violation of rules and practices within the Utah State Industrial School were not recorded, even though many of them, if committed in the community, might have been subjected to official action. Only new arrests were tabulated. Analysis of such data will be made both in terms of frequency and seriousness, and in terms of the proportions of boys in each sample who committed additional delinquent acts while under supervision. The first body of findings has to do with arrest frequency.

Arrest Frequency during Intervention

Table 5-2 presents the mean number of arrests per boy during intervention for each of the samples. It will be observed that in descending order, the probation controls were the most delinquent with a mean of 1.31 arrests per boy, the incarceration experimentals second with .80 offenses, the probation experimentals third with .68, and the incarcerated controls last with .54 offenses. Thus, quite aside from the content of any program, the amount of inprogram delinquency was greatest in that program (probation) which had the least amount of contact with its subjects, and the lowest in that program (incarceration) where contact and surveillance were the greatest.

This finding is not especially surprising, except for the fact that some new violations were recorded for the incarceration controls. Since they were confined, the arrest rates reflect the fact that despite institutional restrictions, some of these boys committed new offenses, either when they were on some kind of home, work or educational furlough in the community, or when they were charged with unlawful escape from confinement. (These figures do *not* include the parole violation rates for the boys who were confined because they will be considered in the analysis of postrelease behavior.)

Table 5-2
Mean Number of Arrests per Boy During Intervention

Sample	Number of Boys	Mean Number of Arrests	Standard Deviations
Probation Experimental	71	.68	1.03
Probation Control	79	1.31	1.51
Incarceration Experimental	44	.80	1.50
Incarceration Control	132	.54	1.68

More important, perhaps, are the offense rates when graduates and dropouts are considered separately in comparing experimental and control groups. The data are revealed in Table 5-3.

With respect to *graduates*, the mean number of arrests per boy for the probation control group (1.28) was more than twice as high as that for the experimental group (.58), a difference that was highly significant ($z = 3.56; p <$ .001). This difference was an important one because almost nine out of ten subjects in these two groups were graduates.

Dropouts in the probation control group also had a higher arrest rate (1.66) than dropouts in the experimental group (1.33), although in this case differences were not statistically significant. Since, however, dropouts comprised only 13 per cent of the total in each group, their impact on the overall group means were not great. Consequently, if one compares these overall means, the differences between the two probation groups were considerable: a mean of .68 for the experimentals vs. 1.31 for the controls ($z = 2.99; p < .01$). Given this finding, plus the fact that the experimentals had been somewhat more delinquent than the controls prior to intervention (a mean of 5.4 vs. 4.6 arrests per boy), the experimental program seems to have been more effective than probation in controlling arrest volume during intervention.

A comparison of the two *incarceration* groups presents a more complicated picture. On one hand, if *graduates* alone are considered, differences are not significant ($z = .29$). The mean number of arrests per boy among incarceration experimentals (.62) was only slightly higher than that for the control group (.54). Surprisingly, this would suggest that despite their incarceration, the control group had not been less delinquent than the experimental groups who were free in the community. On the other hand, the control group had no dropouts, while the experimental group did, 16 percent. Thus, when experimental dropouts are included in the comparison, differences between the two groups are widened: .80 arrests per boy among experimentals vs. .54 for controls

Table 5-3
Mean Number of Arrests of Graduates and Dropouts During Intervention

Sample	Mean Number of Arrests		Standard Deviations	
	Graduates	Dropouts	Graduates	Dropouts
Probation Experimental	.58 (N = 62)	1.33 (N = 9)	.94	1.41
Probation Control	1.28 (N = 69)	1.66 (N = 10)	1.55	1.45
Incarceration Experimental	.62 (N = 37)	1.71 (N = 7)	1.38	1.90
Incarceration Control	.54 (N = 132)	0 (N = 0)	–	–

($z = .96; p > .05$). While these differences favor the controls, the most striking thing about them is that they were not of even greater magnitude, given the fact that the experimental group was free in the community. One might have expected considerably more inprogram delinquency from them.

Such findings suggest that the experimental program may have had approximately the same effect on the more serious incarceration experimentals as it had on the probation experimentals. For example, consider the inprogram arrests for these two groups. Although prior to the experiment the incarceration experimentals had been more delinquent (6.39 vs. 5.35 offenses), Table 5-2 shows that their inprogram arrest rates were not much greater—.80 arrests for the incarceration experimental group vs. .68 for the probation experimental group—a difference that was not significant. Despite initial differences between the two groups, the experimental program seems to have been almost as effective in controlling the inprogram violations of the more delinquent, incarceration experimental group as it was in controlling those of the probation experimental group.

By way of summary then, these findings suggest two things: (1) that the experimental program was more effective than probation in controlling arrest frequency during exposure to the program; and (2) that the experimental program may have been almost as effective as incarceration. However, there is another factor that has not been considered that may well have affected the inprogram arrest rates that were observed—length of exposure to programming.

Length of Exposure to Programming

Length of exposure is important in making comparisons, both within and between programs. Within any program, a major task is that of discovering what the effects of complete, as contrasted to partial, exposure are. Exposure is important not only to those who graduate from the program, but those who fail to complete it—those who become dropouts.

As may be seen in Table 5-4, there were significant exposure variations both within and between the programs under study. Within the probation experimental program, for example, graduates were exposed almost a third longer than dropouts (39 vs. 28 weeks); and in the control program, almost twice as long (49 vs. 25 weeks). In the incarceration experimental program, however, the picture was different. Graduates were exposed for lesser rather than greater periods of time (25 vs. 31 weeks). Finally, there were no dropouts among incarceration controls, so that comparisons in this case cannot be made.

There were important variations *between* programs as well. Considering total samples, probation controls were kept under supervision an average of 11 weeks longer than experimentals, a difference that was statistically significant ($z = 2.17; p < .05$). Similarly, the incarceration control group was kept significantly

Table 5-4
Lengths of Exposure to Intervention

Sample	Mean No. of Weeks			Standard Deviation		
	Grads.	D.O's.	Total	Grads.	D.O's.	Total
Probation Experimental	39 (N = 62)	28 (N = 9)	37 (N = 71)	14	17	15
Probation Control	49 (N = 69)	25 (N = 10)	46 (N = 79)	34	11	33
Incarceration Experimental	25 (N = 37)	31 (N = 7)	26 (N = 44)	13	15	13
Incarceration Control	46 (N = 132)	0 (N = 0)	46 (N = 132)	25	–	25

longer than the community experimental group ($z = 6.78$; $p < .001$), a difference of twenty weeks.[1] Thus, some effort to control for the effects of exposure upon effectiveness rates would seem to be important. It could be that the violation rates described above were as much the function of the amounts of time boys spent in the various programs as the natures of the programs themselves. Hence, that particular issue is explored in the next section.

Violation Rates with Exposure Controlled

Within-Program Comparisons

Consider first the within-program differences between graduates and dropouts. Although one can never know for certain what the offense rates for the two groups would have been had they been exposed to the same programming for equivalent lengths of time, a rough estimate can be made. This can be accomplished by standardizing the mean arrest rates for graduates and dropouts according to a common, average length of stay.[2]

Since dropouts in the probation experimental program were under supervision approximately 28 per cent less time than graduates, their mean number of arrests had to be inflated by the same amount to make it equivalent with that of the graduates. In the case of the probation control program, the required inflation was 49 per cent. As may be seen in Table 5-5, an educated guess would be that the rates of delinquency for dropouts in both programs would have been considerably higher had they remained in their respective programs as long as graduates. In the experimental program, the rate for dropouts would have raised from a mean of 1.33 to a mean of 1.70, and in the control program from a mean of 1.66 to a mean of 2.47.

The picture was different for the incarceration experimental program where dropouts were exposed for longer rather than shorter periods of time than

Table 5-5

Estimated Mean Number of Arrests for Graduates and Dropouts, Controlling for Length of Exposure

Sample	Mean No. of Recorded Arrests		Standardized (Estimated) Means*	
	Grads.	D.O's.	Grads.	D.O's.
Probation Experimental	.58	1.33	.58	1.70
Probation Control	1.28	1.66	1.28	2.47
Incarceration Experimental	.62	1.71	.62	1.39
Incarceration** Controls	.54	0	.54	0

*Means for graduates remain the same. Only the means for dropouts are estimated.
**Comparisons for incarceration control group not applicable because there were no dropouts.

graduates. Thus, if means are standardized in this case, the mean for the dropouts is deflated rather than inflated, by 19 per cent. The consequence is a lowering of the actual mean of 1.71 arrests per boy to an estimated mean of 1.39. Even so, this new estimated mean is still more than twice as high as the actual mean for the graduate group.

Since there were no dropouts from the incarcerated group, no analysis for them can be made. But in the case of the other three groups, the findings imply that when length of exposure is controlled *within* programs, dropouts are likely to be more delinquent than graduates. Most dropout cases were apparently due to an excessive amount of delinquency. While such findings are tentative, they suggest that some serious problems might be encountered in community programs for a small proportion of the boys involved.

Between-Program Comparisons

Since there were no dropouts from the incarceration control program, all between-program comparisons on length of exposure will include total samples. That is the only way a fair comparison can be made. Using the same standardization procedures described above, the findings were as follows.

With regard to the *probation* experimental and control group, Table 5-5 shows that the experimental group was under supervision 19 per cent less time than the control group (37 vs. 46 weeks). If the mean number of arrests for the experimental group (.68) is inflated by 19 per cent, the result is an estimated mean of .81 arrests. Tests of significance, using this estimated mean and the actual mean of the control group (1.31), show that the mean for the controls is still significantly larger ($z = 2.42; p < .02$). Even after making an adjustment for length of exposure, probation experimentals seem to have committed less inprogram delinquency than controls.

The same is not true of the two incarceration groups. When the mean of the experimental group is inflated to match the much longer time that controls spent in confinement (26 vs. 46 weeks), a mean of 1.24 arrests for the experimentals is derived. Comparing this with the actual mean of .54 for the controls, a difference is observed that is statistically significant ($z = 2.73; p < .01$). This finding obviously requires a reinterpretation of the inprogram effectiveness of the incarceration experimental program. It suggests that if experimentals had been exposed to community programming for a period of time that was equivalent to the time controls were incarcerated, their inprogram violation rates would have been significantly higher.

Conclusions

When length of exposure is controlled, the findings suggest that intensity of supervision is a vital force in delinquency control, and that to the degree this intensity is diminished, inprogram arrest rates will increase. While this may be an important finding, it still remains to be seen whether intensity and length of supervision have any discernible impact on postprogram delinquency rates, whether these differences carry over into the period after offenders are released from supervision. Before that can be done, however, we must complete our analysis of inprogram delinquency. Our next concern, for example, is with the proportion of boys in each sample who were involved in delinquency while still under supervision.

Proportions of Offenders and Delinquency

The foregoing analysis of arrest frequency using sample means could be misleading because such means tend to suggest that all boys had inprogram arrests when, in fact, the means may have been highly influenced by the contributions of a relatively few extreme cases. Consequently, another way of measuring inprogram effectiveness is to determine the proportions of each sample who were arrested. The data for such an analysis are presented in Table 5-6.

First, consider the findings for the total samples. The table shows that the percentage of boys in each sample who were involved in delinquency during intervention varied systematically with the amount of supervision and contact they received. Almost seven out of ten (68 per cent) of the probation control

Table 5-6
Percent of Samples Arrested During Intervention

Sample	Number in Sample		Percent Arrested		Mean No. of Arrests	
	Total	Grads.	Total	Grads.	Total	Grads.
Probation Experimental	71	62	48%	30%	2.04	1.67
Probation Control	79	69	68	54	2.68	2.38
Incarceration Experimental	44	37	46	27	3.15	2.30
Incarceration Control	132	132	19	19	2.88	2.88

group were arrested another time, followed by the probation experimentals with 48 per cent, the incarceration experimentals with 46 per cent, and the incarceration controls with 19 per cent. The findings confirm the point that intensity of supervision seems to be an important influence in controlling inprogram delinquency. Perhaps the most striking confirmation is not the sharp contrasts between the probationers, on one extreme and the incarcerated boys on the other, but the striking similarity between the two experimental groups. Despite the fact that the incarceration experimentals had been more delinquent than the probation experimentals prior to intervention, the proportions of boys in these samples who were delinquent during the intervention period were almost identical. It seems likely that their experience in a common program had an almost equal effect upon them.

Contrasts between Experimentals and Controls

When comparisons are made between the two *probation* groups, differences are significant past the .05 level ($z = 2.29$). Fewer experimentals had been arrested. The opposite was true of the two incarceration groups. A larger proportion of the experimentals had been arrested in this case, such that they differed significantly from the controls ($z = 3.35$; $p < .001$). Overall, then, the findings suggest that the experimental program was an effective control device for a larger number of delinquents than probation, but that it was less effective than incarceration.

If one considers only program graduates—those who received full exposure to the various programs—much the same picture is presented. However, as Table 5-6 indicates, the proportions of graduates who had inprogram arrests were much lower than the proportions for the samples as a whole. The findings indicate that the few dropouts in each sample were the ones who were excessively delinquent.

When these graduate proportions were compared, the differences between the two probation groups were even more significant ($z = 2.77; p < .01$), indicating that the experimental graduates were considerably less delinquent than controls during intervention (54 vs. 30 per cent). On the other hand, the differences between the two incarceration groups narrowed (27 vs. 19 per cent), indicating that they did not differ significantly ($z = 1.06$). Graduates in the experimental program were little more delinquent than graduates from incarceration. Consequently, the relative effectiveness of the experimental program is enhanced in both comparisons, but while the comparison is especially relevant for the two probation groups, it is less relevant for the other two, since there were no dropouts from the incarceration control group.

Offense Seriousness during Intervention

The final important dimension to be considered in evaluating inprogram effectiveness is the seriousness of the offenses that occurred. The question that needs answering is to what extent the various programs were able to control offenses of varying degrees of seriousness during intervention. Table 5-7 presents the findings.

For the graduates who were fully exposed to the methods of each program, it is clear that their offenses during intervention were mostly of a low-serious variety—truancy, "incorrigibility," curfew, traffic, and similar types of violations. About eight out of ten offenses among the three community samples were of this type, and for the incarcerated boys, it was seven out of ten.

Some interesting things relative to the more serious kinds of violations may be observed. First, virtually all of them were of the medium-serious variety, involving such things as auto theft, burglary, petty theft and, for several of the incarcerated boys, escape from incarceration with subsequent offenses associated

Table 5-7
Seriousness of Official Offenses During Intervention

Sample		Seriousness Categories							
		Low			Medium			High	
	Grads.	D.O's.	Total	Grads.	D.O's.	Total	Grads.	D.O's.	Total
Probation Experimentals	83%	69%	81%	17%	23%	19%	0%	0%	0%
Probation Controls	80	50	76	21	50	24	0	0	0
Incarceration Experimentals	78	58	71	22	42	29	0	0	0
Incarceration Controls	70	–	70	30	–	30	2	0	2

with their efforts to remain free. Secondly, larger proportions of the dropout group were involved in these more serious offenses than the graduates, especially among the probation controls and the incarceration experimentals. Finally, there was a gradient of involvement which reflected the prior delinquent histories of the various groups. The probation groups were the least delinquent, while the incarceration groups were the most delinquent. Even so, there were no statistically significant differences between graduates from the two sets of experimental and control groups. Moreover, it is probably significant that the preponderant majority of all four groups did not commit offenses during intervention of the most serious character.

Effects of Age and Status

It was suggested in Chapter 2 that age and social status might have an impact on correctional effectiveness. As a result, the relationships of both variables to inprogram delinquency were assessed.

With respect to age, about the only finding of any significance was the tendency for boys in the two probation groups to be somewhat more delinquent than older boys, while just the reverse was true in the two incarceration groups. There, it was the 17-year-olds who were the more delinquent. These tendencies were not of sufficient strength to warrant either acceptance or rejection of the notion that significant trends were at work.

There were some differences with respect to social status, but again they were reflective more of slight tendencies than of important trends. In both of the traditional control programs—probation and incarceration—the mean number of inprogram offenses decreased as social status increased: for probation, the means were 1.69 for lower status, 1.23 for middle, and 1.00 for upper; for incarceration, they were .42 for lower, .24 for middle, and .20 for upper status. This may say something about these two programs because there were no consistent trends in the two experimental groups. Social status did not seem to have discernible impact. While there may have been a tendency for offense behavior in the two traditional programs to be inversely related to status, that tendency was not a highly significant one.

Implications

This chapter has several implications for corrections: whether community programs pose a serious danger to others; whether efforts to use the group as a medium for change poses serious problems; and why dropouts occur and what can be done to decrease them. By devoting some attention to these issues, the findings for this study can be placed into a larger perspective.

Organizational Salience and Dangers to Community

As suggested earlier, the use of community programs for serious delinquents generates fears that the community will not be well protected because it is assumed that the programs are not salient enough to the offenders involved. In this case, however, those fears were not entirely substantiated. Although fairly large proportions of some groups were arrested during intervention, the mean number of offenses per boy was not great, nor were offenses of an especially serious character. Ironically, the most serious offenses were committed by escapees from incarceration, not by the experimental groups who never left the community.

The trouble with being overly sanguine about such findings, is that they are not readily confirmed by other studies. There is a dearth of such studies, and the few that are available do not always support these findings. For example, in her evaluation of the Los Angeles Community Delinquency Control Project, conducted by the California Youth Authority, Pond (1970) recorded a great deal of inprogram delinquency.

This experiment covered a three-year period in which selected California Youth Authority wards were paroled to two intensive community programs in lieu of incarceration, and the usual release to regular parole which follows it. The findings in this study are particularly relevant because its experimental and control groups were analogous to the incarceration experimental and control groups at Provo. The findings, however, were much different.

First, about three-fourths of both of the Los Angeles experimental groups had one or more arrests during the first 15 months of supervision, and over half had from two to six arrests (Pond, 1970:20). Arrest data were not provided on the incarcerated controls covering the period of their incarceration, but they were provided for the period during which controls were on parole. That data indicated that the controls were somewhat less delinquent than the experimentals. While about as many of them as experimentals were arrested at least once while still on parole, significantly fewer were arrested more than once. These high rates of inprogram delinquency, especially among experimentals, contrast sharply with those at Provo where the incarceration experimentals had an average of less than one offense per boy while under supervision. About four out of ten delinquents in both experimental and control groups in Los Angeles were arrested for offenses of a relatively serious nature.

The result was that over half (53 percent) of all experimentals and controls in Los Angeles had their paroles revoked within the first 15 months, a figure that is sharply at odds with the dropout rates at Provo (Pond, 1970:26). Very few of these revocations were for "technical" violations; they were for new arrests. Even though strict comparisons between the Los Angeles and Provo findings are impossible, such findings warn against excessive optimism as a result of the Provo findings. Perhaps the variations were due to differences between the Utah and Los Angeles boys or environments, to the natures of the programs involved, or to the fact that individuals were followed longer in Los Angeles. But until more studies of a careful nature are conducted, one cannot be confident that community programs for serious offenders do not pose some danger.

With respect to the more specific issue of program salience and organizational type, the findings were provocative. They indicated that, even though three out of the four groups under study at Provo were in the community, rates of arrest were inversely related to the kinds and amounts of supervision that were exercised.

This finding was most pronounced for the two probation groups. The delinquency rates for those boys who participated in the experimental program were significantly less than the rates for the controls who were on regular probation. However, it was somewhat less true for the two incarceration groups. On one hand, significantly more of the experimentals than the incarcerated controls were delinquent. On the other hand, the number of delinquent acts committed by the experimentals was not significantly greater than those committed by the incarcerated controls. It was only when length of exposure to programming was controlled that the number of delinquent acts became greater for the experimentals.

These findings are important because they suggest that if the negative effects of involuntary institutional living can be avoided, it may be possible to develop alternative kinds of organizations for the *serious offender* that are more successful in reducing inprogram delinquency than some of the more traditional ones. These empirical findings supported the perceptions of delinquents that efforts to define and reinforce basic expectations, coupled with an effort to enhance the normative power of the organization, were quite effective in controlling delinquency, at least during the supervisory period. It would seem that any solution as to what should be done with the small minority who are the most serious delinquents may lie less in the direction of constructing more and costly institutions in order to control youngsters than in the direction of better matching adolescent needs to different kinds of organizations in the community.

In support of this idea, one of the most impressive findings in the Silverlake Experiment (Empey and Lubeck, 1971:306-307) was that there did not seem to be any uniform sets of personal or background variables that were consistently predictive of offender behavior in every kind of organizational setting. Instead, that behavior (indeed, correctional effectiveness) seemed to be the product of the proper match between personal and social systems. The findings were such as to argue against the common and simplistic conclusion that because dropout or recidivism rates for different programs are approximately equal, they produce essentially the same effect on all offenders. While overall rates among programs may be much the same, it is likely that the personal and organizational factors that interact to produce them will be different. Boys who do well in one program may not do well in another, and *vice versa.* By beginning to document more carefully what those factors are, we might ultimately reach a stage where we could be less concerned with intensity of supervision, because of the controls it provides, than with supervision that is effective because it solves childhood problems.

Use of Group Methods

These findings were at odds with those described by Klein (1971), in which efforts to work through and with delinquent groups produced an increase rather than a decrease in delinquency. In this case, attempts to enhance group participation and solidarity did not seem to increase delinquent tendencies. It seems quite clear, therefore, that differences were due to the types of programs involved.

In less structured street work with gangs where many boys are not adjudicated offenders, as they were at Provo, it is probably impossible, if not unwise, to duplicate Provo methods in their entirety. It is more difficult to set clear expectations, to reinforce those expectations at times with negative sanctions, and to involve the boys themselves in exercising normative controls. Yet, there are some principles inherent in this general approach that may have utility.

These empirical findings tend to support the recent studies cited in the previous chapter which indicate that the fear of punishment, as well as the anticipation of reward gained by observing others being punished or rewarded, has a deterrent effect on deviant acts. When negative as well as positive sanctions are personalized, the likelihood of deviant behavior, at least for the near future, is decreased. Hence, if these principles could be operationalized in a less coercive way than at Provo, where the direct concern is more with prevention prior to adjudication, they may be useful for street work.

Street work, in many cases, has been so unstructured that it may have been difficult for boys to know what was expected of them. As a result, there has been no focal point around which to build a normatively-oriented and prosocial organization. It is unlikely that boys might see the relevance either of negative or positive sanctions. Neither prosocial nor delinquent behavior can be reinforced effectively unless there are norms that clearly set forth what is expected of a person. Many boys who are inclined to drift anyway may have been left in limbo where the only expectations that were very clear were those that were delinquent in character. Efforts to remedy these deficiencies might enhance the effectiveness of work with street groups.

Program Dropouts

The final implication has to do with the low dropout rate observed in this study. Only about 13 percent of the 194 boys assigned to the three community programs, it will be recalled, did not successfully complete them.

While it is often assumed that dropouts occur because of new arrests, this is often not the case. As Lerman's findings suggested earlier (1970:321), correctional organizations may discharge some delinquents unfavorably because they resist treatment, or because of some other internal consideration. Such unfavorable discharge rates, he found, varied from 18 to 31 percent.

Another contributor to dropout rates is runaway behavior. In their study of juvenile correctional organizations, Street, et al., (1966:197) found a wide variation of runaway rates between six different institutional programs and interpreted the varied rates to be a function of differences in the organizations studied. They found that the two organizations that placed the highest emphasis upon control had relatively low runaway rates (16 and 20 percent), while the two organizations that emphasized "treatment" over control had relatively high runaway rates (50 and 29 percent), rates that were much higher than at Provo.

These rates, however, were similar to the runaway rates observed in the Silverlake Experiment (Empey and Lubeck, 1971:Chaps. 10-11). In that study, a community-based experimental program had a surprisingly high runaway rate of 37 percent. In addition, there was a failure rate of 17 percent, largely due to technical reasons, not new arrests. When the two rates were added together, the total dropout rate became 54 percent. Interestingly, the dropout rate for the control group, which was placed in an open, but institutional setting, was almost identical: 40 percent runaways and 10 percent failures, a total of 50 percent in all.

These rather high and strikingly similar rates are especially relevant for this analysis. The reason is that there was only one major difference between the Silverlake and Provo *experimental* programs: the Silverlake program, although located in the community, was residential, while the Provo program was not. About 20 boys were required to live together in a common household. It seems highly possible that one of the primary reasons for the high dropout rate at Silverlake and other places, as contrasted to the low rate at Provo, was the fact that boys were required to live involuntarily in a correctional residence or institution.

One would not have to have a population of delinquents to anticipate problems if he required them to live against their wills in a correctional setting. One could only imagine what the problems would be if that population were college students, and if one attempted to require them to adhere to the same regimen to which delinquents usually have to adhere—lights out at a certain time, regular attendance at work or school, no fights, drunkenness or smoking pot. Under these conditions, it seems highly likely that the dropout rate would be even higher. College students (perhaps even girl scouts) would be more likely to run away or be defined as incorrigible, especially if they were in a community setting where they could walk away at any time.

As if this were not enough, even more problems might be anticipated if the same pressures to conform and yet to change were put on a nondelinquent population as are put on a delinquent one. In both the Silverlake and Provo Experiments, our data indicated that as these programs evolved, the number of critical incidents and actual delinquent acts began to decrease (Empey and Lubeck, 1971:193-199).

On one hand, this development has its positive side. Many of the boys who had been in these programs for some time began to play a reformation role and wanted to stay out of trouble. They supported the idea that deviance should be decreased and that they, as well as staff, should be involved in bringing this about. Prosocial group norms began to develop. On the other hand, this state of affairs seems to have had an adverse effect on some of the boys, especially newcomers, who were unprepared for the new environment in which they found themselves. They were unused to a setting in which their peers, like staff, were playing a reformer role. This problem was worsened by the fact that boys and staff who had been in the program for longer periods of time were not sensitive enough to the uncertainties that confronted newcomers.

But the problems were not merely those of the newcomer. As the Silverlake data showed, there were difficulties that confronted delinquent reformers as well—those boys who seemed to buy the notion of staying out of trouble. They were in need of stability, and seemed to feel threatened by the minority who continued to get into trouble and who inevitably made the group and reformation processes turbulent. The result was some polarization in the programs between the majority whose delinquencies were decreasing, and the minority whose delinquencies were not.

This was not a new phenomenon in corrections. Other investigators have reported that, even in open and innovative correctional settings, there is a continual oscillation from a condition of permissiveness to one in which program ideals are discarded in favor of an arbitrary removal or suppression of the deviant (Street, Vinter and Perrow, 1966:159-190; Rapoport, Rapoport and Rosow, 1960:135-142). In programs in which the offender is sponsored in a reformation role, there is a strong and understandable tendency for the reformer group to be concerned about their own needs for support, and to be rigid in response to deviants. There is merit in the old cliché that there is no one so straight-laced as a reformed sinner. Such persons seem to require strong social and psychological supports in the process of acquiring and maintaining a new self-conception.

Obviously, problems such as these are not always characteristic of more traditional programs in which delinquents do play a reformation role. There are tensions of another variety in such places which may be equally compelling in their need for resolution. This is evidenced by the high dropout rates reported by Street, et al., and by the Silverlake institutional control group whose rates were virtually identical with those of the community experimental group. What, then, is the major point of the discussion?

The major point seems to hinge on whether programs are residential or not—whether offenders are forced to live together, or are free to return home each night after the daily correctional experience. Even though the boys in the Provo Experiment went through a daily experience much like that at Silverlake, they could return to home and community each night while those at Silverlake could not. They could realize some surcease from the pressures of the day, and did not have to spend all of their time in the same confined setting with people with whom their experiences were so often trying. One major reason for the low dropout rate among Provo experimentals—one that was only about one-third of that reported by others—would seem to be the fact that it was not a residential program. This would be even more true for the probation group whose correctional experiences very seldom approached the intensity of those in the experimental program, or those controls who were incarcerated. Clearly, though narrow in scope, these organizations managed tensions better than did broader ones.

On the other hand, the data clearly documented the fact that, if a place of confinement can be made quite secure, such as the incarceration group in the Provo Experiment, the dropout rate can be eliminated entirely. However, that is quite another issue. The issue that is paramount is what the effects are on the delinquent of being submitted to various kinds of programming in open residential and nonresidential settings where he can either walk away or commit new delinquent acts rather easily. In that event, these findings would suggest that it is the highly narrow, nonresidential program that provides the most desirable result. Paradoxically, perhaps, it is this kind of organization that seems to be most successful in preventing dropout problems.

6

Guidelines for Group Development

One cornerstone of the experimental program at Provo was the use of group techniques designed to increase the participation of delinquents and to enhance a sense of organizational solidarity. Chapter 4 suggested that delinquents felt these techniques had been the most valuable part of the program. They felt that they had gained more from them than from any other activity. That may be one reason why the delinquency rates for the two experimental groups were relatively low during the intervention period.

This chapter is devoted to a description of the particular approach to the use of groups that was taken. It is *not* meant to be an objective and empirical assessment of program operation, but rather an enlarged statement of the guidelines that were developed to assist staff members in working with groups.

As indicated earlier, there was a body of theory suggesting that group techniques might provide an effective tool, but provocative though that theory was, it did not by itself provide appropriate guidelines for action. It was one thing to suggest that staff members should sit down with delinquents and try to produce a more effective correctional organization, and quite another to have them do so successfully.

This chapter is a hypothetical guide to group and program development. Part of the chapter was originally prepared to assist staff in the conduct of the experiment, but it has been enlarged by a series of illustrative excerpts from actual group meetings. It is presented to provide an understanding of the program, but because it was designed to indicate what should happen if conditions are ideal, it is only partially accurate in its portrayal of reality.

A fundamental premise was the idea that each new group of boys would go through a series of developmental stages. At the outset, group relations would be characterized by suspicion, distrust, and resentment. But because of the pressing need for some new mode of adjustment, it was felt that the group might be moved through a series of stages until it reached a relatively high degree of understanding, normative control, and shared problem-solving. What was needed, therefore, was some kind of conceptual road map for staff members that would indicate the place for a group to begin, and where it was expected to go. If a group leader were to stay on the right road, he would need some signposts along the way.

Based partly on experience and partly on a theory of group development by Martin and Hill (1957), some guidelines were constructed.[1] But since Martin and Hills' statement was concerned primarily with the inner workings of relatively traditional therapy groups, it had to be made applicable to delinquent groups, to their daily participation in community activities, and to their involvement in group decision-making. The final guidelines that were developed suggested that group, and in a sense organizational development, might be seen as occurring, at least theoretically, in a series of five stages. In order to help operationalize the nature of these five stages, each one of them was described in terms of a common set of categories: (1) the particular *objectives* for the stage in question; (2) the nature of the *group structure* at that stage; (3) the kind of *group process* that might be expected; and (4) the kinds of *discussion content* that should be fostered. This framework is sketched below.

Before proceeding to it, however, it may be useful for the reader to recall that the population of offenders assigned to the program included no more than twenty boys at any one time, and that this group of twenty was broken down into two smaller groups of ten each. Thus, the theoretical statement would be especially pertinent to the operation of each of these small groups as a separate unit. An attempt would be made to keep membership constant so that the anticipated development might be enhanced. As much as possible, members would enter and leave the program at approximately the same time. In addition, it was anticipated that as the program developed, there would be greater and greater carryover from one group to the other. The program itself would go through an evolutionary process parallel to the evolution of each small group. The postulated stages of development had relevance for the overall program as well as for each small unit within it.

Stage 1—Search for Structure

Objectives

It was anticipated that when offenders were first assigned to the experimental program and to a small group within it, they would have neither the experience nor the trust to exercise much effective decision-making or power. Such a condition would be temporary, of course, but a major mistake could be made if too much were expected of the group at this time—if it were expected, for example, that interaction would be without conflict, or that difficult decisions could be readily made. Rather, behavior would be erratic and defensive and, as a result, the concern of a group leader should be with fostering interaction among group members and instilling some confidence that it might eventually be effective and rewarding. Consequently, the objectives set for Stage 1 were twofold: (1) to foster and reward interaction; and (2) to teach delinquent group members that whatever interaction took place in a group and whatever progress was made, would depend upon them, not just staff.

Structural Context

The structural context would be one of relative *anomie*. To be sure, delinquents would be constrained by their involuntary assignment to the program, but they would have few clues beyond that as to how they should behave. The only actual evidence of structure would be their location in a strange correctional setting, and the expectation that they would remain a part of it.

Beyond this, there would be little formal structure. In fact, the group leader should make a conscious effort to avoid providing too much structure at this point. He should avoid playing traditional adult roles: the stern disciplinarian, the loving father, the kindly friend, or the all-wise doctor. While such a refusal might violate the expectations that delinquents have of him, it would help to dispel the efforts of group members either to become dependent upon him or to start immediately to manipulate him. The idea is to upset the reciprocal patterns that have tended to characterize relations between adults and offenders in the past, and to lay the groundwork for new relations.

At first, such an approach would appear to be contrary to the stated objective of fostering interaction in this stage. The point, however, is that while interaction is desirable, it should be interaction based upon newly emerging patterns, not traditional ones. If the group is to become a viable mechanism for shared power and decision-making, the group leader should not go out of his way to make group members comfortable by playing traditional roles.

Once interaction is initiated by others, he can ease tensions and reward comments by asking questions and by showing interest in what is said. But, at first, it may be necessary for him to sit silent for long periods in order to suggest that he does not wish to foster dependency by assuming the kind of stereotyped leadership role that is expected. He is not nearly so concerned with the content of that which is spoken, as with the fact that something is instigated by group members. When the group leader does intervene, he is anxious to support individuals rather than to evaluate or judge what is said. He should convey an acceptance of the importance of interaction by acknowledging the comments of group members.

Two problems might emerge for which conclusive answers do not exist. The first has to do with the extent to which the lack of structure and subsequent anxiety might stimulate resistance in some delinquents to such a degree that they will never participate effectively because of the defenses which they build up. Boys may well respond by doing nothing. The second problem is a group problem. Heightened anxiety and the lack of structure could produce subgroups that might be undesirable. It may be that the ties which delinquents bring with them to the group can serve as a focal point around which delinquent tendencies and solutions are encouraged, not new and nondelinquent patterns established.

Neither kind of response, however, should be cause for alarm. People usually respond to new situations in ways that are common to them. The possibility, for example, that delinquent cliques might develop was considered to be desirable, not unwelcome. Only after they appear, can they become the subject of group analysis and their implications assessed. Since it was considered inevitable that resistive offender cliques would develop anyway, one of the major objectives of the new system was to precipitate such responses, not to drive them underground. The task of weighing the alternatives open to delinquent boys can only be accomplished by having both alternatives clearly demonstrated.

Group Process

Perhaps the most pronounced dynamic of Stage 1 is the *search for structure*. General experience seems to indicate that, whenever individuals are placed in a group setting with which they have had little previous experience, they tend to respond to each other in terms of previously held stereotypes. The traditional concept of transference in psychotherapy is used to connote the interactive effect of this kind of response. A person's reactions are determined by his former patterns and experiences, rather than by the stimulus present in the context of the current relationship.

If this is so, individual group members will find themselves in an awkward spot, one which will result in a groping, noncommital and often angry kind of interaction. They will engage in testing to determine whether their gestures will elicit acceptance, rejection, or a guarded invitation to further exploration. The behavior they exhibit may well be based largely on the private and verbally unshared fantasies which they hold about other members of the group. The strain of this stage will be heightened by the efforts of group members to balance what appear to be contradictory expectations: the conformist expectations of a conventional group leader and the deviant expectations of delinquent peers. Group members will not be interested in responding to each other as individuals or in seriously trying to meet individual needs. Each will be too involved with his own private search for meaning.

Productive communication under such conditions will be virtually impossible, not because there is a lack of verbal interaction, but because people are interacting in terms of their own private frames of reference. When this occurs, the group will attempt to have the group leader assume an authoritarian role; but while he might offer suggestions, he should not assume responsibility for organizing and leading the interaction. If he does not go out of his way to make the group comfortable, he is more likely to set the stage for the development of an effective group, one in which everyone struggles with the problems at hand. It is not as though offenders were being provided with a license to be more delinquent. They are confronted with a difficult situation for which some different mode of adaptation is necessary.

Discussion Content

Discussion content in the early parts of this phase will not appear to be going anywhere, although considerable frustration lies just under the surface. Consider the following interaction taken from a newly formed group.

Jack: What happens if you miss one of these meetings?
Phil: I don't know.
Jack: Do you go to jail?
George: I wish we had a gym up here.
Leader: Why is that?
George: 'Cause we could take five and go play ball.
          (long pause)
Hersh: Here we don't get five.
Group: Giggles
          (long pause)
Joe: I don't like gym.
Rog: What I'd like to know is how we get out of here.
Leader: Do you have any ideas?
Rog: Yeah, I got big ideas, but so far none have worked out.

Obviously, people who engage in interaction of this type are not task-oriented, and are not yet prepared to try to understand what is going on or to try to make the group efficient in terms of resolving important questions. The interaction is characteristic of that found in temporary groups, like cocktail parties, where a common sense of identity and trust has not been established.

Boys will often ask questions that are of considerable importance to them: "How long do we have to stay here?" "What are we supposed to be doing in these meetings?" "What should we talk about?" And while the group leader may feel inclined to respond, there is little that he can do to provide satisfying answers. Even if he tries, underlying tensions often prevent the group from dealing constructively with his answers. Above all, therefore, he must be completely honest in the answers he does give. For example, he does not know with certainty how long boys will have to stay. Past experience indicates that with daily group meetings, much progress can be made in a relatively short time, but even then, much depends on the nature and quality of group interaction. At best, he can point to obvious problems that he knows that group members share and suggest that they might start on them. Beyond that, his answers cannot be totally satisfying, since most people in this stage are in search of short-run, not long-run, solutions.

In addition, the group leader is in a terribly difficult position. His group is a captive group; members would not be present were it not for legal constraints. He represents authority. He is interested in building a group climate which will foster both candor and trust. In such a position, he can do little else than demonstrate that interaction is desirable and that he has confidence that new solutions can be found.

He is not without any resources. One technique is to encourage boys to talk about things of greatest interest to them; their delinquent careers, their feelings about the new program, what they do on weekends. These things are of lively interest to boys and are often provocative as well. The following excerpts illustrate this point. They are taken from a single boy's description of his delinquent history which, because of its length, took the better part of three meetings to recount. This history was of obvious interest to other boys because it was filled with humor, childishness, interest, and even danger. It started with a discussion of childhood pranks and ended up very seriously.

Jim: The first thing I done is steal a can full of pennies from my neighbor. There was about $10 in it.

Morrie: What did you do with all them pennies?

Jim: I went down to the service station, and put 'em in this peanut machine.

Hank: (incredulous) All of 'em?

Jim: Not all of 'em. It run out of peanuts (laughter).

George: What else did you do?

Jim: Well, when I was going to the Franklin School, when I was in the sixth grade, me and _____ and _____ used to go over to this little store, the _____ market, and have our dinner every day. We'd go and take candy bars and soda pop and ice cream and these big packages of candy.

Rich: Did they ever catch ya?

Jim: Yes and no. I got caught stealing in there once. I went in an' I thugged a 10¢ package of candy and an ice cream, and I had the ice cream in my back pocket and the candy in my front pocket an' the lady walked over to me an' asked if I was going to pay for the candy and I said, "no," and she said "well you better give it back then hadn't you?" And I said, "yah," an' I gave her back the candy and then walked out and thought it was pretty neat that I didn't get caught for the ice cream too. I thought it was pretty funny that she didn't know I had the ice cream. I never did steal anything in the store again but there was another one about a block away. We'd go over to that one, in _____ market; it wasn't as easy to steal over there. They'd follow us around in there.

Morrie: Well, didn't ya have enough money to buy your dinner?

Jim: Yah, but we'd spend it in the morning on candy 'n stuff and then at noon we wouldn't have any money to eat lunch in school so we'd go over to the store and steal it. One day we snitched a pound of weenies 'n some weenie buns 'n some catchup and had a weenie roast. We got caught doing' that cause we was all black and everything when we went back to school, (snicker) 'n had to go down and see the Principal 'n everything.

· · ·

Hank: Did you ever steal any cars or anything?

Jim: Yah, that's what I'm gonna talk about right now, how I got stealin' bigger stuff. Me 'n _____ , one Sunday night we went ridin' around, and we went to all the churches we could think of.

Pres: Did ya have a car?

Jim: Yah, we had my car and we went to this new church to siphon some gas and _____ was with us an' we got up there at these cars up at this _____ Church out by where _____ lives, and, uh, pulled up between a bunch of cars and then_____ jumped out with two gas cans 'n hoses and started siphoning gas out of these cars and_____was always standing watch and while he was standing watch he decided to get in this car and see what he could see in it. And it had some real pretty floor mats in it and they go clear across the car in the front and the back, and he got them out, and got some stuff out of the jockey box, some Blue Chip stamps and stuff, and got them over and after we got the gas, ya know, I seen the stuff that he got, so I decided that I'd go through some and all three of us started going through them then. We went through every car that was there, I think, and got all kinds of stuff.

George: Did ya get any money out of them?

Jim: No, we never did find no money. We got a lot of Blue Chip stamps and that, and we'd take the stamps to the store and trade 'em in for tool boxes and stuff . . . . 'cept for it was illegal and we could get in trouble. We never did git caught though.

• • •

Hank: What's that bit about the cop car?

Jim: I shot a cop car one night with my pistol. We was goin' down the highway, and this cop car passed us, and_____was with us that time, and he said, "we'll shoot that sonofabitch," and I said, "all right." And I pulled my .22 pistol and shot at it. I don't know if I hit it or not but it started chasin' us and I just took off up to the mountains in my jeep. He couldn't go up there, so we lost 'im.

(laughter)

It is impossible to sort out, at this stage of group development, what is fact and what is fancy in a recitation of this type. But that is not an important issue at this point. Rather, the material that is described will come up later when it is as important for delinquents to deal realistically with their delinquent image-gilding. A norm developed at Provo, as well as at Highfields, in which it was expected that each boy would eventually recount his delinquent history accurately, gradually separating fact from fancy. In fact, this process became a kind of rite-of-passage for the full acceptance of an individual into the group.

Two benefits seemed to accrue. First, group members became much better informed about each other. This awareness is not always verbalized at this point, but the group does learn a lot about the styles and backgrounds of its members. Second, the open discussion of sensitive material becomes a method of testing the group leader to see whether he will be overly moralistic and condemnatory. In fact, this testing can become the basis upon which an important norm is developed: that whatever is said in the group meeting is sacred. If problems are to be solved, people should feel free to reveal them without censure. Only in this way can a sense of social trust and solidarity be developed. It is important for the group leader to reinforce the notion that the sharing of information, which is to be held in confidence, is a desirable thing.

It must always be kept in mind, however, that the incorporation of these ideas by group members is a vague and gradual process. As Cohen (1959:467) has noted,

Deviant behavior and conformity are kinds of behavior that evolve in the course of an interaction process. When we say that deviant (or conformist) behavior is an attempt to reduce strain or to solve a problem of adjustment, we do not mean that an actor finds himself in an awkward spot, considers a number of alternatives, and then makes a choice. The break with the routine and the institutionalized is more typically half-conscious, tentative and groping. Ambivalence motivates exploratory but noncommital gestures. The gestures elicit from others responses which tend to reduce the original strain, responses which only make it worse, responses which signify that further movement in the same direction will receive a cold welcome, or responses which guardedly suggest that alter has problems akin to ego's and would like to explore with ego the possibility of new solutions.

As Cohen implies, it is not so much a willing and rational commitment to change that may eventually begin to move the group to another, more complex level of development as it is the fact that the story-telling and gripes inherent in these early meetings begin to lose their interest and to bore the members. The reason is that the group process itself is wandering and idiosyncratic. The remarks of each speaker are cued off by something in the previous speaker's remarks, but the material that is cued off is highly personal, indirect, tentative and not in the context of the previous speaker who provided the stimulus. In other words, the discussion does not seem to be going anywhere. Hearing about each other, or giving the group leader a hard time, may have been interesting for a while, but these things by themselves do not point the way to escape from the program which, after all, is the major goal of every boy. As a result, another kind of tension begins to mount in the group—one which arises for two reasons.

First, delinquents find daily, enforced attendance galling. They want to find some magic solution to their predicament. They want to escape the system in which they find themselves. Yet, the wandering and idiosyncratic character of the group process to this point seems to help little. It rambles, it is frustrating, and it provides little assurance that the group is accomplishing anything.

Second, in terms of group process, most people seek a variety of satisfactions from interpersonal interaction. Wandering interaction is limited in its capacity to provide these satisfactions. A member may enjoy the opportunity to talk about himself, but when, time after time, no one builds much on what he has to say, his satisfactions decrease. His remarks seem to have little lasting importance other than that he is the center of attention while he is speaking. This attention is gratifying for a period, but when his remarks seem to have little meaning to others, interaction becomes increasingly frustrating.

Transition from Stage 1 to Stage 2

These two sources of dissatisfaction comprise the force which, in most cases, may eventually move a group from its initial phase of operation to a more functional, collective approach. The success of the attempt will depend heavily upon the group leader. Patience and constant attention to group process are highly important. If he is aware of the growing dissatisfaction, he can begin the task of helping the group to move to another level by exploring with members what the group is doing and why there seems to be little movement. There is no lack of examples of the need for the group to focus its attention—the failure to build on what others say, or the skirting of important issues. By supporting those who express their dissatisfactions, he can help members to communicate any insights they have gained regarding their present dilemma. If he is able to do this, his role as a group leader can begin to emerge. In becoming somewhat more functional than authoritarian, it is a means of allaying anxiety and providing structure.

The group leader should be aware that any actual transition from the beginning to a second stage does not result in a sharp change of behavior, since the transition is motivated more by discomfort with the past than by a sense of confidence in the future. Thus, group members will still tend to react to each other in terms of social stereotypes, will still be frustrated and angry, and their ability to analyze and get at the root of basic problems will be extremely limited. If, at first, he is unsuccessful in effecting a transition, he will have to wait for a new opportunity.

Stage 2—Stereotyped Problem-Solving

Objectives

Eventually, a transition can be effected. It will be observable when delinquents begin to verbalize, in a superficial way, the notion that the group exists to find some solutions. They are not so unattuned to the purposes of the group that they will not begin to say the kinds of things they think the group leader wants them to say. They may begin to discuss problems and to be somewhat more confrontive in inquiring about the past histories and current behaviors of members. However, the group leader may make a serious mistake if he misreads this interaction and interprets it to mean that significant changes and solutions will be immediately forthcoming. Instead, he must retain a long-range perspective allowing him to see that, under the best of circumstances, not answers, but a base for answers, is what is being laid.

The reason is that the type of interaction being described is likely to be stylized and stereotyped, often in highly conventional ways. Group members may actually preach to each other. They may seek a patent medicine solution. Some of their conclusions are likely to be so conventional that they really do not speak to basic issues. In fact, as Scott (1965:58) suggests, " . . . the didactic advise-giving [present in this stage] appears to be almost a satire of typical adult reactions to adolescents. The entire behavior of group members later often proves to be hilarious to the group as they reflect over this period of the group process. At this time, however, there is no humor to be found in the situation."

The basic objective in this stage is to help group members gain confidence, to support their conventional role-playing, and perhaps to learn something of the complexities of delinquent behavior and of finding solutions for it. Even for those who are serious in their conventional behavior, it soon becomes apparent that solutions will not be easily found. Unlike those people who have simplistic solutions for difficult problems, they soon discover that platitudes and cliches do not help much.

Structural Context

One should not view with total cynicism the tendency for boys to exhibit contradictory behavior during this stage. The fact that some boys now begin to play a reformer role—even if highly stereotyped—is important. It signals the beginning of structural and psychological change. The assumption of a reformer role, though often motivated by a desire to gain points with the leader, is a necessary precedent to a deeper, *personal* commitment. Before the expectations associated with the role can be internalized, the role itself must be tried. Moreover, any tendency for an individual to take leadership in adopting a conventional, rather than a delinquent stance, entails risks. While it may please the leader, it can alienate one's peers because it signifies some support, even if small, for nondelinquent views and behaviors. It is almost certain that other boys will hold the neophyte reformers accountable for making his acts consistent with his words.

The degree of commitment to conventionality may receive a real test when the group is confronted with everyday problems brought into the group from outside. One of the realities of dealing with serious delinquents in the community is that problems develop that simply cannot be ignored: some boys continue to violate the law, others cannot get along at school or at home; or others fail to attend the program. When a group encounters such problems, basic loyalties, basic beliefs and commitments are subjected to strain. Boys are torn between their own self-interests and those of others. In a prison, a rule that is enforced by staff as well as offenders is that everyone should do his own "time", and not mess with the "time" of others. Some of the same behavior can be expected in a community program. The pressures against those who would assume a reformer's role is considerable. That is why group members, at this stage of development, cannot be expected to run much risk in dealing with the problems that emerge. They cannot be expected to react very constructively since they have neither a sound basis for trusting the deliberations of the group nor the motivations of the leader. Not only would they be intruding into domains that have never been theirs, but they have never seen the group, itself, deal successfully with difficult issues. At best, therefore, group development can be assisted by presenting emergent problems in particular ways, not by expecting that the group will be ready to take over.

One such way is for the group leader to assume responsibility, in early stages of development, for reinforcing the basic ground rules when such steps are called for, such as imposing sanctions on the persistently deviant individual: making demands upon him, restricting his activities, or in serious cases, even arranging for him to be detained. Following that, the group may be involved in dealing with the problem if the leader seeks the group's advice, not on how further sanctions should be imposed, but on how they might be removed in the most helpful way. What lies behind the boy's difficulties? How can the group act to keep him out of trouble? Did the group leader make mistakes?

Any attempt to deal with such problems is likely to be slow, painful and frustrating. In many ways, it is an overt attack upon the informal, delinquent system. It confronts delinquents with problems from which heretofore they have been protected. Now, however, they are under the strain of choosing between conventional and delinquent expectations, of totally reversing their usual roles. Such a predicament is one from which many boys are likely to shrink. They will refuse to render an opinion or to make a decision (cf. Scott, 1965:64).

Phil: Do you want to let George off work detail, Mack?
Mac: I kinda want to let him off, but yet I don't know.
(long pause)
Mac: I still can't make up my mind.
Rog: You act like you feel trapped.
Leader: You don't like this situation?
Mac: No. It makes me feel kinda shitty. Kinda way back deep. I just don't feel he's ready to get off work detail, and yet, I have the feelin' he can make it. Why don't somebody else say what he thinks?

There is a tendency for many group leaders to become frustrated and angry with interaction like this. They see it as calculated, albeit passive, resistance. Group members are not willing to do the "right" things. Such an interpretation, however, grossly underestimates the pressures under which group members find themselves. In the foregoing discussion, for example, Mac said he felt "shitty", when asked to deal with George's problems. He was probably expressing an honest and common feeling. Like most members, he was not unaware that real problems existed, nor that George may have merited some censure. Nevertheless, it is one thing to recognize that possibility, and quite another to share in deciding George's fate, even on a relatively small issue. Hence, he was uncertain and conflicted.

Mac's self-interest was also at stake, not just George's. When it comes to the point of considering another boy's fate, each group member recognizes that, but for the grace of God, there goes he. It is possible that he will be the next person whom the group will be considering. Any action he takes now cannot help but be reflected in decisions that will be made by the group at some later date about him. Whether his decisions have a conventional or delinquent flavor, they cannot help but have adverse as well as positive consequences.

In terms of possible harm, many would argue that the presentation of the group with difficult real-life issues like this only impedes change. There is one argument, for example, which suggests that clinical personnel should not become embroiled in the daily struggles of controlling deviant acts, nor should they let those struggles impinge upon their interaction with their clients. Rather, by remaining neutral, they can be more effective. Any therapy, personal or group, should provide a kind of moratorium in which psychological healing can take place unimpeded by the need for action.

Whether correct or not, this stance is inconsistent with the theoretical underpinnings of the methods used at Provo, especially those concerned with changing the offender's traditional consumer role—a role in which he has no power and in which authorities do all the diagnosing and prescribing of what is best. How, it might be asked, can delinquents ever acquire the skills and kind of personal autonomy that will permit them to stay out of trouble if they are never involved in dealing with the problems that delinquent acts precipitate? Beyond that, there is the ethical issue as to whether delinquents should not have some right to make fundamental decisions affecting their own lives. Can or should officials make all these decisions?

Initial excursions in Stage 2 into the issues of change and control are one means of (1) introducing group members to the reformation role; (2) attempting to make the group, not just authorities, the medium of change; and (3) attempting to alter the traditional relationship of staff and offenders in correctional programs. Unless pressures favoring change are generated within the delinquent group, the usual exhortations or clinical interpretations by correctional workers may do little to change the subcultural standards. What may happen, instead, is that delinquents will have an official repertoire for the worker and a delinquent repertoire for peers. This means effective use of the group as the medium for change is imperative.

By beginning to share responsibility, delinquents are introduced to the complexities of the control function and to the complexities of finding more productive alternatives. They learn that some concern for others is the price that one must pay for reciprocal concern when one's own problems are the center of attention.

Group Process

In terms of group process, it should be recognized that both the introduction of outside problems and the style of interaction in Stage 2 is more in the service of building an effective group than it is in actually solving basic problems. For example, at this stage, the group is still inclined to be distrustful. As a result, members may interpret the leader's effort to involve them either as a sign of personal weakness or as a clever device for manipulating them. Thus, the testing operation continues.

One symptom of it is the introduction of verbally aggressive behavior. Actually, verbal aggression represents several things. First, and somewhat paradoxically, it may represent a growing sense of freedom in the meeting—a continuing tendency to test the boundaries of what will be tolerated.

Rog:　　I feel most of my trouble is Mr. G. (group leader).
Jack:　　Why?
Phil:　　Yeah, fuck, I see everybody trying to find the right answers but him.
Rog:　　Yeah, he really pisses me off.
George: What did he do?
Rog:　　Whenever a problem comes up, he expects us to figure the goddam thing out for ourselves.

The willingness to openly criticize, or attack the group leader is something that is new to this stage. Second, of course, is the fact that many delinquent boys are used to verbal agression and to getting advice. Parents give advice freely all the time, and boys are verbally aggressive with each other. There are several things, therefore, that must be considered about this behavior as it relates to group process.

The appearance of verbal aggression in Stage 2 may appear to the middle-class adult, who is used to manipulative rather than aggressive interaction, to be constructive. Consider the following interaction which, on the surface, may seem to be highly confrontive and perhaps productive because it challenges a boy whom the group knew was continuing to get into trouble.

Fuzz: How come you say you turned down trouble the other night when them guys wanted you to go with them? How come you keep saying that? We know different.
Mac: Because I don't know. That's why.
Dan: What do you mean, you don't know?
Mac: I don't even know what in the fuck you guys are talkin' about.
Joe: Aren't you payin' attention?
Mac: Yah, I'm payin' attention, Joe. You can stick it in your fuckin' ass.
Fuzz: We just want to know what happened that night.
Mo: We come up here to tell the fuckin' truth so you come up here and bullshit like a bastard.
Mac: I don't know what the fuck you're talkin' about. You did the same God damned thing the other night, Mo.
Joe: We're not talkin' about Mo, we're talkin' about you.
Mo: Just 'cause I done it, that don't give you the God damned right to do it. It ain't gonna get you out doin' somethin' I do. You're not going to help anybody in this meeting by just sitting there bullshittin'. (Pause) We're not going to find anything out about you we don't already know.

Mac: What the fuck are you telling us all this shit for when you do the same God damned thing?

Mo: You're God damned right! That's right. I was doin' it. You're doin' it now.

Fuzz: Well, why are you bullshittin'?

Mac: I'm just tryin' to get out of the fuckin' question, that's what.

Group members are obviously pressuring Mac who was in serious trouble, but the manner in which they did it may have different meaning to *him* than to the leader. The basic issue is whether the group's behavior reflects a consensus that one should really stay out of trouble, and that Mac should change, or whether it merely reflects a style of interaction that is fairly common among many of these boys. The point is that a group leader can ill-afford to assume that there is a direct relationship at this stage between verbally confrontive behavior and a commitment to change.

Beyond that, it will be seen later that a group may have to come to terms with denigrating, verbally aggressive behavior if they are to become an effective and helpful unit. Verbal aggressivity on the streets is often a defensive device by which to avoid, not build, close personal relationships. If the group is to become a cohesive unit, therefore, its members and the leader will have to learn the difference between the kind of aggressive behavior that is highly stylized and primarily defensive, and that which reflects an interest in dealing with group and personal problems. However, despite the limitations of stereotyped and aggressive behavior, group process in Stage 2 continues to perform a socialization function.

The introduction of problems from the outside, the exchange of points of view, and the revelation of personal ways of behaving inevitably result in the exchange of personal and social data. Although there may not be much overt evidence that exchange is taking place, members do become more aware, in a personal sense, of individual differences and more aware of their actions in the community. For example, Mac's frank admission that he is merely trying to avoid a difficult question might even be significant. Thus, the nature of group interaction, and the depth of the discussion at later stages will depend to a considerable extent on things that are learned in this stage.

Discussion Content

Discussion content in this stage may involve any one of a number of things: further recitation and examination of delinquent histories and personal problems, group frustration over a lack of progress, attacks against the leader, or decisions as to what should be done over the various problems that have arisen. The content that will draw the greatest amount of attention is that which has to do with relatively superficial issues, or the problems resulting from reinforcement of the ground rules. One way of helping boys to gain some confidence in group interaction, and at the same time to exchange information is to encourage them to continue to talk about their past and current behaviors: what trouble they have been in, who their friends are, how they get along at home or at school. The involvement of the group in dealing with emergent problems also provokes considerable discussion. Any boy, for example, who finds himself in trouble is usually left on his own to approach the group regarding ways to deal with his problems or to have a sanction removed. Ordinarily, if he does nothing, the sanction remains in force. Thus, boys soon learn to turn to the group for resolution.

Since, however, the group is uncertain of its power at this stage, any number of things may happen. The group may seek to avoid the issue; it may make a tentative attack on the leader; or it may begin an exploration of what can be done. As explained above, one should not have aspirations which exceed the capacity of the group to produce. What is likely to happen is a guarded and superficial exploration of issues and an eventual recommendation that any sanction be lifted. Consider, for example, the results of a long discussion about a boy whose continued drinking and stealing had gotten him into trouble again.

Hersh: Joe, You don't think you'll be arrested again?
Joe: No.
Phil::   Why?
Joe: I don't plan on doin' nothing wrong. I learned my lesson.
George: I believe you.
Jack: Me too. If he'll just listen to what his mother says and quit runnin' around with those hood friends of his, his problems will be solved.
Hersh: He may drink again, but I think his stealing will stop.
George: I believe he should be let out of the detention home.

Though not insightful nor especially productive, some important things can be learned from interaction of this type. Delinquents are not so stupid that some do not recognize the limitations of a discussion like this. In fact, it provides an excellent opportunity to begin evaluating the progress of the group. One way to do that is to ask boys to explain their decisions, to explain why Joe, for example, might not be worse rather than better off if the group's recommendations are followed. What behavioral evidence is there that Joe will stop stealing, if not drinking? What will be the consequences if the group is wrong and Joe is arrested again? How can a group have some confidence in the decisions it makes?

Hersh: What makes you think Joe can stay out of trouble if he goes home tonight?
George: He can turn down trouble at work can't he. He's been workin' damn good on the job.
Jack: If he can do that around us, then I'm sure he can do it around his friends on the outside.

Phil: What makes you so sure about that?

George: Jesus Christ! What in the hell do you think he is, Phil?

Phil: If he's puttin' on a God damned front, he's gonna come up here and act different around the kids up here than he will with his friends on the outside.

George: Christ, I don't know whether he's puttin' on a front or not. What in the hell are you gettin' at?

Joe: Go ahead and say what you want. It's not botherin' me none.
           (Pause)

Hersh: George, you said if he could stay out of trouble around the kids up here, he could with his friends on the outside.

George: I know damn well he can.

Hersh: All right. If he was puttin' on a front he wouldn't get in trouble would he? I want to know what makes you so sure that that's . . .

Jack: Because if he gets in trouble on the job it's brought up in a meeting, isn't it?

Phil: How do you know it's brought up in a meeting?

George: I think he oughta be given a chance to change on the outside.

Leader: Well, what do you think's gonna do him most good about helping him change and stay out of trouble, going home or staying in detention another night or two?

George: I don't know which one . . . but I said to give him a chance to try to show us.

Joe: How'n hell am I goin' to show you I can stay out of trouble if I sit in that tank another night?

Bill: So, Christ, do you want him to stay in jail the rest of his life?

Phil: One thing he could do is to try to help somebody else rather than always thinkin' of hisself.

George: Yeah? He does that already. He bitches at me and Fred all the time. Tells us about getting in trouble for smoking on the job when we're spose'd to be working.

Phil: Does it do any good?

George: No it don't.

Joe: How about you, Roy?

Roy: Well, I want you to go home in a way, but in a way I don't.

Joe: Why's that Roy?

Roy: One thing I'm not sure on. I remember you told us before you come here that you was in detention. Then the very night you got out, you went 'n got in trouble. Is that what you'd do tonight?

Joe: I don't know. Maybe I just want to see my parents. Maybe I want to go out too. I don't know if that's it.

Phil: Christ, you go out every night.

Joe: All right. But I haven't had a God damned chance to prove myself yet neither.

Even though the group is obviously uncomfortable, and its decision-making is halting, a form of socialization is taking place. One significant aspect of this socialization involves the search for criteria by which to evaluate behavior. Note, for example, that the group has considered the influence of Joe's associates on him, both inside and outside of the program, how he behaves on the job, whether he helps other boys, whether he is putting on a "front," and whether he will behave as he has in the past. These are all important issues that almost every boy must face; moreover, the group is becoming far more conscious of ways to look at, and evaluate behavior than they have been in the past. The process is a valuable resource for individual and group learning.

It is not merely boys who can be tortured with difficult problems like this. Group members can, and should, feel free to ask the group leader to justify his point of view. Of what value is detention for a boy like Joe? How does the leader know when a problem is solved? And, finally, Joe, himself can be asked to explain what he means when he relies on a cliche by saying that "he has learned his lesson." What does that mean? Does it have any value at all? Is the group really acting in his best interest if it does only as he wishes?

Questions such as these provide the basis for a greater awareness of individual motivation and the relevance and utility of the group process. In fact, a group like this is on the threshold of recognizing the limitations of the stereotyped kinds of interaction that characterize Stage 2. To deal with difficult issues, they need to consider matters along other dimensions.

Transition from Stage 2 to Stage 3

Recall that interaction in Stage 2 has tended to be relatively superficial, stereotyped and verbally aggressive. Interaction of this type is not very productive, nor is it satisfying in a personal sense. Not only is the individual caught squarely between his own personal interests in wanting to get out of the program, and the stereotypic way the group is going about its business, but stereotyping itself is burdensome and even degrading.

One boy resents being pegged as a "greaser," another as "punk," or another as a "snitch." Even a high-status boy may dislike the role into which he is cast, such as "fighter," of whom everyone expects repeated exhibits of his prowess. One boy claimed that this image of him continued to get him into trouble, even though he was trying to stay out of it. Everywhere he went, someone was trying to arrange a fight for him. He resented the fact that, even in the program, he could not discard his reputation even though he hated fighting.

Circumstances like this provide the basis for a growing, although admittedly vague, recognition that there are better ways for dealing with people. As some of the stylized defenses may begin to come down—the bluster and "sounding" of street life—other sides of the human personality begin to come through. Delinquents, like anyone else, do not enjoy a group in which daily interaction is characterized by perpetual tension, though they may not know what to do about it. By using examples from the group process, the group leader may be able to document the dysfunction of overly aggressive and stereotypic behavior. He may be able to point out that neither individual nor group self-interest is served by it—at least in the present setting.

In addition to the personal discomforts associated with the present mode of operation, stereotyping hinders group efforts to clarify and examine alternatives, delinquent or conventional. In order to examine alternatives, greater candor will be required—an effort to get behind existing facades in the interest of exploring the mixed feelings that members have about their delinquent status. In order to do that, members should feel free to say what they believe and feel, not merely play the role that is assigned to them. Otherwise, important issues remain hidden and are never dealt with.

Any movement to a more complex level of operation will hinge on a complex mixture of forces. If further involvement is seen as overly dangerous by most boys, a significant number may focus around a strong delinquent leader. If that happens, the delinquent status and power system may be ascendent. The group will center around people who strongly resist the influence of either the group leader or those members who are pushing for other kinds of interaction.

If stereotyped reactions can gradually be replaced with more realistic expression of individual differences and alternatives, broader perspectives will be opened up. The group can move into a period in which solidarity is based on new potentialities and the attitude that the boys are people with choices to make. There can be a recognition that not only has society labeled them as delinquents, *but they have labeled each other this way*.

The group leader should not be surprised, however, if the group tends to resist change. It may come to the transitorial period being described here and then retreat—again and again. But contrary to the notion that the conflict inherent in this process is destructive, the position is taken here that it is an inevitable part of the group and organization-building task. The point is that the build-up of pressure for change is a gradual one. Eventually, there is likely to be a gradual movement into a new stage because there are individuals who feel an honest need to begin dealing with their own problems, and because the internal cohesion of delinquent subgroups tends to be weak (Short and Strodtbeck, 1965:231; Klein and Crawford, 1967). Under most circumstances, such groups are held together more by external pressure from police, families and community than by gratifying internal relations. To the extent that delinquents begin to gain some trust in the group leader and the group itself, there will be inclinations to want to seek out some new mode of adjustment. However, the progress of the group oscillates and is in no way linear.

Stage 3—Awareness of Individual Differences and Alternatives

Objectives

Whereas the objectives in Stage 2 were to bring delinquents to the place where they could recognize some of the complexities of human problems, and that stereotyped, formalistic responses would not provide the solutions, the objectives of Stage 3 are to clarify alternatives for them and to help them become aware of individual differences. A recognition of both would be a necessary part of any effective developmental process.

Structural Context

In a structural sense, several matters of significance may occur in this stage. In the first place, there is likely to be an increasing rejection of the rigid and stereotyped ways of responding to people which have characterized much of the interaction to this point. New norms, favoring the importance of individual differences and needs, will begin to appear. Greater openness and candor in group meetings, a greater willingness to explore individual problems without rigid reservation, will be encouraged. However, the more open a group becomes, the more likely this openness will generate resistance. A conservative force will also assert itself. In other words, two rather important subgroups are likely to appear within the group.

The first will support the notion that instead of safe speculations and advice-giving, group members should be candid, analyze what is happening to them, and be willing to consider conventional alternatives. The second subgroup will be resistive, more in favor of the status-quo than of candor and confrontation. Thus, if subgroups are built around these conflicting patterns, there will be an increasing dramatization of the alternatives open to group members—the one alternative favoring further exploration in the reformation process and the second favoring resistance to collaboration, perhaps the continuation of delinquent behavior. Such a dramatization provides an excellent opportunity for the group to explore the significance of each alternative for them and to consider it in relation to the program itself and to the larger community.

Phil: I ain't goin' to say nothin' about myself, 'cause sure as hell I do, I'll be in trouble.
Hersh: I don't think so. I was told you're spose to say what you think in here, and I agree.
Mac: Oh yeah, I agree with Phil. Speak up and you'll see what you get for it.
Jack: I don't know. I think Hersh might be right.
Phil: I ain't talkin'!

The significance of subgroup struggles, and the alternatives associated with them, can be further heightened for group members by their involvement in the search for solutions to day-to-day problems. With even one part of a group willing to consider individual differences, decision-making in this stage can now be utilized in a much more comprehensive way: in solving work problems, in suggesting ways to improve school performance, or in considering familial or peer problems. For those group members who exhibit increasing acceptance of the reformation process, this decision-making can be a rewarding experience. It is rewarding both for those about whom decisions are made, and for those who do the decision-making. By contrast, those who have not fully accepted the process will exhibit increasing ambivalence and obstructionism.

The point is that, during this stage, there may be increasing evidence of social control by at least one segment of the group. Even though all of its members may not be in agreement with the trend toward conventionality, the fact that alternatives are being openly considered and that some delinquents are playing more of a reformation role, means that their split with staff members is not a clean one. What is more, changing norms may no longer afford the more delinquent members in the group with a blanket of silence and security.

The loosening of traditional patterns among some offenders, and between staff and offenders, means that greater opportunity is provided for individuals to evaluate the courses of action open to them. Group abstractions and levels of analysis will not be used much in this stage. That will come later. Group members are still preoccupied with individual insights, feelings, and gratifications. But while this may be true for group members, the leader should be conscious of group phenomena and should be prepared to introduce new concepts when the time is right.

Group Process

Unless by some chance the conflict between reformation and resistive subgroups overwhelms the operations of the total group and causes it to regress to earlier phases of type-casting and advice-giving, there will be an increasing tendency for group members to respond to each other in terms of personal differences. If they do, personally rewarding, rather than stereotyped exchanges, will be more likely to occur, exchanges over personal problems, feelings and alternatives. Even if there is resistance to free exchange, such exchange will be far more common in this stage than they were earlier.

Sam: Mr. G. (group leader) pisses me off. I keep askin' him what I should do an' he won't tell me.

George: Isn't that what your mother does—always front for you? You want him to do that?

Phil: Yeah, that's somethin' Sam has to decide.

Sam: What do you mean?

George: Can't you see that you don't think for yourself?

Sam: (Shouts) Well, fuck! If you want me to do something different you got to tell me what to do. If I don't know how, how the fuck can I change?

Leader: You want me to be your mama? I'm trying to tell you that you're somebody and should learn to think like somebody.

Phil: You're Sam, not some punk that everybody tells how to live.

Even though the exchange was painful for Sam, it revealed attention to him as a person and respect for his individuality—responses he had obviously not had in the past. His remarks, even though emotional may also have revealed a desire to learn more about himself. The responses of the other boys, in turn, indicated a respect for that desire.

In addition to concerns with self, an interesting characteristic of Stage 3 which probably will not have been common earlier, is increased concern for the welfare of the group. This concern, however, is likely to be highly personal rather than collective; the individual is worried about what might happen to himself rather than others if the group should disband. What is reflected, of course, is the self-gratification that occurs at this stage, the satisfactions associated with emotional expression and the receipt of feedback. While it would be a serious problem for a group of delinquents to flounder and remain in this stage, its significance is important.

Evidence from different sources has suggested that the organizational skills of delinquents are low, that their ties to normal institutions are tenuous, that interaction among them is often stylized and defensive, and that their own groups may not be especially cohesive and internally gratifying. If this is the case a reformation group which could provide some solidarity and a sense of personal satisfaction might have much to offer.

Discussion Content

Theoretically, discussion content in this stage should involve more sensitive and personal problems and feelings than prior stages. Individuals will likely be more concerned than they have been with the reasons they became delinquent, how others see them, and what their personal strengths and weaknesses are. On a group level, there should also be some evidence of a greater willingness to help and understand others, as well as to receive help and understanding. The time is one in which considerable information will be exchanged, some new relationships established, and some new satisfactions realized.

Jack: I think we have been expecting things from Rocky that we shouldn't.
Rog: What do you mean?
Jack: I don't know how to say it. Damn. But I don't think he is always lyin' to us. I just think he don't know too much—that he can't think too clear.
Phil: You think he's lost his marbles, or somethin'?
Jack: (shouting) No, he just ain't as bright as some others. You shouldn't expect too much from him.
George: I think I know what Jack is trying to say. Rocky just hasn't been around. We're makin' him somethin' he isn't.
Tony: I think we need to get behind it a little better, then, if we're goin' to help him.

Rog: Are you tryin' to say that all that trouble he was having at school is 'cause he didn't understand.

Jack: That is exactly what I'm saying plus more. Rock is not as smart as some kids, yet he is a good "head."

As a matter of fact, Rocky was not a bright boy, was probably retarded; yet, although some members of the group had known him for years, this was the first time he was understood, and with some compassion as well.

But while understanding is important, it is not the only thing with which the group might be concerned at this stage. The group must still deal with ideological differences within it, and with pressing daily problems. To ignore such realities is to isolate the group process from the other aspects of program operation, and from the community itself. Insular, ingroup ties without outside contacts are to be avoided.

The best way to reality-test the occasional sense of euphoria which characterizes a group that becomes preoccupied with self-gratification and its own internal workings is to turn the context of group discussion to outside matters—to use the here-and-now problems of group members as a means of relating group discussion to the outside world.

George: You don't like to rat nobody off, do you Hersh?

Hersh: Hell, no.

Sam: I can see that—like you and Mike stole that purse. You wouldn't rat on him even though you was both in trouble.

Hersh: I feel like shit if I fink on anybody. I've always been taught never to fink.

Phil: Yeah, but I see it a little different in here. How we goin' to solve Mike's problems if we don't know what they are?

Hersh: I've thought of that. That's what bugs me, especially since he's in trouble again. My keepin' quiet don't help him none.

Thus, a concern with the individual may extend, indeed should, extend beyond intragroup relations and phenomena.

Some past clinical programs have advocated the avoidance of the confrontation of a group with this kind of material. But to do so in this case would not only be contrary to theoretical design, but could be harmful as well. Unless a group is gradually introduced first to difficult problems and then to difficult decisions, it may witness the loss of some of its members to a deeper involvement with the law and life in an institution. Moreover, without the involvement of group members, the staff must assume responsibility for all the daily decisions which seriously affect boys' lives. This approach to group operation suggests that delinquents should be involved deeply in such matters if they are to play a reformation role.

Since, in this stage, the willingness of a group to involve itself is mixed, the group leader's role will not be without tension and difficulty. It was pointed out that in Stages 1 and 2 he would have to be largely responsible for the control function in his group, asking the group to become involved only in the removal of sanctions. Now, however, he might begin the long process of asking the group to help with all aspects of any problem, before as well as after action is taken. The group would be presented with the issue and asked to participate in any decisions that were made: What should be done with a group member who does not show up? What about the request of a group member to drop from school? Why does an individual continually fight with the work supervisor and how can the problem be corrected?

In approaching these issues he will need to recognize that a willingness to participate will not be unanimous. His objective is to keep working toward that end, not to expect it at the outset. At the same time, he must also be concerned lest his actions tend to stamp out expressions of resistance and delinquent points of view. These are as important to a weighing of alternatives as conventional ones. The worst thing that could happen would be to conduct a group in which the pretense of being conventional was fostered when members felt to the contrary. The group leader's comments can help to forestall this.

George: Are you going to answer our questions, Phil?
Phil: Hell, no. I'd rather go back to court and take my chances. This place is too goodie-goodie for me.
Leader: You mean people aren't being themselves?
Phil: That's right, everybody's got a front.
George: Maybe so, but I don't agree with you all the way. Some people are putting it out front.
Leader: What's good about Phil's opinion though is it shows the problems we have. We can't deal with some things because people have fronts.

The real dangers to the group are when delinquent points of view are driven underground. But if the system can legitimize the opportunity to reveal feelings and to recognize their implications, the objective of understanding both self and available alternatives can be achieved. This particular aspect of group development is important because it can help to crystallize basic issues and pose a choice. Growth and understanding are a product of conflict and struggle.

Although involvement and support for emerging group norms will not always be present, either in the form of candor or support for an antidelinquent stance, the hope is that the general trend will be in that direction. If the group continues to progress through Stage 3, decision-making will become more complex, goal-setting will be more realistic, and group ties will be strengthened.

Transition from Stage 3 to Stage 4

Until now, it is quite clear that the group has been engaged in a group-building task: encouraging interaction, trying to overcome the rigid defenses that hinder productive interaction, and exploring individual needs and differences. Assuming the group has gotten this far, it could be argued that much has been accomplished. To paraphrase a comment that was made by different boys on several occasions, "It is hard to describe for other people what this place is trying to do. My parents ask me what we do all the time up here, but I can't explain it to them. When I tell them that we sit around and discuss our problems, they look at me like I'm crazy. People just don't understand that kids can help each other, or that this place is different than any other place I ever seen. In fact, my 'ole man could use it hisself."

Many group programs attempt to go no further in pushing group development than trying to deal with personal feelings and development. The objectives of the group process end here. In a community program, however, an effort should be made to go further. In theory, at least, more can be accomplished. The need, for example, to build strong reference group support for delinquents, or to foster a truly normative organization requires that further steps be taken. As the group moves toward the end of Stage 3, it often becomes apparent that subgroup conflict and concern over selfish and personal ends has important and sometimes dysfunctional consequences. Paradoxically, the sole pursuit of personal satisfaction often hinders the solution of other important problems, especially those having to do with building strong organizational norms and making their influence outwardly pervasive into the community. To do that, group members must be concerned with collective and group phenomena, not just personal and psychological ones. This requires that the group leader make group members aware of the structural and processual characteristics of the group: the presence of conflicting individual or subgroup points of view; the tendency for certain boys to center around particular opinion leaders; or the existence of competing expectations which often hinder the development of trust and solidarity.

The group leader's task at this point is to help the group become more aware of the limitations of factionalism, and to recognize that internal power struggles continually interfere with the ability of the group to resolve important issues. He can do so by introducing abstractions and by articulating some of the things group members have seen going on around them. By focussing upon the group as well as personal aspects of group operation, he may be able to introduce the group to another stage of group development.

There is no end of examples from the community, as well as from within the program, that he can use to assist him: the conflicts some boys face in trying to reconcile the expectations of some of their friends outside of the program with expectations that arise from within it; the system of stratification that exists in the school where a boy finds himself on the bottom of the ladder; or the persistent tendency for the leader and some boys to oppose each other on certain issues. By calling the attention of members to these matters, another dimension of the group process can be introduced and eventually used as a tool in trying to resolve important problems. Any attempt to provide delinquents with such a tool is ambitious, but if they are to understand the nature of organizational and community life and to exercise power effectively in them, a knowledge of these things is important. An attempt should be made toward the end of Stage 3 to provide members with the means to attack a higher level of operation in which organizational as well as personal issues come into play.

Stage 4—Group Awareness

Objectives

The major objective in this stage is to increase understanding of group structure and process and to maximize group problem-solving. It is important for the group to consider the process problems, the subgroupings, and the power structures that have developed within the group because of their relevance for the understanding of individual and group behavior in a general sense.

One of the central theoretical propositions of this Experiment asserted that group phenomena are associated with the causation of delinquency and with the problems which the offender must confront in the community: status differences, competing and shifting group structures, complex role expectations and group conflicts. It is likely that much can be gained from learning about these things in a group setting, and attempting to relate them to the larger society.

Similarly, an understanding of group structure and process would assist in the task of helping the group to deal with its own internal problems. The ability of the group member to see himself in relation to these power structures, to see their impingement on him, and to recognize and try out new role alternatives in dealing with them, are presumed to be helpful. This would be especially true if efforts to develop a reformative and rewarding corrective culture are to be successful. The effective exercise of power, by offenders as well as staff, requires group understanding and insight.

Structural Context

The most noticeable thing about group structure in this stage is the increasing concern of group members with the group as an entity in its own right. The prior lack of trust and the preoccupation of members with their own personal problems and gratifications is diminished somewhat by a growing awareness of the importance of group-level problems and issues. The difficulties with which the group has had to deal, and the decisions it has had to make, have been marked by ideological splits and competing subgroups as well as by personality conflicts and private resistances to change. Without always knowing why, group members tend to become increasingly aware of group phenomena, of informal norms and expectations and of the effects of collective behavior.

Leader:	You say you want us to decide whether you should stay in school.
Sam:	Yeah, I want to quit. I can get a job.
Rog:	Well, why are you goin' to quit now?
Sam:	I figure I'll work a while, then go back.
Phil:	How you going to prove that? People don't go back to the 10th grade.
Sam:	You'll just have to take my word for it.
Jerry:	Your word for it? What are your reasons? There's got to be reasons.
Sam:	You're a hell of a one to be sayin' that. Fuck, half you guys are failin', and you're givin' me a hard time.
Rog:	You're just usin' that as an excuse.
Sam:	I don't have to answer that.
Phil:	He's got a point. It doesn't do much good to tell him to do things we won't do. Even though I'm against his droppin' out, I feel like a . . . a hypocrite.
Jerry:	You mean our actions talk louder than our words?
Rog:	He's still usin' us as an excuse.

The group leader may be able to facilitate an understanding of group phenomena by playing a teaching role, in this case to help members see that behavior is very much a function of unwritten norms which are discernible primarily in behavioral, not verbal terms. As Jerry indicated, what a group does is a better indication of what its members believe than what they say. In exploring any issue, the leader may now try to help the group avoid being caught up entirely in emotional and substantive issues at the expense of missing the subtle interworkings of the group process. It might be useful for the group to learn that the silence of some members is as significant for the workings of the group as the verbal behavior of others. Satellite boys in orbit about a leader are as important as the leader. Withdrawn or dominating members may be seen not only as particular kinds of people, but people whose characteristics are a cause and effect of the way the group operates. By wearing a new set of spectacles, the group can come to recognize that adjustive changes occurring in the group structure are produced by changes in any part of the group; that there is a strong interdependence of group and individual; that modification in one results in modification of the other; and that problems for one are problems for the other.

Assuming that movement through the various stages has been achieved, a noticeable change in the group leader's role might be observed. If he can continue to help a group understand its own inner workings, and to deal more effectively with its own problems, he decreases his own authority and influence, and increases those of the group. Consider the half-humorous, half-serious assertion of the group's ability to correct the group leader.

Rocky:	You said you thought Mr. _____ (group leader) is not always right. What you got against him?
Marty:	I can't think of anything right off hand. Oh, yes, parking on the wrong side of the road (laughter).
George:	Yeah, we told you about it once. It's against the law.

Leader: What are you going to do, put me in jail?
Phil: That wasn't funny. That pisses me off.
Rog: Why?
Phil: 'Cause adults always expect so much from teenagers but when they're wrong, they make a smart crack like that.
Marty: Yeah, it seems to me us Goddam kid drivers are better than you adults.
Leader: You're right. I'm in the wrong.
Phil: Well how come you keep parking on the wrong side of the road?
Leader: That's a good question.
George: I know why. He's too fuckin' lazy to turn around.
Rocky: Well, maybe we can help him to stop breakin' the law.

Interaction of this type retains the aggressive flavor of prior stages and some obvious hostility toward the leader and the adults whom he represents. It also indicates a confidence in being able to criticize without fear of reprisal, and a hint that the group may be able to stop even the leader from breaking the law. Expectations appropriate for delinquent members are also appropriate for authority. While the group may be in the process of developing a sense of identity, and a willingness to attack problems openly, its style of operation is tinged with all kinds of messages.

Group Process

These conditions reflect the fact that any change in process will be relative. While there is some greater evidence of collaboration and cooperation, subgroup and individual conflict in this stage will not have disappeared. Some conflict is inevitable and ubiquitous in any setting where candor is important, especially in one like this where the stakes are so high for everyone. For most boys, it is often a choice between the pressures of this kind of correctional setting versus incarceration elsewhere. For staff, anxieties are associated with changes in role, with fears of the loss of control, with a diminution of power. In many cases, points of view become polarized between those who prefer to play the game according to traditional rules and those who favor some kind of change.

In some cases, the group will be faced with the prospect of seeing that some of its members cannot succeed in this kind of process; they adhere to delinquent behavior and get in further trouble with the law. While they cannot be spared the pains of such a prospect, they can learn from it. Group interaction, and the community freedoms that go with it, must inevitably be constrained by the delinquent histories of the boys and the fact that they are in a correctional program.

There are always dangers that staff and offenders under such pressures will be short-sighted and arbitrary in their action, that they will overreact to difficult situations. But that is a risk that must be run in an attempt to build a group with enough confidence and strength to improve the problem-solving process, and to serve as a nondelinquent reference group.

With the pains of group process and decision-making may also come strengths. Boys may discover that the official group leader is not the best leader in all situations. They may become aware of his personal inadequacies, an awareness which makes him appear more human, decreases group dependency, and assists in building a sense of group solidarity and competency. An important consequence of a group-oriented approach may be that it is capable of building solidarity, not only upon a sense of affect and self-gratification, but upon a sense of satisfaction gained from collective action. If so, these developments could begin to temper some of the strains, resistances and conflicts of previous stages with a greater sense of cooperation and achievement in this stage. Conceivably the group could provide a sense of dignity not usually found in the correctional settings in which delinquents are placed. Theoretically, it is a means of decreasing both the dependence and sense of alienation which delinquents so often experience.

Discussion Content

Many of the things which have been discussed in previous stages will be discussed in this stage—personal problems, delinquent acts, problems at school and so on. These kinds of matters provide much of the substantive grist for discussion in every stage. In contrast to Stage 3, where discussions were devoted heavily to personal feelings and private points of view, the discussion in this stage will also include an analysis of group operation, using group-level abstractions. What is going on in the group? What is hindering communication? What roles are different people playing? By discussing these phenomena openly and candidly, substantive issues can be solved more efficiently. Hidden agendas and opposing subgroups, which often block the resolution of difficult problems, can be brought into the open and dealt with.

Rog: Hersh, has Phil ever been with you when you have been stealing or drinking?
Hersh: I go with him, but when I get in trouble I always leave him and go with those other guys. I don't want to cause no trouble for him 'cause he's really tryin' in here.
Leader: I don't believe you.
Hersh: No. I never took him with me.
George: It don't look right to me. When the guys in the other group told me about that nonsquealers club, I began to get suspicious of you. You're bullshitting us.
Hersh: Fuck you.
Jack: Have you been getting in trouble with him, Phil?
Phil: Well . . .

George: Was Hersh trying to protect you, Phil?
Phil: Yep.
Joe: I was too.
George: Well, what in hell has been goin' on in the group then?
Rog: We've been split right down the middle, that's what. I don't know how the fuck we're ever goin' to get out of here with this kind of shit going on.
George: Are you tellin' me that the reason you was always dragging your feet in here is because you had that thing going on on the outside . . . 'cause you were coverin' up for each other?
Phil: I guess that's about it.
Rog: That's what I mean. We were split right down the middle. No wonder we couldn't put it all together. These guys had their own private club goin'!
Mac: The thing that pisses me off is that these guys have been holding up everything we been tryin' to do. They were frontin' it.

Discussions such as these reveal the ambivalent positions into which delinquents are put. They are not unaware of conventional points of view; they are not without feeling for them; and they are certainly not happy with their official status as delinquent. Therefore, one of the potential benefits of discussions like the foregoing is their ability to cast in sharp relief the contrasting alternatives open to the group. A very real possibility is that the delinquent alternative may be chosen by some boys. If so, they may be lost to the program unless, as in this case, others discover what is going on. Yet, this possibility poses the opportunity for the remainder to make a realistic assessment of the relative merits of a nondelinquent choice, its costs and its advantages.

It should also be remembered that if the group process has operated at all consistently with theoretical design, there should have been considerable socialization of staff as well as offenders. They will have changed also. A group which has developed somewhat according to the stages described here will have acquired tools that will enable it to better understand individual and group problems, and to relate these to the choices which must be made daily. There is a possibility that the group may operate on another plane which could be considered as a further stage of development.

Transition from Stage 4 to Stage 5

The earlier theoretical guidelines stressed the importance of avoiding insularity in any correctional program and the conduct of a group operation that is not integrated with other program activities. It is important for staff and offenders to keep these matters in mind. That is why the kind of group operation suggested here emphasized the importance of using here-and-now material as the grist for group discussion, and of observing the actual behavior of individuals as the means by which to evaluate their progress toward release. To what degree are they able to stay out of trouble, to play a reformation role in helping others, and to adjust in the community? These are the criteria by which a group can determine most successfully whether its activities are achieving the major objectives for which it exists.

If a group has been able to operate successfully in both Stages 3 and 4, it will begin to recognize the obvious fact that, unless it can extend its influence into other components of the program, even to achieve better linkage for its members in the community, its success, at best, will be limited.

Rog: One trouble Rocky has been havin' is that his 'ole man thinks he don't belong here and that his little boy will be corrupted by "hoods" like us.

Jack: Is that right, Rocky?

Rocky: Yeah. Actually, I'd like to go out with Rog and George. Since I been here, they're my best friends, but my dad won't let me go out with 'em.

George: He won't let Rocky go no place. It makes him all the more rebellious— an' that's bad 'cause he needs some friends like us.

Jack: What can *we* do?

Rog: Your dad always makes you stay home and work all weekend, right, Rocky? What's he got planned for you this week?

Rocky: We got to put in a driveway, lay cement.

Phil: I got an idea. Why don't we show up an' help? I'm willin' to do it.

Rog: We could show his old man we ain't so bad.

(A long discussion followed as to whether the group could do cement work, whether group members really wanted to help, or whether Rocky's dad would let them.)

George: Bullshit! We said enough. How many will go?

Phil: We'll all show up, an' any sonofabitch don't show up has got to answer for it.

The results of this session were so contrary to the usual pattern that they bear repetition. Most of the boys did show up; they did help to lay the cement; and they completed the job in one day rather than two. If more results of this type had been achieved, the experiment may have had more success. Rocky's father was so impressed with the unexpected help that he showed up on Monday for the group meeting, and entered into a discussion regarding the reasons he did not want his boy to associate with others in the program. As a result, the father was less fearful of the harmful effect of the other boys and Rocky's association with them. But what is more important was the fact that members had been able to accomplish something as a group and to derive a sense of satisfaction from it.

Not many groups can or will do things of this type, but the incident is illustrative of the way in which a cohesive group might begin to exert its influence in a constructive way, outside of as well as within a program. In some cases, individual group members will be in need of control or support; in other cases, the norms and values of a reformation culture will have to be carried to all aspects of program operation. Assuming that it might be possible to accomplish more things of this type, a group could be moved to yet another, more complex level of operation.

Stage 5—Integration of Group and Program Culture

Objectives

Although it is by no means certain that a more complex level can be achieved, it would certainly be desirable because it would serve as a means for linking the operations of the small group with other program and community activities. Theoretically at least, it would be the stage at which the small group could contribute most to the overall organization-building task. To some degree, every new group in the program would have to go through the developmental process just described, but once having done so, the members of older and more mature groups would help to provide support and guidance to the members of new and incoming groups.

The transmission of norms, the discussion of problems, the providing of support should not be limited only to the members of one's own small group. Once group members have come to recognize the interrelatedness of individual, group, and institutional behavior, they can do much to build and maintain a total operation in which problem-solving is a part of all program activities. In fact, unless they are committed at least somewhat to that task, theory suggests that staff members cannot, by themselves, accomplish it. In other words, group members in Stage 5 could become the medium rather than the target of change. Theoretically they have achieved a level which enables them to be culture builders and maintainers for others.

Structural Context

More than at any previous stage of development, group members should now be aware of the group as an entity in its own right. Subgroup struggles have been analyzed; decisions have been made; and the group, itself, has exercised influence, both over its members and in the program itself. But beyond that, group norms can be extended outward more and more into the community.

One actual step that was taken to accomplish this at Provo was to replace adult group supervisors in the city work program with boys from an older group. Because of continual friction between delinquent workers and the adult supervisors, the decision was made to put boys from this group in charge of the work crews. Only by reversing roles, and by permitting boys to occupy a superordinate rather than subordinate position, did it seem possible for them to experience some of the difficulties associated with both roles.

When this decision was made in a group meeting, and two boys were selected to occupy the position of "foreman," the decision was greeted with pleasure, especially by the two boys who were to be the foremen. Not only would they be in charge, but they would receive twice the pay. They thought it would be a "ball" to be the king pin. But this joy was short-lived. An excerpt taken from the group meeting the following day illustrates what happened.

One boy who had been a foreman walked in, sat down and said the following:

Foreman: You can have your foreman's job and, by god, you know what you can do with it.

Leader: Why? What happened?

Foreman: I thought all I'd have to do is go out there, sit on my ass, and tell these bastards what to do. But you know what they did? Everytime I told somebody like that new kid, Marty, to do something he'd tell me to go get fucked. Even these guys, who ought to know better, gave me a hard time.

Rog: You know why, don't you? You acted like you were king—like your ass weighed a ton.

Skip: Yeah, you pissed me off. Those other guys used to show us how to do something, but not you.

Foreman: Bullshit! I never worked so fucking hard in my life—running around trying to keep those new kids in line, and tryin' to get that septic tank cleaned. Besides, I never saw so many guys wantin' to go get a drink or just goof off. You can keep your job. I quit!!

The discussion went on and on, and around and around. But the group leader took the position that the foreman should not resign. Since he had accepted the obligation, he should honor it. More than that, other boys could help with the problem if they would. By not placing all the burden on one individual, they could help to eliminate some of the problems, especially since others would likely occupy the foreman's role in the future.

Fortunately, the group had enough experience and cohesion to rise to the occasion. Other members rallied around the foreman and helped to maintain order. In fact, this change turned out to be one of the most significant aspects of the program. Friction on the job decreased, work productivity went up, and the rotating foreman's job provided a kind of experience that these young adolescents might never have had.

Once the boys were placed on their own, the work program took on a "no nonsense" air that was quite impressive. But, if the group from which the foreman was originally selected had not possesed a sense of solidarity, it is our opinion that change would not have occurred. Or had boys been placed in this situation at an early stage of group development, chaos might have resulted—chaos that could have served to eliminate rather than strengthen the work program.

Group Process

Group process in this stage will be characterized by some periods of more highly motivated and cooperative problem-solving than has previously been the case. The group will be concerned not only with its own internal problems. but with external problems as well. Pressures generated for change within the group will be evident in the outside activities of its members, individually and collectively. There will be greater evidence than at any other time of delinquents involved in playing a reformation role, at work, school or in the community.

Marty: I think we got to set up some new system to help them new kids in the other group.
George: How come?
Marty: You know that new kid, Buster? Well we either got to help him with that new English teacher he has, or he'll fuck it up sure.
Phil: Which one is that?
Marty: You know. The teacher that gave Phil and George such a hard time. She's all right so long as you keep your mouth shut, but if you don't she'll get you in all kinds of trouble.
Rog: What can we do?
Ike: I think we got to stick close to him and keep him cool. Teach him to "cool it".
Marty: If we can help him cool there, we'll have a better chance to work on his problems here.

At the same time, no group can be expected to operate without periods of wandering and unfocused discussion, stereotyping and conflict. In some cases, the group might be seeking escape from the pressures of the group task. In other cases, it might require new information either about individuals or issues, and when that occurs, it might operate for prolonged periods on other levels. The point is that even though conflicts and other obstacles are still present, the ability to communicate in the group will have increased and there will be a greater sense of social trust. Members should be in a better position than ever before to understand the relevance of the correctional task and to have confidence in its objectives.

Discussion Content

Discussion content in this stage will remain much the same as in previous stages regarding internal group operation. However, it is to be hoped that the group will have become more cosmopolitan, more concerned with the operation of the total program, with maintaining a collaborative system, and with problems to be addressed in the community. If the group has solved some of its internal problems, it should be able to exert a greater influence over all phases of the correctional operation. It should also be in a better position to judge when an individual is ready for complete release to the community. It is that aspect of this stage that is of greatest interest to the boys. Although it has been a subject for discussion throughout all phases of the group's operation, it reaches its apex during this period. Even though the group leader is legally responsible for the task, the group shares power with him in actually carrying it out.

When a boy feels he is ready for release, it is his responsibility to raise the issue. The leader or other group members may also do it. The criteria applied to the decision should be weighted heavily toward behavior. What has the boy actually been doing? What were his problems in the first place? What evidence is there that they have been corrected? Has his delinquent behavior decreased? Does he get along better in school or work? Has he been of assistance to others? These are the kinds of questions that must be explored and answered satisfactorily before the group renders a favorable decision.

Phil: Why don't you explain that a little further, I think that's important.

Rog: How I see Pinehills?

Phil: Yeah, and yourself.

Rog: Well, when I first come here, I thought I could just come up here and serve time, just being here. I asked how long kids usually stayed in here and they said from 3 to 6 months and I figured if I come up here and was a good kid for 3 months, then I'd be out and I figured I'd just come up here and serve time, and I thought that at the meeting, we could get together, you know, and go around the meeting and say everybody was ready to get out. I thought I could come up here and get out without solving my problems, just be what I used to be all the time, . . . and drinking all the time. And I didn't think it was doing any good. I always say shit, Pinehills doesn't do any good.

Joe: But I know how you was livin' when you come in, an' I think that had some drawbacks.

Rog: Before, I was living in a world where all I was living for was just bullshittin' all the time and tryin' to be a big shot, and just trying to be something different. I didn't care about anybody else but myself, and just looking at every thing all wrong. Living in a different world, thinking normal people were just shit and stuff like that.

Mac: What about the world you're living in now?

Rog: I learned somethin' that has made me feel pretty good. Now that I'm not actin' the hard-ass, my neighbors, an' my friends' parents are lookin' at me friendly, an' they're talkin' to me. They never used to do that. An' I found out they're important to me. I just like bein' friends with them, an' don't want them lookin' down at me as a criminal, and let me run around with their sons and daughters.

Jack: That worries me—what you said sounds kinda phony. Are you tryin' to tell us you're happier now? What about the bad old days when you were the king-shit of the South part of town?

Rog: I'll tell you somethin' about that. Before I was just scared all the time. I was always worried about the police and that, worried about 'em coming down. I'd go out and do something wrong then I'd always worry about it for a couple of days after that. A couple of days, or a week, I'd worry about every time somebody'd knock on the door. I'd wonder, Oh, God, is that the cops for what I done, for stealing or something. Now I just got a clean conscience. When somebody knocks on the door, I don't worry about it. When a cop comes, I don't worry about nothin'. I don't worry about him taking me away. There for awhile, when the cops'd come knockin' at the door right at first, they'd come and knock on the door and I'd see 'em out there and I'd say well here I go to jail again. That's no way to live.

Mac: I thought you was just a great big prick when I first seen you. I was just walking by the car and you come over and you says "you want to fight?" I didn't see any sense in that, and you was drunk while you said it. Just the impression I got of him there. He was just a drunken asshole. Didn't care what he'd done or who he went with, or what he did. Now he respects people that respect him and he gets along with his mother a lot better now. I used to feel sorry for her—all alone with this ass walkin' on her. Now, I know for a fact that he is even givin' her some of the money he earns on the job.

Rocky: You wasn't goin' to school then was yuh? An now you got back in.

Rog: Yeah, for a little while.

Sam: I come into the group after you guys, and Rog was the first guy I looked up to. Seemed like he knew more about what was goin' on than anybody.

Phil: He's got something over on the rest of us I kinda admired before, too. He can talk about himself easier than the rest of us could, or at least me, and it seemed like he didn't have nothin' to hold back. When we had a meeting, he told us everything and that, everything he did, so I believed him, the things he said.

George: Well, what used to get me was when I'd say somethin' that was out an' out bullshit, he'd cram it right back down my throat. I mean, I'd say somethin', and he'd flash an answer back that really cut me low.

Rog: One thing that maybe you didn't like was when I was rattin' on ya. I ratted on ya quite a few times didn't I?

George: Yeah. That's another thing too, I didn't like.

Jack: Do you know why he did it now?

George: Yeah, it was to help me. He was tryin' to get me to tell the truth about things I did. When he asked a question it seems like it was a good one; he'd get good points out . . .

Sam: Hasn't Rog ever helped you out, Hersh?

Hersh: I can't count the times he's helped. When I was drinkin' too much, he helped quite a bit and when I got out of jail.

Sam: He's been helping you ever since he's been at the meeting hasn't he?

Hersh: He's been helping me ever since I can remember . . . He's told me things to do on the job an' what to do about those old buddies of ours.

Phil: Even when he was hard on you . . . he was still helping you?

Hersh: That's when he helped me the most.

If our experience is any criterion, innumerable hours will have been spent by the time the group reaches this stage in discussing upon what evidence one can base effective decisions. Prior to this time, the group will have been engaged in deciding the imposition and elimination of sanctions, how to evaluate individual behavior within and outside the group, or to what extent there are differences between verbal and other kinds of behavior. These are productive discussions because almost inevitably it becomes apparent that words and acts are different things, and that acts provide a much better criterion upon which to base decisions than words. This criterion is a brake on the tendency of delinquents to get hung up on the motivations of individuals rather than what they do.

In group sessions, for example, it is quite common for members to agree that a person like Rog is doing all the right things: staying out of trouble, going to school, getting along better with his family, and helping other members of the group. Yet, there will be members who argue that these things do not count because the person's motivations are wrong. The reason he is doing these things is because he is just trying to please the group leader or the group itself, or to gain points with the judge. In other words, he is conning everybody. He is behaving conventionally, not because he thinks it is the right thing to do, but because he wants to get out of the program or because he is just "sucking around."

To be sure, there are boys who do these things—boys who are effective con men. Perhaps Rog was one of them. But when a boy makes rather significant changes in several areas of his life and does so for a considerable period of time, such changes are probably a better criterion upon which to make decisions than the reasons he had for making them. Endless explorations of motivations usually turn out to be an exercise in futility. Often, in fact, a group learns that it is not a boy's motivation they have trouble with, but his way of relating to people. No matter how hard he tries, he only alienates others. Hence, it is important that they learn to distinguish consistent and personal behavior from interpersonal style, and not hold the latter against the individual. They may be able to help him with the latter problem, but even if they are not entirely successful, he should not be punished for it.

A fear of being conned, however, is one that tortures most correctional workers, perhaps because they have little confidence in themselves and what they are doing. Our experience, by contrast, indicates that it is possible in most cases, to identify the rare con man because he is living a double life—a life that is difficult to keep hidden from a group of intimates who spend every day with him. Eventually, his double life will out, and usually because of his acts, not his words. It is not so much the act of conning that causes the greatest difficulty, but in knowing what to do about it. In some ways, a successful con artist has more social skills than most other boys. The task then becomes one of trying to get him to cross over the very fine line that separates the illegitimate aspects of conning behavior from those that are legitimate in a host of sales and related occupations. The most difficult thing about this endeavor, is when a boy refuses to believe that his conning behavior is obvious to those who know him well—that others actually recognize his manipulation of others. Should that be the case, the program and his peers may have little effect on him.

Summary and Implications

In summary, this chapter has described and illustrated, in ideal-typical terms, the guidelines that were developed as an aid to the use of groups in the Provo Experiment. For the sake of convenience, these guidelines are summarized in Table 6-1.

Our experience coincides with that of others who suggest that not every group will be able to progress all the way through the five stages that are described there. Some group leaders, for example, have argued that traditional therapy groups rarely get beyond Stage 3, which is the stage at which there is a great deal of concern for individual need and gratification. But even if that is the case, it is our feeling that, when working with delinquents, the principle of having the group help to decide when an individual should be released from the program should remain in force. It is a principle of great importance if the objective of promoting the consumer's trust in the program is to be realized. Beyond that, every effort should be made to continue group development beyond Stage 3 because of its obvious relevance for addressing the traditional problems of correctional programs and enhancing organizational solidarity.

In terms of a brief evaluation of the guidelines, two things might be noted. First, it is our impression that one major difficulty in using group techniques with delinquents is that of overcoming their initial resistances to serious involvement at least on a voluntary basis. So long as they are free in the community, many will not stick around long enough to become involved or to participate in the steps necessary to build a functioning group. In order to deal with this problem, we tried to structure the necessary conditions by reinforcing the three basic ground rules mentioned earlier sometimes through the use of coercive means.

On one hand, these means seemed to have the desired effect. Prior chapters have indicated that they not only helped to maintain organizational stability and to reduce delinquent behavior, but they seemed to highlight the importance of the group as a problem-solving, even tension-reducing, mechanism. Such findings, as a result, tended to support those who have argued that aversive controls may have some role to play in setting the stage for, if not actually accomplishing, new learning.

On the other hand, other means would obviously be preferable. Aversive controls may be limited more to the suppression of undesirable and prior forms of behavior than to alternative ways of behaving. We observed a defect in group function that may have been exacerbated by the use of coercive means.

Despite our concern with promoting trust and solidarity, our groups never did come up with a system of rewards that seemed to be equal in impact to the negative sanctions that were used. Both boys and staff found it far easier to punish the deviant than to reward the conformist. Part of the problem was

Table 6-1
Summary Description of Stages of Group Development in the Provo Experiment

	Stage 1: Search for Structure	Transition	Stage 2: Stereotyped Problem Solving	Transition	Stage 3: Awareness of Individual Differences and Alternatives	Transition	Stage 4: Group Awareness	Transition	Stage 5: Integration of group and program culture
Objectives	1. Foster and reward interaction. 2. Teach members that the level of group performance depends heavily on them. 3. Instill confidence in the group.		1. Learn complexities of delinquent behavior. 2. Introduction of substantive problems. 3. Gather information on individual group members.		1. Clarify alternatives. 2. Make group members more aware of individual differences.		1. Increase understanding of group structure and process to maximize group problem-solving. 2. Increase capacity of offender to see himself in relation to group structure.		1. Link the operation of the small group with program and community activities. 2. Group members who have reached this stage become culture-builders and maintainers for others.
Structural Context	1. Anomie expected. 2. Minimum of structure provided. 3. Group leader refrains from being authoritarian, does not foster dependency.	*Transition* 1. Dissatisfaction with Stage 1. 2. Enforced attendance is galling and escape is sought. 3. Role of group leader emerges as important. He becomes functional in reducing anxiety by suggesting ways to proceed.	1. Some group members take risks—attempt to play leadership role. 2. Group leader poses problems for which solutions must be found; refuses to accept all responsibility for control function. 3. Delinquents experiment with decision-making.	*Transition* 1. Dissatisfaction w/ stereotyping in Stage 2. 2. Group leader attempts to crystallize dilemmas & point out dysfunctions of type of interaction going on. 3. Explore alternative modes of interaction & behavior.	1. Two types of group members emerge: RESISTERS and REFORMERS. 2. Leader attempts to enrich interaction by providing involvement in complex decision-making. 3. Evidence of social control by the group.	*Transition* 1. Increasing group awareness of the dysfunction of selfish individual pursuits. 2. Leader helps group become aware of consequences of factionalism.	1. Group is seen as special entity. 2. Status of adult leader continues to change—his power and authority decreases and becomes shared by the group. 3. Leader continues to play teaching role.	*Transition* 1. Group recognizes need to establish linkage for its members in the community and to extend its influence into other components of the program. 2. Achievement of this transition depends more than any other phase upon the readiness of group members to assist in the task.	1. Increased awareness of group as an entity. 2. Group members share power with leader in deciding when boys can be released from program and other important issues. 3. Adult leader is seen more as a group member. 4. Roles are assigned on the basis of competence.

Group Process	1. Search for structure. 2. Testing. 3. Private search for meaning. 4. Leader sets stage for emergence of group culture.	1. Distrust of leader. 2. Testing continues. 3. Aggressive behavior; assertiveness. 4. Group members become aware of differences and problems they share with others. 4. Members more comfortable w/ leader and his role is better understood. 5. Candor is encouraged & rewarded.	1. Concern with conflicts between subgroups. 2. More free exchange than Stages 1 or 2. 3. Increased concern for welfare of group.	1. Interaction more candid and satisfying than at any previous stage. 2. Greater collaboration and cooperation than at earlier stages. 3. Conflict among subgroups still present, but to lesser degree.	1. Periods of highly cooperative and motivated problem-solving. 2. Greater evidence of active reformation role than at any other time. 3. Greater trust and communication than earlier stages.
Discussion Content	1. Safe, non-threatening material. 2. Leader does not provide conclusive answers, but sponsors discussion matter of interest to boys. 3. Interaction wandering and idiosyncratic. 4. Recitation of delinquent histories and personal problems.	1. Same as Stage 1 except for introduction of substantive problems: school problems, new delinquent acts, family problems, gripes about program demands.	1. Involves more sensitive and personal problems and feelings than prior stages. 2. Considerable amount of personal information is exchanged. 3. A more involved and persistent examination of problems and decisions.	1. Same as Stage 3, except that content is put more in context of group phenomena and their relation to total program and community.	1. Same as other stages, except there is greater concern for total program operation, maintaining a collaborative system and addressing problems of boys in the community.

*This summary table was originally presented in the Silverlake Experiment (Empey and Lubeck, 1971: 94-95).

inherent in the nature of the organization itself—it was a correctional organization. Yet, staff members were perpetually troubled over the inability of the groups to foster a greater sense of sympathetic understanding, patience, and mutual respect. Somehow, these kinds of rewards were never adequately developed. The problem may have been due in part to the interpersonal styles of adolescents, especially seriously delinquent boys, and part may have been due to the fact that the groups were not a part of such regular institutions as the school or a place of employment where there is a common understanding of the traditional relationship between rewards and activities. Groups that are designed for the specific purpose of introducing change are atypical, and young people are not as used to dealing with them. Whatever the reason, it is our impression that the group function could have been improved had as much attention been paid to the deliberate structuring of rewards as was paid to the deliberate creation of controls.

A second evaluative issue has to do with the nature of group development itself. From a scientific standpoint, it would be important to know whether groups are characterized by phases of development that are anything at all like those set forth in this chapter, or whether group development is a myth. From an applied standpoint, it was assumed that group members could benefit most if they experienced the entire developmental process from beginning to end. It would provide a learning experience, not only with respect to the problems of behavioral change, but with respect to the nature of group structure and process as well. By working with staff and other members through difficult as well as satisfying times, the individual boy might benefit most.

An empirical study of a 15 per cent sample of almost 1000 recorded group sessions, representing 10 different groups that were a part of the Provo Experiment revealed some suggestive findings (cf. Gruner, 1972). First, it was found that when groups remained closed, there was some rather clear-cut evidence that a developmental process does take place—a process in which therapist participation decreases, group-centered comments increase, greater member-risks occur in which candid and confrontive statements are made, and nontask-oriented comments decrease. The analysis revealed that this process is better described in terms of a developmental trend than in terms of sharply demarcated stages. The pattern fluctuated from idiosyncratic and nonproductive to group-centered and task-oriented interaction. Although the trend tended to conform to the stages set forth in the guidelines, it was also characterized by occasional regressions to prior modes of behavior. In its development, a group does not go through each progressive stage never to return. Rather, it gradually changes its overall mode of operation and never is entirely free of what seem to be some of its less desirable kinds of behavior. Its development, as a result, is staggered, characterized by a general trend, not a step progression.

By contrast, it was found that when groups were constituted of both new and experienced group members, a trendlike pattern of development was much less discernable. In fact, when the process patterns of overlapping and contiguous groups were placed side-by-side, it appeared that each following group tended to start where the preceding group had left off. Apparently, the few experienced members who were carried over from a preceding group into a new one tended to dictate the mode of interaction in that new group, not inexperienced members.

In one sense, this was a desirable outcome because it meant that the new groups started to interact immediately on a relatively high level of operation. Experienced members seemed to be bearers of organizational traditions which tended to block some of the conflicts and idiosyncratic behaviors that were characteristic of entirely inexperienced groups. The entire burden for exercising controls, and guiding interactions was not placed solely upon the shoulders of the group leader. Rather, older group members exercised a normative influence.

On the other hand, the empirical analysis revealed that these mixed groups did not move to levels of operation that were much higher in a developmental sense than those on which they began. Unlike the closed groups, evidence of development was much less dramatic. As a result, two limitations were implied. The first was the possibility of a high level of frustration for the experienced member who was unlikely to see his new group move to any new and more productive level of operation beyond that which he had already experienced. The second was the fact that new members were denied the learning associated with the struggles and conflicts inherent in early and primitive levels of operation. In fact, once the pattern of using mixed groups reached its second generation of operation, no group members, including experienced ones, even had the chance to experience the problems of early stages of development. Not only was there something to be said for them to have the chance for doing so, but members may have needed the rewards associated with seeing their group make significant progress, rather than remaining relatively static, and of seeing them move to higher levels of operation.

As a consequence, these findings suggest that the relative merits of closed versus mixed groups should be carefully considered. While the presence of some experienced members in every group may assist in the task of maintaining a relatively high level of organizational control and normative expectations, it may also inhibit higher levels of group operation and learning. Greater organizational conflict is implied in the latter alternative—conflict that will be replicated with every group—but the potentialities for reward and learning may also be inherent in it. The basic question, at its most fundamental level, is that of deciding what the proper mix of structure and consensus versus conflict and discovery should be.

7

Utilitarian Features: The City Work Program

One segment of the Provo Experiment was utilitarian in character. By having a city work program, by paying wages for it, and by seeking employment for boys after they left the program, an effort was made to provide some conventional opportunities for them. Hopefully, a work experience accompanied by monetary rewards would not only develop a more willing commitment to conventional behavior, but would increase the noncoercive power of the experimental organization. Along with the normative features of the daily group meeting, this would be another way of substituting for coercive controls.

This chapter is devoted to a discussion of the employment program: how it was set up, how well it worked, and whether it seemed to accomplish the objectives set for it.

Finding Work

The first major problem was that of finding a source of employment where all boys assigned to the experimental program could be put to work. There were several things that made the task less than easy. In the first place, not all the boys assigned to the experimental program were available for day-long employment during the winter months. On the average, over half of them were still in school, although their performance was usually marginal. In order to give this group as well as the dropouts some work experience, it was necessary to provide Saturday along with week-day, employment. In summer, of course, all boys could be employed during the week; but since most of them stayed in the program only a few months, Saturday work during the winter was a necessity if all were to make any money and to gain any work experience.

Second, in order to maintain the normative power of the organization, it seemed wise, if possible, to have the boys work together, or at least in two groups, each of which would be comprised of those individuals who made up one of the daily discussion sessions. Although our approach to the use of groups could scarcely be equated with what has traditionally been called group therapy, it was our opinion that one of the limitations of that treatment had been the fact that members seldom had much to do with each other except when they met for sessions. In many institutional settings, members are chosen on the basis of some psychological abnormality, not whether they work or live together. Or if they are outpatients, they may live in divergent parts of a city, coming

137

together only when the group meets. As a consequence, group members have very little experience with each other in a behavioral sense, and really do not know each other very well. It is next to impossible to build the normative power of the group to deal with many of the collective and instrumental, as well as psychological, problems that members share. For these reasons, it is important to provide means by which group members could learn how each person behaved. Work activities like the group meeting were a source of socialization, and a means of enhancing the normative and utilitarian power of the organization.

Third, in trying to find a work program, we were confronted with the bewildering and paradoxical array of barriers that have been set up in modern society to make it difficult for young people to find gainful employment. Dropouts are often criticized for not doing something "constructive," but we found it extremely difficult to find something constructive for them to do. Child labor laws, written originally to prevent the exploitation of children, now make many of the most desirable jobs unavailable to young people, especially those involving machinery or other features that make employment inherently attractive. In addition a work permit from the school must be obtained before any dropout may become eligible for employment. Even though the permit can usually be obtained, it represents another bit of bureaucratic red tape that must be unwound before an employer will consider a prospective candidate.

A special citizens' committee had been set up to assist the Experiment with these problems, but it was powerless. Confronted with the existing range of problems, it was neither innovative nor aggressive in finding solutions. In the small town of Provo, there were few industrial enterprises where all of the boys could be employed, and among the few that did exist, such as U.S. Steel, child labor laws and union contracts made employment impossible. The recommendations of the committee tended to reflect the kind of rural and depression-oriented society in which most of its members had grown up.

Among other things, committee members suggested that the boys might be organized into lawn-mowing teams, going from door to door soliciting work. Or they might find seasonal work picking fruit, or working in agricultural areas. Perhaps the committee's best suggestion was that Pinehills set up and run a car wash, although it had neither the capital nor facilities to make the enterprise really work. Nevertheless, a car wash was tried for a while, but it was more like the occasional church group that one sees trying to make a few dollars washing cars than a regular place of employment. In fact, all of the suggestions would only have provided temporary palliatives, not work opportunities of some substance.

Finally, a helpful city manager, at some risk to himself, helped to provide a solution. Through his efforts, a city work program, providing regular employment, was eventually set up. When the idea was first conceived, he knew full well that he could not put regular city employees out of work to employ delinquents.

At the same time, he recognized that there were certain needs in the city that were being left unattended—the beautification of vacant lots and parks, temporary repairs on city streets or sidewalks, seasonal needs for special crews at the city cemetery before and after Decoration Day, needed repairs or improvements at the city golf course, the baseball park, or the city skating rink. He reasoned that by using the boys as a trouble-shooting crew, some persistent, but often ignored, problems could be attended. With the help of Pinehills staff, a proposal was developed and taken to the City Council.

In approaching the Council on this matter, the City Manager and the staff of the Experiment made it clear that neither wanted a special favor, least of all a phony, make-work project. Although there were obvious needs that could be met by delinquent workers, the program would be a failure if they were made to feel that the work was unimportant, or that the city fathers really did not expect that they could render a service. An attempt was made to have the Council take the matter seriously, as they would if any other program were being considered.

The City Council, after some debate, gave its approval for a work program, subject to two conditions: (1) that the necessary funds could somehow be found; and (2) that all existing legal restrictions with respect to the employment of juveniles could be met. Despite this approval, it was given in a somewhat condescending and paternalistic manner. While believing that hard work would be good for delinquents, the Council implied that it did not think that much would be accomplished. It was clear, therefore, that, if the work program were to be put on a secure footing, Pinehills and the boys in it would have to deliver.

Budgetary and Legal Restrictions

As it turned out, the two conditions set by the City Council posed some problems. Since the funds to pay for the program had to be squeezed out of some rather empty pockets, and since two adults had to be hired to supervise the work crews, the wage that could be paid to delinquents was low—fifty cents an hour.

While this rate was low by the prevailing standards of that time, it was not as bad as it would be today—over ten years later. In a small town, with an excess labor supply, juveniles might have gotten seventy-five cents, perhaps a dollar an hour, if they could have found unskilled work. But under the circumstances, we accepted the offer because it was the best that could be provided, and because it would provide Saturday as well as regular employment. (However, if one contrasted the offer with the few cents a day that were paid by the state to adults or juveniles in prison, the offer was downright generous.) Even so, the proferred wage was extremely low in terms of the hope that some strong utilitarian rewards could be built into the program.

Legal and technical barriers posed even greater problems. One set had to do with any effort to place a transient labor supply of delinquents on the city employment roles. Even though each boy would be in the program only a few months, any attempt to hire him through regular channels would require that fringe benefits, unemployment insurance, retirement costs, and other technicalities be met. If that had to be done, the cost would be prohibitive, to say nothing of the resistances that might be generated among regular employees. It was necessary to devise another procedure—one which involved a quasilegal end run.

Rather than placing each boy on the city work roles, an agreement between the city and Pinehills was drawn up in which Pinehills, not individual boys, contracted to provide services to the city. As the prime contractor, Pinehills would hire its own workers, perform the required services, and be paid for them. In turn, it would have to pay its own workers and insure them against possible injury. In essence, this meant that Pinehills simply acted as a middle man who kept the books, and paid employees everything that was earned. But, in addition, Pinehills had to take out medical and liability insurance with a private carrier. The cost for this insurance was not especially great because it was arranged with an insurance agent at no profit to him, but it had to be squeezed out of other funds, nevertheless.

Once the contractual model was developed, it served as the basis for later contracts with two neighboring cities. As a result, it was possible to ensure that employment for boys would be maintained throughout the life of the Experiment. Nevertheless, it may well have been that these contractual arrangements, or the relatively low wages paid to the boys, were contrary to the spirit of the Experiment if not the letter of the law. Certainly, the arrangements were less than ideal as a means of illustrating some of the rewarding features of a good job. Yet, the choice was a difficult one—either to make the best of what was available, or to drop the utilitarian feature of the Experiment altogether. While this part of the program may have been inestimably preferable to the dismal and unrewarding work features of most places of incarceration, the problems associated with setting it up illustrate just how difficult it is to introduce constructive changes, or to implement a program consistent with theoretical design.

Parenthetically, it should be noted that, although a decade has passed since the Provo Experiment began, very little has been done to overcome problems of this type. With all its difficulties, the process of trying to employ delinquents at Provo was nothing compared with that which one might observe today in a number of federal, state and local programs, all of which are designed, ostensibly, to put exconvicts and other poverty groups to work. Aside from economics, perhaps the greatest problem is bureaucratic. The mazes of government that must be run, and the often confused and frightened people who operate them, are nothing short of amazing. It may take months, even years, to get a project off the ground after funds are actually appropriated. As a result, the impact on the morale of an initially hopeful client group is terribly destructive. It would be difficult to construct deliberately any procedures that better symbolize the reactions of an impersonal society to its low-status members than those that continue to prevail.

Operation of Work Program

Once the actual work got under way at Provo, an effort was made to symbolize its importance to boys, and to establish the work norms that would prevail. This was done by having the staff leaders of the discussion groups, as well as the supervisors hired by the city, participate in the work program. But rather than merely supervising, the Pinehills group leaders did the same work that delinquents did. They attempted to show boys not only how to work, but to indicate, through example, that boys would be expected to perform at an adult level.

Hopefully, two things might be accomplished. First, the city work endeavor could serve as a training ground for higher paid, private employment later on, after the correctional experience was over. Second, boys could learn that any issues or problems that arose on the job might be addressed in the group sessions as well as at work. The task of enhancing the normative character of the overall program required that boys see the relationships among its parts, and that they take a part in them.

The work participation of group leaders went on for some time, and while it did, the work went reasonably well. There was the usual bitching from different boys, but in the main, the experience seemed to be a constructive one. But when the group leaders discontinued their work participation and turned to other important experimental tasks—research, training, community organization—problems of two types arose immediately.

Problems with Delinquents

The first had to do with delinquents themselves. Our experiences during the first two years caused us to question whether we were perpetuating or changing delinquent behavior. Many of the boys did not know how to work and others hated the daily grind. The physical labor made them so tired that it interfered with their extracurricular activities at night. As a result, it was difficult for some boys to get to work on time, and others did not work well when they got there.

More important was the continual friction between the boys and the adults who had been hired to supervise them. Unused to the dress, the language, and often the aggression of the boys, some supervisors tended to adopt an unbending, authoritarian stance in dealing with them. As can be imagined, the results were not good. In one case, when the crews were working several miles from the city on a reclamation project, the boys removed the distributor cap from the city truck so that it, and the crews, were immobilized all day. The frustrated supervisor never did find out what was wrong because the boys replaced the cap about the time for returning home. In other cases, supervisors were seduced by their crews in an apparent attempt to become "one of the boys." This did not work either, but only created problems of another type.

The unfortunate result of the general inability of supervisors to deal with their own management problems resulted in their shifting responsibility for work problems from themselves and their crews to the group leaders at Pinehills. Unable to manage the problems of a deviant minority, they expected other staff members to maintain control and prevent difficulties. Consequently, rather than work becoming a productive experience, it became a thorn in the side.

These circumstances served primarily to reinforce rather than to diminish the salience of the underdog, delinquent perspective among the boys. So long as adults assumed responsibility for trying to manage all difficulties, a wide gap between offenders and staff continued to persist. Boys were free, indeed encouraged, to place blame on anyone else but themselves. This state of affairs, led, in the beginning of the third year of the Experiment, to a rather dangerous innovation.

It all began one day when, about noon, a particularly abrasive and foul-mouthed boy suddenly appeared at Pinehills when he should have been working several miles away. When asked by one of the staff members what he was doing there, he replied that once again he had been kicked off the job by a work supervisor for abusive behavior and an unwillingness to work. When asked if this was true, he said "yes," and inquired what he was supposed to do now. The supervisor had told him to report to his group leader at Pinehills.

The usual practice in such cases was to put the offending individual to work around the house for which he received no pay. But this boy had been penalized so many times and his problems had been discussed so often in the group sessions, that it was obvious that a repetition of those procedures would again be a waste of time. Whereas they worked with most boys, they did not with him.

On the spur of the moment, and in response to the boy's question as to what he should do, the staff member said, "I don't give a damn what you do. Don't come to me with your problems." The staff member then appeared to turn his attention back to his work.

This response was disconcerting to the boy who stood in pained silence for several moments. Then, in what was a subdued voice for him, he again asked, "What do you want me to do?" Again, the response was the same: "I don't care what you do. From now on, that's up to you to decide."

The long silence was repeated. Then, the boy walked into an adjoining room and began to vacuum the floor. He did that, and other jobs, until the work crews arrived for the afternoon meeting. But the incident did not end there. In the interim, the staff member talked to the other group leader and it was decided that from then on they would stop being the "fall guys" for the problems that the work supervisors and crews could not handle. If the work program was to survive, its problems would have to be handled in some other way. But how was this to be done?

It was decided that, rather than dividing into two separate groups for the evening meeting, everyone would meet together. Then, using the incident of the afternoon as a case in point, the two staff members disavowed their responsibility for handling this or similar problems unilaterally. Why should they always be put into the role of disciplinarian? How could they act fairly and objectively over an issue about which they knew little? How could they decide who was at fault—the supervisor, the boy, or the group as a whole? They took the position that the best time to deal with a problem was when it occurred, not several hours later when it was difficult to pinpoint the issues.

Secondly, the two staff members suggested that each work crew itself should deal with its problems on the spot. And, in order to do that, especially to locate final responsibility for getting the work done, the regular work supervisors should be removed, and two of the more experienced boys hired to take their place. One delinquent member of each group, in other words, would become the supervisor for his crew. Moreover, this offender-supervisor should receive $1.50 an hour in lieu of the usual 50¢.

Perhaps it is not surprising that this recommendation was accepted by the groups with boyish enthusiasm, especially when it was also suggested that the supervisory job should rotate so that as many boys as possible could have a chance to occupy the position. The boys felt that the new procedure would not only mean that the crews would be freed from the direction of a stupid adult, but almost everyone would have a chance to make more money. Without paying any attention to the implications inherent in the plan, the boys wanted to implement it immediately.

As quickly as possible, their recommendation was followed. Since the two supervisors were college students who would be quitting soon anyway, a termination of their employment was not a special problem. The greater problem was that of effecting a transition with the city foremen who were responsible for assigning the crews their work, either daily, weekly, or monthly depending on the job. These foremen were concerned about the absence of adult supervisors and questioned whether boy supervisors could be trusted. Hence, until that trust could be built—if indeed it could—it was necessary for a regular staff member to act as an intermediary between city employees and work crews. When a new job was assigned, for example, a staff member had to be present to receive instructions, to check out tools and so on. Eventually, this was changed so that boy supervisors fulfilled this function, but that was not for some time.

Once the change was made, however, the loudest protest was heard, not from city foremen nor Pinehills' staff, but from the two boys who were chosen to be the first offender supervisors. Beginning their first day with scarcely concealed glee, they finished it in total depression. They disavowed the job and wanted to quit. According to their own accounts, their expectations were rudely shattered (see Chapter 6). They were unable to sit around all day as they had expected; few of their peers would follow directions; and those that did were colorfully disrespectful. The only way the supervisors could get anything done, they said, was to do it themselves.

This reaction was not unanticipated by Pinehills staff, but it created considerable apprehension nevertheless. A great deal was riding on the success of this radical innovation. Having delinquents working as a group in the open community was bad enough, but having them work there unsupervised was likely to bring a startled councilman, an unhappy citizen, or an enraged police chief down upon them. Consequently, while these early adjustments were being carried out, the actual change in the program was made with as little public announcement as possible, the philosophy being that what officials did not know *might* now hurt them. As it turned out, some heat was generated, but it had to do with many issues, not just this one. More important, the innovation was eventually a success.

Its success, we believe, can be attributed to two things. The first was the existence of the basic ground rules of the program. Unlike any unorganized and inexperienced group of juveniles picked up off the street to work, these boys were under some constraints and they knew it. They were not totally free to do as they wished, and did not really behave much worse under the new arrangement than they had before.

Secondly, and far more important, the normative strengths that had been cultivated through the mechanism of the group meeting helped to save the day. Without prior group ties and the daily meeting, it is unlikely that the change in work procedures would have worked. The way in which group norms and processes helped to resolve problems went as follows.

After their first dismal experience on the job, the two new supervisors turned to the group meetings themselves (whose memberships were coterminous with the memberships of their work crews) for help. They not only vented their frustrations, but confronted their peers with what they felt was traitorous behavior. How could one's supposed friends treat a person the way they had been treated? Conversely, some members of the crews confronted the supervisors with what they thought was stupid and unhelpful behavior. The supervisors, they felt, had acted in a high-handed manner, had not set a good example for their crews, and had failed to provide work instructions in a detailed and understandable way.

The provocative thing about the discussion was its concern with ways to do things in a more effective conventional, not delinquent, manner. In fact, discussions of the type that ensued probably would not have been possible had the usual adult supervisors remained in charge. The upshot was that the group discussions became much more focused and relevant because they dealt with issues that were of direct importance to everyone. There was never enough time in the group meetings to handle all of them. Discussions spilled over into the work and other activities during the day. To be sure, there were some boys who continued to create difficulties, but once the crews themselves, rather than just a single supervisor, had to deal with day-to-day problems, the occasional deviant had fewer reinforcements. Peer controls were more in evidence where they counted.

One basic reason was that, for the first time, there were striking role reversals in which boy supervisors found themselves in the difficult position of an adult attempting to direct a recalcitrant crew. Conversely, when there was friction and when mistakes were made, members of the crews did not have an adult to blame. They either had to bear some of the responsibility themselves, or see both wages and a speedy release from the program go down the drain.

Such conditions provided an insightful experience. Boys began to recognize their parts in any difficulty and the extent to which they were responsible for the success or failure of the work. It was much easier in the group meetings to examine fundamental work and other problems: who the poor workers were, what delinquent manipulations were taking place, and what it meant to be an adult rather than a child. Furthermore, the members of each group began to recognize that if the work was to be done, and if they were to obtain release from the program, there would have to be a greater exercise of collective control and responsibility. The work supervisors could not maintain a reasonable level of productivity and order by themselves.

The importance of this kind of normative, peer control was further illustrated when the role of work supervisor was rotated. Anticipating that they might soon be in that role themselves, most boys began to watch what the current supervisor did, to observe which behaviors on their parts were helpful and which were not, so that they might perform more efficiently when their turns came. The selection of each new supervisor became a group rather than a staff function. After gaining some experience with the matter, the groups were willing to appoint weaker, often retiring, boys to the supervisory job on the premise that these boys badly needed the experience of occupying a leadership role. In order to make such appointments work, stronger and more experienced boys often had to assist weaker ones on the job, further extending the normative power of the group.

There is some concrete evidence, other than these comments, that this change had a salutory effect. The most notable was the fact that, as knowledge of the work program got around, increasing pressure was put on the City Council and City Manager to expand the summer work program to include "good" boys as well as delinquents. After obtaining a matching grant from state funds, this step was taken.

Perhaps surprisingly, the Pinehills staff was apprehensive about this expansion. The new program would have few of the means that Pinehills did for ensuring that "good" boys would show up regularly, or would work well on the job. Nondelinquent crews would be without the benefit of group ties. If the new crews worked poorly and sporadically, the relatively high degree of morale among the Pinehills boys working alongside them would be weakened. If the new program did not work well, the Pinehills program might be endangered.

As it turned out, some of the staff fears were confirmed. Many of the same problems encountered earlier by Pinehills were repeated in this case, but were often worse. When city officials turned to Pinehills for assistance, two suggestions were made that had a helpful effect. The most notable was that the city should hire some carefully selected former Pinehills boys as work supervisors. The second was that, if these supervisors were hired, they should be permitted to set some work standards which, if not observed, could result in termination of employment for the offending individual.

These procedures were followed and the work program improved. Not all Pinehills boys could have played the supervisory role well, but the prior experiences of the few who were hired enabled them to take a no-nonsense attitude toward their work that seemed to provide the needed structure. Unlike those who had never been delinquent and never been through some of the trials of the Pinehills experience, these young supervisors were not cowed by the problems that arose. Their prior careers, in other words, turned out to be an asset rather than a liability.

A second kind of evidence regarding the possible desirability of a work program had to do with the fact that some of the better workers on the Pinehills crews were hired by the city on a regular basis. Without exception, this opportunity was extended, not because boys applied for employment through regular channels, but because they were observed on the job by some city foreman who was impressed by their work.

In some cases, an offer was proffered to a boy before he had been released from Pinehills. When this occurred, the boy's group was consulted and, if it concurred, the boy was permitted to accept the new, higher-paying job in lieu of working with his regular crew. This did not mean that he was automatically released from Pinehills. He had to continue until it was agreed that he was ready for release. Several boys worked in this way on several different kinds of city and other jobs. In terms of long-term, career opportunities, however, these jobs were far too scarce to help any but a very few boys. Most of the available positions involved low-paying, largely unskilled work.

Problems with the Community

There were some problems relative to the task of gaining community acceptance that bear mentioning as well, because those problems have probably gotten worse the past few years, not better. The first had to do with the fears that offenders generate in people. They were most in evidence when boys worked in plain view on city streets, parks, and places of recreation. Because the Pinehills crews were in work clothes, because they worked in groups (which often frighten people terribly), and because they were often boisterous and obscene in their language, protests were received at Pinehills, the Juvenile Court and City Hall. Mothers resented, with some justification, the use of obscenity in front of their children. They were also concerned, with less justification, for the safety of their persons and property.

These problems were discussed openly in the groups, and once some of the more garrulous and obscene features of the crews' behavior were reduced, the number of protests diminished. So long as boys paid attention to their work, conditions improved. Yet, the protests did not end. A second set had to do with problems that were more difficult to solve.

Whenever boys sat down to take a mid-morning or mid-afternoon break or to eat their lunches, they were also criticized. Protests in this case came from citizens and officials who believed that the Pinehills crews were loafing at city expense. On one occasion a charge was made before the City Council that water rates were too high because Pinehills boys were employed, at times, for the City Water Department. The charges stemmed from observations that boys were "sitting around on the job." To make matters worse, the Pinehills crews were sometimes confused with an occasional delinquent who was required by the juvenile court to work off a fine, or with crews of "good" boys hired by the city in its summer work program. In some cases, the charges were justified because neither of the last two groups was noted for its diligence.

All effort to quiet these kinds of problems through public relations efforts failed. On occasion, a favorable newspaper article by a reporter who made it her business to find out whether the charges were true did not help. It was not until all obvious evidence of boys resting or eating near their places of work were removed that the protests died down. When boys were working in a residential neighborhood, which fortunately was not often, the rest periods for that day had to be cancelled. And during the noon hour, they either had to eat their lunches in a staff member's car, or be transported to some other location. When the crews were working in some more remote place, the problems were not so great, but even then boys had to learn circumspection, especially to control their inclinations to want to separate and roam around during the break.

These kinds of unreasonable and often unwarranted difficulties are not only frustrating, but often interfere with efforts to deal with more fundamental problems. Yet, on balance, they may have done some good. In contrast to the usual pattern where convicted offenders are as foreign to the average citizen as a man from Mars, the occasional conflicts over their presence in the city not only kept their needs in the public eye, but sometimes generated additional support for the Experiment. At least there was some publicity where before there had been none. Since not all citizens were opposed to the work program, criticisms provided a rallying point for their support. Because citizen complaints were discussed in the daily meetings at Pinehills, the boys tried to do something about them, especially when some boys became work supervisors. Since work crews were often at fault, this fact provided another means for highlighting the need for boys to come to grips with childlike and obstreperous behavior which, though not always delinquent, did interfere with their adjustments at school and home as well as at work. The resistances of the community to the work program were not all destructive.

Postprogram Employment

It will be recalled that the operational design of the Provo Experiment was divided into two phases. The first phase involved the group and city work programs that have just been described. The second phase involved an effort to provide full-time employment for boys once they completed Phase 1. Because most repeat offenders have done so poorly in school and seemed to dislike it so intensely, it was assumed that the most productive thing that could be done would be to find jobs for them. This would be the most effective way of opening up some conventional alternatives for delinquents.

As it turned out, this set of assumptions not only proved to be incorrect, but the effort to find employment was a failure. The following chronology will help to clarify this conclusion.

At first, some strenuous efforts were made to find regular employment for Pinehills graduates. Repeated meetings were held with the Citizens' Employment Committee, but the effort was fruitless. Not only were there few promising jobs available for teenagers, but the committee itself rarely did anything except attend meetings. They simply did not contact employers and solicit jobs as we had hoped. As a consequence, the staff of the Experiment recognized that if any jobs were to be found, they, or the boys themselves, would have to find them.

On occasion, some interested and helpful employers provided solid assistance. One was a building contractor with a small business who did everything he could to keep one or two boys employed. Another was a service station owner who did the same thing. A few boys, as mentioned earlier, were also employed by the city, or found jobs themselves. But, in the main, the number of boys needing employment grossly exceeded the supply of jobs.

Two major problems hindered most efforts to find employment. The first was the youthfulness of the group. Since the average age was only sixteen, most boys were simply too young for any employer to give them serious consideration. The second was their lack of education and a saleable skill. They qualified for nothing but the most unskilled of jobs for which there was already an excess labor supply.

It became increasingly clear, as a result, that efforts to find permanent employment simply would not work and the basic focus of that effort was changed. While attempts to place older individuals in available jobs did continue, experiment staff sought to replace the job-hunting with enrollment for boys in a nearby vocational school. In that way, they might acquire a saleable skill.

It was assumed that, despite their poor educational problems, this population might benefit from a curriculum which offered training in auto mechanics, electronics, or drafting. Not only might it be more interesting, but it could serve as a stepping-stone to more promising employment later on. Much to the chagrin of everyone, it was found that most Pinehills boys lacked the necessary entrance requirements for enrollment in the school. Its students either had to have a high school diploma, or its equivalent in terms of verbal and quantitative skills.

When efforts were made to have Pinehills boys treated as exceptions, at least on a trial basis, school officials argued that their classes were already filled with high school graduates. There was, in fact, some competition for a relatively scarce number of positions. More important, school administrators noted that most skilled occupations today cannot be learned or practiced without the capacity to read instructions, to make arithmetic computations, or to utilize and interpret some rather complicated instruments. And, since this particular vocational school did not provide the necessary means for acquiring the necessary academic skills, Pinehills boys would have to acquire it elsewhere. Once having done so, they would then be welcome to enroll.

There was institutional inflexibility and dislike for delinquents reflected in this response, but there was some truth in it as well. A careful study of the school revealed that both its students, and the courses being offered, were beyond the maturity and abilities of most of the Pinehills boys. It seemed likely that they would fail once again unless their training included a great deal of remedial help with computational and reading skills, something that the vocational school did not provide.

This series of events clearly highlighted a basic correctional dilemma. One of the arguments that is often made in favor of community programs, like the Provo Experiment, is that they can utilize the resources that already exist in a community rather than trying (but usually failing) to replicate all of them in a closed institution. But what this experience revealed was that such resources did not exist.

The longer we worked with this admittedly small minority of adolescents, the more we found that they simply fell between the institutional cracks of the community fabric. There were no means by which to match their needs with existing resources. Most of the boys were failing in, or had dropped out of school; they were too young or too unskilled to find decent employment; and they could not qualify for enrollment in a trade school. The implication, of course, is that future community programs, if they are to be successful, will have to do something to alter this state of affairs. A strategy designed to change institutional patterns would seem to be an absolute necessity.

Insofar as the Provo Experiment is concerned, the findings mean that there was a serious failure to implement one segment of the basic operational design; namely, to open up a greater range of conventional alternatives for delinquents. The Experiment, in fact, was naive in its approach. The magnitude of the problems it would face were grossly underestimated, and the structures it set up to help provide employment and other opportunities were entirely inadequate.

Consumer Perceptions

In earlier chapters, it was argued that, if correctional programs could not do more than was done in this case to alter community structures, they would not be perceived as credible by their delinquent or criminal consumers. The ways in which delinquents viewed both the city work program and the attempts of staff to find employment for them are instructive.

First of all, delinquents were far less inclined to view the city work program with enthusiasm than they were to be supportive of group problem-solving and decision-making. When asked to evaluate these two major components of the overall program, they were not especially critical of the work activities. They simply placed much greater stress upon the values of the group function. Some of them advocated that work demands be made even more stringent than they were, but just as many failed to make suggestions of any type. When discussed solely in utilitarian terms, in other words, the work program was not of special importance to delinquents.

This finding may be attributed in part to the fact that hourly wages were so low. Had the rate of remuneration been higher, support may have been higher. Yet, there is another more subtle point that merits consideration.

The employment of delinquents as work supervisors, and the involvement of virtually all the boys in dealing with work problems, may have had a paradoxical but significant result. Rather than enhancing the virtues of the work program in the eyes of the boys, it enhanced the virtues of the group segment. That may be why boys felt that group activities occupied such a preeminent position. In struggling, both in the group meetings and on the job, to overcome conflict and disunity, group cohesiveness and solidarity were seen as the most rewarding results, not better work performance. If so, the salience of the normative rather than utilitarian features of the program would have been increased, despite the fact that work activities were the focus of attention.

This interpretation is interesting in light of the fact that, if one is concerned with an efficient accomplishment of some instrumental task, he is not well advised ordinarily to rely upon democratic procedures involving quite large numbers of people by which to get it done. In the discussion of a simple work problem, Pinehills boys often spent hours, even days, in search of a solution. The process seemed interminable. Yet, if this interpretation is correct, it suggests that, in the eyes of group members, the greatest by-product of these interminable discussions was not the accomplishment of the instrumental task, but the sense of personal and group satisfaction that was gained from it. Although work performance was actually increased, it was not this instrumental change that was most important to delinquents, but the fact that they participated successfully in it. Normative, not utilitarian results, were the most important.

Another result growing out of the work program, and the failure of staff to find long-term employment for graduates, is also noteworthy. Contrary to theoretical assumptions made about the negative aspects of the school experience and to the surprise of staff members, there was a growing tendency throughout the life of the program for delinquents to advocate the importance of remaining in, or returning to, school. When the Experiment first started, that was not the case. But the more delinquents discussed the matter, and the more capable they became of getting to the heart of their problems, the more they tended to emphasize the importance of school.

This change may simply have reflected a response on the parts of delinquents to what it was they thought staff members wanted to hear. But in light of the concern of staff for sticking to the theoretical importance of employment, that interpretation is not entirely satisfying. There seemed to be other reasons for the position that delinquents took.

The first was a frank, albeit conventional, admission that, without some rudiments of an education, they could not get a decent job. Most of them had no difficulty with this idea in a philosophical sense, especially since they had seen so many boys fail to get a decent job. What bothered them were its pragmatic implications whether they could make it in school, or whether the school would accept them. Most were keenly aware of and sensitive about their own low levels of achievement. Nevertheless, there was growing peer pressure, as the program aged, for boys to remain in school. This was especially true of boys who were still hanging on, but were considering dropping from school. Any attempts on their parts to drop out were met with an increasing wall of resistance. Their peers tended increasingly to judge their abilities to stay in school as a sign they were making significant progress in the Experiment.

A second reason had to do with the school as a place where interesting things happen, where friends are made, and where girls can be found. As many youth workers can attest, dropouts often congregate at school during lunch breaks, during football games, or at other times when classes are not in session. In fact, they often get into trouble with administrators for doing so. In their more candid moments, Pinehills boys often expressed regret that they were separated from the youth-oriented functions of the school and wished they could return. Life on the streets was often incredibly boring while, at school, there was action.

A final reason that school seemed to increase in importance probably had to do with the work experience. Many boys found the eight-hour work grind much worse than the school grind. Once the initial euphoria wore off, work was a drag.

Summary and Conclusions

This chapter has been concerned with the extent to which the utilitarian objectives of the Provo Experiment were realized. The evidence is mixed.

Once a host of legal and economic obstructions were overcome, a work program for all experimental boys was started and maintained. There was constant friction between delinquents and work supervisors, however, so long as the latter were left in charge. It was only when these supervisors were eliminated and some of the boys themselves put into the supervisory role that the problems declined. Some Pinehills boys went on to become supervisors in a summer work program for nondelinquents run by the city.

While this outcome was salutory in the sense that it increased work productivity and demonstrated that delinquents may be able to perform well in new kinds of careers, it was our impression that the greatest benefits were normative rather than utilitarian. Were it not for the increase in group controls and possibly group satisfactions gained by the delinquent workers, the work innovation may have failed. There is considerable reason to believe, therefore, that while the group discussion and work segments of the program were highly complimentary, boys were inclined to attribute most of the desirable results to the group discussions and problem-solving.

Their work in the community put delinquents, indeed the Pinehills organization, into a goldfish bowl. Wherever the workers went, they were observed critically by citizens and often officials. Besides making it necessary for delinquents to be highly circumspect about their behavior, it was often necessary to adopt the appearance of unique virtue and diligence, even if the appearance was somewhat deceptive.

Following their graduation from the program, Pinehills was unsuccessful in providing employment for delinquents. This phase of the experiment was a failure. Moreover, some of the assumptions emphasizing the importance (or even feasibility) of career-oriented employment for adolescent delinquent boys seemed to be incorrect. Coupled with the extreme difficulties of finding jobs, the reactions of delinquents themselves seemed to favor a much greater concentration upon trying to provide educational rather than work opportunities. Given their youthfulness and their inabilities to write and read well, these boys would have been better served had the same effort gone into an alteration of educational structures.

Relatively little contact with the schools found administrators generally in favor of the Experiment. What pleased them most was the fact that those Pinehills boys who were still in school were much less a behavioral problem than they had been before. But while these administrators often waxed eloquent about their need to be less concerned with the control problems that had plagued them before, we could find little evidence that the academic performance of the boys in question had improved, primarily because they needed so much remedial help before they could perform on a grade level equivalent to that of their peers. If the Experiment were to be repeated, therefore, we would probably make every effort to make it a part of, not separate from, the school.

By design, we would seek both funding and school support by which delinquents, living in their own homes, might have a better chance of making it in school. With all the miseries of their prior educational experiences, it is our impression that delinquents feel more at home in the school setting than in any correctional setting one could devise. The latter, especially when residential in character, is the most alien of all to young people.

Along with obvious changes in formal school procedures and structures that would have to be made, it would be equally important to alter informal peer structures. Research has indicated that the latter are highly important in determining the norms by which the performance of pupils in any school is guided. Since the group aspect of the Provo Experiment was better received by delinquents than any other, it might well be used again in the school setting, and for many of the same kinds of purposes. In fact, one added characteristic not found at Pinehills would be the incorporation of nondelinquents and even school personnel, as well as delinquents, into the group process of analyzing and solving school rather than employment problems. The idea would be to build as strong a set of ties as possible between the normative and instrumental features of the educational experience. In that way, both kinds of school functions would be strengthened. More will be said on this subject in the concluding chapter.

8

The Struggle for Survival

Any experimental organization like Pinehills must constantly struggle to survive. As an alternative to incarceration, it may avoid some of the traditional problems of a large and impersonal correctional system, and may be of relatively greater service to offenders. Yet, if it deliberately sets out, as the Provo Experiment did, to remain small in size, to avoid the excessive use of physical controls, and to keep its members well integrated into the community, it may also be sowing the seeds of its own destruction.

The reason, as suggested earlier, is that a small, noncoercive organization like Pinehills is narrow rather than broad in scope. It possesses neither the means to exercise a high degree of control over its delinquent members nor the means to exercise much social, economic, or political power. Unless it is tied to a large public bureaucracy, which the Provo Experiment was not, its capacity to survive a host of large and often competing vested interests may be severely constrained. At least this was certainly true in the case of the Provo Experiment.

Such an incredible series of events occurred that it would seem wise to present them in detail. All too often the power struggles in which innovative programs become embroiled remain undocumented in the literature (Miller, 1958; Miller, 1962; Klein, 1971:205-221 for some of the few accounts available). In this case, a natural history of the political and ideological conflicts of the Provo Experiment will be presented. At the conclusion of the chapter, it will be possible to relate the events of that history back to a more general set of issues. Perhaps in the future, it may be possible for others to avoid some of the problems that were involved.

The Organizational Strategy

In order to understand the problems that Pinehills encountered, it is necessary to be acquainted with the strategy that was followed in setting it up. Of importance, first of all, is the way in which the juvenile court system and correctional services are structured in Utah.

Utah is one of the few states in the nation where the juvenile judiciary and all correctional resources, including probation, are organized on a state, not a local, level. At the pinnacle of responsibility, these services are under the direction of the Utah State Welfare Commission, but are administered by the Director and staff of the Bureau of Services for Children. Under ordinary circumstances, any change in correctional practices would be the responsibility of these state officials. The Provo Experiment, however, was not organized under their direction—nor even with their blessing.

The actual foundation for the experiment was laid a few years prior to the time it actually began. The initial impetus came from the judge of the Fourth District Juvenile Court, whose headquarters were in Provo. Unhappy with incarceration, he had sought for several years to find some community alternative. He had organized a Citizens' Advisory Council whose purpose was to provide support and advice, and he had obtained an annual small budgetary allotment of $10,000-$12,000 from Utah County in whose jurisdiction his court was located. Even though the county fathers had no official responsibility for helping in the correctional task, they made these funds available as a form of service to the children of their county.

Once these financial resources had been obtained, the Judge, along with the Advisory Council, sought some professional help from Dr. Ray R. Canning under whose direction the initial community program in Provo was set up. Outside of the state structure, it became a forerunner to the Provo Experiment.

On paper, this new program appeared to be a good one: boys continued to live at home and were required to meet each day in the late afternoon; public school teachers assisted with remedial reading and handicrafts; Dr. Canning conducted group counseling sessions; college students provided the transportation each day to and from the boys' homes; and Brigham Young University made athletic facilities available. But with all its promise, many of the time-worn problems were present. Since the group of boys was comprised only of the most serious offenders, they often either failed to attend the daily sessions as required by the court, or created chaos when they did. Some of the staff volunteers were not reliable, and those that were reliable were often ill-prepared for the kinds of treatment they received. Two well-intentioned female teachers were often reduced to tears. The negative reactions of delinquents to them did not square with their preconceptions as to how they should be treated for "doing good." Given these kinds of difficulties, Dr. Canning felt obliged to reconceptualize and reorganize his program, but before that could be done, he became ill and had to resign as director for the program.

When that occurred, the time seemed propitious to rethink the program and, if possible, to set up research procedures by which it could be evaluated. The Provo Experiment was the result. A new director was selected; intervention procedures were restructured in terms of the theoretical assumptions described in earlier chapters; an experimental design was created; a foundation grant to supplement county funds was obtained; and a small permanent staff was hired. In taking all these steps, attention was focused more upon theoretical issues and program design than upon the politics of intervention. The ultimate destiny of the experiment may have been determined by this omission.

It is true that, in reconceptualizing the program, some thought was given to the possibility of soliciting support at the state level, and perhaps having the Welfare Commission and State Bureau of Services for Children act as cosponsors of, and participants in, the experiment. But this alternative was rejected for several reasons.

First, it was assumed, perhaps naively, that, because the experiment was being conducted in conjunction with the Fourth District Juvenile Court, the blessing of the state was implied. In fact, in accordance with powers granted to him by state law, the judge of the District Court had appointed the staff of the Experiment as deputy probation officers, and had required that they act in a way consonant with the restrictions placed upon any probation officers.

Second, because it was assumed that local funds would continue in support of the program, state sources would not be needed. In fact, the investment of local funds in the program was precisely what was desired so that the community might have a stake in the success of the new endeavor. People who spend their own money on a program are more likely to take an interest in it.

Third, there were, from a scientific standpoint, a number of reasons why it seemed wise to conduct the experiment apart from the state. State involvement might entail so many compromises that it would be impossible to design a program alone new theoretical lines and to adopt and implement an experimental design in which experimental and control groups were selected.

The emphasis upon involving serious offenders in solving problems and making decisions, still viewed with skepticism today, was even more radical at that time. It coincided with neither the generic casework approach of regular state probation, nor with the institutional practices of the Utah State Industrial School. There was serious question as to whether sufficient resolution could be made of these differences in order to permit the new program to follow its original design. Likewise, the practice of randomly selecting serious offenders to be kept in the community in lieu of incarceration was also radical. Unless the practice could be kept as unsullied as possible, objective evaluation would be jeopardized.

Other reasons for seeking independence were staff-related. If the experiment could retain its autonomy, it would not have to become involved in the hiring practices, the promotion procedures, and the conflicting loyalties that decimate the ranks of any experimental staff that is set up within a state bureaucracy. Any experiment requires a degree of organizational flexibility that is often hard to find in a large state system. Personal flexibility in staff members was also needed. People were required who were not already used to a prior set of intervention practices, who had a high degree of intellectual and emotional resiliency, and who had a willingness to take some personal risks. These staff characteristics were not necessarily those of a long record of prior service or a particular professional training.[1]

Finally, the staff of the experiment itself were tentative about their chances for success. This probably contributed to a kind of organizational myopia; little thought was given to the needs and perceptions of outside state officials. It was naively assumed that, if a local program could be successful, they would welcome and support it.

In the account that follows, some of the limitations of this strategy will be revealed. In order to ensure that it will not be overly biased from the perspective of those who ran the experiment, most of the details will be drawn from the reporting of a third party; namely, the newspaper community. Because the struggles of the Provo Experiment were often newsworthy, a rather good chronology of events can be found in the files of three different newspapers: the *Daily Herald* in Provo, and the *Deseret News* and *Salt Lake Tribune* in Salt Lake City.

The Experiment is Announced

While the juvenile court in Provo, and its Citizens' Advisory Council, had struggled in relative obscurity for several years to establish and maintain the community program for delinquents that was the progenitor of the Provo Experiment, the sudden announcement of a large grant from the Ford Foundation to fund the latter brought immediate and unexpected attention. Extended reports of the grant and the program appeared not only in the local Provo papers, but in the two major newspapers published in Salt Lake City.

There were two things about these accounts that were significant. They reflected the usual tendency for newspapers to overstate the potential outcome of any research endeavor. They probably generated expectations among the citizenry that could not possibly have been fulfilled. But the reports were gratifying in the sense that they helped to legitimate, to popularize, and to generate support for the new program.

An editorial appearing in the *Deseret News* (June 28, 1959), a Mormon-sponsored daily in Salt Lake City, reflected both of these characteristics. Interestingly, the editorial also lamented the fact that such juvenile problems as truancy, incorrigibility, and vandalism had become matters of legal rather than domestic concern—a philosophy that was not entirely alien to that of the experiment. "Our grandparents," it noted

would have found it hard to believe that truancy, incorrigibility and vandalism were matters for a court or judge.

Now come the Provo Juvenile Court District, Brigham Young University and the Ford Foundation with a research program to ascertain the effectiveness of recreated home environment, youth-level group discussions, and vocational guidance. This is an almost revolutionary approach in this age where the machinery of social control moves further and further away from domestic responsibility.

With a six-year program cut out for them and $182,000 added to their regular funds with which to carry on the work, who knows but that the Provo

Experiment will contribute something of great importance to the campaign against juvenile delinquency?

Like the *Deseret News* editorial, other newspaper reports in the first year and a half of the experiment reflected the relative political quietude of its honeymoon period. Delinquents and staff members may have had their domestic quarrels, but people in the community seemed to feel that the union was a blissful one. Then, problems of two types loomed on the horizon.

The first was a shift in power and philosophy on the local county commission from liberal to conservative. Following an election in November 1960, a new commission was seated in January 1961. With this shift in power, a former deputy sheriff was selected as the commission's chairman. This new chairman was less inclined philosophically than had been his predecessor to continue supporting the experiment with even a few thousand dollars from local funds.

A more serious problem provided the new chairman with a legitimate rationale for cutting off support; namely, the possibility of a budget deficit in the ensuing year (1962). Reductions had to be made somewhere, it appeared, or taxes increased. And since the county had no legal responsibility for supporting juvenile court functions, Pinehills became the chairman's major target.

Strong Public Support

The reactions of both the public and press to the announcement by county officials that funds for Pinehills were to be cut off were almost universally negative. "A project, like a prophet," wrote a reporter in the *Daily Herald* (Dec. 8, 1961),

may not be without honor, except at home.
Pinehills project for rehabilitation of delinquent boys has been drawing national and even international attention recently but faces possible loss of financial support from Utah County next year . . .

Likewise, the Women's Legislative Council of Utah County, in response to these problems, convened a special public session to which the judge of the Juvenile Court, the chairman of the county commission, the state director of the Bureau of Services for Children, and the director of the Experiment were invited to present their views on Pinehills' financial problems. The result, of course, was to bring about a confrontation among the various parties and to pinpoint their particular views.

In a newspaper article (*Daily Herald*, no. 5, 1961), headlined LACK OF FUNDS THREATENS PINEHILLS TREATMENT CENTER, an account of the meeting was provided. As might be expected, each speaker hewed to his party line. While the judge of the court and the director of the Experiment argued the merits of support, the county chairman, as the newspaper account noted, said that, "The County cannot continue its financial support of Pinehills because it (the County) must take care of its legal responsibilities and keep within the budget."

The state director of the Bureau of Services for Children was more diplomatic, but he gave little help. He

acknowledged that philosophy is changing on how best to deal with offenders, traditional methods are being discarded, there is need to support research along the lines of Pinehills, and to train personnel to staff such institutions.

He felt that, although Pinehills is a desirable project, there will be no monies from state welfare commission available at this time for its support.

In sum, the chickens of the project strategy had come home to roost. The local sources of funds upon which Pinehills had depended now seemed to be drying up, and the state sources, which had not been sought in the first place, were being denied.

In fairness to both governmental officials, it should be noted that they had taken positions that, to them, seemed entirely sensible, especially since they had not been a party to initiating the project in the first place. In the face of appeals to revise their priorities and to support this community endeavor, they stood firm in rejecting that notion.

It was ironical that this whole tempest was being created over a paltry sum of only $8,300. The amount loomed large only to Pinehills; it would scarcely represent a threat to the solvency of either county or state government. For that reason, it seemed likely that an unwillingness to provide continued funding was based upon grounds that were political and ideological, as well as financial.

This conclusion was confirmed by the unbelievable sequence of events that followed. This first public confrontation was the initial shot in a political war over the Experiment that never ended until the Experiment was dead. The meeting at the Women's Legislative Council occurred in November 1961. The following is a month-by-month chronicle of what happened in an action-packed period that followed. In light of the viewpoint often expressed in the tumultuous years of the 1960s and 1970s that government often remains insensitive to the expressed wishes of its citizenry, this chronicle is an interesting document.

December 1961

Recognizing that there was considerable community support for Pinehills, the chairman of the county commission took a different tack in opposing it. In addition to his public utterances on the shortage of funds for 1962, he began to stress the possible *il*legality of the experiment. Since court and corrective functions were a state responsibility, he doubted whether a program should be run under local sponsorship. The excerpts from newspaper accounts indicate what happened.

WOMEN SUPPORT YOUTH UNITS
(Daily Herald, December 10, 1961)

Pinehills Treatment Center and the local juvenile court received resolutions of support this week from the Utah County Women's Legislative Council.

The resolutions were passed . . . unanimously [and] urged the county commission to support the agencies . . . on a par with the past several years.

A local educator and civic leader of considerable influence wrote an open letter to the county commission which was published in the *Daily Herald* (December 10, 1961). In her letter, this lady appealed to the long tradition of leadership in the state which the county and local juvenile court had exercised. A short excerpt indicates the tenor of her comments:

Editor, Herald:

I would like to submit the following statement as an open letter to the Utah County Commission.

During the past several years, Utah County has become a leader in the state—perhaps even in the nation—in the enlightened treatment of youth problems. . . .

Much of this has been made possible through the Utah County Commission, which has seen the importance of human values as well as the other necessities of county government. By making funds available for these things, the county commission has blazed the trail of conserving human resources which should stand as a monument to it for many years to come. . . .

The money is there, if you will but allot it. We repeat, government is more than roads and sewers. It is the conservatism and development of human resources. And the agencies now threatened by fund curtailment have proven their worth in conserving these resources.

In addition to the support of the press, many citizens, as well as the judge of the court, attended budget hearings and petitioned the commission directly for support of Pinehills. An account of these efforts appeared in the *Daily Herald* (December 15, 1961). And since the question of the legality of Pinehills was being raised, the judge also presented detailed testimony on the legal statutes that made the program possible. Among other things, the relevant statutes were presented in the press (*Daily Herald*, Dec. 18, 1961).

. . . The judge said today that he believed it is not illegal for the county to contribute to Pinehills, quoting from Utah Code Annotated 1953, in a statement filed with the commission:

"Section 55-10-9:

"Any city or county on recommendation of the judge of the juvenile court may provide for the payment of the salary and expenses of any assistant probation officer or officers to serve within the area of such city or county, to be appointed as other paid probation officers are appointed.

"Section 55-10-62 Juvenile Court Entitled—Every county, town or municipal officer or department shall render all assistance and cooperation within his or its jurisdiction or power to further the objects of this chapter, and the juvenile courts are authorized to seek the cooperation of all societies or organizations, public or private, having for their object the protection or aid of children. . . .

"Section 55-10-1: . . . Cost of maintaining juvenile courts and the expenses of the probation work shall be paid out of the general funds of the state or other funds available to the commission for such purposes. . . .

"55-10-17: Service of summons, process or notice required by this chapter shall be made by a probation officer, peace officer or by any suitable person directed by the court. The court may authorize the payment of necessary traveling expenses and witness fees incurred by any person summoned or otherwise required to appear, and such expenses and fees when approved by the court shall be a charge upon the county wherein the hearing is had and shall be paid from the treasury of such county as other such charges are paid."

Finally, because of the stress that was being placed upon community-based programs by the new Kennedy administration in Washington, and because the new President's Committee on Juvenile Delinquency and Youth Crime knew about the Provo Experiment, its Executive Director wrote a letter in support of Pinehills. His entire letter was reprinted (*Daily Herald*, Dec. 26, 1961):

"The President's Committee on Juvenile Delinquency and Youth Crime is seeking to involve total communities in the prevention and rehabilitation of delinquents.

"The Pinehills program of Utah County is one of the forerunners of this approach. It has nationwide attention. I would like to congratulate officials and citizens of Utah County for their efforts. It is not easy to obtain the kind of public support which you have.

"Now that there is some question regarding future financial support for Pinehills, I would hope that the program would not be dropped just as it is coming into its own. Its loss at this time would not only be a detriment to the County, but to many others throughout the country who are looking to Pinehills for new techniques. May I suggest, therefore, that the relatively small expenditure in dollars being asked at this time is a small price to pay for the new approaches which you are opening up.

"Best wishes for your success.

Sincerely yours,
David L. Hackett
Executive Director
President's Committee on
Juvenile Delinquency and Youth Crime."

As a result of public and media support from every quarter, the county commission, if not its chairman, appeared to bow to this influence. But the gesture was in form only, not substance. The commission announced approval for the Pinehills budget, but then proceeded to set another set of conditions that made the actual release of funds impossible (*Daily Herald*, Dec. 29, 1961).

[The] County Commission Chairman . . . said he still feels it is a state function, not county, to support the juvenile court. . . .
The stipulation by [the] County Attorney is that no money would be spent . . . until and unless approved by the [state] attorney general, who is being asked to interpret whether the county may legally contribute. . . . (Italics ours.)

In other words, funds were not really being released for Pinehills' use. Yet, because there appeared to be little doubt that Pinehills was legal, it seemed only a matter of time until the attorney-general would release a favorable ruling. But this was a naive interpretation. The political game was being played by an entirely different set of rules.

February 1962

It was not until two months later, in February 1962, that we found out what the rules were. Rather than presenting a clear set of legal issues for the attorney general to rule upon, this is the way the county commission phrased the "legal" question for him (*Daily Herald*, Feb. 18, 1962): *"May the Utah County Commission appropriate $8,000 for use by the juvenile court in connection with research being conducted by the Ford Foundation?"* (Italics ours.)

It was difficult to conclude other than that the question had been phrased in a deliberately misleading way, and subsequent events confirmed that conclusion. No reference was made to Pinehills, its purpose, or the enabling statutes in the Utah code which made local community programs possible. It came as no surprise when the attorney-general's ruling was negative.

Upon receiving this news, the county commission announced that the Pinehills' funds would be used for *flood control* (*Daily Herald*, Feb. 18, 1962). The judge of the juvenile court replied that he would appeal the ruling by posing the needed legal evidence on them, and by pointing out that the Ford Foundation was not conducting research in Provo.

March 1962

After reviewing the new evidence, the attorney-general ruled that Utah County could pay the salaries and expenses of any probation officer associated with the experimental Pinehills program. It could not contribute funds directly to the program in any other way (*UPI*, May 7, 1962). But, by now, the whole issue had achieved considerable notoriety, and was picked up not only by the United Press, but by the two major papers in Salt Lake City.

The metropolitan papers got into the act because of some inconsistency they saw between an announcement by the State Welfare Commission regarding some grand new plans they had for dealing with delinquency, and the fact that Pinehills might be going under. The Welfare Commission had announced that, with federal funds, it would like to select a medium-sized community in the state and make an "all-out attempt to control delinquent conduct" (*Salt Lake Tribune*, March 15, 1962). Why, asked the *Tribune*, should not the Pinehills' concept be supported and expanded, since it seemed to have some promise and since it was in need?

The *Deseret News* (March 15, 1962) was more direct. Regarding any plan to start a large new endeavor, when Pinehills was still struggling for survival, it editorialized, in part, as follows:

Tentative plans to set up a model study and treatment center in Utah to get at the causes and cures of juvenile delinquency should have all necessary support.

All this sounds good. No one can deny the need of getting to the root of this serious and growing problem . . .

But while those concerned with juvenile problems are thinking about pushing ahead in a new study program, an existing study program, one with great promise, is in danger of folding up.

This is Utah County's so-called "Pinehills" experiment . . . The program is on shaky ground because anticipated financial support from Utah County has not been forthcoming. County funds were held up originally pending a decision from the state attorney-general . . . Last week [the attorney-general] ruled that the county can legally pay the cost of salaries and expenses for workers in the program.

. . . [Utah County's] proud record of leadership should not be marred by allowing this important and promising experiment to be starved out.

With strong editorial support of this kind, backed by a favorable legal ruling and local public endorsement, one might have predicted that the long struggle over a few dollars for Pinehills would end—that even the state might move to provide some support. But that was not to be. Each time the staff of the Experiment, and the judge of the court, felt they had finally reached some kind of plateau where they could catch their breaths, they were soon tossed back to the foot of the financial mountain.

April 1962

The plunge this time occurred when the county commission chairman received the attorney-general's favorable ruling. Pursuing his current argument that everything about Pinehills should be legal, he demanded that any staff members at Pinehills who would be receiving any county funds whatsoever should be fully qualified as a state probation officer. Therefore, he should take the State Merit

System Exam to determine his qualifications. Only if qualified, would county funds be used to pay him. To the chairman, the whole matter had apparently become a test of endurance and a contest of wills.

Still thinking that they might really win, two Pinehills staff members took the exam and not only passed, but one of them achieved the highest score among all applicants for that year. The whole process introduced another delay of several months, during which time all support for the experiment came from foundation funds.

October 1962

The struggle went on. Once the county commission had the documented proof of the staff's professional qualifications, they introduced another roadblock. This time, they would not release the beleaguered funds until they received a letter of endorsement for Pinehills from the State Welfare Commission under whose jurisdiction the entire juvenile system operated (cf. *Daily Herald*, Nov. 7, 1962 and Dec. 2, 1962 for a summary of all these matters). This was a politically astute move because the county commission knew that the Welfare Commissioners were less than enthusiastic in their support for Pinehills. The staff of the experiment, the judge, and others had tried repeatedly to get members of the Welfare Commission and the director of the Bureau of Services for Children to visit Pinehills so that they might become better acquainted with it. Perhaps then they would be willing to support it. Once their letter of endorsement was needed, therefore, efforts were increased to bring this about.

November 1962

Finally, in November 1962, a meeting was arranged, largely through the support and offices of the Speaker of the House of Representatives who was from Utah County. It is questionable, in fact, whether the meeting would have been held without his intercession. The Speaker, an educator, was well acquainted with Pinehills and was active in its support. He also attended the meeting, along with the Chief of the Bureau of Services for Children.

Some of the reasons the state officials were inclined to be doubtful about Pinehills came out during the November meeting (*Daily Herald*, Nov. 7, 1962). The first was ideological resistance to the use of group techniques. One commissioner argued that "brainwashing" was involved, and that in the Utah State Industrial School no such pressures, especially from peers, were put upon the individual. While his concern over the use of group techniques may have been reasonable, it seemed that he was highly uninformed regarding the pressures that are put upon the individual in a place of incarceration, by his peers as well as others. In the commissioner's mind, at least, the Utah State Industrial School was a place in which juveniles had a great deal of free choice.

The second reason concerned the experimental design of the study where Pinehills boys were being compared with boys on probation and the Utah State Industrial School. An attempt was made to explain the tentative approach that was being taken by the research staff toward Pinehills as well as the two control programs, but this did not allay some of the anxiety state officials felt at having their own programs assessed. They understandably expressed some concern over the ability of the research staff at Pinehills to be objective, but the Chief of Children's Services did verbalize the importance of research.

The Welfare Commission agreed to write a letter to the county commission, but, when questioned by the Speaker, declined to provide any financial aid themselves to Pinehills. They did agree to meet again with the Speaker to consider the introduction of legislation that might assist Pinehills, or other research of that type.

Eventually, a letter was written by the commission to the county chairman, but it was so hedged with qualifications that it could scarcely be considered a ringing endorsement for Pinehills. "We do not presume," said the Welfare Commission, "to tell you what you should do but we would be pleased to see Utah County make a financial contribution to this project . . . " (*Daily Herald*, Nov. 28, 1962). The Welfare Commission did express the opinion that Pinehills was desirable research, but they scarcely backed up that opinion because they also said that they had no money to support it themselves.

It really did not matter what was in the letter. The county chairman had no intention of releasing the funds even if it had been stronger. Once he received it, he found another excuse. Since the letter had made no specific reference to the hiring of local probation officers, it did not meet the requirements of the attorney-general. No funds would be released. The next move, said the chairman, should be to get the *legislature* to appropriate funds to Pinehills (*Daily Herald*, Nov. 28, 1962).

December 1962

In response to this turn of events, a letter by the Director of Pinehills was written to the county commission and released to the press. It charged the county fathers with duplicity and a failure to act in good faith (*Daily Herald*, Dec. 2, 1962). Their unwillingness to honor the success of Pinehills in meeting every single one of their stipulations, and their arrogance in ignoring public opinion were outlined. A demand was made not only that the 1962 funds be released but that the budget for Pinehills be increased in 1963. By this time, the county chairman had successfully avoided expending any funds for Pinehills during 1962. No county support was ever provided that year.

January 1963

Because of the need for funds, the Pinehills staff turned again to state legislators for political assistance. The Speaker of the House, a Democrat, and the minority leader of the Senate, a Republican, agreed to help. Both were supportive of Pinehills, and privately critical of the state bureaucracy and its unwillingness to participate in research. Both were also from Utah County and thus had some local clout.

First, the Senate minority leader arranged for a meeting with the governor. Along with the director of Pinehills, the minority leader explained the nature and plight of the Provo Experiment to the governor, and its possible potential for reducing correctional costs. But, alas, the necessary behind-the-scenes political work had apparently not been done prior to the meeting. It was a waste. Failing to indicate that he would even explore the matter himself, the governor simply asked the director of Pinehills to take the matter to the same chief of the Children's Bureau who had already refused on repeated occasions to provide support. Left in the hands of the bureaucracy, this effort went nowhere.

Following that failure, the Speaker of the House and the Senate Minority Leader arranged for a meeting in which members of the State Welfare Commission and the Bureau of Services for Children would meet with the Utah County Commission. Privately, these legislators gave some assurances to the county commissioners that they would work on the state level to provide funding for Pinehills in the future. Significantly, this one bit of private assurance worked where all other efforts failed. Because it seemed to be what the local politicians wanted to hear, a motion of the county commission was quickly passed and a sum of $8,000 was made available to Pinehills for 1963 (*Daily Herald*, Jan. 6, 1963).

Later in the month, the proposed meeting of county and state officials was held. Any person viewing it from the outside might have been confused, or amused, or both. State bureaucrats and local politicians alike extolled the virtues of Pinehills, and local services for youth, but each argued that the other should pay for them. Out of this mixture of patriotic pronouncements and practical politics came a deadlock. Consequently, the Speaker of the House proposed a compromise: the county would continue to provide some support for Pinehills which would be matched in amount by an allocation of state funds. The county commissioners tentatively accepted the offer, but the welfare commissioners protested that their budget was already inadequate. They had no funds for Pinehills, however small. Despite the fact that Pinehills had already spared the state the cost of incarcerating or supervising a considerable number of boys, arguments of this type made no headway.

The House Speaker and the Minority Leader then proposed that they introduce a special bill designed solely to provide funds for Pinehills at least until the Experiment could be completed. Since this bill would in no way affect the welfare appropriation, they asked if the commissioners would support it. The latter hesitantly agreed to do so. As a result, the way seemed to be opened by which funding for the completion of the study would be assured. The county and state would provide matching funds.

The Ultimate Outcome

To make a long story short, the compromise never worked out. A new bill was introduced in the state legislature but never got out of committee. While it is difficult to be certain, one major reason seemed to be the failure of the welfare commission to support it. A rumor was, in fact, that one or more influential members of the state bureaucracy worked behind the scenes to kill it. Without state matching funds, the county made no further contributions. The final local allotment to Pinehills was the $8,000 in county funds made in January 1963. The state, which had ultimate responsibility for juvenile corrections, never contributed anything.

The result was that those people who conducted the Provo Experiment—its director, the judge, and the Citizen's Advisory Council—failed in their commitment to the Ford Foundation to match its grant with local operating funds. Nevertheless, the Experiment was completed, largely because its staff existed on small salaries, and because some parts of the research segment of the study were cut out.

By 1965, when grant funds were finally exhausted, a desperate effort was made by the Utah County Mental Health Association to continue supporting the program, but the association itself was in desperate straits so that its spiritually generous, but monetarily small, offer was declined.

Why, it might be asked, did not the staff of the Experiment and its advisory group conduct a local fund-raising drive for private funds? The reasons were that such funds were not only uncertain, but the years of failure to obtain even a token source of matching funds from local or state government were highly demoralizing. Any staff only has so much energy, and when it finally came to a choice between devoting large amounts of energy to obtain a few dollars and working with the delinquents to complete the Experiment, the staff chose the latter.

This decision was affected in part by the fact that the struggle for survival involved not only the unsuccessful effort to find operating funds, but demanded tireless effort in order to maintain the city work program, to find employment for delinquents, and to keep some hard-nosed offenders out of further trouble. All of these things took a heavy toll. In the face of powerful political and bureaucratic opposition, further struggle seemed out of the question. Pinehills died a lingering death in 1965.

Implications and Interpretations

As promised earlier, there is need to relate the happenings of one locality and one experiment to a larger set of issues (cf. Miller, Baum and McNeil, 1968 for analysis of related issues). The first has to do with the delinquent offenders in this case who constituted the client population. On one hand, it is difficult to reach any other conclusion than that the public and news media were solidly behind the Pinehills venture, at least initially. Utah County, under the guidance of a courageous and farsighted judge, had had a long history of improving its court services. The public, as a result, seemed to endorse these kinds of efforts, and desired to see them continued.

By the same token, some readers will be inclined to sympathize with the plight of Pinehills, its staff and offender groups. Certainly, the Pinehills experience illustrates the buffeting and even demoralization that are likely to be associated with any attempt to change existing structures. In our concern with the problems of interorganizational conflict, it is important to consider the fact that criminal and delinquent populations are low-status populations, and that this fact may have contributed to the course of events that was described. When an increasingly scarce number of local funds were being distributed, the needs of a small group of offenders, and those who worked with them, did not rank very high in the existing set of priorities. When a series of astute political moves were made to block even a small innovation like Pinehills, the public eventually grew weary of its role in the struggle. It became increasingly difficult to generate public support. Because few citizens were directly affected by the kinds of budgetary cuts that were made, initial enthusiasm died down and, with it, the pressures upon politicians to maintain services for offenders.

There is a lesson in this for local communities today. Many cities are near bankruptcy. This suggests that, although there has been a wave of new community programs for offenders, there may be an increasing number of serious problems unless some powerful lobbies for those programs can be developed and sustained. Without adequate local funds, municipalities turn to state or federal sources, and when that occurs correctional programs become pawns in the struggles of local versus state or federal governments, just as the Provo Experiment did. In the no man's land, funds for innovative programs are always those most in jeopardy. In an ambiguous structural position, without any powerful voices speaking for them, they are likely to be the first to go. How an effective lobby for offenders can be developed is hard to say. In the case of the Provo Experiment, governmental officials successfully ignored a relatively good one.

Inseparably connected with this issue is the correctional establishment itself. In any existing correctional system like that in Utah, there are structures and beliefs which also inhibit change. It is probably inaccurate to suggest that this resistance to change is always deliberate and cynical. Prevailing beliefs about the best way to help delinquents and criminals determine what any decision-maker will see in a new program, and whether he will accept or reject it.

The difficulties that can be generated were epitomized in the case of the Provo Experiment by such strange bedfellows as a former deputy sheriff on the county commission, and a thoroughly dedicated and high-placed official in the State Bureau of Services for Children. For quite different intellectual reasons, each of these two individuals clung to a strong and unswerving ideology that was harmful to the Pinehills cause, not necessarily for factual reasons but because of the beliefs they held. Although their points of view were polar opposites—one favoring a hard-nosed reaction to delinquents, and the other a highly clinical, even Freudian, approach—both were at odds with the Pinehills philosophy. The former sheriff was inclined to view Pinehills as being too permissive, while the state official much preferred an individualized and highly personal, rather than group, approach. Despite the striking differences between them, the reactions of these two leaders helped to mobilize the Pinehills opposition. For ideological reasons, they could not see that it had much to offer, and ended up opposing it.

The point is that if any new correctional enterprise departs too far from current beliefs and practices, it may not receive official blessing. Ironically, if it fits too well with existing patterns, it is not likely to be very innovative. Even if official approval and funding for an innovation can be obtained, it must still surmount the high degree of inertia that is associated with existing budgetary commitments, staffing patterns and organizational arrangements. High-level policy-makers, no less than their underlings, are often severely constrained by existing institutional patterns. These factors, as well as the ideologies of key decision-makers, were instrumental in Pinehills' problems. This leads us to the strategy that was adopted in organizing the Provo Experiment outside of the regular state bureaucracy. What might have been done, both to ensure that it would be innovative, and yet to make certain that it would obtain continual financial support? There is no clear-cut answer, only a host of questions.

It is abundantly clear that important policy-makers on the state level never did understand, nor sympathize with, the methods of intervention used at Pinehills. But since those methods were new and without prior test, some resistance was understandable. What was not understandable, however, was the unwillingness of these important gatekeepers to invest even a pittance in seeing Pinehills evaluated. While they did not block the gathering of background and follow-up information on experimental and control groups, and while they paid some lip service to the importance of research, their failure to provide actual support for it, when the chips were down, scarcely made their pronouncements convincing. One basic question, therefore, is whether they would have acted differently had their support been solicited before the Experiment began.

After several years of experience with them, it is our feeling that an early solicitation of support would have made little difference—at least insofar as this particular kind of experiment was involved. State officials might have been willing to support the evaluation of a program that was more traditional in character, but this one was far too radical for them. If their participation had actually been involved, it is unlikely that this particular study would even have been conducted. What should one do if faced with that possibility prior to, rather than after, an experiment?

One alternative, of course, would be to work out a compromise approach. Although such an approach might be less innovative, it would have the virtue of adding research and experimentation to a system in which none had previously existed. Although the process of change would be slow, at least it would have been introduced into, and perhaps become a part of, the official structure. Traditionally, there have been many problems with even a collaborative approach—one in which the high-level policy-maker, along with the investigator, has a great deal of say about the nature of the Experiment itself. Most of these problems are related to the conflicting perspectives and needs of the actors involved. Just as they occur when an innovation is started outside the system, as at Provo, they also occur within it.

While the investigator may be motivated by the same humanitarian interests that policy-makers and practitioners are, he also possesses a commitment to knowledge that can scarcely be shared at the same level by others. In fact, there is serious reason to question whether, in a highly political world, the policy-maker, even the practitioner, can ever be expected to live with the tentativity that is required in scientific work, especially where that work is conducted in the goldfish bowl in which correctional programs operate. While the success and prestige of the scientist require it, those of the policy-maker (and politician) do not. An everchanging political climate is incongruent with the time it takes to collect, analyze, and publish research findings. The rules of the scientific game are incongruent with the rules of politics and bureaucracy.

An example from the Provo Experiment provides a case in point. In their dealings with county and state officials, experimental staff usually tried to be as candid as possible regarding the controversial methods that were being used at Pinehills, and the likelihood that they would provide some kind of correctional panacea. Since, in the past, few programs had ever been highly successful, that fact was freely admitted. Much to the chagrin of the investigators, however, this candor boomeranged. Even among state officials, where greater understanding might have been expected since they were in the correctional business themselves, objective information was used, not in the spirit in which it was presented, but as a weapon against the Experiment. It was as though a scientist studying cancer was being punished because he expressed reservations about the chances he would find a cure. The lesson that was learned is that any investigator who openly shares information according to scientific rules may, according to political rules, find himself hoisted on his own petard.

This was not an isolated case. The same thing happened in the Silverlake

Experiment in Los Angeles (Empey and Lubeck, 1971:169-70), where opponents used freely shared information from one of the study's annual progress reports to try to shut the experiment down. Although a number of details were taken out of context, facts that are required in a scientific report became weapons against scientific study.

The issues seem clear. In a highly political arena, the scientific game is an anomaly. In its most traditional form, it prescribes a set of standards with which it is impossible to fully comply.

The scientific community has contributed to this problem. Its standards, at least when expressed in classical positivistic terms, imply that any correctional experiment should be evaluated solely in terms of its adherence to rigorous scientific procedures. Even though the existence of a host of political, economic, and ideological barriers may be acknowledged, the idea persists that these barriers should somehow be incorporated into the plan of study and rendered impotent. The only thing that really counts is how well the effects of the experimental stimulus were assessed, and how sophisticated the methods of analysis were. It is often striking how often a difficult field experiment is evaluated almost entirely in terms of narrow criteria that are appropriate only to the laboratory. If laboratory procedures are not followed, the experiment will be of dubious quality. But what are accepted and proven canons in the realm of field experimentation? In what text on methods can one find them? How does one account for, and control, all of the forces that impinge upon experimental subjects in a "normal" social environment?

The obvious answer is that totally effective controls cannot be exercised. A number of compromises are inevitable. Our summary of the problems encountered in the Provo Experiment, for example, has indicated: (1) that it was difficult to sustain a high level of public support for this particular field study; (2) that the rules by which the scientific game were played were incongruent with the rules by which the political game was played; and (3) that, in the absence of effective and politically supported models for field experimentation, it was necessary for the investigator to play a host of conflicting roles: scientist, politician, public relations man, agent of social control, therapist, and others. In short, efforts to maintain a reasonable degree of scientific rigor were often made difficult by a long list of nonscientific impediments.

These impediments illustrate the fact that scientific endeavor is inevitably constrained by prevailing political and social climates. If science appears capable of solving some pressing social problem, it tends to be supported. If social and scientific perspectives do not coincide, the kinds of problems just described can be anticipated. What are the implications for future field experimentation? Is there hope that fruitful studies can be conducted?

Two things might be suggested. The first is the possibility that social scientists can take better advantage than they have of a number of significant "naturalistic" experiments that occur with increasing frequency in modern society.

These kinds of experiments are initiated not by scientists, but by legislative, executive and policy-making groups. A good example in the area of crime and delinquency is California's probation subsidy program (Smith, 1972).

In response to the passage of enabling legislation, this program encourages county probation departments to reduce their rates of commitment to state correctional facilities, most of which involve incarceration. In return, the county receives a financial reward for every offender who, though he would be incarcerated otherwise, is retained in the community.

The consequences of this naturalistic experiment have been enormous. Hundreds, if not thousands, of adult and juvenile offenders have remained at home. Some state institutions have been closed or are being phased out, and plans for new facilities have been scrapped. Although overall correctional costs have been reduced, the infusion of state funds into county probation departments has encouraged better training for probation officers, and new community programs for offenders. An experiment of potentially tremendous political, social and economic consequence has been initiated.

Although it would be difficult to impose rigorous experimental controls as a means of evaluating this naturalistic innovation, some important research could be conducted. An attempt could be made to assess its impact on (1) offenders; (2) the entire criminal justice system; (3) policy-making groups; and (4) the populace at large. Because of the obvious practical as well as scientific relevance of such research, it would be less likely than a study like the Provo Experiment to encounter official opposition. By changing the political context in which the study was conducted, it would be far more likely to have official endorsement and support.

A second possibility for improving the conduct of experimental field research might involve the development of new and more protective structures for that kind of study. There is a subtle, yet pervasive, notion among the policy-making groups responsible for the funding and conduct of field experimentation that, if some new and theoretically exciting approach to correctional problems is to be tried, it should require the full participation, as well as endorsement, of some group of established policy-makers and practitioners. The latter, as well as the investigator, should be involved in conceptualizing and designing the experiment.

Applied to other areas of scientific investigation, this would be like saying that a biochemist who suddenly comes up with a defensible and fruitful lead for some terrifying physical disease should be required to ensure the participation of hospital policy-makers and family physicians in the conduct of his study. Obviously, this would be a foolhardy approach. The full endorsement of his research by key decision-makers and professionals would be needed, but not their participation in it. Yet, in a very real sense, that is what is often implied when a correctional experiment is proposed.

The rationale for taking such an approach is that, if correctional people at all levels participate in an experiment, they will be more inclined to incorporate its better features into their ongoing and daily practices. But such a philosophy is totally inconsistent with the realities of scientific study. What if the new approach does not work? Regular correctional people would be involved in implementing a cure for which there was no disease. Meanwhile, the real problem would go unchecked. It is true that correctional policy-makers and professionals must learn to become comfortable with research and must fight to see it implemented. But the acceptance of experimentation, and the provision of funds and facilities by which to carry it out, are different from saying that every experiment will bear fruit. Policy-makers are understandably reluctant to buy experimentation if it means that every study that is conducted will require that they make a radical alteration in their ongoing systems.

If, by contrast, a regular structure devoted to research and development could be treated as a necessary adjunct to ongoing correctional practice, several benefits might result. First, there would be less inclination to hold regular correctional personnel responsible for the failure or problems of any single experiment. The investigator would have to bear that burden. While it would be a heavy one at times, at least it would be consonant with the rules of science. The groundwork might be laid by which the public could come to understand that science in the social realm will probably have to operate in much the same way that it operates in biological and physical realms. Medical hospitals and schools, businesses and industry have come to terms with the need for research and development in their organizations. It might be hoped that legal and welfare structures would do the same thing. If experimental research were given greater institutional support, it would not be subject quite so much to the fluctuating interests of public opinion, as happened in the Provo Experiment. At the same time, greater support would be healthy for social science itself. Many existing beliefs and theories among social scientists badly need empirical test. The presence of support could do much to subject those beliefs to careful scrutiny.

The adoption of regular structures for research and development might also assist in overcoming the ideological problems that a radical innovation usually creates. In the Provo case, for example, the availability of such a structure might have facilitated the conduct of the study, even though state officials were initially wary of its implications. The reason is that it would probably have been easier to sell the idea of research than it was to sell the idea of community intervention. If the Experiment could have been conducted as a pilot venture and its effects assessed, it might have been tolerated more easily. Besides the possibility that some empirical support could have been garnered, officials would have had a longer time to get used to its implications. That this might have been the actual outcome is supported by the fact that community programs have become far more commonplace today than they were 10 years ago, in Utah as well as elsewhere.

In short, it is the need to become comfortable with research and experimentation and to provide a supportive climate that is required as a first step.

Policy-makers and the public would have to endorse the need for research, while social scientists would have to provide the theory and methods. If this were done, any particular investigator would not be placed in the position of trying to sell, and any policy-maker in the position of having to buy, the idea that a single study would constitute a panacea, and that an entire system should be organized immediately to incorporate it. If it eventually proved useful in some way, its incorporation or rejection would be a part of an entirely different political and decision-making process. The conduct of research, as contrasted to the use of its findings, would be a relatively independent endeavor.

Program Salience and Long-Run Control of Delinquency

An analysis of the long-run effectiveness of the experimental program at Provo is of considerable significance. In a very real sense, this program, along with the more traditional programs with which it is being compared, is a modern portrayal of correctional history. Since each of them is representative of a distinct phase in correctional thinking, an assessment of their relative effectiveness in the long-run is of great importance. .

The state training school in which the incarceration controls were placed is a vestigal remnant of society's emphasis upon revenge and incapacitation of the offender. To be sure, this training school was not like the prisons of old. The offenders' loss of freedom and their isolation from common daily pursuits in the community were about the only characteristics that partook of the older pattern. Yet, this same school was relatively traditional in orientation.

In a sense, it was an amalgam of the obedience/conformity and reeducation /development organizations described by Street, Vinter and Perrow (1966:49-66). Delinquency was seen as the product of the corrupting effects of inadequate families, parental laxity, and improper influences in the social order. Intervention combined an emphasis upon indoctrinating offenders with the need for obedience to authority and rules, and moral, education and personal training. Some choice for inmates was permitted, but firm discipline and constant supervision remained highly important. Rewards, on the other hand, were scarce and voluntarism was not greatly encouraged.

Probation, by contrast, partook more of the reform ideology in corrections, with its emphasis upon generic casework, and the personal disabilities of the offender. Both the philosophy and administration of probation were an uncertain mixture of psychotherapeutic theory and a general concern with helping the offender to adjust socially and economically to his environment. The ideology was one of generalized beneficence. Ideally, probation was supposed to help the offender with all phases of his life, as well as monitor his capacity for self-discipline and control. In practice, probation officers were hampered by large caseloads and excessive paperwork.

Last, the experimental program was based on contemporary theory and philosophy. It attempted to address a number of important organizational and social issues. It sought to avoid some of the negative aspects of incarceration by remaining nonresidential in character, and by trying to alter the community so that the ties of the delinquent to it might be maintained and strengthened. The experimental program also differed considerably from regular probation because

177

of its concern with making the delinquent group both the medium and the target of change. Of significance was the fact that, in order to accomplish that task, the traditional roles of both staff and offenders had to change considerably. A new organization was created in which the effects of *intra*organizational and *inter*organizational change and struggle were considerable.

The experimental design of this study provides a unique opportunity to assess their relative merits. Of special concern is whether the experimental program was any more salient to delinquents in the long-run than more traditional approaches. Given the conflicted context in which it operated, could it develop enough normative power or utilitarian rewards to have a lasting impact? First, however, consider some issues that bear on the assessment of program efficiency.

The most important has to do with the prevailing ambiguity as to how the long-run effectiveness of correctional programs can best be measured. This ambiguity stems from the problems inherent in defining and operationalizing effectiveness, in deciding who should be included in the analysis and in deciding over what time periods effectiveness should be measured. For example, one might contend that correctional efficiency should be based upon all individuals assigned to a given program. From an administrative perspective, this is a perfectly sound position since failures from a program, be they dropouts or recidivists, ordinarily necessitate new actions of the parts of the agents of control and perhaps reassignment to another program. The extent to which a program works effectively with all individuals assigned to it is an important criterion upon which to judge the program's adequacy.

From a scientific viewpoint, however, any assessment could be seen as contaminated that includes those persons who are not fully exposed to program stimuli as well as those who are. To use a medical analogy, it could not really be said that the effects of experimental treatment were really assessed if several members of the test group failed to complete the treatment. In fact, it could be argued that a partial exposure might be worse than no exposure at all.

While the same is somewhat true in corrections, there are other matters to be considered. For one thing, the tendency for offenders to drop out of, or to fail, a correctional program says something about the program as well as about the dropout. Dropping out is a function of programmatic as well as personal inadequacies. Unless dropouts are considered, tests of effectiveness can be highly misleading. When an open community program, in which dropouts are common, is compared with an incarceration program where they are often nonexistent, comparisons would not really be valid unless dropouts were included. The comparison would be unfair.[1]

For these reasons, steps were taken in this analysis to provide several measures of effectiveness, some of which include dropouts and some which exclude them. It will permit an evaluation of effectiveness from several different perspectives.

Measurement of Technical Efficiency

The first is a measure of technical efficiency. It is based upon a technical efficiency rating which takes into account those who drop out of a given program as well as those who, though they complete it, are rearrested. The rating for any given program can be calculated using the following formula:

$$\text{Technical Efficiency Rating (TER)} = 1 - \frac{\text{No. of Dropouts} + \text{No. of Arrestees}}{\text{Total No. of Individuals Assigned}}$$

Note that the Technical Efficiency Rating could vary from 0 to 1. It would be 0 in that case where all individuals either dropped out of a program or were arrested after completing it. Conversely, it would be 1 if there were no dropouts and if no one recidivated. Since technical efficiency, in this case, is based upon *arrest*, not conviction data, the success rates observed below will be somewhat lower than they would have been had conviction data been used; that is the programs will not appear as efficient as they might have had the less stringent criterion been used.

The technical efficiency rating is also a very stringent measure of efficiency since it equates dropping out of a program with recidivating, even though the dropout may not have been arrested for any new offenses. It would be most applicable to community programs, probation or parole, where offenders run away or are defined as failures by staff members for such "technical" reasons as failing to be cooperative or to live up to conditions set by court or correctional personnel relative to associating with old friends, refusing to go to school, or staying out late.

Findings

The findings, when the Technical Efficiency Rating was applied, are displayed first in Figure 9-1. That figure compares the four samples taking into account the number of dropouts in each sample, plus the number of graduates who had one or more recorded arrests of any kind, serious or nonserious. It includes followup data for each of four years after release.[2]

Several things about Figure 9-1 are worth noting. First, when this stringent criterion of effectiveness is applied, none of the programs appears to have been especially successful. Only the two probation groups were above the 50 percent success level after one year. In subsequent years, the success rates did not go down precipitously for most of the samples, but they did go down.

Second, the similarity in the technical efficiency of the two probation samples is striking. The findings could be reflective of one, not two programs.

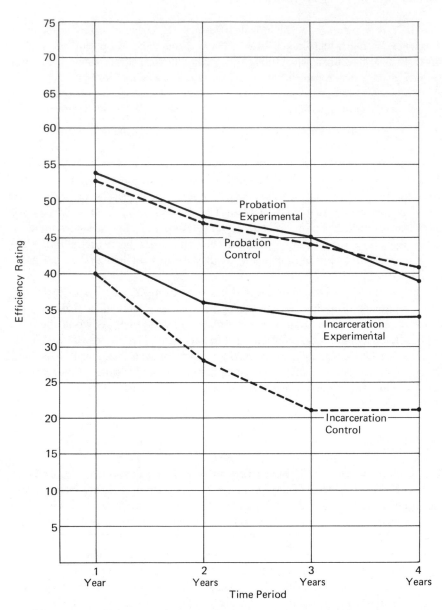

Figure 9–1. Technical Efficiency Rating on Dropouts Plus Graduate Recidivists With One or More Arrests.

On this comparison, it cannot be said that one was more successful than the other.

Third, and perhaps most important, is the finding that the technical efficiency of the incarceration controls was the lowest of all, despite the fact that they had no dropouts as an initial encumbrance. Obviously, their rate of recidivism was somewhat higher, such that after 4 years only 21 percent had no new arrests. At the same time, it should be noted that, while differences between them and the experimentals approached statistical significance, it is possible that they were due to chance. Caution should be exercised in assuming that the technical efficiency rating of the controls was greatly lower than the experimentals.

This conclusion is borne out by an examination of Figure 9-2. In this case, technical efficiency is based upon number of dropouts, plus those individuals who were arrested for *three or more* offenses after release. The rating indicates that the efficiencies of the two incarceration groups were approximately equal as were those of the two probation groups. In addition, it can be seen that the ratings for all samples rise sharply when this less stringent criterion is applied. After four years, the rating for the two probation groups was over 75 percent, and for the two incarceration groups over 55 percent.

There is evidence that the highest violation rates seem to occur during the first year or two. After that, they tend to decline. This was especially true for the two probation groups and the incarceration experimental group. It was less true for the incarceration controls whose rate of arrest continued at a rather high pace into the third and fourth years.

Overall, the findings indicate that when the technical rating is applied, and dropout as well as recidivism rates considered, the results are not especially encouraging. It remains to be seen whether this bleak picture will prevail when recidivism rates only are examined and when seriousness is considered as well. The next section is concerned with what we call "correctional" rather than "technical" efficiency.

Measurement of Correctional Efficiency

Correctional efficiency is measured in two ways, first, in terms of the mean number of new arrests per boy in each of the samples and, then, in terms of three indexes especially constructed for the purpose. In looking at means, the analysis will concentrate upon graduates only, those who were fully exposed to each of the programs. Then, when the three indexes are used, recidivism rates for dropouts and total samples, as well as graduates, will be studied. Again, arrest data were used to calculate the means.

Before presenting findings on sample means, however, a word on sample comparability is in order. It will be recalled that 13 percent of the two probation

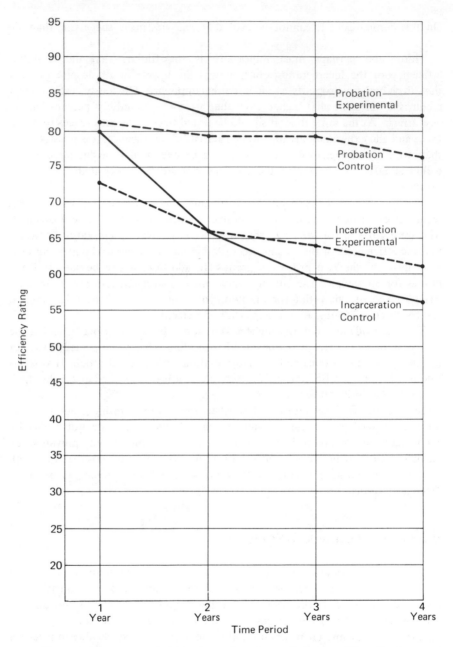

Figure 9–2. Technical Efficiency Based on Dropouts Plus Graduate Recidivists With Three or More Arrests.

groups, and 16 percent of the incarceration experimental group became dropouts. Therefore, before comparing graduates from the various samples, it is important to know whether comparability was altered by the dropout losses.

Briefly, it can be reported that the dropout losses did not alter comparability. Not only were there no changes between the two probation groups, but the two incarceration groups seemed to be somewhat more comparable. This was apparently due to the fact that dropouts in the incarceration experimental group were among the less delinquent in that group. The result was not only to make the incarceration groups more alike but to make the two experimental groups less alike. They were significantly different on virtually every measure of frequency and seriousness. The findings will be useful not only in comparing the relative effectiveness of the two sets of experimental and control groups, but the effectiveness of the experimental program in dealing with two distinct samples of offenders, one significantly more delinquent than the other prior to intervention.

Correctional Efficiency: Sample Means

Table 9-1 compares the mean number of new arrests per graduate in the two *probation* groups at one-year intervals for a period of four years. Two things are apparent. First, the arrest rates for neither sample are especially high. After one year, the arrest rate was considerably less than one per boy; and, after four years, it had risen to only about one and one-third arrests per boy.

Second, as the technical efficiency rating implied, the postrelease arrest rates for the two probation groups were very much alike. In none of the four time periods did differences approach statistical significance. While the experimental program was more effective in controlling delinquency in the short run, it does not seem to have been more effective than probation during the long run after intervention.

Table 9-1

Mean Number of New Arrests for Graduates in the Probation Experimental and Control Programs

Time Period	Probation Experimental (N = 62)		Probation Control (N = 69)		Differences	
	Mean	S.D.	Mean	S.D.	$M_1 - M_2$	P
1 Year After	.55	.78	.70	1.08	−.15	NS*
2 Years After	.97	1.46	.93	1.38	.04	NS
3 Years After	1.24	1.87	1.01	1.46	.23	NS
4 Years After	1.32	1.85	1.42	2.14	−.10	NS

*NS = not statistically significant

Table 9-2
Mean Number of New Arrests for Graduates in the Incarceration Experimental and Control Programs

Time Period	Incarceration Experimental (N = 37)		Incarceration Control (N = 132)		Differences	
	Mean	S.D.	Mean	S.D.	$M_1 - M_2$	P
1 Year After	1.11	1.47	1.71	2.08	− .61	.05
2 Years After	1.95	2.78	3.34	3.33	−1.39	.05
3 Years After	2.24	2.98	4.54	4.65	−3.30	.001
4 Years After	2.43	3.13	5.28	5.23	−2.85	.001

Table 9-2 presents comparable data for the two *incarceration* groups. Here, the findings were different on both counts. Arrest rates for both groups were higher, but the rate for experimentals was significantly lower than for controls in every time period. By the ends of the third and fourth years, for example, the mean numbers of arrest for the controls were more than twice as high as those for the experimentals (4.5 vs. 2.2 offenses after 3 years, and 5.3 vs. 2.4 offenses after 4 years). While the arrest rate for the experimentals tended to decline after the first two years, it did not do so for the controls. Although there was a tendency for the controls to have been more delinquent than experimentals prior to intervention, the postprogram differences were much greater than the preprogram differences, especially during the latter time periods.

Another factor might have made these differences even greater. These recidivism rates do not take into account those cases in which new arrests resulted in the incarceration, or reincarceration, of those who were arrested. The net effect, had all samples been free in the community during the entire follow-up period, would have been twofold: (1) the arrest rates for all samples would likely have been higher because the most delinquent boys were incarcerated some of the time; and (2) the disparities between the incarceration controls and experimentals would have been even greater since arrest rates for the controls were the higher. This important qualification should be kept in mind as further comparisons are made.

If one compares the means for the two *experimental* groups, he will discover that the arrest rate for the *incarceration experimental* group was about one arrest higher than that for the *probation experimental* group after two, three, and four years. This disparity was almost exactly the disparity between the two groups prior to intervention. This finding, along with those in which the experimental and control groups were compared, raises some perplexing problems.

On one hand, the experimental program appears to be considerably more effective than incarceration as a mode of intervention for the most serious population of offenders. On the other hand, it was not more efficient than probation for a less serious population, nor did it reduce the offense disparity between the two experimental groups. One is at a loss to know whether the experimental program was actually more constructive as an intervention device or merely avoided the negative aspects of incarceration. This is a crucial question insofar as corrections is concerned. While it would be unwise to attempt to resolve this dilemma without considering more data, especially offense seriousness, it is an issue that should be kept in mind as the analysis progresses. Once all the data have been presented, it can be given careful attention. For now, let us consider some special indexes that were constructed for the analysis of correctional efficiency.

Construction of Efficiency Indexes

In all, three indexes of correctional efficiency were constructed: one to measure program efficiency for graduates, one for dropouts, and one for total samples. The Correctional Efficiency Index for graduates (CEG) is calculated as follows:

$$\text{Correctional Efficiency For Graduates (CEG)} = 1 - \frac{\text{No. of Graduates Arrested}}{\text{Number of Graduates}}$$

This index will apply, then, only to those boys who were fully exposed to, and successfully completed, one of the three forms of intervention. The second index applies only to dropouts and is calculated by the same kind of formula described for graduates:

$$\text{Correctional Efficiency For Dropouts (CED)} = 1 - \frac{\text{No. of Dropouts Arrested}}{\text{No. of Dropouts}}$$

An efficiency rating for dropouts is important because, in a sense, dropouts provide a comparison group for graduates in each of the programs. Hypothetically, if any correctional program is worth having, those delinquents who successfully complete it should exhibit less delinquency after release than those who fail to complete it, those who become dropouts. Therefore, by comparing the efficiency rating for dropouts with that for graduates, this assumption can be tested.

The final index measures program effectiveness when recidivism rates for both dropouts and graduates are considered. Like the others, it is calculated as follows:

$$\text{Correctional Efficiency For Total (CET)} = 1 - \frac{\text{No. of Arrestees}}{\text{Total No. of Delinquents Assigned to Program}}$$

This index, like the Technical Efficiency Rating, is a useful measure of total program effectiveness because it takes the recidivism rates of total samples into account.

Correctional Efficiency: Offense Frequency

One or More Offenses as Criterion

Using all three indexes, correctional efficiency will be measured first in terms of arrest frequency, more specifically, in terms of the percentages of offenders in each sample who had one or more arrests after release. This, like the Technical Efficiency Rating, is a stringent measure of recidivism because it draws no distinctions with respect to seriousness. Minor offenses, of which there were many, are given equal weight to very serious ones. The findings are displayed in Table 9-3.

First, it will be observed that correctional efficiency is not very high for any of the programs. Efficiency for both *probation* groups on the CEG (graduate) and CET (total) indexes was about 60 percent after the first year, and declined to around 45 percent after four years. The results for both groups, moreover, were virtually identical, suggesting little overall difference between the two.

The same was not true, however, for the two *incarceration* groups. Not only were both somewhat more delinquent than the probation groups, but differences between them were greater. Using the CET index which is the most valid for comparing the two, since there were no dropouts from incarceration, the efficiency rating favored the experimentals 55 to 40 percent after one year, and 36 to 21 percent after both three and four years. First impressions are (1) that none of the programs was especially efficient; and (2) that while experimental programming for probationers made little difference, it may have for boys who would have been incarcerated. Since differences between the two incarceration groups were not statistically significant, differences may be due to chance.

Another important comparison is between dropouts and graduates so that the effects of full versus partial exposure might be considered. There appear to be some important findings in this regard, both within and between groups. *Within* the probation controls, there were few, if any, differences in the offense behaviors of graduates and dropouts. This was not true, however, of the two experimental groups. Dropouts in both of them were considerably more delinquent than graduates. After four years, for example, correctional efficiency for graduates was more than twice as high in both cases—45 vs. 22 percent in the

Table 9-3

Correctional Efficiency Based on One or More Arrests After One through Four Years

Sample	No. of Years After Release	Effectiveness Indexes*		
		CEG	CED	CET
Probation Experimental	1	.61	.44	.59
	2	.55	.33	.52
	3	.51	.22	.48
	4	.45	.22	.42
Probation Control	1	.61	.60	.61
	2	.54	.60	.54
	3	.51	.40	.49
	4	.46	.40	.46
Incarceration Experimental	1	.51	.71	.55
	2	.43	.14	.39
	3	.41	.14	.36
	4	.41	.14	.36
Incarceration Control	1	.40	—**	.40
	2	.27	—	.27
	3	.21	—	.21
	4	.21	—	.21

*CEG—Rating on Graduates Only
CED—Rating on Dropouts Only
CET—Rating on Total Sample
**No Dropouts from Sample; Rating Not Applicable.

probation experimental group and 41 vs. 14 percent in the incarceration experimental group.

The number of dropouts in each case was small—10 in the probation control group, 9 in the probation experimental group, and 7 in the incarceration experimental group—so that it would be unwise to conclude that these are stable findings. Nevertheless, they seem to provide the first real hint of a differential impact resulting from partial vs. full exposure. Dropping out of the experimental program seems to have had a more deleterious effect than dropping out of probation.

There is some utility in comparing the efficiency ratings for the two experimental groups. At issue is the effectiveness of the experimental program as an alternative to incarceration, as contrasted to its effectiveness as an alternative to probation. Whether one applies the CEG or the CET indexes, efficiency for the probation experimental group seems to be the greater. When one considers the fact that the incarceration experimental group was considerably more delinquent prior to the experiment, the differences favoring the probation experimental group are not large. The data suggest that, when each experimental group is compared to its appropriate control group, the incarceration experimental group may have been the most effective one. In other words, the experimental program may have been of greater value as an alternative to incarceration than an alternative to probation.

Three or More Offenses as Criterion

In the next set of comparisons, the criterion will be three or more offenses after release. Although this is a less stringent criterion, it is a useful one for populations like these whose delinquent histories prior to the experiment were considerable. It may be useful in indicating whether the overall rates of delinquency were on the decline as a result of programming. Table 9-4 presents the findings.

It will be noted that efficiency rates generally went up a great deal. After the first year, the CET rating for the *probation experimental* program was almost 100 percent, and that for the control group was over 90 percent. After four years, the rates were 92 and 86 percent, respectively, for these two groups. Although the rates on all the indexes favored the experimental group, only one of them was statistically significant past the .05 level. That was on the CET index after the first year where the contrasting percentages were 99 and 91 percent in favor of the experimentals.

Overall, effectiveness rates for the two *incarceration* groups were not as high, but they also went up markedly. On the CET index, after the first year, the experimental program was 89 percent efficient, while the control group was 80 percent efficient. However, during subsequent time periods, the rates for the incarceration controls went down noticeably, to 66 percent after two years, and to 56 percent after four years. The comparable figures for the experimentals, which were 82 and 77 percent, respectively, were significantly higher in both cases $(P < .05)$. The findings suggest that the experimental program was the more successful, especially over the longer time periods.

While this finding illustrates the importance of applying different evaluative criteria, it is even better illustrated by considering the comparative rates of dropouts and graduates. It will be recalled that, when only one arrest was the criterion, dropouts tended to be considerably more delinquent, particularly in the two experimental groups. When three arrests became the criterion, several significant changes occurred.

Consider dropouts from the probation experimental group. Although they still remained more delinquent than graduates, the disparities between them and

Table 9-4

Correctional Efficiency Based on Three or More Arrests After One, Two and Four Years

Sample	No. of Years After Release	Effectiveness Indexes*		
		CEG	CED	CET
Probation Experimental	1	1.00	.89	.99
	2	.94	.79	.92
	3	.94	.79	.92
	4	.94	.79	.92
Probation Control	1	.93	.80	.91
	2	.90	.80	.89
	3	.90	.80	.89
	4	.87	.80	.86
Incarceration Experimental	1	.87	1.00	.89
	2	.78	1.00	.82
	3	.76	1.00	.80
	4	.73	1.00	.77
Incarceration Control	1	.80	—**	.80
	2	.66	—	.66
	3	.59	—	.59
	4	.56	—	.56

*CEG–Rating on Graduates Only
CED–Rating on Dropouts Only
CET–Rating on Total Sample
**No Dropouts from Sample; Rating Not Applicable.

graduates lessened considerably. This change was important across samples as well. Whereas dropouts from the probation experimental program had been considerably more delinquent than dropouts from the control program, this was no longer true when three or more offenses were considered. In fact, the efficiency rating for dropout experimentals was higher after one year (89 vs. 80 percent), and virtually identical in subsequent years (79 vs. 80 percent).

More significant were changes among dropouts from the incarceration experimental group. When only one arrest was the criterion in the prior comparison, the effectiveness rate after two years was only 14 percent. In this case, it was 100 percent after *four* years. The result was that dropouts in the incarceration experimental group were less delinquent that graduates in every time period. In fact, they were less delinquent, according to this criterion, than any group from any sample.

This finding has several lessons to teach, the most important of which has to do with the task of selecting appropriate evaluative criteria for correctional programs. Had this analysis ended with the use of one arrest as the only criterion, dropouts most assuredly would have appeared to be the most delinquent group. What is more, there would have been a strong inclination, either to conjecture about the reasons for this finding or to assume that full exposure to programming was of vital importance. While there still may be some merit in this assumption, since dropouts in the two probation groups were the most delinquent, the grounds for arriving at such a conclusion have been weakened.

In comparing rates for the two *experimental* groups, it can be seen that the experimental program was more successful with the less delinquent probation group than the more delinquent incarceration group as might be expected. On the CEG index, differences were significant at all three time periods ($P <$ .05), and on the CET index in the first and fourth years ($P < .05$). The findings imply that prior delinquent history does have an impact on correctional efficiency, and that the more delinquent the group, the less likely they will be to experience success in a community program. It should not be forgotten that when the two experimental groups were compared to their appropriate controls, the experimental program seemed to be more effective as an alternative to incarceration than as an alternative to probation.

Correctional Efficiency: Seriousness

All of the analyses thus far have been on offense frequency. Seriousness is another important dimension.

One or More High Serious Offenses as Criterion

In Table 9-5, the three indexes are used to measure correctional efficiency when the criterion is one or more offenses of a *high serious* nature. It will be recalled that this category of offenses, as rated by police and court personnel, included nine delinquent acts: serious assault, child molesting, forceable rape, arson, use of narcotics, robbery, drunk driving, possession of dangerous weapons, and burglary.

As might be expected, efficiency in a general sense was high. Using both the CEG and CET indexes, more than nine out of ten boys in the two *probation* groups had not been charged with any high serious offenses after four years. The performances of these two groups were so much alike that any differences on these indexes did not approach significance.

Some significant differences were found, however, between the two *incarcera-*

Table 9-5
Correctional Efficiency Based on One or More Arrests of a High-Serious Nature

Sample	No. of Years After Release	Effectiveness Indexes*		
		CEG	CED	CET
Probation Experimental	1	.98	.79	.96
	2	.92	.78	.90
	3	.92	.78	.90
	4	.92	.56	.87
Probation Control	1	.99	1.00	.99
	2	.96	1:00	.96
	3	.94	1.00	.95
	4	.90	1.00	.91
Incarceration Experimental	1	.95	.86	.93
	2	.92	.86	.91
	3	.89	.86	.89
	4	.87	.71	.84
Incarceration Control	1	.84	—**	.84
	2	.71	—	.71
	3	.64	—	.64
	4	.61	—	.61

*CEG–Rating on Graduates Only
CED–Rating on Dropouts Only
CET–Rating on Total Sample
**No Dropouts from Sample; Rating Not Applicable.

tion groups. While correctional efficiency for the experimental group was almost as high as that for the two probation groups, it was considerably lower for the control group. After two years, almost 30 percent of the controls had been arrested for a high serious offense, and after four years, the figure was almost 40 percent. Differences between the incarceration experimental and control groups for years two, three and four were significant beyond the .01 level. This may be the most forceful clue yet that incarceration is not a constructive technique, in fact may be a destructive one.

Considering *dropouts*, the one most noticeable finding is that those in the probation experimental group were the most delinquent. In fact, after four years, over half of them had been charged with a high serious offense. Since this represented only 5 of 9 boys, overall rates for the probation experimental group were not much affected. For the few dropouts involved, this rate was as great, or greater, than that for the incarcerated boys. None of the probation control dropouts, by contrast, had a high serious offense.

It may also be important that, according to this seriousness criterion at least, there were no significant differences between the two *experimental* groups, either on the CEG or CET indexes. Despite their more serious histories, the incarceration experimental group did about as well as the probation experimental group.

While there is encouragement in the fact that so few boys in the three community programs committed highly serious delinquent acts, it is not encouraging that the rates for the incarceration controls were so high. The kinds of delinquency they committed, and the fact that significant proportions of them were involved, are things that cannot be taken lightly. It will be important to determine whether the same findings are repeated when the final measure of effectiveness is considered.

Combining Frequency and Seriousness

This measure combines both frequency and seriousness by examining the proportions of boys in each sample who had four or more offenses of a medium or high serious character. The nature of high serious offenses has been described. The medium serious offenses were illegal acts extending all the way from auto theft, on one extreme, through felony theft and forgery in the middle range, to petty theft on the other extreme. The only offenses that are omitted are juvenile-status in character—incorrigibility, truancy, drinking and so on.

The findings, displayed in Table 9-6, are somewhat redundant with those already presented, except that they underscore the conclusions that were reached. Effectiveness for the three community groups, with the possible exception of a few dropouts, was high. After two years, scores on the CET index indicate that almost none of the boys in these programs had four or more arrests for medium or high serious offenses and after four years the figure was, at most, only 8 percent.

By contrast, significant proportions of the incarceration controls had been arrested for a wide range of acts, most of which would be criminal for adults as well as juveniles. After three years, one-third of them had been arrested four or more times, and after four years, the number had reached almost 40 percent. On the CET index, the incarceration controls differed significantly from the experimentals in every time period: after one year, $P < .01$; after two, three and four years, $P < .001$.

More than anything else, the findings question the effectiveness of incarceration as a correctional device. Either they show that the efficiency of the incarceration program was less than that of the experimental program, or that the effects of incarceration were so negative as to cause offenders to become more delinquent. Perhaps both sets of forces were at work. At any rate, the relative inefficiency of incarceration, as contrasted to community programming,

Table 9-6

Correctional Efficiency Based on Four or More Arrests of a Medium- or High-Serious Nature

Sample	No. of Years After Release	Effectiveness Indexes*		
		CEG	CED	CET
Probation				
Experimental	1	1.00	.89	.99
	2	1.00	.78	.97
	3	.95	.78	.93
	4	.95	.78	.93
Probation				
Control	1	1.00	.90	.99
	2	.99	.90	.98
	3	.97	.90	.96
	4	.93	.90	.92
Incarceration				
Experimental	1	1.00	1.00	1.00
	2	1.00	1.00	1.00
	3	.95	1.00	.96
	4	.92	1.00	.93
Incarceration				
Control	1	.87	—**	.87
	2	.74	—	.74
	3	.67	—	.67
	4	.61	—	.61

*CEG–Rating on Graduates Only
CED–Rating on Dropouts Only
CET–Rating on Total Sample
**No Dropouts from Sample; rating not Applicable.

is dramatically illustrated in the next section which has to do with the extent to which new arrests among the different samples resulted in confinements for the boys involved—confinements in juvenile institutions or in adult jails and prison. In contrast to what arrest records revealed, that section reflects the ways in which the courts responded to the boys who were arrested.

Confinements

Number of Boys Confined

Table 9-7 presents the number of boys who were confined during the four-year follow-up period and the types of confinement they received. Looking first at

Table 9-7
Number of Boys Confined and Types of Confinement

	Juvenile Institution		County Jail		Adult Prison		Total	
Sample	N	%	N	%	N	%	N	%
Probation Experimental								
Grads (62)	1	2	1	2	0	0	2	3
Drops (9)	8	89	0	0	2	22	8	89
Total (71)	9	13	1	2	2	3	10	14
Probation Control								
Grads (69)	3	4	9	13	3	4	13	19
Drops (10)	6	60	1	10	2	20	9	90
Total (79)	9	11	10	13	5	6	22	28
Incarceration Experimental								
Grads (37)	6	16	4	11	4	11	11	30
Drops (7)	7	100	0	0	2	29	7	100
Total (44)	13	30	4	9	6	14	18	41
Incarceration Control								
Grads (132)	49	37	47	36	28	21	76	58
Drops (0)	–	–	–	–	–	–	–	–
Total (132)	49	37	47	36	28	21	76	58

*Percents shown in "Total" column are not equal to summation of other columns because some individuals are represented more than once.

the *probation* samples, it will be observed that about equal proportions of these two groups were confined in *juvenile* institutions during the follow-up period: 13 percent of the experimentals and 11 percent of the controls. However, those who were confined came almost exclusively from boys who were dropouts in either group. Only one experimental graduate and three control graduates were eventually sentenced to the state training school.

A perusal of the records suggests that virtually all of the dropouts were confined because of new delinquencies committed while they were still under supervision. In one sense, their confinements could be viewed as resulting from inprogram rather than postprogram difficulties. A crucial question, therefore, is whether they continued to be in any more trouble with the courts following their confinements than program graduates. In fact, one very real test for juvenile correctional programs in general is whether they deter adult criminality.

A review of the numbers of boys who were sent to jail or prison after they reached adulthood reveals that dropouts may have been somewhat more criminal than graduates. About one-fifth of them (only two boys in each group, however), as contrasted to none of the experimental graduates and only 4 percent of the controls, eventually were sentenced to prison. The rate of adult criminality in these two groups seems to have been slight. Perhaps of equal significance is the fact that, considering all types of confinement, the experimental program had fewer confinees than the control program: 14 vs. 28 percent for the total samples, and 3 vs. 19 percent for graduates. There may be grounds for concluding that, from the way officials responded, probation experimentals were somewhat less delinquent than controls.

The same was generally true for the *incarceration* groups. Three out of 10 experimentals vs. almost 4 out of 10 controls were confined in a juvenile institution. Again, a large proportion of the confinees in the experimental group were dropouts (all 7 of them were confined). And again, all of these dropout confinements occurred as a result of inprogram arrests. Later, only 9 percent of the experimentals vs. 36 percent of the controls spent time in jail. (Interestingly, these jail confinees included no dropouts.) Finally, the proportion of experimentals who were eventually sentenced to prison was 14 percent vs. 21 percent for the controls. The results, again tended to favor the experimental program, although it is obvious because of the higher rates that these two were the more delinquent groups.

Number of Confinements

Another way of exploring these same issues is to consider the number of confinements for each sample, in contrast to the number of boys who were confined. This provides a second, perhaps more accurate, estimate of career criminality because it takes account of those individuals who were confined repeatedly as against those who were confined only once.

The findings are displayed in Table 9-8. Since only small proportions of the two *probation* groups were confined at all, the average number of confinements per boy for the total samples was concomitantly small: .17 confinements among experimentals and .34 among controls. For the minority who were confined, the rates were higher: a mean of 1.40 confinements for the 10 experimental confinees, and a mean of 1.23 for the 22 control confinees.

In terms of the career or adult criminality of these two confinee groups, the findings favor the experimentals. Controls were confined a total of 12 times in jail versus only once for experimentals, and 6 times in prison versus only 2 for experimentals. These data on confinements for the two *probation* groups tend to favor the experimentals throughout. What may be even more significant is the fact that the rate of adult confinements for both groups was so low. There was little evidence in the follow-up data that this population of boys ultimately became serious adult offenders.

Table 9-8
Number and Types of Confinement

Sample	Types of Confinement				Average Number of Confinements	
	Juvenile Institution	County Jail	Adult Prison	Total Confinements	Confinees Only	Total Sample
Probation Experimental						
Grads (62)	1	1	0	2	1.00	.03
Drops (9)	8	0	2	10	1.25	1.11
Total (71)	9	1	2	12	1.40	.17
Probation Control						
Grads (69)	3	10	4	17	1.31	.25
Drops (10)	6	2	2	10	1.11	1.00
Total (79)	9	12	6	27	1.23	.34
Incarceration Experimental						
Grads (37)	8	6	6	20	1.82	.54
Drops (7)	8	0	2	10	1.43	1.43
Total (44)	16	6	8	30	1.67	.68
Incarceration Control						
Grads (132)	66	83	46	195	2.57	1.48
Drops (0)	–	–	–	–	–	–
Total (132)	66	83	46	195	2.57	1.48

Rates for the two *incarceration* groups differed considerably. The average number of confinements per boy for the total samples was .68 for epxerimentals and 1.48 for controls, averages that in both cases were higher than those for the probation groups. Even more striking were the means for the 18 experimentals and 76 controls who comprised the confinee groups: 1.67 for the former, and 2.57 for the latter.

The evidence indicates that when confinements carried over into adulthood, it was most often the controls who were involved. For example, 47 control boys were confined a total of 83 times in adult jails, and 28 of them were confined a total of 46 times in prison. The offenses for which this latter group were sent to prison were often very serious. Among the convictions against them were two cases of first degree murder, one kidnap, three rapes, four assaults, 24 burglaries, 18 cases of grand larceny, and four forgeries.

By contrast, only 6 experimentals were confined in prison a total of 8 times. Their convictions included six burglaries, two cases of transporting stolen cars across state lines, and one case of carnal knowledge (a reduced rape charge). The differences between the two groups were such that statistical comparisons between them were highly significant.

Such findings are documentation of serious failures in corrections, especially of incarceration. The data indicate clearly that incarceration was not successful for a significant minority of the boys who received that kind of treatment. The extent and seriousness of their delinquent acts strongly suggest the need for other alternatives. Not only had their lives been disrupted, perhaps spoiled for as long as they live, by repeated crimes and confinements, but they were an obvious danger to society.

Implications

In order to relate these findings to the larger body of correctional theory and research, it might be important to consider three issues.

1. In general terms, it would be useful to determine how the outcomes of programs under study here compare with similar kinds of programs elsewhere. Was probation at Provo, for example, more or less successful than probation elsewhere? The same might be asked about the effects of incarceration.
2. Relatively speaking, it would be important to know whether the differentials observed in this study between community intervention and incarceration have been observed elsewhere. The available literature on this subject is by no means conclusive.
3. Finally, it might be useful to explore the problems of evaluating correctional programs. Existing critiques have raised many questions about evaluative research and they should be considered in light of findings in this chapter.

Let us consider these issues, one by one.

1. Comparative Findings

Probation. Any attempt to compare the outcome findings for the probation groups in this study with probation studies elsewhere indicates just how primitive our knowledge of correctional effectiveness is. Despite hundreds of publications extolling the virtues of probation theory and practice, and the fact that hundreds of thousands of people have been placed on probation, England (1957) was able to locate only 15 accounts of scientific research into the efficacy of this correctional device.

The reported success rates for these studies varied between 60 and 90 percent. Somewhat in support of them, a 1948 survey of such states as Massachusetts, California, New York and several foreign countries reported results with the modal success rate at about 75 percent (Grunhut, 1948:60-82). Considerable caution must be exercised, however, in interpreting these studies.

In the first place, few of them were conducted under carefully controlled experimental conditions nor do the reported results apply solely to juveniles and to their postprobation behavior. For example, in the 15 studies reported by England, six of the accounts were concerned with success *during*, rather than after, intervention. Second, measures of effectiveness varied from study to study, some being based on arrest, some on reconviction, and some, perhaps, on confinement. Valid comparisons between these and the Provo results are difficult to make.

To illustrate how difficult the task of making comparisons is, this chapter has shown that success rates for the probation groups at Provo varied considerably as different measures were applied. For example, when only *one arrest* was the criterion, the success rate for both groups, including dropouts, was only 45 percent, a rate that was much lower than those reported above. If three arrests were used, or if seriousness were taken into account, the success rate would rise precipitously, to around 90 percent *after four years*. If *any kind of institutional confinement* were the criterion, the success rate would be 72 percent for the regular probationers and 86 percent for the experimentals, rates that also compare favorably with those reported above.

With these kinds of rate variations, it is difficult to say what they mean when compared to the rates observed elsewhere. They document Wilkin's observation that we are still at a stage where the nature of our ignorance is only beginning to be revealed (cf. Hood and Sparks, 1970:71). Until some standardized measures are used, and until more of them are applied under experimental conditions, it will be impossible to speak with much precision regarding the exact effects of probation.

Incarceration. A larger number of studies on the general effects of incarceration are available, but they also leave important questions unanswered. In his survey, Glaser (1964: Chap. 2) found that adults and juveniles being released from diverse institutions in Massachusetts, Minnesota, Wisconsin, California, New York, Washington, and the federal system had *reconfinement* rates varying between 15 and 45 percent.

Later reviews, concerned only with juveniles, revealed varying rates: slightly over 40 percent reconfinement rates for the federal system (Costner, 1968:14-15); parole revocation rates of from 31 to 64 percent for nine institutions of the California Youth Authority (Costner, 1968:14-15; Jesness, 1970:32); reconfinement rates varying between 44 and 51 percent in Wisconsin over three time periods (Wisconsin State Department of Public Welfare, 1966);

and a 26 percent rate for boys in Florida who were eventually convicted of adult crimes and confined in an adult institution (Eichman, 1969:9-10).

As Adams (1970) points out, it is difficult to interpret such findings because like probation figures, they are not based upon uniform and standardized reporting procedures, and because the periods of postrelease follow-up are not equivalent. Nevertheless, one gains the feeling that they are somewhat more sound than the probation findings reported above because they are based upon state and federal systems whose record-keeping is more consistent and reliable. If one compares them with the outcome rates for the incarceration controls at Provo, one finds that they are not totally inconsistent: 37 percent of the Provo controls were reconfined in a juvenile institution, a figure that is not greatly at odds with the rate for the federal system (40 percent), but perhaps lower than the California rate (31 to 64 percent); 36 percent were reconfined in jail, a rate that compares very closely with rates observed by Adams (1970:8) for two youth groups in Washington, D.C. (41 and 36 percent); and 21 percent of the Provo controls were reconfined in adult prison, a rate that is close to the 26 percent rate in Florida. The findings suggest that there may be some uniformities in the effects that incarceration has upon juveniles in different jurisdictions; generally common outcomes may be occurring.

2. Relative Rates

Recognizing this as a possibility, a second question is how recidivism rates for incarcerated offenders compare with those for equivalent groups who are placed on probation, or in some other form of community intervention. It is of crucial importance to know whether the latter are more effective, and whether the Provo findings are typical or atypical.

After examining a number of studies in which the recidivism rates of different correctional alternatives were compared, Robison and Smith (1971) concluded that there was little evidence favoring one alternative over another. Considering both juvenile and adult programs, they presented rather convincing evidence that overall outcomes will be about the same when community programs are compared with incarceration, when length of sentence is varied, when offenders are subjected to different kinds of programs within prison, when intensity of supervision on probation and parole is varied, and when outright discharge from prison is used versus release on parole.

Hood and Sparks (1970:186ff.) report similar findings from their survey of corrections in the United States, England and Denmark. Treating only adult males, placed either on probation or incarcerated, the authors found postrelease reconviction rates to be about the same. One form of intervention was not more effective than the other.

It should be noted that the conclusions reached in both surveys were based upon studies in which statistical rather than experimental controls were generally the rule.

Rather than using experimental designs and random assignments, most of the investigators had simply controlled for a number of offender characteristics—prior criminal record, family status, place of residence, etc.—when outcome rates were compared. When this was done, any observable differences tended to wash out. The data seemed to indicate that any differences between programs were due more to kinds of offenders than to kinds of intervention. The implication is that poor risks do poorly, whether incarcerated or placed on probation, while good risks do well in either setting. How or whether the findings might change under experimental conditions is difficult to say. Nevertheless, it is important to consider them in light of the Provo findings.

The more intensive experimental program at Provo did not seem to be greatly superior to regular probation. There was some evidence that it resulted in fewer inprogram arrests (Chapter 5) and fewer postrelease confinements, but its effectiveness was not superior in every circumstance. The *incarceration* experimentals who were actually left in the community had consistently fewer arrests than controls during the follow-up period, and considerably fewer confinements for adult crimes. The two programs did not seem to have equivalent consequences.

Given the lack of definitive differences in the past, it would be pleasant to conclude that these findings provide one bit of conclusive documentation of the superiority of community intervention over incarceration. The difficulty with this conclusion has to do with the fact that the hypothesis of no difference between the incarceration experimental and control groups was given questionable rather than total support in Chapter 2. It is necessary to entertain the possibility that the observed differences, though great on occasion, were due to offender rather than program differences.

The same questions have been raised about other group-oriented programs, like Highfields (Weeks, 1958) or Essexfields (Stephenson and Scarpitti, 1967), where, although experimentals did better than incarcerated controls, random assignments or other experimental devices were not exercised. In the one case where random assignment was successful—the Silverlake Experiment (Empey and Lubeck, 1971)—outcomes for community experimentals and institutionalized controls were essentially the same. It is difficult to say, whether the experimental program at Provo, was an exception to the rule.

The way one reacts to such findings depends as much upon his particular set of values as upon the scientific evidence. One can react with total pessimism to the ambiguity of these findings, or with disbelief in the notion that community alternatives are not superior to incarceration. It is also useful to recognize that, even if one remains cautious in his interpretation of the evidence, it indicates almost always that *community intervention is at least as effective as incarceration.* This is not a matter to be taken lightly.

The likelihood that this is true is important from many standpoints. From a humanitarian standpoint, it is important because it suggests that young offenders may be spared the indignities and deleterious effects of incarceration without any apparent added danger to the community. The usual assessment of program effects on the basis of recidivistic acts tends to ignore the likelihood that community programs are able to avoid some of the lasting harms to the self-concepts and social relations of offenders that result from incarceration, even though these consequences are not readily apparent in the outcome measures that are used.

Findings of no difference are important from a cost standpoint as well. The average length of stay for a boy who was confined in Utah in 1962, the midpoint of the study, was nine and one-half months and cost approximately $2,015. The average stay at the Provo Experiment was approximately seven months and cost about $609. This would mean roughly a saving of $1,406 per boy plus two and one-half months of his time, plus the fact that he never had to experience the negative effects of incarceration.

Stated another way, it was found in the Silverlake Experiment (Empey and Lubeck, 1971:310) that for every 1,000 boys treated in the community rather than in the institution, two million dollars could be saved—two million dollars that could be devoted to the conduct of further research and program improvement. Moreover, this saving would be even greater if regular probation were the sole means of intervention rather than a more expensive community model. In Provo, for example, the average cost per boy on probation was only about $200, an expenditure that was $400 less than the experimental model, and $1,800 less than traditional incarceration.

Despite reasons like these for experimenting further with various kinds of community intervention, there are arguments favoring institutional innovation as well. First, it is possible that there are some offenders for whom some kind of institutionalization is in order, either as a better means of helping them or as a means of protecting society. Improved methods are needed for these groups. Second, Street (1965) for one, has cautioned against overgeneralizations on the negative effects of incarceration. He found that while inmates in juvenile institutions that possess traditional punitive orientations do exhibit the classic internal problems with which everyone is familiar, institutions that were characterized by a minimum of social distance between inmates and staff had no such problems. One might infer that outcome rates in the latter would be superior. As yet there is little support for this assumption.

Several attempts have been made in California institutions to reduce social distance and improve parole performance by using a variety of group and therapeutic community approaches. Careful studies of both adult and juvenile programs have not been able to document an increase in parole performance as a result (cf. Kassebaum, et al., 1971; and Seckel, 1965). Although Jesness (1970) used a much different approach, his findings were the same. In his case, all delinquents were classified into several maturity types and assigned to institutional programs designed specifically to meet their particular needs. While he observed personal changes which favored the experimentals, their parole performances after release were identical with those of the controls (65 percent failure). Of all the evidence available, there is little that supports the notion that institutional treatment, is any more effective in terms of postrelease delinquency than less costly community programs. The only argument that can be made in favor of institutionalization is that it can provide more effective custody during intervention, and that some offender types might eventually be identified for whom it will be superior.

3. Problems of Measuring Outcome

The final issue that merits attention has to do with the problems of measuring correctional effectiveness. This chapter has shown that interpretations of correctional effectiveness will vary markedly depending upon the measures that are used. When the stringent Technical Efficiency Rating was applied—when dropouts as well as recidivists were treated as failures—or when correctional efficiency was measured in terms of only one arrest after release, the efficiency ratings for all programs after four years were low. The three community programs were only about 50 percent successful, and the incarceration controls went as low as 20 percent. When three or more arrests was the criterion, or when offense seriousness was considered, efficiency rates went up markedly. The two probation groups were between 80 and 90 percent successful, and the incarceration experimentals were almost 80 percent successful. Only the incarceration controls remained low at around 56 percent. Variations of equal or even greater magnitude were also observed when program graduates alone were considered, or when long-term confinements was the criterion.

Such findings, as a result, point to two problems that must be solved if accurate pictures of correctional efficiency are to be obtained. The first has to do with the need for some kind of standardized measure or for greater detail in reporting. Since it is difficult at present to obtain standardized indicators, both because of the complexities of the measurement problem and because there are few uniform data collection systems, the next best alternative may be greater detail in reporting. Many of the better state systems rely heavily upon parole revocations or reconfinements for their measures of effectiveness. Unfortunately, such data leave unanswered the question as to what kinds of factors contribute to observed rates; how many are due to new crimes; how many to technical violations; and what the natures of these new crimes and technical violations are. It is not really accurate to treat all reconfinements equally. One offender may be reconfined for a whole new series of violations while another may have only violated some condition of his parole—failed to stay away from his old friends, failed to stop drinking, or gotten into a fight.

There are other kinds of distortions in reconfinement figures. Many studies indicate simply whether offenders are reconfined or not, failing to note that, in some cases, several reconfinements may have occurred while in others only one was observed. The only way to provide better information is to follow offenders for as long a period as possible, to note what kinds of trouble they got into, and to note the kinds of dispositions that are made of their cases.

A second difficulty was noted in Chapter 5. It has to do with the ways in which the actions of correctional agents or research people can affect and distort effectiveness ratings. One source of distortion can occur when dropouts are not included in assessments of program effectiveness.

Lerman (1970:325) cited one example in which some investigators who were studying the effectiveness of a private correctional institution excluded from their follow-up analysis (1) all offenders who were defined as unsuitable for treatment while in the institution; and (2) excluded all offenders who got into trouble during an extended period of aftercare. The only individuals who were included in the assessment of success and failure were those who successfully completed both phases. It should come as little surprise to find that boys from this institution had a higher success rate than those from a neighboring state school. State schools have no means by which to exclude people they do not want or to ignore failures on parole. The investigators in this case eliminated many chances for finding failure, and probably inflated their success rates in a way that was questionable.

An even more difficult problem can occur because of the subtle effects of correctional philosophy and practice upon assessments of outcome. Robison and Smith (1971:69) illustrate this problem in their analysis of outcome findings for the Community Treatment Project of the California Youth Authority. This project, widely acclaimed for its promise, utilized randomly selected experimental and control groups as a means of determining effectiveness rates.

The experimental group was released to the community where each individual was diagnosed according to his maturity level and, on the basis of that diagnosis, assigned to a parole agent who was skilled in working with that type of delinquent (cf. Warren, 1964 and 1968). The control group was assigned to one of the institutions of the California Youth Authority where, after confinement, its members were released on regular parole. While in the community, the caseloads in the experimental program were small, from 9 to 10 offenders per agent, as compared to a caseload of around 55 offenders per parole agent in the control programs (California Legislature, 1969).

A follow-up of the two groups, as Robison and Smith (1971:69) note, strongly favored the experimental community program.

At the fifteen-months period, 30 percent of male experimentals had 'violated parole or had been unfavorably discharged,' compared with 51 percent of male controls . . . At the 24-months period these outcomes were 43 percent and 63 percent, respectively, again favoring the experimental group. If we take these findings at face value, we are forced to conclude that probation has been proven to be a more effective correctional program than imprisonment for reducing recidivism. But has it?

There is considerable evidence that the reported figures were highly a function of parole agent decision-making, not just the behaviors of the delinquent subjects. And since permanent revocation of parole, presumably followed by institutional confinement, was the criterion for failure, this decision-making was of crucial significance.

Warren and Palmer (1966) note that 68 percent of the control failures were due to recommendations by regular parole agents that parole be revoked. By contrast, the same figure for the experimentals was only 29 percent. Instead of using permanent revocations (which would signify failure), the experimental staff was far more inclined to utilize temporary suspensions in which, although offenders were placed in detention for a short while, they still remained under the supervision of the experimental program, and were not considered failures (Palmer and Warren, 1967: Part I, 11-12).

Regular agents in the control program also seemed far more inclined than experimental agents to revoke parole for low or moderately serious offenses. Only when offenses were of high severity were experimental agents inclined to react as control agents did (Lerman, 1968; Palmer and Warren, 1967: Part I, 11-12). The lack of uniformity in this area also contributed to the observed differences.

The picture is complicated by the fact that experimentals actually committed more known offenses than controls. The average per experimental boy was 2.8 offenses versus only 1.6 per control boy—a difference that was highly significant (Lerman, 1968; Palmer and Warren, 1967: Part I, 11-12). The directors of the project feel that these differences were due, at least in part, to the fact that experimentals were more closely supervised than controls. Increased supervision probably resulted in more offenses being observed. Nevertheless, even if this were true, the task of clearing up the measurement problem, and of determining the relative effectiveness of the two programs remains. The findings are by no means definitive.

The issue is not whether the experimental program was wrong in trying new methods. Philosophically speaking, there is no reason why personnel in the Community Treatment Project should not have been given the opportunity to exercise greater latitude in their treatment of delinquents. Correctional effectiveness, in the long run, may have been increased by their methods. The issue, instead, is whether the data warrant any claims for superiority or inferiority at this stage. Probably they do not. Before any such claims could be made, it would be necessary to distinguish more clearly between the effects on outcome of correctional philosophy and practice, on one hand, and the actual behaviors of delinquents on the other.

Unfortunately, the need to make such distinctions is more easily recognized after the fact than before. We are actually indebted to the Community Treatment Project for bringing the problem into sharp relief. Before any final conclusions regarding the relative outcomes of the two programs could be reached, more data and analyses would be required. Can any independent sources of data—police arrest records, or new court dispositions—be brought to bear on the issue? What do these records show, as well as parole revocation rates, regarding the delinquent behaviors of experimental and control groups? What would a long-term follow-up of the two groups reveal after they have been entirely free of parole agent supervision for some time? Perhaps follow-up interviews of subjects by an independent research team regarding new, but undetected, delinquent acts could shed some light on the issues.

If such information were available, it would provide an excellent means by which to assess the consequences of revoking parole, as parole agents did, using different criteria. Some basis would be provided for determining whether their acts were based on adequate evidence, or were merely the consequences of their own, disparate philosophies.

Above all, this brief review has shown how crucial the measurement problem is, and how difficult it will be to be definitive about correctional effectiveness until better measures are developed. There is as much need for innovation and attention in this area as in the area of correctional programming itself.

Future Chapters

It should be noted that two basic questions are unanswered. The first asks whether overall delinquency rates were reduced as a result of the various programs under study. Although recidivism rates were examined, they did not tell us whether postprogram delinquency among the various samples was any less after intervention than before. Consequently, the next chapter will be concerned with that issue. Despite the fact that many delinquents did get into trouble after intervention, it may be that their overall violation rates were less. If so, that possibility should not be ignored in assessing program effectiveness.

A second question has been discussed in part. It has to do with the nagging possibility that correctional programs provide little positive help; that they may be distinguished more by their abilities to avoid doing harm than by their abilities to be constructive. That question, as a result, will be examined in Chapter 11. The various programs will be studied to determine whether any positive impact can be discerned.

10 Relative Effectiveness: Before and After Delinquency Rates

Thus far in the analysis, correctional effectiveness has been examined in absolute terms—whether or not delinquents commit new offenses. This kind of analysis overlooks the evaluative method that is ordinarily associated with the classic experimental design; namely, a relative assessment of effectiveness in which preintervention and postintervention offense rates are compared.

Some studies have evaluated correctional impact by conducting pretests and posttests of educational, attitudinal or personality change, but rarely has a before-and-after analysis been applied to actual delinquent behavior. This is a surprising omission because, by comparing the preintervention and postintervention offense rates of any given program, it is possible to determine whether significant reductions were produced by it. Even though many offenders recidivate, it is entirely possible that the rate at which they commit crimes after intervention is lower than it was before. Consequently, if relative changes of this type are ignored, which an analysis in absolute terms does, some of the actual effects of intervention may be missed entirely.

Second, a before-and-after analysis is an excellent method of making comparisons between programs, of indicating whether one program is any more effective than another. Preintervention and postintervention rates provide the means by which relative degrees of change can first be calculated, and then compared. Consequently, this chapter is devoted to a detailed exploration of both issues.

The amount and seriousness of official delinquency associated with each of the experimental and control groups, during the four-year follow-up period, will be compared with similar data for an equivalent period prior to intervention. An attempt will be made to determine whether delinquency rates went up or down, and whether there were differences between programs.

Before-and-After Arrest Frequency

Figure 10-1 provides a summary statement of findings comparing the total number of arrests for each sample four years before, versus four years after intervention.[1] Because the four samples were not equal in size, some method had to be found for standardizing the comparisons. This was done by treating the preintervention arrests for each sample as a base rate of 100 percent, and then comparing the postintervention arrests with that base. Figure 10-1 indicates that there was a reduction in arrest rate for every sample.

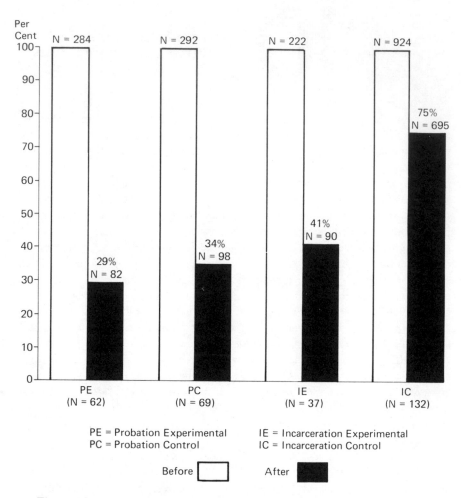

Figure 10-1. Postintervention Offenses as Proportion of Preintervention Offenses, Four Years Before Vs. Four Years After.

The number of postintervention arrests for the probation experimental group was only 29 percent of the preintervention figure; for the probation control group only 34 percent; and for the incarceration experimental group, only 41 percent. In the case only of the incarceration control group did the postintervention figure of 75 percent come close to approximating the earlier figure. These figures indicate that arrest rates following intervention were reduced considerably in at least three of the four cases—71 percent for the probation experimental group, 66 percent for the probation control group, and 49 percent for the incarceration experimental group versus only 25 percent for the incarceration control group. Whether these reductions were entirely and directly attributable to the programs involved is difficult to say, but they were generally striking, nevertheless.

Mean Number of Offenses

A more precise picture of the findings and a method of assessing the relative effectiveness of the programs can be determined by examining the mean number of arrests per boy, in one-year intervals, before and after intervention. Two kinds of tests can be run: (1) *within-group* tests that tell us whether reductions in the number of arrests for each group are statistically significant when its preintervention and postintervention means are compared; and (2) *between-group* tests that tell us whether the reductions that occurred in the experimental groups differed significantly from those of their respective control groups.

Comparisons of Probation Groups

Table 10-1 presents the findings for the *within*-group changes for the two *probation* groups. It shows that the mean number of arrests per boy in each of them, during each of the four-year follow-up periods, was significantly lower ($P < .001$) than during a corresponding period prior to intervention. After four years the average number of arrests in the experimental group was only 1.32 offenses as compared to 4.63 offenses during the four years prior, a reduction of 3.31 offenses. Comparable figures for the control group were 1.42 offenses after intervention vs. 4.25 offenses before, a reduction of 2.83 offenses. The decline

Table 10-1
Differences in Mean Number of Arrests per Boy Before and After, for Probation Experimental and Control Groups

		Sample Categories									
Time Periods	Probation Experimental (N = 62)						Probation Control (N = 69)					
Before vs. After	Before		After		Difference		Before		After		Difference	
	X_1	S_1	X_2	S_2	$X_1 - X_2$	P	X_1	S_1	X_2	S_2	$X_1 - X_2$	P
1 Year	3.52	1.72	.55	.78	2.97	.001	2.87	1.65	.70	1.08	2.17	.001
2 Years	4.16	2.09	.97	1.46	3.19	.001	3.52	1.95	.93	1.38	2.59	.001
3 Years	4.45	2.20	1.24	1.87	3.21	.001	3.91	2.22	1.01	1.46	2.90	.001
4 Years	4.63	2.32	1.32	1.85	3.31	.001	4.25	2.46	1.42	2.14	2.83	.001

in the number of official arrests *within* each of these two groups was both statistically significant and substantively great.

Of equal significance are comparisons *between* the two groups. It would be useful to know whether the reductions that occurred in the experimental group were greater or lesser than those occurring in the control group, and whether any differences were statistically significant. The findings are displayed in Table 10-2.

It will be observed that the only difference that was statistically significant occurred after one year. Reductions in the experimental group were greater than in the control group. Thereafter, differences tended to decline such that the two groups appeared very much alike. The declines in arrest rates, although considerable, were about the same in both groups.

Table 10-2
Differences in Degrees of Change Between Probation Experimental and Control Groups (4 Years Before vs. 4 Years After)

Time Period	Probation Experimental Difference $(M_1 - M_2)$	Probation Control Difference $(M_1 - M_2)$	Differences Between Samples $(D_e - D_c)$	Level of Significance Z	P
1 Year	2.97	2.17	.80	2.15	$<$.05
2 Years	3.19	2.59	.60	1.28	NS
3 Years	3.21	2.90	.31	.58	NS
4 Years	3.31	2.83	.48	.85	NS

NS = Not Significant

Comparison of Incarceration Groups

The *within*-group comparisons for the two incarceration groups are shown in Table 10-3. Again, the contrasts between before and after rates were great. Even within the incarceration control group, the reductions, although small by comparison with that of the experimental group, were highly significant ($P <$ .001). Any assumption that violation rates would be as great or greater after intervention, especially after confinement in an institution, was not borne out. There was a significant decline, not an increase.

Table 10-4, which indicates whether the year-by-year reductions occurring in the experimental group were any greater than those in the control group, reveals an interesting trend. After one year, the reductions occurring in both groups were approximately equal. From then on, the differences between before and after rates for the experimental group tended to widen, while just the opposite was true for the control group. After one year, the reduction in the experimental group was 2.46 arrests, compared with a similar reduction of 2.72 arrests in the

Table 10-3

Differences in Mean Number of Arrests Before and After, for Incarceration Experimental and Control Groups

Time Periods Before vs. After	Incarceration Experimental (N = 37)						Incarceration Control (N = 132)					
	Before		After		Difference		Before		After		Difference	
	X_1	S_1	X_2	S_2	$X_1 - X_2$	P	X_1	S_1	X_2	S_2	$X_1 - X_2$	P
1 Year	3.57	1.69	1.11	1.47	2.46	.001	4.43	2.83	1.71	2.08	2.72	.001
2 Years	5.05	2.58	1.95	2.78	3.10	.001	6.14	3.67	3.34	3.33	2.80	.001
3 Years	5.70	2.86	2.24	2.98	3.46	.001	6.74	3.90	4.54	4.65	2.20	.001
4 Years	6.00	3.03	2.43	3.13	3.57	.001	7.01	4.12	5.28	5.23	1.73	.001

Table 10-4

Differences in Degrees of Change Between Incarceration Experimental and Control Groups (4 Years Before vs. 4 Years After)

Time Period	Incarceration Experimental Difference $(M_1 - M_2)$	Incarceration Control Difference $(M_1 - M_2)$	Differences Between Samples $(D_e - D_c)$	Level of Significance Z	P
1 Year	2.46	2.72	− .26	.00	NS
2 Years	3.10	2.80	.30	.39	NS
3 Years	3.46	2.20	1.26	1.50	NS
4 Years	3.57	1.73	1.84	2.08	<.05

NS = Not Significant

control group. But by the end of the fourth year, the reduction for experimentals was even greater, 3.57 arrests, while that for the controls was less, 1.73 arrests. The difference in degrees of change at the end of the four-year period was statistically significant ($P < .05$). Table 10-4 shows that the ultimate difference was reflective of distinct trends for the two groups: while the post intervention rate for the experimentals tended to decline when compared with the prior rate, the post intervention rate for the controls tended to catch up. The difference in degrees of change between the two groups, therefore, tended to expand with the passage of time.

Before-After Comparisons by Seriousness

Although significant reductions in the rates of postintervention offenses occurred in all the groups, it is important to determine whether these reductions were characteristic of all kinds of offenses or only some of them. Did offenses of high or medium seriousness decline, as well as those that are strictly juvenile-status in character? If one is interested in crime control, then it is the more serious kinds of offenses with which one is most concerned.

The general findings for the two probation groups are shown in Figure 10-2. It is designed to show the percentage reductions in frequency of arrest for high-, medium- and low-serious offenses. Again, it reveals very little difference between the two samples. *Within* each group, the differences between preintervention and postintervention rates for all kinds of offenses were highly significant ($P < .001$). Decreases ranged from the highest reduction of 86 percent in high-serious offenses for the experimental group to the smallest reduction of 55 percent in low-serious offenses for the control group. In every case, however, important reductions in offense rates were observed.

Although the experimental group had fewer offenses of both a high- and low-serious nature, differences *between* experimentals and controls were not significant. It would appear that, insofar as this set of findings is attributable to the two programs, they both had about the same effect and both may have helped to produce postprogram offense rates that were considerably lower than preprogram rates.

Figure 10-3 presents the same set of findings for the incarceration groups. In this case, findings were not the same. A visual inspection of the figure indicates the point made earlier that the incarceration control program seems to have had the least effect. On high-serious offenses, the percentage reduction for experimentals was 67 percent vs. only 30 percent for the controls; on medium-serious offenses, the differences were 74 vs. 38 percent; and on low-serious offenses, there was actually an increase of 26 percent in the control group in contrast to a reduction of 28 percent for the experimentals. But while these findings indicate that reductions for controls were not so great as those for experimentals, it is still possible that some rate reductions *within* the control group were sufficiently great to be statistically significant. It remains to be seen whether, when individual means are considered, controls were significantly more delinquent than experimentals. They may not have been.

First, consider the changes *within* groups. Table 10-5 shows that on high- and medium-serious offenses, both groups exhibited statistically significant reductions. And while low-serious offenses actually increased in the control group, as they were being reduced in the experimental group, neither of these changes was statistically significant. They could have been due to chance. In any event, it is noteworthy that, on the most serious kinds of delinquency, the postintervention rates for these two groups of persistently delinquent boys were significantly lower than their preintervention rates.

With respect to *between*-group differences, Table 10-5 shows that, while the overall pattern favored the experimentals, it was only on low-serious offenses that mean differences were statistically significant ($P < .05$). As a result, one

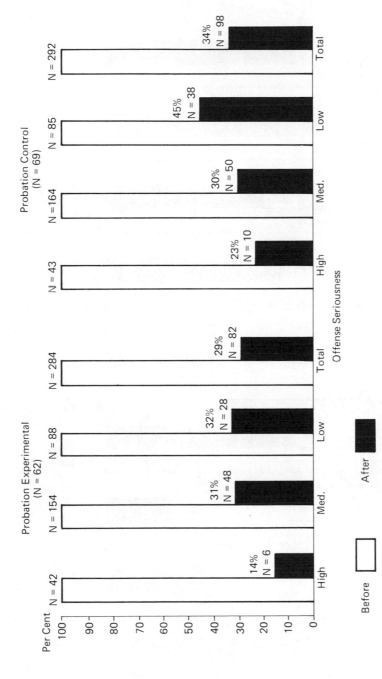

Figure 10-2. Percentage Reductions in Frequency of Arrest in *Probation* Groups for Offenses of Varying Seriousness, Four Years Before Vs. Four Years After.

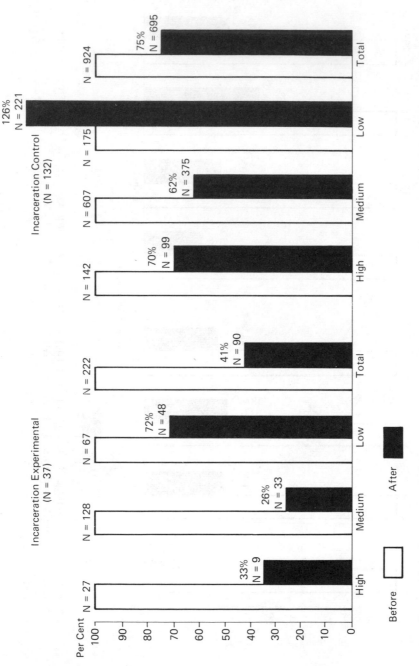

Figure 10-3. Percentage Reductions in Frequency of Arrests in *Incarceration* Groups for Offenses of Varying Seriousness, Four Years Before Vs. Four Years After.

Table 10-5

Significance of Differences Within and Between Incarceration Group Means on Offenses of Varying Seriousness, 4 Years Before vs. 4 Years After

Type of Offense	Sample	Before X_1	S.D.	After X_2	S.D.	Within Difference $X_1 - X_2$	Significance Level Z	P	Between Difference $D_e - D_c$	Significance Level Z	P
High	IE*	.73	.86	.24	.67	.49	2.70	.001	.16	.00	NS
	IC**	1.08	1.27	.75	1.23	.33	2.10	.05			
Medium	IE	3.46	2.25	.89	1.16	2.57	6.09	.001	.81	1.44	NS
	IC	4.60	3.01	2.84	3.40	1.76	4.73	.001			
Low	IE	1.81	1.67	1.30	2.32	.51	1.07	NS	.85	1.64	<.05
	IC	1.33	1.62	1.67	2.23	-.34	.00	NS			

*Incarceration Experimental
**Incarceration Control

could not conclude with certainty that reductions in the most serious kinds of offenses clearly favored the experimentals. One reason is that there is a great deal of variation about the group means, suggesting that while some offenders were highly delinquent, others were not. Consequently, this lack of homogeneity undoubtedly contributed to the finding of insignificant differences. It underscores the importance of determining whether there were differences in the proportions of boys in each sample who remained persistently delinquent after release. What we may be measuring here are the effects primarily of a highly delinquent minority, not the effects of the majority. This matter will be treated later in the analysis.

Relative to the matter of crime control, one can ill afford to ignore the contextual nature of these findings. Reductions, as a whole, for the incarcerated boys were not nearly so great. If attention is directed to Table 10-6, it can be seen that, compared to the other groups, there was a progressive, year-by-year decline in the extent to which reductions occurred in their postintervention, as contrasted to their preintervention rates. On high-serious offenses, the reduction after one year was 76 percent, but it went progressively downward: to 59 percent after two years, 41 percent after three years, and only 30 percent after four years. The decline was much less pronounced for the experimental group where the decline went from 83 percent after one year to only 67 percent after four years. In fact, this particular pattern among the experimentals was much more like that of the two less delinquent probation groups than like that of the incarcerated group with which it was being compared. Whether a lot of boys in the control group, or only a few, were involved in contributing to a higher rate of postrelease delinquency, their pattern was a more serious one. There was a

Table 10-6

Percentage Reductions in Frequency of Arrest in Each Sample for Offenses of Varying Seriousness

Sample Categories	Offense Seriousness	Percent Reductions before vs. after			
		1 Year	2 Years	3 Years	4 Years
Probation Experimental	High	97	83	85	86
	Medium	83	76	71	69
	Low	78	74	68	68
	All	84	77	72	71
Probation Control	High	97	92	90	77
	Medium	75	74	75	70
	Low	60	61	64	55
	All	75	73	74	66
Incarceration Experimental	High	83	81	75	67
	Medium	82	78	77	74
	Low	37	22	21	28
	All	68	61	61	59
Incarceration Control	High	76	59	41	30
	Medium	67	54	45	38
	Low	26	3	−16	−26
	All	61	46	33	25

progressive deterioration that does not seem to be characteristic of the other groups. It will be important to learn in the next section of the analysis what proportion of boys in each sample actually contributed to these differing patterns.

Reductions in Proportions of Offenders Committing Offenses

Of considerable significance to the matter of crime control is not only a reduction in the number of offenses committed, but a reduction in the number of offenders who continue to commit them. Each of the samples under study here included offenders, most of whom had committed a considerable amount of delinquency prior to their assignment to one of the programs. One crucial test of those programs is how they affected numbers of offenders as well as offenses during the follow-up period. If such programs are to be considered effective, some evidence of reductions should be available.

Figure 10-4 presents summary findings on the matter. Without regard to kinds of offenses, it indicates what proportions of all groups had fewer arrests during the four years following intervention (as contrasted with the four years preceding it), what proportions did not change, and what proportions had more arrests. It reveals reductions that may seem surprisingly high, given the general pessimism that is associated with interpretations of correctional effectiveness. Around eight out of ten boys in each of the three community groups, and 64 percent of the incarcerated group had *fewer* arrests. By comparison, the proportion having *more* arrests was small. It varied only between 11 and 16 percent in the community programs, but went as high as 27 percent for the incarcerated boys. Only small proportions made *no change*. The proportions of offenders in each group whose offenses were reduced were sizeable. Reductions *within* each group were highly significant ($P < .01$).

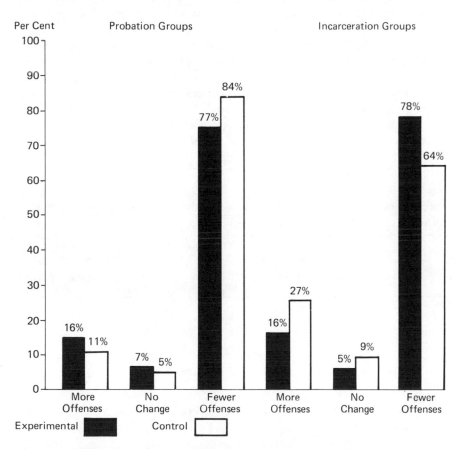

Figure 10-4. Percentages of Each Sample Having More, The Same, or Fewer Offenses, Four Years After Vs. Four Years Before.

Low-Serious Offenses

In a more pointed way, Table 10-7 shows how many of these general changes were attributable to reductions in the numbers of boys involved in *low-serious*, juvenile-status offenses. Three major sets of findings may be observed. First, over half of the three community groups, and about one-third of the incarcerated controls, had fewer arrests following intervention. Most of these reductions involved one or two fewer arrests, although there were sizeable groups of boys in the three community samples who had as many as three, four or even five fewer arrests. The only case in which a statistically significant difference ($P < .01$) appeared in the table was between the incarceration experimental and control groups. Arrests for experimentals were reduced by 59 percent as contrasted to only 34 percent for the controls.

The incarcerated controls also had the highest proportion of boys with more arrests, 39 percent (vs. 22 percent for the experimentals). The probation controls had the fewest arrests, 15 percent (vs. 20 percent for the experimentals): although none of these differences were statistically significant, they tended to follow the pattern that has characterized relationships between groups in the past.

Finally, there were fairly large proportions in all groups—from 19 to 29 percent—whose behaviors did not change. This need not suggest that boys included in this category necessarily remained as delinquent as they were before. In some cases, it meant just the opposite, that they had remained *non*delinquent,

Table 10-7
Percentages of Each Sample Having More, the Same or Fewer Low-Serious Offenses, 4 Years After vs. 4 Years Before

	Percent of Boys with More Arrests				Percent No Change	Percent of Boys with Fewer Arrests			
	Total % With More	Over 5 More	3-4 More	1-2 More	Total	1-2 Less	3-4 Less	Over 5 Less	Total % With Less
Probation Experimentals (N = 69)	20.2	1.4	2.9	15.9	26.1	36.2	14.5	2.9	53.6
Probation Controls (N = 62)	14.5	0	1.6	12.9	29.0	41.9	8.1	6.5	56.5
Incarceration Experimentals (N = 37)	21.6	8.1	2.7	10.8	18.9	37.8	18.9	2.7	59.4*
Incarceration Controls (N = 132)	38.6	8.3	6.8	23.5	27.3	25.0	6.1	3.0	34.1*

*Differences Statistically Significant, $Z = 2.79, P < .01$.

the reason being that those who had no low-serious offenses before intervention, and none after, would be included in the no-change group. The largest discrepancy between samples was again between incarceration experimental and control samples (19 vs. 27 percent) but it was not statistically significant.

Medium-Serious Offenses

The data on the medium-serious offenses may be the most revealing and most salient of all in terms of crime control. Medium-serious offenses, it will be recalled, include a long list of rather common delinquent and criminal acts—auto theft, grand theft, malicious mischief, petty theft, simple assault, or persistent incorrigibility. In fact, prior to intervention, over 90 percent of all the boys included in the analysis had been found guilty of these kinds of offenses. This fact is indication not only of offender behavior but of the extent to which the agents of social control were concerned with this kind of behavior. Therefore, if it could be shown that there was a significant reduction in the number of boys committing these kinds of offenses following intervention, the finding would be a significant one.

Table 10-8 shows that such a reduction occurred. More than 7 out of 10 offenders in every group, including the incarcerated controls, had fewer offenses of this type during the follow-up period. Not only were all the samples strikingly similar relative to reductions in this area, but many of the boys in them had

Table 10-8
Percentages of Each Sample Having More, the Same, or Fewer Medium-Serious Offenses, 4 Years After vs. 4 Years Before

	Percent of Boys with More Arrests			Percent No Change	Percent of Boys with Fewer Arrests			
	Total % With More	Over 5 More	3-4 More	1-2 More	Total	1-2 Less	3-4 Less	Over 5 Less	Total % with Less
Probation Experimentals ($N = 69$)	15.9	0	0	15.9	11.6	39.1	24.6	8.7	72.4
Probation Controls ($N = 62$)	12.9	0	0	12.9	11.3	38.7	32.3	4.8	75.8
Incarceration Experimentals ($N = 37$)	10.8	0	2.7	8.1	16.2*	24.3	24.3	24.3	72.9
Incarceration Controls ($N = 132$)	21.3	7.6	6.1	7.6	4.5*	30.3	19.7	24.2	74.2

*Differences Statistically Significant, $Z = 2.44$, $P < .05$.

three, four and even five fewer arrests. Among the incarceration experimentals and controls, for example, almost one-quarter of the boys had five or more fewer arrests. In many ways this is a striking reduction.

The only difference that was statistically significant in this case ($P < .05$) was between the incarceration experimentals and controls on the no-change category. Fewer of the controls (5 vs. 16 percent) made no change. Since, before intervention, only small and almost identical proportions of each sample (9 percent of the experimentals and 8 percent of the controls) had no medium-serious offenses, the findings suggest that more of the controls who already had arrests of this type continued to have them after intervention. Even so, this finding seems much less noteworthy than the finding that almost three-quarters of every group had fewer medium-serious offenses after intervention.

High-Serious Offenses

Table 10-9 provides the data on the most serious kinds of offenses—such things as aggravated assault, rape, burglary, narcotics use, or arson. In interpreting these data, therefore, it should be kept in mind that, because of the exceptionally delinquent character of these offenses, one might expect the no-change category to include a large proportion of each group, not because they continued to be highly delinquent after intervention, but because they committed such offenses neither before nor after. For example, 48 percent of the incarceration experi-

Table 10-9
Percentages of Each Sample Having More, the Same, or Fewer High-Serious Offenses, 4 Years After vs. 4 Years Before

	Percent of Boys With More Arrests				Percent No Change	Percent of Boys with Fewer Arrests			
	Total % With More	Over 5 More	3-4 More	1-2 More	Total	1-2 Less	3-4 Less	Over 5 Less	Total % with Less
Probation Experimentals (N = 69)	7.2	0	0	7.2	56.5	33.3	0	2.9	36.2
Probation Controls (N = 62)	6.5	0	0	6.5	48.4	43.5	1.6	0	45.1
Incarceration Experimentals (N = 37)	5.4*	0	2.7	2.7	51.4	40.5	2.7	0	43.2
Incarceration Controls (N = 132)	22.7*	1.5	3.0	18.2	38.6	28.8	7.6	2.3	38.7

*Differences Statistically Significant, $Z = 2.38$, $P < .05$.

mentals and 42 percent of the controls had no high-serious arrests prior to intervention (cf. Table A-6). Equivalent figures for the probation experimentals and controls were 56 and 60 percent, respectively. Consequently, unless the effects of intervention were highly deleterious, one would expect this pattern to be repeated during the follow-up years.

Table 10-9 suggests that, in general, it was. The proportion showing no change in each group remained quite high: around 50 percent in the three community groups and 40 percent in the incarcerated control group.

Given this fact, the most crucial question in terms of crime control—and it is a grave question—is whether there is evidence of an increase in the number of boys involved in high-serious offenses following intervention. If, as is often assumed, correctional programs do more to educate offenders in ways of increasing, rather than reducing crime, we could find significant increases. That was not the case, however.

Table 10-9 shows that only about 7 percent of the two probation groups had more high-serious arrests after intervention than they did before. And, in every case, those arrests involved no more than one or two additional violations. Surprisingly, the increase for the incarceration experimentals was slightly lower at 5 percent. The number of boys in these groups who committed more, very serious offenses, therefore, was small.

Only the figures for the boys who were incarcerated proved exceptional. Over one-fifth of them had more arrests after incarceration than before. Although most of these arrests involved only one or two additional violations per boy, many of them were very serious (see Chapter 6). The discrepancy between the controls and the experimentals (23 vs. 5 percent) was considerable. In fact, it was the only case in which a statistically significant difference ($P < .05$) appeared in this table. Once again, there is evidence that incarceration was not as successful in reducing the number of boys involved in postrelease crime as was the experimental community program.

On the more optimistic side, it should not escape unnoticed that almost four out of ten boys in every group, including those who were incarcerated, had fewer high-serious arrests after intervention. And in the case of the incarcerated boys, this included a group of 10 percent who had more than three, even four or five, fewer such arrests. When those boys who had fewer arrests are weighed against those who had more, it can be seen that intervention, even incarceration, may not have had more negative than positive effects.

Implications

This chapter has shown that one's interpretation of correctional effectiveness can vary considerably depending upon its measurement in absolute or relative terms. Earlier chapters were concerned with effectiveness in absolute terms. If this criterion were rigorously applied to the findings, they would suggest that all of the programs under study could easily be labeled failures. For example, it was shown in Chapter 9 (Table 9-3) that if failure were defined as including all offenders who were arrested at least once during the four-year follow-up period, the failure rate for the three community programs would be sixty percent or more, and that for the incarcerated boys as high as 80 percent. The picture would be dismal indeed.

In contrast, by the use of *relative* measurement in this chapter, it was shown that postintervention rates were reduced by as much as from 60 to 70 percent in the three community groups, and by 25 percent in the incarcerated group. In every case, a statistically significant and substantively great reduction in the offense rate was observed, the only exception being on low-serious, juvenile-status offenses for the incarcerated boys. Otherwise, there was little evidence that official arrest rates were anywhere so great following intervention as they were before.

The evidence also indicated that significant reductions were made, not only in the number of postintervention arrests, but in the number of offenders who were arrested. In every program, those delinquents who committed *fewer* offenses after intervention far exceeded the number who committed more offenses. Even though delinquency was not totally cut off, like water through a spigot, the overall flow was diminished considerably.

The implications are manifold. The measurement of effectiveness in absolute terms provided virtually no clues that changes of this magnitude were occurring. The uncovering of such information was precluded by its concern with postintervention behavior. To be sure, the absolute analysis did highlight some of the most important differences between groups, especially the suggestion that incarceration was less effective than experimental community intervention. But even here, some subtleties were missed which the relative form of analysis picked up. One good example had to do with the long-term effects of intervention. When the two probation groups were compared, it was found that reductions in offense behavior after one year in the experimental group were significantly greater than in the control group. The experimental program seemed to have a more immediate impact. Yet, after one year, these immediate effects seemed to wane. Differences in subsequent years were not significant.

By contrast, the pattern of differences between the two incarceration groups was just the opposite. After the first year, offense reductions in both were considerable, and about equal. Each year thereafter, however, differences between them began to increase. For the experimentals, the gap between preintervention and postintervention arrest rates tended to widen with each passing year, while just the opposite was true for the incarceration control group. Their postintervention offense rate tended to catch up with the preintervention rate the longer they were followed. Reductions diminished. And while the analysis showed that most boys in each group tended to commit fewer rather than more offenses after intervention, the general trend favoring the experimentals persisted here as well. No matter what kinds of offenses were looked at, larger numbers of controls than experimentals were involved in committing them. In contrast to the two probation groups, it was the observed differences over the long run that was the most telling thing about this comparison. For whatever reason, the experimental community program seemed to have a more lasting impact on those assigned to it than did the incarceration control program.

As a result of analyzing effectiveness in relative terms, two important conclusions are evident: (1) that important changes occurred *within* groups that would not have been observed had evaluation been conducted exclusively in absolute terms; and (2) that, by using the before and after approach, a number of more definitive differences *between* groups were also uncovered. There seems to be little question that the comparison of preintervention and postintervention rates added a great deal to the analysis.

In speculating on the implications of this finding, one conclusion seems plausible. Since the use of before-and-after analysis is uncommon in corrections, it is possible that evaluative research, like correctional programming itself, may be the victim of a pervasive myth; namely, that absolute and irrevocable change in delinquents is a realistic goal, and that it can be achieved in a relatively short period of time. If that goal is accepted as reasonable, then it follows that research should be designed to determine whether it is achieved. However, if that goal is not reasonable, research will be directed to the uncovering of evidence of limited significance.

Not only does the absolutist approach tend to ignore the complexities associated with changing human behavior and providing realistic opportunities for delinquents, but it raises the haunting possibility that important changes are being overlooked by research. The insensitivity of evaluational measures to relative improvements may be doing harm both to delinquents, and to the correctional programs that work with them. Had only absolute measures been used in this study, significant reductions in criminal behavior would have been missed. The extent to which real changes had taken place would have been missed.

A more reasonable approach would seem to be one that combines both relative measurement and a long-range perspective of change. It should not be forgotten that, quite aside from whatever help correctional programs may be able to give, delinquents, themselves, may go through a period of maturational reform in which their criminal acts are reduced spontaneously, if not eliminated entirely. Not only should correctional programs be designed to facilitate rather than hinder this reform, but correctional research should assist in identifying ways by which it might be encouraged.

With reference to the relevance of a long-range perspective for correctional planning, it should be noted that one of the greatest problems habitual delinquents face is their lack of affective and instrumentally successful ties to the basic institutions of society—to the family, school, conventional friends, or world of work. Having been cut off from these institutions, they have little at stake in them. It may well be, therefore, that the most successful correctional programs will not be those that further disrupt the individual's community ties, but which help to strengthen them. Certainly, the findings of this study would support that conclusion. Banishment to a total institution was the least successful of all the approaches. As a consequence, the best role for corrections may be a facilitator role; e.g., the agency that is both a community change agent and an advocate for the delinquent. It would be the task of corrections to get the offender back on the institutional track, not pull him further from it, as the community would often like.

To be sure, there would be times in which the need to protect the community would require that the offender be removed to a secure place, but perhaps even that should be a part of a larger plan designed to return him as soon as possible, through a series of gradients, to the struggles of community life. Were this approach taken, the task of measuring effectiveness in relative terms would make a great deal of sense. Research could then be concerned with two things: (1) the extent to which progressive changes are observable in offender behavior over longer periods of time; and (2) the extent to which correctional programs, themselves, are able to introduce community change. The successful reintegration of the offender is going to require both—changes on the offender's part but much greater institutional change as well. Evaluational research that is concerned with both is that which is most likely to provide important leads for the future.

Research must confront a difficult problem that is generated as much by nonscientific bias as by methodological complexity. The bias is inherent in the contradictory and inconsistent ways with which evidence on correctional effectiveness is often greeted. It seems to be associated with an absolutist approach to evaluation.

If evidence is presented showing that a correctional program has high recidivism rates, when measured in absolute terms, then that evidence is readily accepted. The program is blamed for failure and the conclusion is made that its methods do not work. On the other hand, if evidence is presented that, in relative terms, postintervention offense rates are lower than preintervention rates, a curious switch takes place. While the reduction in offense behavior is acknowledged, there is a reluctance to give any credit to the program for it. Instead, the tendency is to assume that any constructive changes were due, not to the program itself, but to such outside factors as class membership or maturational reform.

Actually, there are some sound reasons why one must be very cautious in assuming that reductions in offense behavior can automatically be attributed to correctional programs. It is highly possible that, in some cases, the chance factors associated with more arrests, ethnic status, age or other influences were more responsible than programs. Nevertheless, those who cling to the absolutist bias must recognize that they cannot have it both ways. They cannot reasonably assume that all recidivism is due to the failure of correctional programs, while assuming that all reductions in offense behavior are due to factors with which those programs had nothing to do.

Inconsistent biases of this type do little to resolve the problems involved. Instead, what is needed are more sensitive measures designed to sort out the influences that are at work—those influences, good and bad, that can be attributed to correctional programming, and those for which correctional programs can take no credit.

Two examples come immediately to mind. The first is maturational reform, which has already been mentioned. Maturational reform refers to the general assumption that the law violations of young people tend to diminish as they move from adolescence into adulthood. Whether this is due to an increased sense of responsibility attendant to becoming an adult, or to the fact that many juveniles are arrested for acts that are not illegal when they become adults, there is some evidence that age is inversely related to the chances of further law violation (Glaser, 1964:36; Wilkins, 1969:54-56). If that is the case, it is possible that some of the postintervention reductions observed in this study were due to maturational reform, the effects of the various programs notwithstanding. To the extent that this occurred, it would be important to separate the two effects, and to see how much, if any, can be attributed to the programs involved.

The second example has to do with what is known as the "regression effect" (Campbell and Stanley, 1963:10-12). Whenever any subjects are selected for an experimental study because of their extremity on some variable—in this case delinquent acts—there seems to be a tendency for them to regress toward the mean on any subsequent measurement—a tendency for the subjects to appear less extreme than they did initially. To the extent that the regression affect was operant in this study, we would expect the various groups to appear less delinquent on the follow-up than they did on the pretest.

The effects of regression can be controlled in making postintervention comparisons between experimental and control groups when random selection is used. One group might be expected to regress as much as the other. In this particular analysis, there are two problems. First, there is really no way of telling how much of the reductions in offense behavior that occurred *within* groups was due to the regression effect and how much to the effects of programming. The argument could be made that all the reductions were due to the regression effect. Any such argument is weakened by the fact that reductions, especially in the three community groups, were large. It hardly seems possible that they could be due entirely to regression. There is both theory and evidence which suggests that repeat offenders of the type included in this study are well known to the police and are more likely than others to be picked up again after release. Once labeled as serious delinquents, the chances are increased, not decreased, that they will be rearrested. While it is impossible to say that none of the large reductions were due to regression, it seems unlikely that all were due to it.

The second problem has to do with the fact that random selection for the incarcerated groups broke down. While important reductions occurred within each of them, one cannot be completely confident that the large differences *between* them were due to differential programming. It is possible that postintervention differences favoring the experimentals were due to uncontrolled variations in the samples, not to variations in intervention.

Because of the importance of these kinds of problems, the next chapter will be devoted to an analysis of programmatic effects. By controlling for a number of outside variables, an attempt will be made to determine the extent to which the various outcomes were attributable to the programs studied, or to other variables over which they had little control.

11

Outcome Effects Attributable to Intervention

This chapter is devoted to an effort to determine whether the marked reductions in offense and offender rates that were observed earlier can be attributed, at least in part, to the effects of intervention, or whether other factors such as age and social status were the deciding influences. A second objective will be to determine whether the various kinds of programs had differential effects. It is not enough merely to indicate that reductions occurred, or that differences between programs were present. Some effort must be made as well to determine whether the effects of intervention were actually greater than might have been expected otherwise. It is not out of the realm of possibility that some, or even all programs, actually impeded rather than encouraged change. Although reductions did occur, they might have been even greater had the programs not been used.

Given the complexity of such issues, it is impossible to exhaust all possible sources of explanation. It is impossible to say what part of the reductions in offense behavior were due to regression effects—i.e. to the tendency for the behaviors of these serious delinquents to regress spontaneously toward more normal levels. Not only is there an absence of any method for placing a numerical value upon the amount of regression that might be expected, but regression, itself, might be impeded by the fact that the boys under study have been labeled as delinquents. There are many who believe that the chances of being rearrested are greater after an adolescent has become delinquent than they were before. All that one can do is suggest that regression might have occurred but that its magnitude, if it was present, cannot be estimated.

The possible effects of two other relevant factors can be examined: age and social class. Age is presumed to be of crucial significance because of its contribution to maturational reform. The notion of maturational reform generally suggests that, with the onset of adult roles and expectations, the deviant behavior of the adolescent years tends to decline. It is contended, as well, that there is more to maturational reform than the mere fact that juvenile status arrests automatically disappear when the adolescent achieves legal adulthood. Rather, the relation between age and delinquency seems to be curvilinear, starting at a low point at the onset of adolescence, achieving a high point during the period of middle and later adolescence, and declining with the approach of adulthood. If this pattern is a general one, its impact should be apparent in outcome findings, the effects of intervention notwithstanding.

Social status may also be of great importance because of its possible impact upon offender adjustment. Almost without exception, writings on the subject suggest that delinquents of low social status will have the greatest problems of adaption. Born into conditions of poverty, deprived of intellectual and interpersonal stimulation, and officially labeled as deviant, they will be terribly handicapped, if not doomed to failure, both during and following the correctional experience. Not only are they less able to meet educational and work standards, but they are downgraded socially. In contrast to delinquents of higher status, their chances for remaining out of trouble will be seriously hampered. If these assumptions are true, they, too, should have an effect upon outcome findings. In contrast with maturational reform, their effects should be negative rather than positive.

In looking at the effects of age and social class upon delinquency rates—both before and after—two steps will be taken. First, the relationship of each variable to delinquency will be examined in a separate analysis. This will have methodological as well as substantive significance, providing information on possible approaches to measurement as well as indicating how the effects of age and class should be interpreted. Second, a multiple regression analysis will be run that assesses both the independent and joint effects of age, class and intervention upon outcome.

Age and Delinquency

In studying age and delinquency, the first set of correlations are simple, zero order correlations between the age of offenders and the number of official offenses for different time periods. They will help to suggest not only whether the two are related, but whether, if they are, the relationship is linear or curvilinear, positive or negative. These questions will be explored both before and after intervention, and in terms of the whole eight years during which delinquents were followed. The findings are displayed in Table 11-1.

Considering the four years *prior* to intervention, two major findings may be observed. First, they indicate that the relationship between age and delinquency in each sample was positive, whether measured in linear terms by Pearsonian *r*, or in curvilinear terms by *eta*. As age went up, so did delinquency. However, the size of both kinds of coefficients was not large, suggesting that the relationship was not a very strong one. This finding, however, may be the consequence of the method that was used to select the various samples. Before any boy could be included in the study, he already must have had several official offenses. Whether young or old, he would not have been included had this not been the case. It is possible that the findings were affected by this fact and that the sample is not typical of delinquents or adolescents generally.

Second, the sizes of the *eta* coefficients (ranging from a low of .11 for the probation control group to a high of .41 for the incarceration experimentals) were larger than those of the Pearsonian *r*'s (ranging from .05 to .33).

Apparently, the relationship between age and delinquency, prior to intervention, was more curvilinear than linear. Again, because the coefficients were relatively low, the increase in association, using eta, was not dramatic.

When relationships were examined, using official offenses four years *after* intervention, a very different picture emerges. Not only were both kinds of coefficients considerably larger, but all of the linear correlations (Pearsonian *r*'s) were negative. This time the findings suggested that delinquency *decreased* with an increase in age, as the maturational reform hypothesis implies. But perhaps more significant, there is a suggestion that the two experimental programs may have done more to speed up this process than the two control programs.

There are two reasons for this conclusion. First, as indicated in Chapter 2, the two experimental groups were younger than the two control groups by half a year in each instance. This being the case, one might expect that the negative relationship between age and delinquency in the experimental groups would be lower than that of the control groups if maturational reform were the primary influence, the reason being that younger boys would be expected to reform less rapidly than older ones.

This is not what the findings show. The negative relationships for the two experimental groups were considerably greater than those for the control groups— −.41 for the *probation* experimentals versus −.04 for the controls, and −.48 for the incarceration experimentals versus −.16 for the controls. Since the *eta* coefficients also reveal differences of a similar magnitude, the data imply,

Table 11-1

Correlations Between Official Delinquent Offenses and Age* for Experimental and Control Groups According to Various Time Periods

| | Time Periods | | | | | |
| | 4 Years Before | | 4 Years After | | 4 Years Before and After Combined | |
Sample Categories	Pearsonian r	Eta	Pearsonian r	Eta	Pearsonian r	Eta
Probation Experimental	.05	.28	−.41	.60	−.24	.33
Probation Control	.07	.11	−.04	.22	−.07	.19
Incarceration Experimental	.33	.41	−.48	.52	−.06	.24
Incarceration Control	.11	.25	−.16	.20	−.05	.09
All Samples	.15	.16	−.09	.18	−.01	.11

*Age is defined as age to nearest birthday at time of assignment to experimental or control groups.

overall, that maturational reform may have been precipitated at a faster rate by the two experimental programs. It appears that the decline is more likely to be curvilinear than linear.

The pattern for the entire eight-year span also confirms this conclusion. When the relationship between age and delinquency is calculated, covering the periods both before and after intervention, the linear relationship almost washes away. There is clear indication that both overall and within samples, the curvilinear model does fit the distributions more adequately than does the linear model. The linear coefficients are all negative, suggesting that the decline in delinquency with advancing age was greater than the increase. This might have had something to do with intervention, but the small size of the linear coefficients, combined with the more predominant curvilinear relationship precludes the imputation of much meaning to this particular set of findings.

A Synthetic Age Cohort

One reason these findings are not definitive is because the various samples were selected for the purpose of studying experimental intervention, not for studying the relation of age to delinquency. The ideal design for the latter purpose would have been a panel design in which boys of the same age were first selected, and then followed over time in order to study their rates of delinquency as they grew older. Had this been done, the task of assessing the relation of age to delinquency would have been much simpler. All boys in this study were not of the same age when selected, vastly complicating the analysis. For example, the 8-year period covered by the study for a boy who was 17 when he was selected was from age 13 to age 21. By contrast, the period covered by a boy who was 14 when he was selected was from age 10 to age 18. The foregoing analysis was not able to take full advantage of a panel design.

One method for overcoming this problem, at least partially, was to construct a *synthetic age cohort* which could then be treated somewhat like a panel design. This was accomplished by calculating the mean number of delinquent acts for each age group in each sample for a period ranging from age ten to age twenty-one. Once this was done, it was possible to determine whether offense means went up or down in different age groups. Although this was not the same thing as taking a group of ten-year-olds and then studying their offense patterns until they reached 21, it did provide an approximation.

Figure 11-1 provides a graphic representation of the relationship between age and delinquency for the synthetic cohort for the four years *prior* to intervention. The most striking thing is the steepness of the curve. For the two incarceration groups, especially, there was a rapid rise in delinquency rates before intervention, beginning as early as age eleven and continuing on, almost uninterrupted, until age sixteen or seventeen. The rise for the two probation

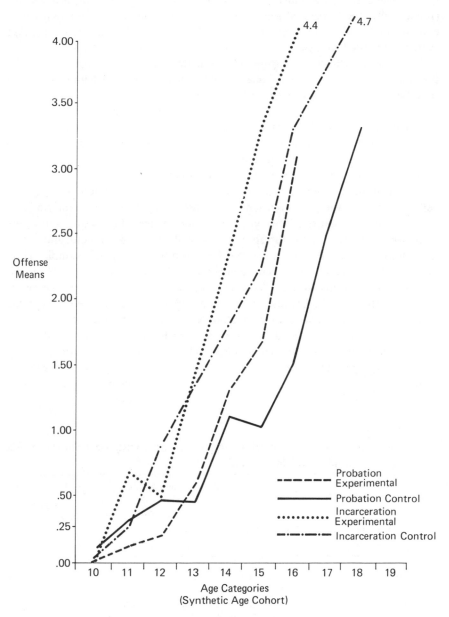

Figure 11-1. Offense Means by Synthetic Cohort Ages, Based on Offense Four Years Before Intervention.

groups, while great, was much less dramatic, especially during the earlier years. (Incidentally, the horizontal gap at the top of the graph between the two sets of experimental and control groups represents the fact that the experimentals averaged about a half a year younger in each case than the controls.)

The pattern shown in Figure 11-1 for the synthetic cohort implies the possibility of a much stronger relationship between age and delinquency than that shown in the first analysis. This can be confirmed by reference to Table 11-2. *Eta* coefficients in that table show that the relationship between age and delinquency prior to intervention ranged in value from .70 to .83, depending upon the sample involved. If all samples were taken collectively, around 70 percent of the variance in delinquency rates before intervention could be explained by knowing the ages of the offenders involved. This is an impressive finding that underscores the importance of assessing the relation of age to delinquency following intervention.[1] In interpreting these and later findings, keep in mind the nature of the synthetic cohort. Since all boys were not of the same age when selected for the study, each of them could not contribute to all the offense means that were calculated. To return to our original example, a boy who was 14 when selected would contribute only to the means for 10- to 18 year-olds, while a boy who was 17 when selected would contribute to the means for 13- to 21 year-olds. The results that were obtained could not be precisely the same as if a real cohort were selected, all of whom were the same age.

With that thought in mind, our next concern is with what happened to the relationship between age and delinquency following intervention. Did the sharp rise in rates continue with age, or was there a downward turn, suggesting maturational reform? Was there any evidence that the postintervention pattern

Table 11-2
Eta Coefficients Between Official Delinquency and Synthetic Cohorts by Age According to Sample and Time Periods

Sample Categories	Time Periods					
	4 Years Before		4 Years After		4 Years Before and After Combined	
	Eta	Eta^2	Eta	Eta^2	Eta	Eta^2
Probation Experimental	.80	.64	.76	.58	.89	.79
Probation Control	.81	.66	.98	.96	.94	.88
Incarceration Experimental	.70	.49	.88	.77	.82	.67
Incarceration Control	.83	.69	.96	.92	.92	.85
All Samples	.84	.70	.98	.95	.93	.87

was affected differentially by variations in intervention? Answers to these questions are shown in Figure 11-2.

Note that, in general, delinquency rates for 14- and 15-year-olds continued to accelerate after intervention, the effects of programming notwithstanding. Then, by contrast, the rates for boys over 16 showed a dramatic decrease. Delinquent acts in every group went down sharply. These data would suggest that age has an effect upon delinquency rates independent of intervention. The rates of younger boys may continue to go up, or at least to remain as high as they were before, even if intervention occurs. Then, at around age 16, the rates may start to decline, perhaps precipitously.

There is no way of saying for certain whether, or how much, intervention may have had a general effect on these patterns, but Figure 11-2 does suggest that different programs had different effects. Consider first the two *incarceration* groups. While the delinquent acts of fourteen- and fifteen-year-olds in those two groups continued to go up dramatically after intervention, the rise for the experimental group was not so great. Then, at age sixteen, and thereafter, there was a precipitous decline in delinquency in both groups as age increased. This decline again favored the experimentals. While crime rates for the experimentals dropped to almost zero at ages eighteen through twenty-one, they remained much higher for the incarcerated controls. Although the rates for the controls declined, they did so at a pace that was much less precipitous than that for the experimentals.

The pattern for the two *probation* groups was not so marked. Most important, the delinquency rates after intervention were nowhere so high for these two groups as they were for the two incarceration groups. Nevertheless, there were some interesting differences between them. The delinquency rate for the 15 year-old probation experimentals went up markedly after intervention, while that for the controls remained about the same. Then, differences began to appear in the opposite direction, primarily because the delinquency rate for older experimental boys went down faster than it did for older control boys. At age sixteen, rates were about the same; at age 17, there was a divergence favoring the experimentals. Thereafter, this divergence, though not great, persisted. In fact, as the crime rate for older experimentals almost reached zero, it actually went up again for controls.

In substantive terms, these findings have several implications. First, there does indeed seem to be some evidence favoring the maturational reform hypothesis. Despite the possible effects of intervention in general terms, delinquency tends to increase with age until boys reach 15 or 16 years, and then it seems to decline precipitously. Significantly, this pattern was most pronounced among the more serious incarceration groups. In both cases, radically different forms of intervention did not seem to be successful in fully deterring the younger boys. It was only when subjects became older that delinquency rates went down.

At the same time, the evidence does not support the notion that this pattern

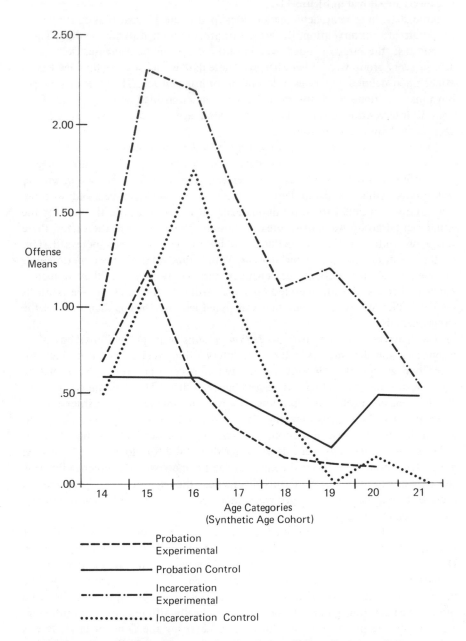

Figure 11–2. Offense Means by Synthetic Age Cohort Based on Offenses Four Years After Intervention.

was totally unaffected by different forms of intervention. That was certainly not the case. There are two good examples to the contrary which have not been explicitly cited. The first has to do with younger offenders, those from 14 to 16 years of age.

The data in Figure 11-2 suggest that, for this group, the less intensive a program is, the more effective it may be. In the experimental community program, for example, the pace at which younger but seriously delinquent boys continued to be delinquent after intervention was not so great as among younger boys who were incarcerated. Similarly, but further down the gradient of controls, the violation rate for younger boys who were assigned to the generally unstructured activities of regular probation remained about the same after intervention as before. The rate for comparable boys in the more intensive experimental program went up. It is possible that intensive programs may do more to hinder maturational reform in young and impressionable boys than to encourage it. Perhaps such programs help to reinforce a delinquent self-concept rather than to eliminate it, something that would be the opposite of that intended. Whatever the explanation, a gradient of effects was suggested by the findings in which there was an increase in violation rates among younger offenders that coincided with an increase in the intensiveness of programming.

By contrast, a quite different pattern was revealed for older boys. For those over sixteen, the experimental program seems to have been more effective than the two control programs. It seemed to accelerate the pace of maturational reform, and, at the same time, to have a more lasting effect. The older the experimental boys became, the lower their violation rates tended to be when compared to boys of equivalent ages in the two control groups. Figure 11-2 shows that while delinquency was almost nonexistent among experimental boys when they reached the ages 18 to 21, boys of similar ages in the two control program were still continuing to commit illegal acts.

It is difficult to know for certain, but it seems likely that two unique features of the experimental program may have accelerated maturational reform for the older boys—e.g., their participation in the problem-solving functions of the daily group sessions, and their participation in a city work program for pay. The fact that they had to find a balance between their habits of the past and the demands of regular work, and that group sessions placed them in the position of having to deal with the many problems precipitated by their delinquent status, may have provided them with a perspective not found in more traditional programs. These activities, taking place in the open community, could have speeded up and sustained the maturational process. Yet, it should not be forgotten that while program activities which thrust offenders into a more mature role were helpful to older boys, they were less helpful to younger ones. Perhaps too much was demanded of the younger ones. In any event, some other form of intervention for them, perhaps less intensive, is suggested.

Finally, it is important for methodological reasons to refer again to Table

11-2. Along with Figures 11-1 and 11-2, it strongly suggests that the relationship of age to delinquency, both following intervention and during the whole period of adolescence, is highly curvilinear. The size of the *eta* coefficients in Table 11-2 strongly supports the notion that delinquency accelerates until about age sixteen, and then curves rapidly downward. The correlation for the entire period, for all samples, was .93 with an explained variance of .87. Even though this general pattern may be affected differentially by programs of different kinds, it is an impressive one, suggesting two things. First, it is clear that age is highly related to delinquent behavior. To ignore its impact in assessing correctional outcome, therefore, may result in serious distortions. Second, since the relation of age to delinquency is curvilinear, analytic methods that did not take that fact into account could also be misleading. These findings, as a result, underscore the importance of a later analysis in which both the independent and interactive effects of age and intervention are assessed.

Social Class and Delinquency

It will be recalled that the second variable to be studied in its relation both to delinquency and the effects of intervention is social class. It has often been suggested that class is a variable whose impact is not only highly important as a cause of delinquency but whose effect is likely to confound the effects of intervention.

Social class in this study was measured by means of a ten-point scale on which each boy's father's occupation was ranked (cf. Empey, 1956:703-709). This ranking then served as the basis for estimating the boy's status, and for determining how that status was related to the commission of delinquent acts, both before and after intervention. Table 11-3 presents a brief summary of the findings.

First, when the relation of class to delinquency was measured both by Pearsonian *r* and *eta* coefficients, the *eta* coefficients were larger for every sample, both before and after intervention. The data clearly suggest that the relationship in these samples is more curvilinear than linear. This finding, as a result, is contrary to the common assumption that class and delinquency are related in a negative and linear fashion; e.g., the lower the class, the higher the delinquency. There is very little support for that notion in these data, however. There were a few instances in which the linear coefficients were negative, but they were so small in size that little confidence could be placed in them.

A careful examination of the scattergram that led to the finding of a curvilinear relationship revealed a complex pattern. The scattergram for the periods both before and after intervention was in the form of an inverted "Z." This meant that delinquency rates were the highest for boys who were at the lowest and middle points of the class spectrum, and lowest for boys whose class

Table 11-3
Correlations Between Official Delinquent Offenses and Social Class for Experimental and Control Groups According to Various Time Periods

Sample Categories	4 Years Before		4 Years After		4 Years Before and After Combined	
	Pearsonian r	Eta	Pearsonian r	Eta	Pearsonian r	Eta
Probation Experimental	.02	.31	.04	.16	.05	.24
Probation Control	.01	.26	−.03	.23	−.12	.36
Incarceration Experimental	−.20	.42	.22	.41	.04	.40
Incarceration Control	.10	.27	−.02	.18	.00	.24
All Samples	.02	.14	.03	.15	−.02	.17

membership was lower-middle and upper. As suggested, this pattern appeared after, as well as before, intervention. In fact the plottings look almost identical. Thus, in addition to the fact that a linear pattern was not observed, the data suggest that intervention, in all its different forms, did very little to change the pattern that prevailed before intervention. Boys whose status was either very low, or was at the midpoint of the prestige continuum, were the most delinquent, while lower-middle and upper-status boys continued to be the least delinquent.

These findings probably have more significance for the purpose of assessing intervention effects upon these particular groups than they do for testing delinquency theory in general. The reason is that the samples are made up entirely of serious delinquents, and include no nondelinquents. Until nondelinquents, and delinquents with less serious records are included, it is impossible to say what the more general relationship between class and delinquency might be. So long as measurement is based upon extreme groups who comprise only the most delinquent end of the spectrum, findings can easily be atypical. The only point that might be made is that there is need for caution in the generalizations that are made about class membership and delinquency. When individuals, rather than groups or demographic units, are the object of analysis, a growing number of studies tend to question the prevailing assumption that delinquency rates are highest among the lower classes and decline progressively as one goes up the class ladder (cf. Empey and Lubeck, 1971 for a summary of this literature). As this analysis has implied, the relationship may be far more complex and less definitive than that.

For this particular analysis, the overriding significance of these findings is twofold: (1) the suggestion that, if social class is to be included in a predictive model for these samples, steps must be taken to treat it as a curvilinear rather than linear variable; and (2) that the relationship between class and delinquency, prior to intervention, seemed relatively unchanged by the intervention experience. It may be that the effects of class membership are relatively unaffected by the correctional experience. Consequently, there is evidence that, along with age and the intervention experience, the effects of class upon correctional outcome should be taken into account. This will be done in the section that follows.

Multiple Regression Analysis of Intervention Effects

Under ordinary circumstances, a multiple regression analysis (Baggaley, 1964; Blalock, 1960; Bryant, 1960; Efroymson, M.A., 1960; Guilford, J.P., 1956; Hoel, 1962; Kelley, 1924; Mandel, 1964; McNemar, 1962; Walker and Lev, 1953) is ideally suited for the task at hand; namely, the determination of the independent and interactive effects of age, class, and different forms of intervention upon official delinquency rates. Unfortunately, however, the application of a multiple regression analysis assumes that the relationships between independent and dependent variables are linear, and that the effects of independent and dependent variables upon the dependent variable are also linear. It is clear that to conduct such an analysis in this case would be to violate basic assumptions. Some other alternative had to be found.

This alternative involved the conduct of a multiple regression analysis using "dummy variables" (Morgan, et al., 1962; Suits, 1957; Gujarati, 1970a,b). Setting up dummy variables is a simple and useful method of introducing into a regression analysis information that is contained in variables that are not conventionally measured on a numerical scale or which do not have a linear relationship to the dependent variable. The technique itself is not new, but its application in sociological analysis is rare (Blau and Duncan, 1967; Curtis, et al., 1967; Ezekiel, 1941; Morgan, et al., 1962; Treiman, 1966).

The procedure involves the conversion of each independent variable—e.g., age, class, and intervention—into a set of dummy variables, one for each of the age categories at which boys were assigned to intervention (14, 15, 16, 17 and 18), one for each social class level (lower, upper-lower, middle, upper-middle, and upper), and one for each kind of intervention (probation experimental, probation control, incarceration experimental and incarceration control). Each of these dummy variables takes the value of "one" if an individual belongs to it and "zero" if he does not. Instead of a single regression coefficient for a value like age, we have a set (one attached to each age category) constrained so that their weighted sum is zero. The advantage of using these dummy variables is that the restrictive assumptions about the linearity of effect can be avoided. It is still possible to determine from the products of the regression analysis the independent and joint effects of each of the dummy variables.

As Suits (1957:551) suggests, one often encounters suspicion when dummy variables are used. Yet, as he points out,

... There is nothing artificial about such variables; indeed, in a fundamental sense, they are more properly scaled than conventionally measured variables. If we can see the task of regression analysis to be that of providing an estimate of the dependent variable, given certain information, the use of linear regression yields biased estimates in the event of curvature. By partitioning the scale of a conventionally measured variable into intervals and defining a set of dummy variables on them, we obtain unbiased estimates since the regression coefficients of the dummy variables conform to any curvature that is present.

This procedure can be fruitfully applied to a variable like age, the influence of which is frequently U shaped. Attempts to use chronological age as a linear variable may lead not only to the bias mentioned above, but to the failure of the variable to show significance in the regression. Although we sometimes resort to the use of a quadratic form in age to capture this curvature, there is little additional difficulty and in general better results in the application of a system of "dummy variables" defined by classes.

The technique of dummy variable analysis is nothing more than a simple extension of multiple correlation to a situation where the explanatory factors are membership in subclasses like age, class or different forms of intervention rather than subclasses characterized by numerical values.[2]

The analysis which follows will be conducted in a series of steps each of which works progressively toward the explication of two major issues: (1) the extent to which intervention, age and social class have an effect on postrelease delinquency, both independently and in combination; and (2) the extent to which the various forms of intervention had differential effects on postrelease delinquency, independent of the effects of age and class. As will be seen, however, the task of explicating these issues is not a simple one.

General Effects of Intervention, Age and Class

The first step involved an assessment of the separate and combined relationships of the three independent variables to delinquency. It is best conceived as requiring five types, or levels, of analysis.

Type 1 is concerned with determining the independent relationships of intervention (without distinction as to kind), age and class to delinquency. The findings derived from this type of analysis ignore the joint and interactive effects of the different kinds of variables taken in combination.

Type 2 analysis increases in complexity. It involves the joint relationships of dual sets of variables to delinquency e.g., the four interventions and five ages together, the five interventions and five classes together, and the five ages and five classes in combination. While this type of analysis moves us a step closer to assessing the total effects of these sets of variables to delinquency, it does not build any interactions among them into the analysis.

Type 3 analysis, however, does attack this problem. It requires the use of dummy variables that reflect in detail the interactive as well as joint characteristics of dual sets of independent variables. For example, the four kinds of intervention and the five age categories would be combined as follows: intervention 1 and age 14 as one dummy variable, intervention 1 and age 15 as a second, and so on until intervention 4 and age 18 are included. In all, twenty new dummy variables would be created. In the same way, the interactions among the two remaining sets of variables—intervention and class, and age and class—were also assessed. When the four intervention and five class categories were joined, another set of 20 dummy variables was created, while the combination of the five age and class categories resulted in a 25 variable set.

This type of analysis will eventually be very useful because it is a necessary step to make definitive interpretations of the effects of intervention on delinquency. In order to do this, we must be able to separate from the total effects of all variables on delinquency, the effects of age, the effects of social class, and the effects of interaction between age and social class.

Type 4 analysis moves us even further in this direction. Along with the twenty-five combination variables of age and social class, it adds the effects of the four kinds of interventions as four independent dummy variables, making 29 variables in all. The eventual utility of this type of analysis will be the assessment of the independent effects of each of the interventions (in the form of beta weights) while controlling for the effects of age and class, and the interactions between them.

Type 5 analysis is the most complex of all. Using all three independent variables, it involves the formation of multiple-variable permutations as dummy variables, e.g., intervention 1, age 14, and lower social class as one dummy variable, intervention 1, age 14 and upper-lower class as a second variable, and so on until intervention 4, age 18 and upper class are included. In all, these three-variable permutations produce a string of 100 dummy variables: four kinds of intervention multipled by five age categories multipled by five class categories. Thus, for each individual, information that goes into the regression analysis is a string of zeros except for the one permutation of intervention, age, and class to which he belongs, in which case a "one" is inserted. By constructing the final data set in this way, the independent effects of each of the dummy variables can be assessed by examining their Beta weights, and a multiple correlation coefficient can be obtained that will ultimately produce the maximum amount of variance that can be explained in delinquency using the three categories of variables, and all interactions among them.

The general results of these five levels of analysis are shown in Table 11-4.

Table 11-4
Multiple Correlations Between Various Combinations of Dummy Variables and Official Delinquency over Four Time Periods

Time Periods After	Type 1 (Independent Relationships)			Type 2 (Joint Relationships)			Type 3 (Interactive Relationships)			Type 4 (Interactive & Joint)	Type 5 (Interactive)
	Interv. (4 Dummy Variables)	Age (5 Dummy Variables)	Class (5 Dummy Variables)	Interv. and Age (9 Dummy Variables)	Interv. and Class (9 Dummy Variables)	Age and Class (10 Dummy Variables)	Interv. and Age (20 Dummy Variables)	Interv. and Class (20 Dummy Variables)	Age and Class (25 Dummy Variables)	Interv., Age, Class (29 Dummy Variables)	Interv., Age, Class (100 Dummy Variables)
1 Year	.30	.10	.15	.31	.35	.20	.33	.38	.27	.41	.49
2 Years	.39	.12	.14	.40	.44	.20	.44	.47	.30	.50	.56
3 Years	.43	.12	.17	.43	.47	.23	.45	.50	.32	.52	.57
4 Years	.43	.14	.17	.44	.48	.24	.46	.51	.34	.53	.58

The dependent variable in this case is all official offenses—ignoring seriousness—for each of the four years after release. The relationships of the various variables, independently and in combination, to postrelease delinquency are shown. It should be remembered, however, that the separate effects of the different programs are not shown in Table 11-4; rather their effects on delinquency are treated as a unit.

Note, first, that there is a general increase in the sizes of the relationships as one moves from the simple to the more complex levels of analysis. Obviously, if there were no increase, the findings would indicate that the prediction of correctional outcome could not be improved by combining the different sets of variables, and taking their interactions into account. However, that was not the case. Age and social class, separately, and intervention when it is added to them, are all related to outcome.

When the effects of different kinds of variables are considered, however, the findings raise some provocative issues. In the Type 1 analysis, for example, the independent relationship of intervention (without distinction as to type) to delinquency was considerably higher than the independent relationship of age and class. After four years of follow-up, for example, the correlation between intervention and delinquency was .43, as contrasted to a correlation of only .14 for the relation of age to delinquency and a value of .17 for the relation of class to delinquency. It seems quite clear that intervention had a definite effect.

When the joint effects of dual sets of these three variables were considered in the Type 2 analysis, the size of the coefficients increased, but the increment that was added by joining the effects of age or class to those of intervention was not great. The original relation of intervention to delinquency, after four years, was .43. When the effects of age were added to it, however, the size of the coefficient rose only by one point to .44. When class was added, it was raised to .48. By contrast, the combined effects of age and class, apart from intervention, were relatively small. The joint relationship of the two to delinquency after four years was only .24.

The size of the coefficients rose again when the interactive, as well as the joint effects of these dual sets, were considered in the Type 3 analysis, but again the rise, even if consistent, was not spectacular. As a consequence, the findings imply, at least initially, that intervention had an effect on postprogram delinquency that was independent of the effects of age and class, and was perhaps of greater size than had been anticipated. For example, the original, independent relationship of intervention to delinquency after four years was .43. After its interactive effects with age had been added to this value, the correlation was only .46. The same was somewhat less true when the interactive effects of class were added, which brought the value to the slightly higher figure of .51. Meanwhile, the interactive effects of age and class, independent of intervention, was only .34.

This is only a suggestive finding since the crucial test will involve the consideration of the joint and interactive effects of all three variables. The findings could change considerably. Nothing has been indicated as to whether the effects of intervention were positive or negative. In order to obtain this information, the Beta coefficients of each of the four different interventions, which will indicate the nature of these effects will have to be considered. This information, however, will be presented later. For now, it is important to consider the remaining information shown in Table 11-4.

The last two columns in that table, representing the fourth and fifth levels of analysis, show two things. First, they show that when the joint and interactive effects of intervention, class and age are examined, the values of the correlation coefficients rise considerably. For example, after 4 years, the relationship of age, class and intervention to delinquency, when their joint and interactive effects are considered in the 100 dummy variable analysis, is .58. By contrast, the dual relationships of intervention and age to delinquency, or of age and class to delinquency, are only .46 and .34 respectively. A reasonably good improvement is made when the effects of intervention, and interactions to intervention, are considered.

Overall, the results shown in Table 11-4 provide information of three types. First, they suggest that intervention does have an effect on postrelease delinquency that is independent of age and class. Second, they indicate the importance of considering the joint and interactive effects of all three independent variables if the maximum amount of variance is to be explained. Finally, the findings provide a good illustration of the flexibility and power of dummy regression analysis for assessing the effects of several independent variables on a dependent variable where curvature is known to exist or is suspected, and where interactions among the independent variables is also suspected. It should be pointed out, however, that it is not entirely necessary to go through all of the steps that were illustrated in Table 11-4. Actually, the last three of the several sets of data shown in the table will suffice. Their potential utility for isolating both the independent and interactive effects of the various forms of intervention, age and class is illustrated in the remaining sections.

Interactive Effects of Age, Class, and Intervention on Offense Seriousness

In this section, the relationships of the three most complex levels of analysis are used to study the joint and interactive effects of the independent variables on offense seriousness. Official delinquency is partitioned into low-, medium- and high-serious levels, and the effects of different combinations of variables upon them are analyzed. The results are shown in Table 11-5.

The first column of the table does not include any indication of intervention effects. Instead, it includes only the 25 dummy variables representing different

Table 11-5
Multiple Correlations Between Various Combinations of Dummy Variables and Three Levels of Offense Seriousness

Time Periods After	Seriousness Categories	Age & Class (25 Dummy Variables)	Age, Class & Intervention (29 Dummy Variables)	Age, Class & Intervention (100 Dummy Variables)
1 Year	Low	.27	.33	.47
	Medium	.26	.38	.48
	High	.20	.29	.40
2 Years	Low	.31	.39	.49
	Medium	.29	.47	.53
	High	.25	.36	.44
3 Years	Low	.30	.42	.52
	Medium	.33	.49	.55
	High	.25	.38	.44
4 Years	Low	.28	.41	.51
	Medium	.33	.50	.56
	High	.32	.42	.47

combinations of age and class, and the interactions between them. Note that the multiple correlations of these two variables with delinquency range in value from a low of .20 to a high of .33. These values represent the effects on delinquency due solely to age and class. Eventually, these effects will have to be extracted from the overall relationship, if the unique effects of intervention are to be made explicit. However, that step is to be taken later. For now, the only thing about them that is of added significance, aside from their general effects, is that the relationship of age and class to medium- and high-serious offenses gradually goes up during the four-year follow-up, while their relationship to low-serious offenses remains about the same. For example, the relationship of age and class to high-serious delinquency after one year was .20, but by the end of the fourth year, it had increased to a value of .32. Meanwhile, the relationship with low-serious delinquency increased only from .27 to .28 over the same time span.

It is possible that this difference is due, at least in part, to the fact that, as boys grew older, they became increasingly less liable for the juvenile-status offenses of which the low-serious offense category was comprised. No longer chargeable with such offenses as they reached adulthood, their commission of such acts would no longer be reflected in the official records. The ability of age, especially, to predict them should not be expected to increase much. This was not true for high-serious offenses, all of which would be reflected in the record. Consequently, this fact would influence the relationships that were observed.

The second column in Table 11-5 represents the effects on delinquency when intervention is first added to the effects of age and class in the form of four dummy variables representing correctional intervention. The coefficients that are shown, however, do *not* reflect the interaction of intervention with age and class, only the joint effects that are produced.

Note that for all levels of seriousness, for all time periods, the size of the coefficients were increased by the introduction of intervention into the model, clearly suggesting that intervention does have an effect, independent of age and class and interactions between age and class. For example, the correlation of age and class with low-serious offenses after four years was .28, but when intervention was added, the relationship rose to a value of .41. Comparable increases for medium-serious offenses were from a value of .33 to a value of .50, and for high-serious offenses from .32 to .42. Furthermore, the sizes of the coefficients, when intervention was included, were not only larger overall, but the differences between them and the first set of coefficients tended to increase with the passage of time; that is, with intervention added to the model, the predictive efficiency of the coefficients gradually increased over the four-year period. This increased efficiency was most pronounced for the medium-serious offenses, which constitute the garden variety of adult as well as juvenile offenses, but it was characteristic of low- and high-serious offenses as well. In fact, the increased ability to predict juvenile-status offenses suggests quite strongly that intervention has an effect, positive or negative, that was not suggested when only age and class alone were considered.

The final column in Table 11-5 (the 100 dummy variable analysis) provides the total relationship of the three variables to delinquency when their interactive as well as their joint effects are taken into account. Again, the size of the coefficients went up, testifying to the impact of intervention and the consequences of interaction among the three independent variables. Obviously, that interaction is important. By taking it into account, an increment was added to the value of every correlation. After four years, for example, the coefficient for low-serious offenses rose from .41 to .51; for medium-serious offenses from .50 to .56; and for high-serious offenses from .42 to .47. While these coefficients, if converted to explained variance, would leave much of the total variance unexplained, they do suggest that intervention, age and class, and the interactions among them, are ones to be reckoned with in any attempt to understand correctional outcome.

Of substantive interest is the fact that the multiple correlations of these three variables with medium-serious delinquency were again the highest correlations observed. This finding may be related to the fact that, of all the three kinds of offenses, the medium-serious offenses were reduced the most after intervention, and thus could be expected to be reflected in these findings. In terms of overall importance, however, the most significant findings were (1) that intervention did seem to add significant increments to observed relationships; and (2) that the interactions among intervention, age and class variables were relatively important ones.

Explained Variance Due to Intervention

Since the analysis has indicated that intervention does seem to have a direct effect on correctional outcome, the next step involves an effort to explicate just what the magnitude of that effect is. The answer can be supplied (1) by converting the multiple correlation coefficients that have already been presented into explained variances; (2) by utilizing the explained variances that included all three independent variables and the interactions among them—e.g., the 100 variable coefficients—as a baseline; and then (3) conducting a series of subtractions which will result in the specification of the relative amounts of explained variance accounted for by the various combinations of variables and interactions among them.

In Table 11-6, these steps are taken. The dependent variable used in the table is all official offenses for the four follow-up years. Since no distinctions with regard to seriousness are made, the data for the analysis are taken from Table 11-4. It provides the correlation coefficients, which after being squared, were converted to explained variance.

Note that the first line in Table 11-6 represents the baseline mentioned above.

Table 11-6
Amounts of Explained Variance in Official Delinquency Attributable to Intervention, Age and Class, and Various Combinations of Them

Sources of Explained Variance	Per Cent of Total Variance by Time Periods			
	1 Year After	2 Years After	3 Years After	4 Years After
1. Total Explained Variance: Intervention-Age-Class and All Interactions [100 Dummy Variables]	24	31	33	33
2. Age-Class and All Interactions [25 Dummy Variables]	7	9	10	10
3. Intervention and Interactions with Intervention [Line 1 minus Line 2]	17	22	23	23
4. Intervention *Plus* Age-Class and Interactions Between Age-Class [29 Dummy Variables]	17	25	27	27
5. Interactions with Intervention [Line 1 minus Line 4]	7	6	6	6
6. Direct Effects of Intervention [Line 1 Minus (Line 2 + Line 5)]	10	16	17	18

Derived from the 100 dummy variables, it represents the maximum amount of variance this model can explain because it includes the total explained variance for all interventions, ages, and classes, and the interactions among them. It will be observed that the amount of variance explained on this line increased over time, from 24 percent after the first year to 33 percent after the third and fourth years. Yet, despite this increase, two-thirds of the variance in delinquency after intervention remains unexplained. Although intervention, age and social class were important, other forces were obviously at work for which this analysis cannot account. The finding illustrates all too clearly the extent to which more information is needed if all of the factors that contribute to correctional outcome are to be explicated.

The second line in Table 11-6 represents that part of the total explained variance that is attributable exclusively to age and social class, and interactions between them. The effects of intervention in this case are left out. The amount of variance contributed by age and class, however, is relatively small, accounting for only 7 percent after the first year, and rising to no more than 10 percent after four years. At first glance, such findings would seem to be contrary to the high curvilinear relationship shown earlier between age and delinquency, but that is not necessarily the case. It is possible that such a relationship may exist and still be consonant with these findings. The reason is that, while age (and class) may contribute to delinquent acts, they may derive their causal effectiveness, at least in part, from their combination with numerous other factors in the environment. While both variables, especially age, are associated with delinquency, that association is not an exclusive one, and not exclusively causal. In this case, it seems highly unlikely that age and class are the sole causes of increases or decreases in postintervention delinquency as an extreme interpretation of the maturational reform hypothesis would suggest. Instead, the relationship of age and class to delinquency is probably affected by the interaction of these variables with other variables, of which intervention would be one.

The information shown on the third line of Table 11-6 seems to substantiate this interpretation. It is obtained by subtracting line two from line one, and represents the explained variance that is due to the direct effects of intervention and its interactions with age and class. As such, it excludes that part of the total explained variance that is due to the direct effects of age and class, and their exclusive interactions with each other.

It can be seen that, of all the variables included in the model, intervention and its interaction with other variables accounted for a large portion of the explained variance. After four years, for example, it accounted for 23 percent of the *total* variance, or 73 percent of all the variance that was explained by this model. In each of the prior years, this same relationship held: at least 70 percent of the *explained* variance was due to intervention and interactions with intervention. These findings provide probably the strongest confirmation of the idea that intervention does have an effect, and that its effect can be sizeable.

The fourth line in Table 11-6 represents another combination of variables, and another way of explicating the sources of explained variance. It represents the effects of intervention, plus the independent effects of age and class, plus the effects produced by the interactions between age and class. The only difference between line four and line one, therefore, is that line four does not include the interactions of intervention with age and class. Thus, it is possible to isolate that portion of the total variance that is due to these interactions by subtracting line four from line one.

The results of the subtraction are shown on line five. It will be noted that the amount of variance due to interaction with intervention is small—7 percent after one year and only 6 percent thereafter. The findings would suggest that the interaction of treatment effects with those of age and class were not of overriding importance. Even though the direct and interactive effects of intervention contributed much more to the total explained variance than did age and social class by themselves, the evidence implies that it was the direct effects of intervention rather than its interaction with age and class that was of greater importance.

This conclusion is confirmed by the findings in line six of Table 11-6. An estimation of the direct effects of intervention is obtained by subtracting lines two and five (the effects of age and class plus the effects of the interactions of age and class with intervention) from line one (the total explained variance). The figures that are derived, ranging from a variance of 10 percent after one year, to variances of 16, 17, and 18 percent after subsequent years, constitute sizeable proportions of the total *explained* variance shown in line one. In all four periods, the direct effects of intervention provide approximately 50 percent of that explained variance. In answering the question whether intervention does have a discernible effect on postintervention delinquency, these findings suggest rather strongly that it does. The direct effects of intervention accounted for about 50 percent of all explained variance, and, when the effects of interactions with treatment were added to the direct effects, the figure rose to 70 percent. Clearly, intervention was an important influence.

This is an important finding because it provides some much needed empirical information. Given the lack of definitive data on correctional effectiveness, the general tendency has been to discount virtually all approaches. At best, the effects of intervention are viewed as making little difference; at worst, they are seen as hindering rather than helping the correctional task.

Since the findings of this chapter have been contrary to the first assumption that the effects of intervention make little difference, there are compelling reasons to examine the second—e.g., that the effects of intervention are negative. Despite evidence that intervention does indeed seem to have a rather strong effect, two basic questions have not been answered: (1) whether the effects that were observed were helpful or harmful; and (2) whether the alternative approaches that were examined had any differential effects on outcome.

Effects of Differential Intervention

A simple way to analyze both the nature and differential effects of the four experimental and control programs is to examine the standardized regression coefficients (Beta weights) of the four intervention dummy variables included in the twenty-nine dummy variable analysis. It will be recalled that these four dummy variables were added to the twenty-five dummy variables representing age and class, and all interactions among them. As a consequence, the Beta weights of these four variables represent the direct effects of the four different programs, controlling for the effects of all other variables and interactions among them. The differences among these Beta weights, both in terms of sign and magnitude, will indicate whether the effects of the various programs were helpful or harmful, and whether there were noticeable differences among them.

In Table 11-7, the Beta coefficients of each of the four intervention variables are presented for all offenses combined, and for each of the three levels of seriousness in each of the four time periods. In reviewing the signs of those Beta coefficients, an important point should be kept in mind; namely, that a negative sign in front of a coefficient means that the form of intervention it represents had a *negative* effect on delinquency—that is, it helped to reduce it. By contrast, a positive sign means that the program in question was associated with an *increase* in delinquency; its effects were harmful rather than helpful. In addition, the size of a coefficient, whether positive or negative, expresses the strength of any relationship between programmatic effects and postintervention delinquency—the greater the size, the greater the relationship.

With these stipulations in mind, consider the findings revealed in Table 11-7 for the two *probation* groups. It will be observed that all of the signs for both the experimental and control groups were negative, suggesting that both tended to reduce delinquency. This is true whether one considers all offenses collectively, or divides them into delinquent acts that are low-, medium- and high-serious in nature. The effects of each program in each case were desirable. As a result, some satisfaction can be taken in the fact that positive consequences were achieved.

The degree of satisfaction must be tempered by the fact that the magnitudes of the observed effects were not great. As may be seen in Table 11-7, the 16 Beta coefficients for the experimental program ranged in size from $-.02$ to $-.12$, while those for the control group ranged from $.00$ to $-.11$. The desirable impact of each program was modest at best. The contribution that each made was far from optimum. One must hasten to add that the failure to note effects of greater magnitude may be due to the methods of measurement that were used. Such methods are in a primitive state and may be insensitive to, or even ignore, a number of other important and possibly desirable effects. Improvements in research and improvements in programming are needed.

With reference to program improvement, it is noteworthy that the effects of

Table 11-7

Standardized Regression Coefficients (Beta Weights) Showing the Direct Effects of Programs on Delinquency During Four Years Following Intervention

Time Periods After	Dependent Variables	Categories			
		Probation Experimental	Probation Control	Incarceration Experimental	Incarceration Control
1 Year	All Offenses	−.10	−.04	.01	.27
2 Years	All Offenses	−.10	−.05	.05	.36
3 Years	All Offenses	−.11	−.08	.01	.35
4 Years	All Offenses	−.11	−.06	.00	.37
	Low Seriousness	−.06	−.02	.11	.15
1 Year	Med Seriousness	−.07	.00	−.04	.25
	High Seriousness	−.09	−.11	−.01	.12
	Low Seriousness	−.10	−.04	.11	.18
2 Years	Med Seriousness	−.10	−.05	−.03	.32
	High Seriousness	−.04	−.08	−.03	.21
	Low Seriousness	−.08	−.04	.10	.25
3 Years	Med Seriousness	−.09	−.07	−.04	.32
	High Seriousness	−.02	−.04	.00	.29
	Low Seriousness	−.10	−.03	.07	.25
4 Years	Med Seriousness	−.12	−.08	−.07	.30
	High Seriousness	−.05	−.04	−.02	.26

the experimental program for probationers were consistently greater than those of regular probation. In the list of 16 comparisons shown in Table 11-7, there were only three instances in which the effects of the control program were greater. Otherwise, in the remaining 13 comparisons, the effects of the experimental program predominated. This is reflected by the fact that the median desirable effect for the experimental group was −.09, while that for the control group was only −.04.

While these differences were not great in absolute terms, the fact that they occurred consistently has important implications for evaluating the relative merits of the experimental program and regular probation in dealing with repeat rather than first offenders. In all previous comparisons of these two groups, when recidivism rates alone were the criterion, the groups appeared more alike than different. There may have been some evidence favoring the experimental program but it was slight. Therefore, one might infer that their effects were essentially the same. In this case, however, where the effects of age and class have been controlled and separated from those of intervention, the evidence suggests that effects were not the same. Instead, the desirable effects of the experimental program seem somewhat greater, suggesting that for probationers with longer histories of delinquency, that program may be somewhat more effective.

Turning now to an assessment of the effects of incarceration versus those of community programming on the two *incarceration* groups, it will be observed in Table 11-7 that seven of the 16 coefficients (44 percent) for the experimental group were negative, suggesting that some of its effects at least were desirable— e.g., were associated with a decrease in delinquency. Interestingly, the kinds of offenses on which the experimental program had the greatest desirable effects were medium- and high-serious offenses—offenses with which the community is most concerned, and for which the greatest changes are sought. Too much significance should not be attributed to this finding, since the sizes of the desirable coefficients were small—smaller than those observed for the two probation groups. The effects of the experimental program were not associated with a reduction in low-serious offenses, those that were almost entirely juvenile-status in character. Why this occurred among the more serious population of offenders is difficult to say because it had occurred among probationers assigned to the experimental program. But because low-serious offense behavior was not sufficiently affected, the Beta coefficients that reflect the impact of the experimental program on all offenses combined were slightly positive—slightly undesirable.

These particular findings clearly suggest that the impact of the experimental program, as an alternative to incarceration, was not all that had been hoped for it. Nevertheless, when compared to the impact of the incarceration control program, it appears in a much different light. The signs of the Beta coefficients for that group of boys who were incarcerated, without exception, were positive—meaning that the effects of confinement were associated with an increase in delinquency. In not one instance was a desirable effect noted. Furthermore, if one compares the sizes of the effects of this program with those of the experimental program, or with the two probation programs, one will find that they were much greater—anywhere from two, to six or even twelve times greater. The effects of incarceration were not only in an undesirable direction, but were, by far, the greatest of all effects observed.

This finding is probably the most striking of all those that have emerged in this chapter. It indicates that while the experimental community program at least had a modest impact on the reduction of ordinary and serious criminal acts, the effects of traditional incarceration were totally and highly undesirable. It may actually tend to increase further criminality.

That the finding should not be taken lightly is confirmed by the fact that it is the product of a method for assessing the differential effects of experimental and control programs that was less reliant upon group comparability than the mere comparison of recidivism rates. The reason is that by controlling for the effects of other variables, such as age and class, it was possible to isolate with greater precision the direct effects of intervention. And, when this was done, the consequences of incarceration were shown to be considerably more harmful than the consequences of community intervention. Even though the experimental and control groups may not have been totally comparable at the outset, the disparity in the effects of the two programs upon them seems to have outweighed any initial differences. The effects of the control program were much less desirable than those of the experimental program.

Summary and Implications

To recapitulate briefly, the findings of this chapter indicated that both age and social class were related independently to correctional outcome. If the independent and direct effects of intervention were to be isolated, the effects of social class and age would have to be controlled. This was accomplished through the use of a dummy variable regression analysis which controlled the effects of age and class and took account of the fact that the relationships of these two variables to the dependent variable, delinquency, were curvilinear.

When controls were exercised, it was discovered that the direct and interactive effects of intervention accounted for 70 percent of the *explained variance* derived from the model. One important objective was realized: clear evidence was provided that the effects of intervention could be isolated and that their impact was sizeable, considerably greater than the direct and interactive effects of age and class. Such evidence was the first in a series that was contrary to the assumption, long held by some, that age and class, not intervention, are the major factors determining correctional outcome. But while some question was raised about the overriding effects of age and class, the evidence to this point lacked two things. It had not indicated whether the effects of intervention were positive or negative, and it left considerable variance unexplained; that is, the total variance explained by intervention, age and social class was only about one-third of all that might have been explained. Undoubtedly, there are other factors that have great impact on outcome that were not included in the model.

As the analysis progressed, no further evidence was supplied regarding this second inadequacy. It was suggested, however, that if the dummy regression analysis, or some similar technique, is extended in the future to include additional variables, it may be possible to be more definitive regarding the sources of the unexplained variance. Research of this type is badly needed.

In regard to the effects of intervention, additional evidence of two types was presented: (1) whether they were helpful or harmful; and (2) whether the experimental and control programs had differential effects. With reference to the first, the findings indicated that the effects of the experimental and control programs for the two probation groups were helpful. Both programs seemed to be influential in bringing about a reduction in delinquent behavior. The same was true, although to a lesser degree, for the incarceration experimental program. Its greatest effects were on the deterrence of medium and high serious delinquent acts, but it did not help to deter juvenile status offenses. By contrast, the effects of incarceration were just the opposite of those of the three community programs. Not only were its effects associated with an *increase* in delinquency, but they were, by far, the largest effects observed. They were both contrary to major correctional goals, and of considerable size in their undesirable consequences.

With regard to differential effects, both experimental programs were superior to their respective controls. Although the effects of both probation programs were desirable, those of the experimental program were greater. Second, the differences in effect between the two incarceration groups were the greatest of all, due largely to the harmful effects of incarceration, but due, as well to the helpful deterrence of medium- and high-serious offenses by the experimental program. The findings provide badly needed empirical evidence of two types. First, they help to isolate both the direction and magnitude of intervention effects, and indicate that one can ill afford to write off those effects either as totally negligible or totally harmful. In some instances, they are helpful, and in others they are harmful; but in either case, they are present and should be studied. Second, this particular set provided rather conclusive evidence that correctional programming might be considerably more effective if it utilizes community rather than institutional alternatives. To be sure, improvements are badly needed in the modest effects that community programs have, but at least they are not burdened by the strong harmful effects with which places of confinement are burdened. Before the latter can even begin to produce effects of a desirable nature, harmful consequences of considerable size must be undone. Given the fact that this has not occurred throughout the long history of corrections, the evidence in favor of community experimentation is much more persuasive.

12 Implications for Future Experimentation

This chapter is devoted to an assessment of the implications of the Provo Experiment for future correctional experimentation and programming. In approaching this task, it will depart from the usual method of relying solely upon the impressions and interpretations of the investigators, but will turn as well to some suggestions from offenders. To be sure, delinquent adolescents have no magical panaceas to suggest, but their comments do reveal useful insights. Before turning to them, let us review the major theoretical issues and empirical findings that have been generated by the study. They will provide a useful foundation upon which to lay the comments and suggestions of delinquents.

Theoretical Issues

The first basic question is whether an organization like Pinehills, in comparison with more traditional forms of intervention like probation or incarceration, can control delinquency successfully, and yet provide other kinds of help for offenders as well. The question is a pertinent one theoretically because the experimental organization at Provo embodied many contradictory features.

On one hand, the new program was expected to control delinquency—clearly an "order" goal for which some forms of coercive power were used. Boys were assigned to Pinehills involuntarily and required by the court to attend. If they did not, overt punishments were sometimes used. On the other hand, the program also sought normative and utilitarian objectives for which it used noncoercive means of social control such as group decision-making and wages from an employment program. In short, Pinehills was a crossbred organization. Even though, in the absence of walls and guards, it relied primarily upon the use of group methods as a means of building and maintaining normative controls, it also used some coercive and utilitarian methods as well.

In considering the possibility that organizations of this type could be used successfully in corrections, Etzioni (1961:84-85) was not optimistic. Based upon his review of correctional research, he felt that it would be difficult to substitute normative for coercive controls, even in part. A small number of offenders might be affected positively by the exercise of normative power, but a prevailing sense of loyalty to peers among the majority would make it difficult for them to share a set of norms with, and be affected by, correctional staff members. Differences in social and cultural backgrounds, reinforced by the subordinate position of the offender, generates a high degree of alienation that does not allow the normative power of the organization to develop. For a host of reasons, the offender group tends instead to negate the acceptance of the conventional ideology and the means of intervention used by staff.

By the same token, Etzioni was pessimistic regarding the chances that a utilitarian system of rewards inherent in a work program would be successful either. Although the interest and involvement of some offenders might be enhanced, the violation of rules by the majority would still be too frequent, and in many cases, too severe to be controlled by remuneration. Furthermore, the public, even staff and offenders, are so accustomed to the idea that correctional organizations must be coercive that they virtually insist upon maintaining a climate of deprivation. Because everyone *expects* deprivation to be present, they tend to foster it. Even among offenders, there is a tendency to stress deterrence through punishment for wrongdoing rather than adherence to norms through rewards for right doing.

Finally, there are impediments associated with the general level of control that the community expects any correctional organization to maintain. Even though the following comments by Etzioni (1961:85) are meant to apply to total institutions, they apply, at least in part, to community correctional organizations as well.

One reason for the prevalence of coercion seems to lie in the level of effectiveness demanded by society or the community in which the organization is situated. These external collectivities tend to ask both of prisons and of custodial mental hospitals one hundred per cent effectiveness in controlling escapes and suicides. This requirement leads to the need to apply coercion, and to apply more coercion than would otherwise be necessary. Lindsay (1947:92) has pointed out that mores, which in other circumstances can rest on what we have referred to here as moral commitments and normative powers, require the support of coercion . . . when they are expected to hold for *all* of the people *all* the time. Even when the large majority of people are willing to comply, there are some people, all the time, and most people sometimes, who are not willing to comply. Hence, even when in general normative compliance would do, the expectation of "one hundred per cent" performance increases the use of coercion, since the deviant minority can rarely be specified with complete assurance.

Other investigators (Sykes, 1958:18 and 20; and Grusky, 1959:458) have made essentially the same point, indicating why, along with the other impediments cited above, the task of developing new organizational arrangements for corrections has proceeded so slowly. In fact, it is Etzioni's (1961:87) opinion that when attempts are made to incorporate the characteristics of different organizational types, especially normative and utilitarian, into a single organization, such as was the case in Provo, the result is not likely to be good. Wasted means, social and psychological tension, and a lack of coordination will often be the result.

These are not encouraging conclusions in light of the basic assumptions adopted at Pinehills: (1) that coercive means should be used only to reinforce basic ground rules; (2) that group techniques, stressing the use of normative power, should be the primary medium of change; and (3) that remuneration from a work program would help to solidify a commitment to conventionality among delinquents. The actual findings of the study are important as a means of shedding light upon these difficult issues.

Joint Use of Coercive and Normative Power

The first issue has to do with the consequences that were observed when an attempt was made to use coercive and normative means in the same program. If the perceptions of the delinquent consumers are considered, it will be recalled that they did not reveal the degree of pessimism expressed by Etzioni. Delinquents disliked and often resented the use of coercion in the form of unpaid work detail, and the occasional use of detention for the violation of basic ground rules. They repeatedly said that these coercive techniques had a controlling influence upon them. In their words, limited coercive methods "kept them in line." They were less inclined, as a result, to be delinquent.

This conclusion was confirmed by arrest data which indicated that, at least while delinquents were a part of the experimental organization, their delinquent acts were curtailed. The rates of arrest for both experimental groups were only about half the rate for the probation controls, and almost as low as the rate for the control boys who were actually incarcerated. It was only when length of exposure to programming was controlled that the boys in the experimental program appeared to be more delinquent than those who had been removed from the community entirely. The finding that Pinehills could afford protection to the community during the intervention period that was almost as good as total incarceration was a suprising one. As further evidence of this fact, only a small proportion of community experimental and control groups had to be eliminated from these programs because they were excessively delinquent. The implication is that delinquents did not overreact, as Etzioni implied they might, by becoming even more delinquent than they were. Yet, as important as this possibility may be, it probably does not constitute the most important finding.

Etzioni's suggestion that normative means would be unlikely to work in correctional organizations was strongly denied by offenders. In fact, the one organizational component from which they said they learned the most, and gained the greatest personal benefits, was the component in which they helped to solve problems, to make decisions, and even to impose controls. In contrast to Etzioni's conclusion, their participation in these activities seemed to reduce their sense of alienation, and to promote the development of the normative power of the organization. It was that aspect for which delinquents felt the greatest affinity. This may yet be another important reason that inprogram delinquency rates were so low.

This is suggested by the fact that delinquents also noted that the presence of a normatively oriented group mechanism in the program provided them with the means to better understand, and learn from the occasional imposition of coercive controls. Rather than representing wasted means and a lack of coordination, the exercise of both coercive and normative power in the same organization was not entirely dysfunctional. When efforts were made to demonstrate the relation between the two, and to have boys participate actively in implementing them, they seemed to understand and benefit from them.

Where some of Etzioni's comments were most pertinent, however, had to do with the possible excessive use of coercive methods. He noted that, because of the unique character of correctional organizations, people may demand higher levels of conformity from their members than from the members of noncorrectional organizations. Persons tend, in other words, to expect one hundred per cent effectiveness. When deviance occurs, there is an inclination to resort more quickly to coercive methods than would be the case in other organizations.

In some ways, that may have been true at Pinehills. As the analysis indicated, both boys and staff tended to rely heavily upon coercive methods when normative means did not seem to be working. Yet, this may have been a self-induced reaction because, contrary to the one hundred per cent hypothesis, there was relatively little pressure from the community to be entirely successful. Rather, the members of Pinehills seemed to be reacting more to the possibility that such pressures could arise than the fact that they actually did so. It is possible that had a Pinehills boy committed a bizarre crime, negative reactions would have been much greater. If so, the hypothesis may have been given a more valid test. Yet, even without it, fears regarding possible community reactions were omnipresent. This seemed to be another reason that the use of coercive means may have been overdone.

It is difficult to be certain about this matter because another issue which Etzioni did not mention has to do with the need for any open correctional organization to maintain its own sense of social solidarity. There is little security for anyone unless the organization possesses a sense of community. In the Pinehills case, a few persistently deviant individuals were a threat to all the boys who were going through the difficult trials of trying to change themselves. They seemed to require a great deal of certainty and social support—more than people in other organizations normally do where the stakes are not so high. When any boy seemed to threaten the security and welfare of others by continuing to get into trouble, reactions were likely to be severe. This reaction has also been common in other organizations such as Synanon or other self-help programs where addicts and offenders play key roles.

The problem was exacerbated by the general absence of culturally sanctioned, organizational rewards for prosocial behavior. While all kinds of negative reinforcement were available when deviance was observed, means for the positive reinforcement for desirable behavior were harder to find. If Pinehills had had more such rewards available, perhaps questions regarding the use of coercive controls would have been less troublesome.

Contribution of Utilitarian Features

One might have expected the utilitarian features of the Provo Experiment to have fulfilled this function. Their effects were not entirely what one might have expected. The work experience, and the wages paid for it, seemed to be the least salient aspect of the program to delinquents. They felt neither hot nor cold about them. As a consequence, the amount of social control that was exercised by monetary remuneration, per se, was relatively small.

The types of work in which the boys engaged and the relatively low wages they received may have accounted for this outcome. It was not just monetary reward that delinquents seemed to be looking for. The more open they became in sharing their feelings, the more they seemed to be concerned with becoming better integrated into the youthful activities of the school and community rather than into the adult world of work. The basic theoretical assumption that what they wanted was more economic opportunity was simply not confirmed. They were young, and their reactions reflected this youthfulness.

On the other hand, utilitarian activities did serve other, unanticipated functions. One was to contribute to, and strengthen, the normative aspects of the program. When troubles with adult supervisors occurred on the job, and when delinquents were confronted, as a group, with the task of doing something about them, the result was to strengthen the normative controls of the organization. Individual delinquents were placed in charge of the work crews, and when they could not function well without the support of others, the group features of the organization became a means of providing this support. Peer rather than official forms of social control became the main source of structure.

In a sense, this was a provocative finding because most of the small group literature has suggested that task achievement and social solidarity in a group tend to be opposed. Most writers have suggested that simultaneous attempts to solve instrumental and expressive problems will not be successful. At the very least, a group will swing like a pendulum from an emphasis upon task achievement to an emphasis upon building social solidarity.

While this kind of behavior was not uncommon at Pinehills, it was our impression, at least, that the task of dealing with, and solving, instrumental problems was not always opposed, but contributed to the maintenance of group solidarity. In fact, without instrumental issues to consider, groups often tended to become insular, and to wander further and further from the realities of day-to-day life. When this occurred, boys became bored and began to question the utility of the whole operation. To them, too much emphasis was being placed upon issues that had relatively little relevance. When by contrast, they could relate the persons and happenings of the small group to the outside activities of work and other behaviors, they could not only make better sense out of what was going on, but could take some satisfaction in doing something about it. A consideration of instrumental work problems often contributed as much to the building of the normative as to the building of the utilitarian features of the organization.

The work program also helped to dramatize for the community the particular needs of delinquents. In its struggle to develop and maintain a city work program, Pinehills brought to the attention of both policy-makers and the public a set of problems that were not then being addressed. Even though the resultant changes in existing community structures were small, at least some changes were made.

In deciding whether utilitarian features had a role to play at Pinehills, it would seem that they did. In fact, they might have had an even greater impact if rewards had been related to the kinds of instrumental activities that were more salient to adolescents than was unskilled employment—perhaps more to school relationships, to relationships with friends, or to family. In that way, the normative as well as the utilitarian power of the organization might have been strengthened even more than it was.

Overall, this review has suggested that it may be possible to design new programs in which an admixture of normative and utilitarian features is used. Although reason dictates that the exercise of some coercive power may be necessary, especially where a population of serious and persistent offenders is involved, it seems clear that the heavy reliance that has been placed traditionally upon coercion and physical restraint is not entirely necessary. Evidence in favor of this conclusion is not derived solely from this particular part of the analysis, but from the long-term follow-up of experimental and control groups.

Outcome Findings

From the large body of outcome data that was provided, three major findings stood out. The first was the fact that the experimental community program seemed to be associated far less with postprogram delinquency and adult crime than incarceration. Especially pertinent was the fact that boys who had been incarcerated tended to continue to violate the law long after their period of incarceration was over, while the offense rates of boys who had remained in the community declined at a more rapid rate. By implication, the finding seems to confirm the suspicion that imprisonment results in a kind of socialization that is negative rather than poisitive, at least for a significant number of those who experience it.

The second major finding was that, when preprogram and postprogram delinquency rates were compared, significant reductions in every program were noted, even incarceration. However, these reductions were again greater for those boys who remained in the community than for those who were incarcerated. Nevertheless, the finding raised serious question regarding the long-held assumption that correctional programs do not correct. It was this question, at least, that made the third major finding an important one.

In an endeavor to determine whether the large disparity between preprogram and postprogram delinquency rates was actually attributable to intervention, the effects of age and social class upon outcome were controlled. When this was done, it was found that intervention did indeed have a significant impact. But, alas, that impact was not uniformly desirable.

As implied by the first finding, the discovery did more to indicate that incarceration clearly had an *un*desirable impact than to indicate that the experimental program had a desirable one. Nevertheless, the effects of the latter, even though smaller, were the kinds that were being sought. While incarceration was clearly harmful, community intervention had been somewhat helpful. All data seemed to indicate that efforts to improve correctional programs might be far more fruitful if they concentrated upon the improvement of community rather than institutional designs. Since the effects of the experimental program seemed to be only slightly better than regular probation, the difficulty is in deciding on the kinds of community programs. Although they might be preferable, how shall they be organized?

One way to consider that question is to examine a number of problems from the unique perspective of the offender. An examination of the difficulties he faced, even in the community-based, Pinehills program, illustrates two things: (1) the absence of an interface of that program with a number of important community networks and institutions; and (2) the resultant burden that this lack of interface placed upon the delinquent boy.

The Family

The lack of an adequate interface with community networks was illustrated, first, where the families of delinquents were concerned. When sociological theory was used in designing the Provo Experiment, it suggested that, while family problems may have been important at an early stage in the genesis of official delinquent behavior, the tendency for older, adolescent delinquents to find alternative sources of satisfaction with their peers would rule out the necessity to concentrate heavily upon family relationships. If anything, a program would be most successful if it taught the delinquent how best to deal with his family. An effort to alter all delinquents' families would be a hopeless task. A series of findings suggest that such a point of view may need some modification.

The first was a careful examination of the antecedents of delinquent behavior among all the delinquents included in this study, along with a sample of nondelinquents (cf. Empey and Lubeck, 1971a:passim). Signs of family strain were not always mediated by peer relationships, but possessed strong and direct relationships to delinquency itself. As a number of other investigators have indicated (Bordua, 1962; Monahan, 1957; Toby, 1957), these findings suggested that contemporary sociological theory may have underestimated the extent to which family problems are important to a still youthful population. If so, what should the response of the community programs be?

A few comments by delinquents may provide some clues. At the very least, they indicate the need to do more than Pinehills did to at least inform parents about what is happening to their children. As one boy said, "My mom don't know nothing about Pinehills and yet she is always saying something bad about it. It pisses me off."

Another said, "My dad thinks it [Pinehills] is punishment. He thinks it is something to get over as quick as you can. Mother thinks its a pain in the ass."

Comments of this type suggested that, not only may Pinehills have been failing to improve relations within the family, but actually could have been making them worse. Few parents ever really understood what went on in the program. The reason is that Pinehills policy was never to divert interest or power from peer group, problem-solving unless it was absolutely necessary. Yet, in those few cases where meetings were held with a boy and his parents, subsequent comments by boys reflected a different parental outlook.

My folks and I had some talks with Mr. _____. I found out they were telling me about the same thing as the meeting did. I still don't have much in common with them as far as things to talk about, but both of us feel the program has done me a lot of good.

There were also cases in which some discussion with parents was needed, not just to improve Pinehills familial relationships, but to deal with some of the hypocritical and deceitful methods parents were using to try to protect their children. They may have been making the correctional problem worse, not better.

God, Mom came to court one day and really lied for me. I didn't even know what she was talkin' about. God, I was ready to spill the beans, but I thought— 'Well, she's lyin' for me, so why shouldn't I lay out a nice neat pile of shit.' So I did.

It became clear that, as the program progressed, boys were actually gaining a greater understanding of parent-child relationships in their families than their parents were. It would seem that parents deserved the opportunity to benefit from some of the same insights. At the very least, they had the right to be better informed about the program itself. Beyond that, they might have been given the opportunity to participate voluntarily in some form of program activity, either to request and receive some kind of help when they needed it, to engage in regularly scheduled sessions, or even to act as a pressure group for Pinehills.

In the Silverlake Experiment (Empey and Lubeck, 1971b), we were amazed to find as many people as forty—parents, guardians, and all their other children—turning up for a regular group session with delinquents on a weekday night. In this case, parents and delinquents alike became problem-solvers, or at least sharers of information. By no means were the results salutory for everyone, but striking changes occurred in some instances. The voluntary response by a significant number of parents was more than anticipated.

The School

Another arena of equal, if not greater, importance, is the school. In the study of delinquency causation mentioned earlier (Empey and Lubeck, 1971a), it was found that in Utah, as well as Los Angeles, poor academic achievement was probably related more strongly and more directly to official delinquency than any other single variable. Similarly, Call (1965) and Polk and Halferty (1966) found that, while delinquency was uniformly low among boys from all social class levels who were doing well in school, it was uniformly high among those who were doing poorly. Along with the earlier findings on the family, these kinds of discoveries tend to support the opinions of Hirschi (1969) and DeFleur (1969) that marginal integration in basic institutions is more predictive of deviant behavior and associations than other antecedents. Interestingly, these conclusions were also supported, in an indirect way, by Pinehills boys themselves. It will be recalled that they expressed frequent concern over their failure to make it in school. Why, then, has not more been done to integrate correctional and school functions?

Discussions of, and attempts to deal with, educational problems were common at Pinehills. But, like most other correctional programs, Pinehills was so far removed from the school, that it could do little to affect that school itself. Efforts to deal with school difficulties concentrated upon what the individual, Pinehills boy might do to adjust to the school, not the reverse. Despite the one-sidedness of this effort, it paid large dividends. School administrators became solid supporters of Pinehills because many of the boys with whom they had had trouble for years were much less a control problem. The liability was, however, that boys' academic achievement did not improve much.

In considering what might be done in the future to correct this problem, it is clear that remedial educational programs that are far more imaginative than current ones will have to be devised. Most Pinehills boys, for example, were so retarded academically that their levels of performance were far below their actual class levels. But before considering what might be done about educational techniques, per se, consider some other kinds of issues that delinquents themselves identified. If they are correct, it would be naive in the extreme to suggest that more remedial effort by itself would be adequate.

One obvious problem has to do with the school's stratification system. The usual tendency is to assume a direct correlation between a boy's social class membership, and his status position in the school, but that seems to be an oversimplification. Shafer, Olexa and Polk (1970) found that students could be classified by their placement in two general "track positions" in the school. The first track was college preparatory and stressed the acquisition of academic skills. The second, by contrast, emphasized business and vocational training. It was found that these track positions were virtually irreversible once they were started, and that there was very little mobility between them. Furthermore, track position was found to have a relatively strong, but inverse relationship to the violation of school rules and to delinquency itself; that is, rule violations were highest among the low-track students, and lowest among the high-track students.

Although these investigators found that upper- and middle-class whites were more likely to be found in the college prep track than lower class and black students, they found that the effects of this system were largely independent of such factors as social class and I.Q. In other words, it was the tracking system itself, more than students' generic social status on their basic abilities, that seemed to be at fault.

In many ways, that same sort of pattern was observed in Provo. In this case, however, delinquents alluded to three rather than two classes of students: (1) the "pansy asses"; (2) the "good kids"; and (3) the "hoods."

In describing their reactions to the "pansy asses," delinquents provided a clear message. They wanted nothing to do with them. They were an elitist group who concentrated upon academic matters to the exclusion of everything else. However, the expression of feelings toward the "good kids" and the "hoods" painted an ambivalent and sometimes surprising picture. In simplest terms, delinquents wanted to be accepted by *both* groups.

The "good kids," delinquents felt, were solid citizens who, though they did well in school, were worthy of admiration. They were generally equalitarian, and possessed characteristics that the delinquents wished they had. Yet, delinquents also wanted to be admired by the hoods." Their approval was also important.

George: What kinds of kids would you rather have look up to you—the good kids or the hoods?

Al: I guess I'd rather have—well—I would like hoods to look up to me, but there's a lot of good kids I'd also like to look up to me.

Fritz: Who would you *rather* have look up to you more?

Al: Both.

Mel: Which one in particular?

Al: (Long Pause) It depends on which one I'm around. I can change. One minute I can be a goody-goody, and—

Fritz: —and the next you can be a greasy vandal, huh?

Al: Yeah!

This theme was played over and over, and may have illustrated Matza's (1964: 27-30) contention that delinquents are "drifters," wed neither to a delinquent nor a conventional self-image. It would imply that they do not feel strongly about either alternative. On the other hand, the theme may suggest that delinquents are highly ambivalent about their status, as Cohen (1955:13) has suggested. If this is so, delinquents may not be drifters at all, but may be persons who feel rather strongly about their ties to both delinquent and nondelinquent groups. They simply have not resolved their ambivalence fully in favor of either group.

Whatever the interpretation, it seemed that Pinehills delinquents were well aware of both conventional and delinquent expectations and, depending upon circumstance, wanted to appear to adhere to the appropriate set. In some cases, they liked the attention they got from being deviant; in others, they appreciated the approbation of successful students.

Mark: Hey, Phil, what friends are most treasured by you—the ones you win by fightin' an' bein' the big tough guy, or the ones you make by goin' through your school work?

Phil: I really couldn't say. It used to be about the only way I could get friends was to show I was big an' tough. Even the teachers would start smilin' sometimes when I was the big smart ass. But I've made a lot of friends with good kids too.

Sully: Why do you call them "good" kids?

Sandy: Do you think they're better 'n you, or somethin' like that?

Phil: Yeah, I think they are.

Sandy: Why do you think they are?

Phil: 'Cause they can read a lot better'n me, an' get a lot better grades than I can.

Sully: So you think kids that make higher grades an' that are better than you.

Phil: I look up to them kids.

In terms of its implications for corrections, this dialogue suggest that the basic socializing institutions have not succeeded in providing delinquent boys with sufficient rewards for making a stronger and more exclusive commitment to conventional expectations. While they may look up to "good kids," they still have an affinity for the rewards that a deviant status provides.

Sam: M._____, my history teacher, still thinks I'm gettin' in trouble more than anybody in the school. The other day he was givin' us a lecture on how bad we was, an' he said, 'Can I use you as an example?' He said he couldn't understand kids like me.

Rocky: He said it like *that*?

Mac: Did you care?

Sam: I said, 'I don't care.'

Charlie: Well, then, how did it make you feel when Mr._____used you for an example.

Sam: I guess it really made me feel kinda good.

Tom: God! It seems to me it would make you feel bad.

Mac: I think Sam still likes people to look up to him for bein' the big, bad hood.

Sam: *Sometimes* I do.

Even though it appears that delinquents like Sam have not really won in either the conventional or deviant games, they seem to feel that they should continue playing in both. Perhaps feeling that they are not successful in winning the conventional game, they retain a series of side bets in the deviant one. If this is the case, it reaffirms the notion suggested above that they have not experienced sufficient rewards for conventional behavior to cause them to give up their gambling behavior. At the same time, it also illustrates a major weakness of the Pinehills program.

Because Pinehills was separated largely from the school and the adolescent world of which it is comprised, it was unable to affect a social context that was of great significance to delinquent boys. It simply did not have as much influence as it might in helping them to stop gambling, and to invest greater energies in winning the conventional game. That is why Pinehills might have had greater impact had it been tied more closely to the school rather than to the adult world of work. While it is difficult to generalize about such matters, the evidence was sufficiently compelling to suggest that if a second experiment were to be conducted in the same community, efforts would be made to make it a part of, not separate from, the school. Were that done, delinquents might have received greater help in making up their minds.

The following kinds of features might be encouraged in such a program. First, the emphasis would be upon educational and general adolescent adjustment, not simply upon "correcting" law violators. Second, funding would be sought so that the limited resources of the school could be expanded considerably. Most schools are now in serious financial trouble, and need additional resources if they are to assist in remedying the delinquency problem. Third, the utilitarian goals of the program would be educational rather than occupational. The principles of learning theory and contingency reinforcement could bolster an effort to help delinquents do better by increasing their academic and vocational skills.

In a similar experiment conducted by Cohen (1968), and Cohen, et al. (1968), the following kinds of steps were taken. Each boy's educational program was based upon the results of a large series of tests given not only upon his arrival, but throughout his stay in the program. Depending upon his level of performance in a number of areas, his educational program was determined. He was given a set of programmed instructional material upon which he could work at his own level and at his own speed. Any evidence of progress was then elaborately reinforced through a series of instrumental means. Mainly there were points which could be redeemed in the purchase of food, clothing, radios or other goods. This would be the kinds of remuneration that would help to symbolize the importance of playing the conventional game.

A step that Cohen, et al., did not take, however, would be the fourth feature of the new experimental program. It would involve a strong normative component of the type used in the Provo Experiment. This time, however, rather than delinquents and correctional staff remaining in splendid isolation, an attempt would be made to promote daily group interaction in which nondelinquents and school personnel, as well as delinquents, would participate. By promoting the normative power of the new organization, it might be possible to reduce some of the gratifications that delinquents obtain from a retention of their former deviant status. Hopefully, they could be tied more strongly to the "good" kids, and to school personnel, so that their deviant images would no longer retain such salience for them.

If this were done, it would probably be necessary for nondelinquents, as well as delinquents, to participate in the innovative, educational components of the pilot endeavor. In other words, "good kids" as well as "hoods" should be able to benefit from it. By wedding utilitarian and normative features in this way, the overall school itself might benefit. Just as the Pinehills staff learned a great deal from penetrating discussions with delinquents, so school people might likewise have much to learn. They would then be in a better position to assist in enhancing the normative power of the school.

It is likely as well that, with some imagination, there could be other beneficial spinoffs. By working jointly, "good kids," and "hoods" might improve their own relationships. They might have helpful suggestions to make regarding the stratification system in the school so that other young people might be prevented from becoming delinquent. They might help to build better bridges between school and home, especially if parents were involved. The complex networks of home, school, friends and community might be more effectively and humanely integrated. The socializing effects of the basic institutions upon which society so heavily depends might become more functional.

In considering issues such as these, there is also the difficult question as to whether any coercive features should be built into the program. If serious delinquents like those at Pinehills were involved, it is hard to imagine how all use of coercive power could be avoided, or even if it were, whether that would be wise. Few organizations are able to operate without negative as well as positive reinforcement of some kind. Delinquents, for example, would likely have to participate as a condition of their probation. Failure to do so might result in a revocation of it. Likewise, the longevity and integrity of the program might be endangered if any individual, "good kid" or "hood," happened to threaten the program through persistently deviant acts. Organizational members, as a result, would be likely to develop and impose some control measures of their own.

Any program of the type being suggested would also be viewed with a great deal of trepidation by the community, as well as the school. And while it might provide a much improved structure than the school now actually possesses for working with the delinquents who are already there, that possibility would have to be proven. For the program to survive, it would have to be concerned with establishing its credibility in the community. To convince the parents of "good kids," that they should be permitted to interact daily with known delinquents would require assurances of some kind that at least a few ground rules would be defined and reinforced, and that "good kids" could benefit as well.

Finally, there is the "labeling" question. Many people, concerned with the welfare of delinquents, might be fearful of any program in which the status of the latter was common knowledge. It might do them more harm than good. Since delinquents at Pinehills often talked about this issue, some different ways of perceiving the issue were revealed.

Friends, Labeling and Self-Image

Certain threads in the discussion make the question of labeling, and what to do about it, a difficult one. On one hand, there was little question but that the delinquent status of Pinehills boys was well known. Virtually all their acquaintances, adolescent and adult alike, knew about it. On the other hand, Pinehills boys did not, by any means, express universal concern over this label. Instead, as indicated above, they still tended to seek the attention and approbation of both "good kids" and "hoods." As a result, a curious dilemma was presented when it came to the matter of relating the question of labeling to what seemed to be an uncertain self-image.

Stated briefly, it involved the question as to whether an attempt should be made to convince boys that they were in serious trouble, and thus run the risk of having them internalize a delinquent self-image, or to ignore their tendency to gamble and with that gambling run the risk of their being arrested again and perhaps incarcerated. The issue was not an inconsequential one.

On repeated occasions, for example, it would come to the attention of a Pinehills group that, in a very thoughtless way, one of their members was continuing to do things that could get him into worse trouble than he was already in. In an attempt to deal with this problem, the group would try to convince the boy that he was behaving in a delinquent way, and that, even if he did not see himself as delinquent, others would. But try as it might, the group was often unsuccessful in getting the individual to acknowledge this possibility. While he would deny that he really was a delinquent at heart, his actions often suggested otherwise. As a result, there seemed to be far less danger that most boys would internalize a delinquent self-image by being labeled by the group, than there was the danger that they would get into further trouble because of their continuing to gamble in a situation where the odds against them were great. If this is so, it suggests the need to rethink some of our notions about labeling, and the ease with which the individual is likely to accept a delinquent self-concept.

In one sense, it was our impression that delinquents were strikingly like most respected citizens in the community. If one asked these citizens whether they were delinquent or criminal, they would hotly deny that they were. Yet, many would not hesitate to violate traffic laws, to cheat on the income tax, or steal petty items from the company for which they worked. The only major difference between them and the Pinehills boys, therefore, would be the strengths of their assertations about their own virtuous and nondelinquent identities. Hence, in dealing with the labeling question, it would seem that the best approach would be to worry less about the possibility that one would be reinforcing a delinquent self-image, and to concentrate more upon ways to enhance a nondelinquent one.

Rather than dwelling solely upon the negative aspects of deviant behavior, as is so often done in isolated and highly insular programs, a more positive approach would require the availability of ties to conventional institutions, peers and adults so that the status of the delinquent can be changed. This requires alterations in patterns of interaction, not just changes in the personal predisposition of the delinquent. And since most of a delinquent's associates are likely to know about his deviant status anyway, the basic problem is that of getting both parties to deal openly and honestly with that status. It is only when each tends to stereotype the other, and to retain structures that inhibit the integration of the offender, that insurmountable problems are created. Hopefully, by making correctional programs a part of basic socializing institutions, some of these problems could be overcome.

Some Closing Comments

The failure of the Provo Experiment to accomplish these very things seems to represent its greatest weakness. Because it was not better integrated into important community networks, Pinehills may have left delinquents to resolve difficult problems on their own with which it could have helped. Hence, it was suggested that, by linking offenders more closely to their families, to their schools, communities and nondelinquent friends, future programs might achieve better results. However, the principle that is implied is far more important than the specific suggestions that were made.

The reason that this is so is because the application of the principle may have to vary greatly from place to place and time to time. For example, it was suggested that work with families might be important. Yet, it is unlikely that any one monolithic style for working with families would be appropriate in all instances. Existing evidence suggests that careful consideration should be given to the effects of any family's membership in different class, ethnic and neighborhood groups. Short and Strodtbeck (1965:105-6), for example, found that

> ... Negro gang delinquency tends not to be clearly *differentiated from nondelinquent behavior*—that participation in the "good" aspects of lower class Negro life (responsibility in domestic chores and organized sports activities) is closely interwoven with "bad" aspects (conflict, illicit sex, drug use, and auto theft).
>
> The literature on lower-class Negro life is rich in detail which supports such a conclusion among adults as well as children and adolescents. As compared with lower-class white communities, delinquency among lower-class Negroes is more of a total life pattern in which delinquent behaviors are not likely to create disjunctures with other types of behavior.

There was evidence throughout their study that family and community life for both adults and children was held much more in common among blacks than in other racial and neighborhood settings.

By contrast, white gang boys have been found to be more openly at odds with adults in their community (Short and Strodtbeck, 1965:105-112). They were at odds in terms of their activities, which were often seen as rowdy and delinquent, and they were unwelcome in adult hangouts and groups. Much more than among black boys, their delinquent acts represented a protest against, rather than being more nearly a part of, conventional family and community obligations. Thus, the subcultural variations that surround adult-child relations as well as intrafamily disruptions, are but one of a number of interdependent variables for which better account might be taken, and for which programs would have to vary.

Closely related to and often inseparable from family influences is the neighborhood as a socializing institution. There has long been a disagreement in the literature whether those neighborhoods with the highest rates of law violations are disorganized or organized. On one hand, Thrasher (1963:20-21) concluded that illegal acts are most likely to occur in "what is often called the 'poverty belt'—a region characterized by deteriorating neighborhoods, shifting populations, and the mobility and disorganization of the slum." On the other hand, it was Whyte's (1955:viii) opinion that the slum may be highly organized, but not in the way that conventional people conceive of social organization. The point is that the degree of organization in any neighborhood may not only vary from place to place, but be characterized by sharply different patterns as well. In some cases, the traditional institutions of socialization and control found in the larger community are ineffective. In others, new patterns are generated or are imported by the particular subcultural or ethnic groups who live there. These patterns are often conducive to behavior that is illegal and disturbing to the larger community. Such behavior may be disturbing to local residents as well, but this will depend upon the extent to which juvenile conduct is well integrated with, or is contrary to, adult expectation. Some of the behavior, as suggested above, may not be especially atypical under certain circumstances.

Virtually equal in impact to, and often inseparable from, the family and neighborhood, are illegitimate structures in the community. A number of different investigators have observed that a great deal of illegal behavior results from the transmission to the juvenile of local traditions of group-supported delinquency, some of it criminally and career oriented (Cressey, 1964; Kobrin, 1951; McKay, 1949; Thrasher, 1963).

By way of illustration, Short (1963) refers to a question posed for the staff of a YMCA gang program in Chicago: "What are the most significant institutions for your boys?" The answer from a detached worker was revealing. "I guess," he said, "I'd have say the gang, the hangouts, drinking, parties in the area, and the police." While these would scarcely be acknowledged as "institutions" in the conventional sense, there was agreement among other workers that the answer of the first worker was correct. One of them would have added the boys' families to the list, but the overall conclusion was that the most viable places for the boys were the street corners, the pool halls, taverns, and "quarter parties" in which adults as well as juveniles often participated. Relating this back to the system of formal norms, it is easy to see why law violations would be high in such an area. Many of the regular activities of these juveniles, although a normal part of daily life, were officially illegal. Without any deliberate intent on their parts to be delinquent, they were law violators by definition. Because of this fact, problems of social organization for the larger society as well as the juvenile are created. The potential for conflict is high.

Information regarding the network of informal institutions for middle- and upper-class juveniles is not so readily available, documenting a serious omission in the literature. But with the advent of the drug scene, pot parties, underground protest, and changes in sexual mores, it is undoubtedly the case that there are parallel associations on these social strata as well. Illegal structures, very much a part of the lives of juveniles, undoubtedly contribute to what is officially defined as illegal.

Given these variations, both in degree and kind of neighborhood and family organization, it is not difficult to understand why the school has become a focal point for adolescent difficulty. The school usually operates on policies set up and administered by middle-class people whose ways of viewing the world may be greatly at odds with those of the people whom they are trying to educate. Operating from a central headquarters, they attempt to impose uniform policies and practices on widely divergent groups who have little in common. These attempts result in a lack of communication, in conflict, and eventually in law violation.

But if these comments are pertinent to the school, they are no less pertinent to correctional organizations. Every bit as much as the school, they exhibit the same centralized kind of policy and decision-making, the same narrowness of perspective, and the same inability to deal in a way with their clients that makes sense to them. That is why it is being suggested that correctional programs should adhere to the principle of working right in the community. And since local communities, neighborhoods, families and schools are likely to vary, so correctional programs will have to vary in the way they operate. Rather than remaining monolithic in character, they will have to adapt to a range of different environments. Through better integration into these environments, they might then achieve a greater level of effectiveness in providing a satisfying and enriching adjustment for all juveniles.

Appendixes

Appendix: Comparability of Experimental and Control Groups

Two fundamental questions were examined relative to the comparability of experimental and control groups: (1) whether the division of the total population of repeat offenders into probation and incarceration subpopulations was warranted; and (2) whether experimental and control groups within each subpopulation are comparable.

Comparison of Probation and Incarceration Populations

The question as to whether the total population of repeat offenders should have been divided into probation and incarceration subpopulations was answered by examining their delinquent histories both in terms of frequency and seriousness.

Frequency

In Table A-1, it will be observed that the total population of 326 boys in the study had committed a large number of official delinquent acts—2,025—before being selected. The result was an average of 6.21 offenses per boy. But the data also indicate that the incarceration population contributed disproportionately to that average.

Table A-1 shows that the average number of offenses per boy in the incarceration population was 7.27, as contrasted to a mean of only 4.96 for the probation population. Thus, there was a mean difference of 2.31 offenses between the two populations. Moreover, the table indicates that, while the probation population constituted 46 percent of the total number of subjects, these subjects had committed only 37 percent of the violations. By contrast, the incarceration population, which included 54 percent of all subjects, had committed 63 percent of the violations. In terms of frequency, then, the latter population was considerably more delinquent.

Table A-1
Official Offenses of Probation and Incarceration Groups

Boys			Offenses		
Population	No.	% of Total	No.	% of Total	Mean Number of Offenses
Probation	150	46	745	37	4.96
Incarceration	176	54	1280	63	7.27
Totals	326	100	2025	100	6.21

Table A-2
Offense Seriousness Judgments

Offense	Judgments				
	City Police N = 17	County Sheriff N = 20	Juvenile Court N = 13	Total N = 50	
Aggravated Assault; possibility of great harm; use of weapons	4.9	4.8	4.5	4.7	
Child Molesting	5.0	4.7	4.5	4.7	
Forceable Rape	5.0	4.6	4.6	4.7	
Arson	4.9	4.6	4.5	4.7	
Narcotics Use (excluding glue)	4.8	4.5	4.5	4.6	
Robbery	4.7	4.8	4.5	4.6	High
Drunk Driving	4.0	3.6	3.8	3.7	
Possession of Dangerous Weapons	3.9	3.6	3.5	3.7	
Breaking and Entering; Burglary	4.4	3.7	2.7	3.7	
Glue Sniffing	4.0	3.5	2.8	3.5	
Association with Known Narcotics Users	3.9	3.4	2.9	3.4	
Automobile Theft	4.1	3.4	2.8	3.4	
Nonforceable Homosexual Behavior	3.7	3.6	2.7	3.4	
Probation Violation; i.e., Ineffective Rehabilitation	3.7	3.6	2.5	3.3	
Grand Theft (greater than $50 and excluding auto)	3.7	3.4	2.5	3.3	
Forgery (re: fictitious checks)	3.6	2.9	3.0	3.1	
Runaway from Correctional Program	3.5	3.0	2.8	3.0	Medium
Assault and Battery	3.5	2.7	2.9	3.0	
Incorrigibility: defiance of teachers, parents and others	3.7	2.7	2.7	3.0	
Damaging Property; Malicious Mischief	2.8	2.4	2.3	2.5	
Nonforceable Heterosexual Behavior	2.1	2.6	1.8	2.2	
Liquor Violations (possession, drinking)	2.4	2.2	2.2	2.2	
Fighting; Disturbing the Peace	2.6	2.0	2.0	2.1	
Runaway from Home	2.6	1.8	1.8	2.1	
Petty Theft	2.8	1.7	1.9	2.1	

Table A-2 (cont.)

Offense	Judgments			
	City Police N = 17	County Sheriff N = 20	Juvenile Court N = 13	Total N = 50
Truancy from School	2.3	1.6	2.0	2.0	
Gambling, Loitering, Improper Companions	2.2	2.0	1.5	1.9	
Driving without a License	1.5	1.8	1.8	1.7	Low
Other Traffic Violations	1.8	1.2	1.6	1.5	
Curfew Violations	1.7	1.2	1.1	1.4	
Smoking	1.1	.5	.3	.7	

Seriousness

Seriousness was examined by means of the specially constructed seriousness scale shown in Table A-2. Based upon the judgments of 50 juvenile police and court personnel, this scale ranks 31 of the most common juvenile offenses from high to low. For the purposes of this analysis, it was arbitrarily divided into three seriousness categores: "low," "medium" and "high." By design, the "low" category includes only 6 offenses, most of which apply only to juveniles, not adults—smoking, curfew violations, truancy, improper companions, and two kinds of traffic violations. The "medium" category includes 16 offenses such as auto theft, nonforceable homosexuality, grand theft, forgery, correctional escape, and petty theft. All of these, it will be noted, are offenses for which adults as well as juveniles could be tried. Finally, the "high" category includes 9 offenses, examples of which are serious assault, forceable rape, arson, narcotics, robbery or burglary. By dividing the scale in this way, it is possible not only to categorize offenses in different ways but to separate those which are predominantly juvenile-status in character from those which apply to everyone, juvenile or adult.

Table A-3 presents the findings when the offenses of the two populations are grouped into the three seriousness categories. It indicates that the incarceration population committed more violations of a high-serious nature (15 vs. 13 percent), more of a medium-seriousness nature (64 vs. 58 percent), and fewer of a low-serious nature (21 vs. 29 percent).

The findings, as a result, provide general support for the hypothesis that the two populations did differ. Not only had the incarceration population committed more violations than the probation group, but they were of a more serious type. Boys who would have been, or were incarcerated, had longer and more serious histories of delinquency than probationers. Thus, based upon court decision, their separation into two populations for the purpose of selecting experimental and control groups seems to have been a reasonable one.

Table A-3
Seriousness of Offenses of Probation and Incarceration Groups

Population	No. of Boys	No. of Offenses	Per Cents of Offenses By Seriousness		
			High	Med.	Low
Probation	150	745	13	58	29
Incarceration	276	1280	15	64	21

There are other findings which also support this conclusion, but rather than considering them twice, they will be presented in the next section which is also concerned with the comparability of the experimental and control groups within each population.

Comparability of Experimental and Control Groups

The hypothesis that the experimental and control groups did not differ will be tested by comparing, not only the delinquent histories of the relevant groups, but their ages and social statuses as well. First consider offense frequency as a measure of delinquent history.

Offense Frequency

In Table A-4, the prior delinquent histories of all boys are broken down into the four sample categories. If the samples are ranked according to mean number of offenses per boy, the incarceration control group ranks first with 7.57 offenses, the incarceration experimental group second with 6.39, the probation experimental group third with 5.35, and the probation control group last with 4.2. This rank ordering tends to confirm the point made above that the incarceration groups were the more delinquent. However, since there are some differences between the experimental and control groups within each population, the crucial question in this case is whether these differences are real, or could be due to chance.

One method of answering this question is a test of the significance of differences between sample means.[1] If one accepts the standards that are often used in social science for comparing means, those for the probation experimental and control groups did not differ significantly ($z = 1.47; p < .13$). The same was true for the two incarceration groups ($z = 1.80; p < .07$). The findings would suggest that the two sets of groups could have come from common populations and that comparisons can be made with some confidence. However,

Table A-4
Official Offenses of the Four Experimental and Control Groups

Sample Categories	Number of Boys in Sample	Number of Official Offenses	Mean Number of Official Offenses	Standard Deviation
Probation Experimental	71	380	5.35	3.16
Probation Control	79	365	4.62	2.83
Incarceration Experimental	44	281	6.39	3.36
Incarceration Control	132	999	7.61	4.65
All Samples	326	2025	6.21	4.00

since standards are arbitrary for judging comparability, and since these means are not so close as we would have liked, we felt that final judgments should be based upon an examination of more data.

If the reader will examine the deviations about the mean shown in Table A-4, he will discover that they are considerable. They illustrate the problems engendered when the offense histories of delinquents are pooled and averages calculated. They suggest the possibility that there were individuals in the groups, especially the incarceration groups, for whom the means may not be an accurate reflection. There could be a few individuals, for example, whose histories are so extreme that they seriously distort the averages. Consequently, two things were done to determine whether this was true.

The first was to test the samples for homogeneity of variance. Were the two groups in each set sufficiently homogeneous to warrant comparison or did they differ significantly? Using the variance ratio method (McNemar, 1962:247), the difference between the probation experimentals and controls was not significant ($F = 1.25; p > .05$). However, the two incarceration groups did differ significantly ($F = 1.91; p < .002$). Thus, while the test lent further support to the hypothesis of no difference for the probation groups, it underscored the importance of determining whether the lack of homogeneity between the incarceration groups was reflective of the total groups or due to the excesses of a few individuals.

This was done by providing frequency distributions of the total number of official offenses for the individuals in each group. Once their delinquent histories were distributed along a continuum, cumulative percentages at different points along the continuum could be easily compared. The results for all four samples are provided in Figures A-1 and A-2.

Figure A-1 for the incarceration groups shows the ways in which the two incarceration groups were both similar and different. While fully two-thirds of the boys in both groups were highly similar in the numbers of delinquent acts

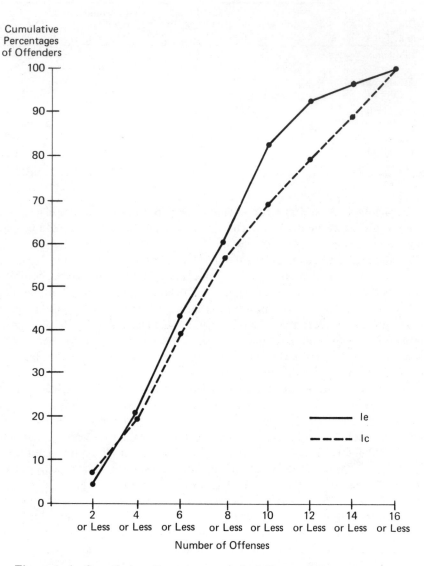

Figure A-1. Cumulative Percentages and Offenses of Incarceration Groups.

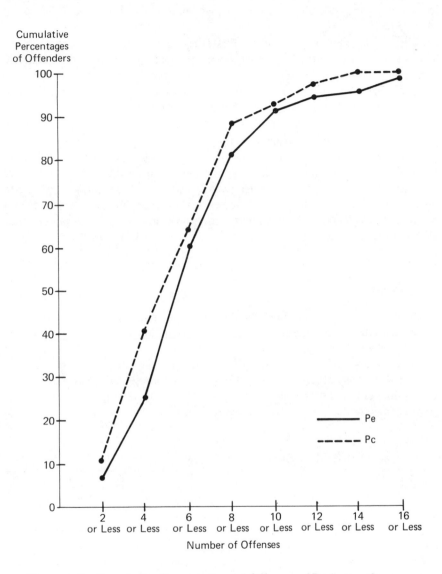

Figure A-2. Cumulative Percentages and Offenses of Probation Groups.

they had committed, about one-third of the controls had been somewhat more delinquent. Even so, tests of significance of difference between proportions at all points along the distribution indicated that none of the differences was beyond the .05 level.

The findings illustrate two things. First, they indicate that when the effects of extreme cases are controlled by distributing their offenses in terms of frequency rather than pooling them, the two samples appear more alike than different. But, second, they also suggest that careful attention will have to be paid to these extreme cases in drawing conclusions about comparability.

By contrast, Figure A-2 again shows that the probation groups were very much alike. While the experimental group had been somewhat more delinquent, the two groups were highly similar when the effects of extreme cases were controlled. The only difference of any significance occurred in the category of four-or-less delinquencies, where significantly more of the control group fell into this category, i.e., had been less delinquent. Otherwise, the two groups do not seem to pose serious comparability problems insofar as volume of prior delinquency is concerned.

Seriousness

Table A-5 presents the findings when the delinquent acts of the different groups are placed into the three seriousness categories described earlier. The first finding of note is the striking similarity between the two probation groups. The percentage distributions in each of the seriousness categories are virtually identical, testifying again to the utility of random selection as a means of controlling sample differences. By contrast, differences were greater between the two incarceration groups where random selection broke down.

Table A-5
Percentages of Official Offenses by Seriousness

Sample Categories	Number of Boys	Number of Offenses	Per Cents of Offenses by Seriousness		
			High	Med.	Low
Probation Experimental	71	380	14	57	29
Probation Control	79	365	13	58	29
Incarceration Experimental	44	281	12	58	30
Incarceration Control	132	999	16	66	18
Total	326	2025	14	62	24

The incarceration control group was more heavily involved in medium-serious delinquency than the experimental group (66 vs. 58 per cent; $z = 2.48; p<.01$), and less involved in low-serious delinquency (18 vs. 30 percent; $z = 4.39$; $p<.001$). And, although the two did not differ significantly on the most serious delinquency, the control group was also higher in this category (16 vs. 12 percent).

In an effort to trace down the sources of these differences, especially the possibility that a few extreme cases were accounting for the lack of homogeneity, we conducted a number of additional tests much like those used in assessing offense frequency.

By calculating means and standard deviations for each of the samples on the high-, medium-, and low-seriousness categories, two things were discovered. First, the findings again corroborated that which has already been shown, i.e., the high comparability of the probation groups, but the tendency for the incarceration groups to vary. Second, however, tests for homogeneity of variance indicated that a few individuals in each of the groups, rather than the groups as a whole, might be accounting for the observed differences. Consequently, an effort was made to control for the effects of extreme cases when the samples were compared.

This was done by determining what proportion of each group had committed no offenses of a given seriousness category, had committed one such offense, two, three, four, five or more. By taking this step, the precise nature of the delinquent histories of the different samples could be better understood and compared. Insofar as the probation groups are concerned, no statistically significant differences were found, either in the proportions of the samples that had committed no offenses of a given seriousness category, or had committed several. There seems to be little doubt that confidence can be placed in the comparability of these groups.

The results for the incarceration groups are displayed in Table A-6. While they do not entirely eliminate the concerns over comparability that have been raised, they do indicate that when the contributions of extreme cases are controlled, the two groups are quite similar. In only two of eighteen comparisons were differences beyond the .05 level: (1) more controls than experimentals had committed five or more of the medium serious offenses (47 vs. 25 percent; $p<.05$); and (2) fewer of the experimentals than the controls had been charged with no low serious offenses (25 vs. 44 percent; $p<.05$). Otherwise, in the remaining sixteen cases in which comparisons of degrees of delinquency in the three seriousness categories were made, differences were not significant. Consequently, if one considers the total set of findings, they would suggest that there may still be grounds for assuming comparability. Nevertheless, the fact remains that, overall, the offenses of the incarceration controls tended to be more serious than those of the experimentals, suggesting that if comparisons are made they will have to be treated conservatively and cautiously.

Table A-6
Proportions of Ie* and Ic* Groups by Categories of Seriousness

Number of Offenses	High Serious			Med. Serious			Low Serious		
	Ie	Ic	P	Ie	Ic	P	Ie	Ic	P
0	48%	42%	N.S.	9%	8%	N.S.	25%	44%	.05
1	36	30	N.S.	11	5	N.S.	32	21	N.S.
2	11	14	N.S.	16	10	N.S.	16	14	N.S.
3	5	8	N.S.	16	22	N.S.	7	11	N.S.
4	0	3	N.S.	23	8	N.S.	11	7	N.S.
5 or More	0	2	N.S.	25	47	.05	9	4	N.S.

*Ie = Incarceration Experimental
Ic = Incarceration Control

Age and Sample Comparability

There has been considerable documentation of the fact that age is inversely related to delinquency, especially during the latter years of adolescence (cf. Glaser, 1964:36; Wilkins, 1969:54-56; Bernard, 1957:421 and 444; McCord, McCord and Zola, 1959:21; Dunham and Knauer, 1954:490-496). The law violations of most young people tend to diminish as they move into adulthood. The term that has been used to describe this phenomenon is "maturational reform" (cf. Matza, 1964:22-26). Consequently, it is possible that the subjects of this study, especially the older ones, would undergo a certain degree of maturational reform, the effects of the experimental and control groups notwithstanding (cf. Dunham and Knauer, 1954; McCord and McCord, 1959). Therefore, it is of some importance to determine whether the groups were initially comparable in terms of age, and, if not, to make provision for that fact.

Table A-7 indicates that the mean age for all samples was about sixteen and one-half years. A comparison of the two sets of experimental and control groups shows that the controls were about five months older than the experimentals in each case. Although these differences are small in substantive terms, they were significant in statistical terms ($p<.05$). The reason is that, although the mean difference between the two groups was small, the relatively large size of the samples would indicate that we should expect the obtained means to be very close to each other. That they were not suggests the possibility of real rather than chance differences.

In attempting to trace down the sources of these differences, we found that there were more 17-year-olds in both control than in both experimental groups. Otherwise, differences in sample proportions at each age level were not statistically significant. Moreover, no significant differences were found between

Table A-7

Means and Standard Deviations of Ages of Offenders at Time of Assignment to Experimental or Control Groups

Samples	N	Mean Age	Standard Deviation
Probation Experimental	71	16.2	1.11
Probation Control	79	16.7	1.13
Incarceration Experimental	44	16.3	1.10
Incarceration Control	132	16.8	1.08
Total	326	16.5	1.13

either set of experimentals and controls on the mean amounts of delinquency in all age categories.

Given this overall set of findings, there is some question about the significance of the mean age differences that were observed. The age differentials between both sets of experimentals and controls were not great, and the samples with respect to age were quite homogeneous—much more so than they were with respect to delinquency. Consequently, the major issue seems to be that of determining whether the size of the age differences had a significant impact upon experimental outcome. Because these differences were relatively small, one might question whether their effects will be discernible. Nevertheless, since there may be merit in the notion of maturational reform, we might expect delinquency during the followup period to be greater among the younger, experimental groups than among the controls. Thus, steps will be taken to control for age differentials when effects are assessed.

Social Status

Socioeconomic status was the final variable considered in examining sample comparability. It was viewed as important, first, because of the heavy emphasis placed upon it in the program assumptions upon which the experiment was based and, second, because social status is thought to have an overriding effect on the life chances of a young person (President's Crime Commission, 1967; Cohen, 1955; Cloward and Ohlin, 1960, Deutsch, 1967), to affect the way officials respond to him (Goldman, 1969; Piliavin and Briar, 1964; Wilson, 1970; Reckless, 1955) and to determine in part his ultimate reintegration into the community after being processed as an offender (Reckless, 1955; Lemert, 1951). Therefore, it seemed wise to determine whether the various samples were comparable with respect to social status.

Social status was measured in terms of a ten-point scale on which the prestige of each subject's father's occupation was ranked (cf. Empey, 1956). This permitted a rather wide and detailed distribution of the samples in terms of status.

Table A-8 presents the findings. It reveals that the mean status levels of the four groups were remarkably similar. The overall mean on the 10-point scale was 3.11, with a range of only .27, and with no significant differences between groups. The population with which we are dealing, then, tends to be highly homogeneous with respect to status and concentrated toward the lower-middle, or upper-lower segment of the status scale.

Moreover, when the four samples were divided into low-middle- and high-status categories, and the mean amounts of delinquency in each category recorded, there were no significant differences, either within or between samples. Although the number of upper-status individuals was underrepresented, those who were included had been about as delinquent as their lower- and middle-status counterparts. Thus, with respect to social status, the hypothesis of no difference between appropriate samples is strongly supported.

Table A-8
Means and Standard Deviations of Socioeconomic Status Levels of Offenders Assigned to Experimental or Control Groups

Samples	N	Mean S.E.S.	Standard Deviation
Probation Experimental	71	3.14	1.29
Probation Control	79	3.08	1.28
Incarceration Experimental	44	3.00	1.49
Incarceration Control	132	3.27	1.24
Total	326	3.11	1.13

Conclusions

This analysis has suggested that there were grounds for separating probation and incarceration groups into two populations from which experimental and control groups were chosen. The incarceration population had not only committed considerably more violations than the probation population, but their violations were of a more serious nature. Consequently, the procedure of using official decision-making as a means for separating the two populations prior to selecting experimental and control groups seems to have been a reasonable one.

With respect to the comparability of the experimental and control groups, Glaser (1970:539) has noted that the value of an experimental design, when comparing different ways of handling offenders, is that it reduces the prospect of statistically uncontrolled factors accounting for the results that are observed.

This seems to have been the case where the probation groups were concerned. Randomization seems to have had the desired effect. The analysis indicated that they can be compared in assessing experimental effects without serious distortion.

The analysis of the two incarceration groups, by contrast, raised several problems. On one hand, gross comparisons between them revealed some statistically significant differences. On the other hand, the analysis also showed that many of these differences disappeared when the effects of a few extreme cases were controlled. As a result, the overall findings were ambiguous.

Since there are no universally accepted standards for resolving findings of this type, it is our opinion that an extreme position should not be taken in responding to this ambiguity; that is, either fully accepting the hypothesis of comparability or fully rejecting it. Instead, the findings suggest that the hypothesis should be treated as questionable, with subsequent analyses taking that categorization into account. Thus, rather than fully aborting any subsequent comparisons or accepting them without qualification, the procedure that would seem most consistent with the data would be that of presenting comparative followup findings, but of treating them conservatively and with reservation. If that were done, it seems to us, the advantages of comparing the two incarceration groups would seem to outweigh the disadvantages of omitting them entirely from the analysis.

There are other investigators, of course, who might disagree with this opinion. Such a disagreement, in the absence of standard criteria, is certainly legitimate.

Notes

Notes

Chapter 1
Theoretical and Operational Guidelines

1. Daniel Glaser (1958:697) maintains that the prison social system has not received the study it merits. Most writing about prisons, he says, is "impressionistic," "moralistic," "superficial," and "biased," rather than "systematic" and "objective."

2. As Glaser (1958) points out, sociologists have tended to be deterministic and to ally themselves with psychiatrists in the struggle against classical legalists and religious leaders over the free will versus determinism issue. He labels this struggle as a "phony war," involving polemics more than reality. However, he says the war is losing its intensity because of a declining interest in metaphysical issues and a recognition of the importance of voluntaristic rather than reflexive conceptions of human behavior. Contrary to their protestations, the determinists, for example, recognize that humans are aware of alternative possible courses of behavior and make deliberate choices between them.

3. Sutherland (1947:6-7), it will be recalled, maintained that "While criminal behavior is an expression of general needs and values, it is not explained by those general needs and values since noncriminal behavior is an expression of the *same needs and values*." (Italics ours.) The accuracy of the statement would hinge on the definition of "needs" and "values."

4. Except for the community aspects, the assumptions outlined and the treatment system are similar to those pioneered at Highfields (McCorkle, Elias, and Bixby, 1958). The Provo Experiment was especially indebted to Albert Elias, Director of Highfields at that time, not only for his knowledge about treatment techniques, but for his criticisms during the life of the Provo Experiment.

5. Vold (1951:360) maintains that guided group interaction assumes that there is something wrong inside the individual and attempts to correct that. He is right in the sense that it emphasizes that an individual must accept responsibility for his own delinquencies and that no one can keep him out of prison unless he himself is ready to stay out. Vold, in our opinion, is incorrect if his remarks are taken to mean that the group does not discuss groups and group processes, what peers mean to a boy or how the orientations of delinquent groups differ from that of conventional society.

6. Cooperation of this type between the Juvenile Courts and rehabilitative agencies is not always forthcoming. However, it also reflects two things: (1) the fact that the judge sentenced only those boys to Pinehills who were habitual offenders; and (2) the fact that it was his conviction that rehabilitation must inevitably involve the Court's participation, both in posing alternatives for boys and in determining the effectiveness of various approaches.

7. Gwynn Nettler (1959) has raised a question as to who perceives reality most accurately, deviants or "good" people.

8. Support for this idea can be found in a matrix developed by William and Ida Hill (1960), designed to measure the impact of group interaction.

Chapter 2
The Experimental Design

1. A four-year analysis of commitment rates from each of the juvenile court districts in Utah revealed that the judge of Utah County committed proportionately fewer boys to the State Industrial School than any other juvenile court judge in Utah. This analysis was made on the records available at the State Industrial School covering the four-year period from 1956 through 1960.

2. Since all the Utah County subjects were Caucasian, no black or Mexican-American boys from the State Training School were included in the sample (they were very few in number anyway, constituting only a tiny proportion of the population in Utah, delinquent or nondelinquent). In addition to the matter of race, it was also necessary to exclude any boys that were committed to the State Industrial School from another state or were being returned to the State Industrial School for parole violations. Since the original design was to include only individuals who would be sentenced to the Industrial School for the first time, the criteria were limited to first-time commitments in the hopes of ensuring better sample comparability.

3. Offenses were categorized into levels of seriousness by means of a specially constructed seriousness scale. The "high" seriousness category includes 9 offenses, examples of which are serious assault, forceable rape, arson, narcotics, robbery or burglary. The "medium" category includes 16 offenses such as auto theft, forgery, grand theft, forceable homosexuality, escape from a correctional institution, and petty theft. The "low" category is made up almost entirely of 6 juvenile-status offenses—smoking, curfew, truancy, improper companions, etc. The scale, and the means by which is was constructed, may be found in Appendix A.

4. Even though the percentage of cases lost is surprisingly small, some explanation of the reasons behind their not being included may be necessary. Investigation of the cases that were eliminated from the analysis shows that a number of them are accounted for by death, including several suicides. Others appear to be the product of mysterious dissappearance of juvenile court records, linked with the fact that the boys were never officially involved in any delinquent activities or crimes, subsequently, or they had moved permanently without leaving any record of such a movement in official records. In any case, we dropped those few cases only after considerable effort to try to locate them and/or their records, and in so doing concluded that their loss was due to factors

beyond our control. It should also be pointed out that we are well aware of many weaknesses in the official data regarding the delinquency of the boys that are included in the analyses. For example, we did not find it feasible to take into account the fact that some of the boys in all samples spent time in the military service during at least part of the time period that we examined. However, in most cases where individuals and/or their families moved out of state while the boys were on official probation or parole, it was necessary for them to clear their movement with official agencies, and therefore it was possible to obtain official records in new locations regarding the official delinquent activity of the individuals in the different samples. Nonetheless, we are painfully aware of the inadequacies of official records, especially over a long period of time. At the same time, however, there are few feasible alternatives for improving on our data collection and follow-up procedures.

Chapter 4
Rules of the Game: The Consumer's View

1. It is difficult to say as yet whether, in fact, delinquents are highly ambivalent, but considerable evidence has been generated showing that they have internalized conventional expectations to a high degree. Short and Strodt-beck (1965:59,74,271), for example, note that theorists may have seriously underestimated the degree to which this is the case. The implication is that prior theories may have been overly deterministic in suggesting a radical separation between delinquent and conventional systems, and that the repertoires of values and norms used by delinquents in different settings may be far more like (rather than different from) the repertoires used by nondelinquents (Matza, 1964:33; Empey, 1967:37-39).

Chapter 5
Program Salience and the Short-Run
Control of Delinquency

1. In order to determine whether these differing patterns might be associated some way with age and status differences, exhaustive tests of within-sample and between-sample differences were run. *Within* samples, there was a tendency for the probation control group to expose younger boys to probation longer than older ones, although differences were not statistically significant. The same was somewhat true of the probation experimental group where 14-year-olds, especially, were kept the longest. Within the two incarceration groups, there were no pronounced age differences.

The only pronounced age difference *between* samples was due to the fact that incarcerated controls of all ages, except 17-year-olds, were kept under supervision significantly longer than controls. However, these differences were not really a function of age, per se, but of differences in correctional policy in the two programs. Thus, age did not seem to be of much overall influence in determining length of stay in any of the programs.

With respect to social status, there were even fewer differences. The two control groups were inclined to retain lower-status and middle-status offenders longer than the experimental groups, but this was a function less of status differentials than it was of the fact that the probation and incarceration groups tended to retain all offenders for longer periods of time. Consequently, the common tendency to assume status bias on the parts of correctional agencies was not supported. Rather, the greatest difference was inherent in the difference between traditional correctional programs—probation and incarceration—and the experimental approach.

2. In order to take such a step, two assumptions are required: (1) that the observed standard deviations of the group would remain constant; and (2) that offense behavior would remain constant over time. To the extent that these assumptions are not met, error is introduced. Error is likely to be high in this case, since the number of dropouts is small. Nevertheless, an approximation is probably worthwhile.

Chapter 6
Guidelines for Group Development

1. Appreciation is expressed to Max L. Scott, presently Director of Treatment, Boys Republic, California, and formerly Treatment Director in the Provo Experiment, for his help and suggestions in the preparation of this chapter. For his own treatment of the same subject, see Scott (1965).

Chapter 8
The Struggle for Survival

1. The search for flexibility among staff members, and the desire to try a new approach, did result in the hiring of a mixed bag of staff members. In all, only four group leaders ever practiced at Pinehills. Of these, two were sociologists, one was a psychologist, and one a social worker. One had a Ph.D. degree, one a Masters degree, and two Bachelor's degrees.

Chapter 9
Program Salience and Long-Run
Control of Delinquency

1. In their discussion of this issue, Campbell and Stanley (1963:16) point out that the procedure of including dropouts, those who are not fully exposed

to program stimuli, obviously attenuates their apparent effects. Nevertheless, it avoids sampling bias and prevents distortions that may be even greater if dropouts were not included.

2. The recidivism data include all the offenses committed by a given boy from the time of his release until a maximum of four years later. Although follow-up data were collected on some boys for as long as 8 years after release, the four-year period had to become the standard because it represented the maximum amount of time information was available on those individuals who were released last at the very end of the experimental period.

Chapter 10
Relative Effectiveness: Before-and-After
Delinquency Rates

1. Dropouts were not included in this analysis, for several reasons. Their contributions to overall effectiveness rates have already been presented, and their influence assessed. The data in Chapter 9 indicated, however, that outcome rates were not greatly affected by their inclusion, since their numbers were small. For that reason, and because the assessment of experimental effects on a before-and-after basis is more defensible, if only those who were fully exposed to programming are included, dropouts were eliminated and the analysis limited to graduates.

Chapter 11
Outcome Effects Attributable to
Intervention

1. It would have been desirable to include Pearsonian r values in the analysis, since Table 11-1 suggests that the relationship between age and delinquency is linear. But this could not be done for the following reasons: (1) for each case (y values), there were 8 x values (offenses for each of 8 time periods); and (2) the ages of boys varied from 14-18 and the number of cases contributing to the means of the time periods also varied. These two characteristics of the synthetic cohorts make calculations using Pearsonian r problematic. However, the calculation of *eta* coefficients can be accomplished easily by merely treating each of the time periods as separate classes within which means are calculated. In this way, adjustments for the variation in number of cases within each time period can be made. Once this is done, the application of the formula for *eta* is straightforward. Thus, even though Pearsonian r could not be calculated using synthetic age cohorts, *eta* coefficients will serve as a good

substitute because when *r* is high, *eta* is also high. Usually the relationship is almost classically curvilinear when average number-or-offenses-per-age category is plotted.

2. The actual means of the dependent variable for each of the partitioned sets (dummy variable conditions) of each of the explanatory (independent) variables are presented in the form of adjusted deviations from the grand mean (of all categories), as well as the adjusted coefficients—adjusted simultaneously for the effects of all of the other factors and intercorrelations among them. One can then see, for example, whether those in a given treatment category have higher or lower levels of delinquency than the average of all treatments and at the same time determine whether these differences persist in an analysis that also takes into account age and social class (and logically any other variable(s) that one wanted to include in the model). In addition, the differences between the unadjusted and the adjusted deviations provide evidence about the extent to which intercorrelations among the explanatory factors required adjustment, and hence the extent to which the unadjusted deviations were biased as a result of these intercorrelations. The predicting formula permits estimations of expected values for each individual by starting with the overall average and adding or subtracting the suggested deviations for each explanatory factor, depending on which partitioned set each individual belongs for each variable. In other words, the prediction for an individual uses only one adjusted deviation from each "dummy variable" set.

The most important restriction in this type of analysis is the assumption that each explanatory factor affects the dependent variable in an independent manner, regardless of the values of the other explanatory factor(s). The assumption that the effects of various factors are independent (additive) is only an approximation of reality. Where two factors are suspected of interacting with each other but not affecting any other factors, combination variables can be formed. For example, on the next level of analysis, combination variables are formed based on joint membership in age and socioeconomic status categories. The result is a string of 25 dummy variables representing each of the combinations of age and socioeconomic status classifications taken together. Thus, for a given individual, he would have a one representing his membership in one of the 25 combination sets and zero in all of the others. This same logic can be extended to three variable combinations for treatment, age and social class. The result of forming combination variables for the three variables would be a string of 100 dummy variables (25 dummy variables for age and social class) for each of the four treatment classifications. Thus, an individual would have only a one representing his membership in a treatment, social class, and age category and the remaining 99 dummy variables for this individual would all have zeroes in them.

Appendix
Comparability of Experimental and
Control Groups

1. In using a test of significance, and investigator's hypothesis, ordinarily, is substantively based and implies a difference (and perhaps specifies the direction) between two samples. Thus, the null hypothesis, which is the obverse of the researcher's hypothesis, is stated in terms of no difference. In this case, just the reverse is true. Our hypothesis in testing the comparability of the two experimental and control groups is one of no difference, making the null hypothesis one that assumes a difference. Consequently, it is clear that the larger we set our error rate, the greater will be the probability of accepting the hypothesis of no difference (and thus affirming the comparability of the groups). However, the setting of a large error rate would also have the effect of increasing the probability of accepting the hypothesis incorrectly. If this occurs, then considerable error might be introduced into the assessment of experimental effects.

In this analysis, a relatively conservative level of significance (.05) was selected as the basis upon which to accept or reject the hypothesis. This makes it easier to reject the hypothesis of no difference if such a rejection is warranted. But since the choice is an arbitrary one, p values are also provided so that the reader can draw his own conclusions. Moreover, we will also conduct a number of different tests so that acceptance or rejection of the hypothesis will rest, not just on one measure, but on several, on the total configuration of findings, not just one or two (cf. Labovitz, 1968, for further discussion).

References

References

Chapter 1
Theoretical and Operational Guidelines

Abrahams, Joseph, and Lloyd W. McCorkle
  1946 "Group psychotherapy on military offenders," *American Journal of Sociology* 51 (March):455-464.
Adamson, LaMay, and H. Warren Dunham
  1956 "Clinical treatment of male delinquents: a case study in effort and result," *American Sociological Review* 21 (June):312-320.
Bixby, F. Lovell, and Lloyd W. McCorkle
  1951 "Guided group interaction and correctional work," *American Sociological Review* 16 (August):455-459.
Bordua, David J.
  1960 *Sociological Theories and Their Implications for Juvenile Delinquency* (Washington, D.C.: U.S. Department of Health, Education, and Welfare).
Cloward, Richard A.
  1959 "Illegitimate means, anomie, and deviant behavior," *American Sociological Review* 24 (April):164-176.
  1960 "Social control in the prison," in Theoretical Studies in Social Organization of the Prison. Social Science Research Council Pamphlet No. 15 (March):20-48.
Cloward, Richard A., and Lloyd E. Ohlin
  1960 *Delinquency and Opportunity: A Theory of Delinquent Gangs* (Glencoe, Illinois: The Free Press).
Cohen, Albert K.
  1955 *Delinquent Boys—The Culture of the Gang* (Glencoe, Ill.: The Free Press).
Cohen, Albert K., and James F. Short, Jr.
  1958 "Research in delinquent subcultures," *Journal of Social Issues* 14:20-37.
Cressey, Donald R.
  1955 "Changing criminals: the application of the theory of differential association," *American Journal of Sociology 61* (July):116-120.
Dubin, Robert
  1959 "Deviant behavior and social structure: continuities in social theory," *American Sociological Review* 24 (April):147-164.
Elias, Albert, and Jerome Rabow
  1960 "Post-release adjustment of Highfields boys, 1955-57," *Welfare Reporter* (January):7-11.

301

Empey, LaMar T., and Jerome Rabow
   1961   "The Provo experiment in delinquency rehabilitation," *American Sociological Review* 26 (October):679-695.
Erikson, Erik H.
   1955   "Ego identity and the psycho-social moratorium," in *New Perspectives for Research on Juvenile Delinquency,* Helen Kotinsky ed. (Washington, D.C.: U.S. Department of Health, Education, and Welfare), pp. 1-23.
Glaser, Daniel
   1956   "Criminality theories and behavioral images," *American Journal of Sociology* 61:443-444.
   1958   "The sociological approach to crime and corrections," *Law and Contemporary Problems* 23 (Autumn):685-697.
Hakeem, Michael
   1958   "A critique of the psychiatric approach to juvenile delinquency," in *Juvenile Delinquency,* Joseph S. Roucek ed. (New York: Philosophical Library).
Hill, William Fawcett, and Ida Hill
   1960   "Interaction Matrix for Group Psychotherapy," mimeographed (Provo, Utah: Utah State Mental Hospital).
Kitsuse, John I., and David C. Dietrick
   1959   "Delinquent boys: a critique," *American Sociological Review* 24 (April):211.
Kobrin, Solomon
   1951   "The conflict of values in delinquency areas," *American Sociological Review* 16 (October):653-661.
McCleery, Richard
   1957   "Policy change in prison management," (Michigan: Michigan State University Political Research Studies, No. 5).
McCorkle, Lloyd W., and Richard Korn
   1954   "Resocialization within walls," *Annals of the American Academy of Political and Social Science* 293 (May):88-98.
McCorkle, Lloyd W., Albert Elias, and F. Lovell Bixby
   1958   *The Highfields Story: a Unique Experiment in the Treatment of Juvenile Delinquency* (New York: Henry Holt & Co.).
Merton, Robert K.
   1955   "The social-cultural environment and anomie," in *New Perspectives for Research on Juvenile Delinquency*, Helen Kotinsky, ed. (Washington, D.C.: U.S. Department of Health, Education and Welfare), pp. 24-50.
   1957   *Social Theory and Social Structure* (Glencoe: The Free Press).
   1959   "Social conformity, deviation, and opportunity-structures: a comment on the contributions of Dubin and Cloward." *American Sociological Review* 24 (April):177-189.

Miller, Walter B.
  1958 "Lower class culture as a generating milieu of gang delinquency,"
        Journal of Social Issues 14:5-19.
Milner, John G.
  1959 "Report on an evaluated study of the citizenship training program,
        island of Hawaii," (Los Angeles: University of Southern California
        School of Social Work).
Moran, Mark R.
  1953 "Inmate concept of self in a reformatory society," (Ph.D. Diss. Ohio:
        Ohio State University).
Nettler, Gwynn
  1959 "Good men, bad men and the perception of reality" (Paper delivered at
        the meetings of the American Sociological Association, Chicago).
Nye, F. Ivan
  1958 *Family Relationships and Delinquent Behavior* (New York: John Wiley
        and Sons).
Schur, Edwin M.
  1957 "Sociological analysis in confidence swindling," *Journal of Criminal
        Law, Criminology and Police Science* 48 (September-October):304.
Shaw, Clifford R.
  1929 *Delinquency Areas* (Chicago: University of Chicago Press).
Shaw, Clifford R., Henry D. McKay, et al.
  1931 *Delinquency Areas* (Chicago: University of Chicago Press).
Sutherland, Edwin H.
  1947 *Principles of Criminology*, 4th ed. (Philadelphia: Lippincott).
Sykes, Gresham M., and David Matza Techniques of neutralization: a theory of
  1957 delinquency. *American Sociological Review* 22 (December):664-670.
Sykes, Gresham M., and Sheldon Messinger
  1960 "Inmate social systems," in *Theoretical Studies in Social Organization
        of the Prison*, (Social Science Research Council Pamphlet No. 15
        (March)), pp. 5-19.
Tannenbaum, Frank
  1938 *Crime and the Community* (Boston: Ginn and Co.).
Thrasher, F.M.
  1936 *The Gang* (Chicago: University of Chicago Press).
Toby, Jackson
  1957 "The differential impact of family disorganization," *American Socio-
        logical Review* 22 (October):505-511.
Vold, George B.
  1951 "Discussion of guided group interaction and correctional work,"
        American Sociological Review 16 (August):460.
Weeks, H. Ashley
  1958 *Youthful Offenders at Highfields* (Ann Arbor: University of Michigan
        Press).

Wheeler, Stanton
    1961   "Socialization in correctional communities," *American Sociological Review* 26, 5 (October):697-712.

Whyte, William F.
    1943   *Street Corner Society* (Chicago: University of Chicago Press).

Williams, Robin M., Jr.
    1955   *American Society* (New York: Alfred A. Knopf).

Chapter 2
The Experimental Design

Berelman, William C., and Thomas W. Steinburn
    1968   *Delinquency Prevention Experiments: A Reappraisal* (Seattle: Seattle Atlantic Street Settlement).

Bernard, Jesse
    1957   *Social Problems at Midcentury* (New York: Dryden).

Cohen, Albert K.
    1955   *Delinquent Boys: The Culture of the Gang* (Glencoe: Free Press).

Dunham, Warren H., and M.E. Knauer
    1954   "The juvenile court and its relationship to adult criminality" *Social Forces* 33 (March):290-296.

Empey, LaMar T.
    1969   "Contemporary programs for convicted juvenile offenders: problems of theory, practice and research," in *Crimes of Violence*, Staff Report to the National Commission on the Causes and Prevention of Violence, Vol. 13 (Washington, D.C.: U.S. Government Printing Office), pp. 1377-1426.

Empey, LaMar T., and Steven G. Lubeck
    1971   *The Silverlake Experiment: Testing Delinquency Theory and Community Intervention* (Chicago: Aldine-Atherton Press).

England, Ralph
    1957   "What is responsible for satisfactory probation and post-probation outcome?" *Journal of Criminal Law, Criminology and Police Science* 47 (March-April):667-677.

Glaser, Daniel
    1964   *The Effectiveness of a Prison and Parole System* (Indianapolis: Bobbs-Merrill).

Grunhut, Max
    1948   *Penal Reform* (New York: The Clarendon Press).

Lemert, Edwin M.
    1951   *Social Pathology* (New York: McGraw-Hill).

Matza, David
    1964   *Delinquency and Drift* (New York: John Wiley).

McCord, William, Joan McCord and Irving Zola
    1959   *Origins of Crime* (New York: Columbia University Press).

McCorkle, Lloyd W., and Richard Korn
   1954   "Resocialization within walls," *Annals of the American Academy of Political Science* 293 (May):94-95.
Wheeler, Stanton, and Leonard S. Cottrell, Jr.
   1966   *Juvenile Delinquency: Its Prevention and Control* (New York: Russell Sage Foundation).
Wilkins, Leslie T.
   1969   *Evaluation of Penal Measures* (New York: Random House).
Wilson, James Q.
   1970   "The police and the delinquent in two cities," in *Becoming Delinquent: Young Offenders and the Correctional System*, Peter G. Garabedian and Don C. Gibbons eds. (Chicago: Aldine).

Chapter 3
A Framework for Organizational Assessment

Cohen, Albert K.
   1955   *Delinquent Boys: The Culture of the Gang* (New York: Free Press).
   1966   *Deviance and Control* (Englewood Cliffs, N.J.: Prentice Hall, Inc.).
Empey, LaMar T., and Steven G. Lubeck
   1971   *The Silverlake Experiment: Testing Delinquency Theory and Community Intervention* (Chicago: Aldine-Atherton).
Erikson, Kai T.
   1964   "Notes on the sociology of deviance," in *The Other Side*, Howard S. Becker, ed. (New York: Free Press).
Etzioni, Amitai
   1961   *A Comparative Analysis of Complex Organizations* (New York: The Free Press).
Joint Commission on Correctional Manpower and Training
   1968   *The Public Looks at Crime and Corrections* (Washington, D.C.: United States Government Printing Office).
Goffman, Erving
   1961   "On the characteristics of total institutions," in *The Prison*, Donald R. Cressey, ed. (New York: Holt, Rinehart and Winston), pp. 68-106.
Parsons, Talcott
   1970   "How are clients integrated in service organizations?" in *Organizations and Clients: Essays in the Sociology of Service*, William R. Rosengren and Mark Lefton, eds. (Columbus: Charles E. Merrill), pp. 1-16.

Chapter 4
Rules of the Game: The Consumer's View

Ball, John C.
   1955   "The deterrence concept in criminology and law," *Journal of Criminal*

Law, Criminology and Police Science 46 (September-October):347-354.

Bandura, Albert
1969 *Principles of Behavior Modification* (New York: Holt, Rinehart and Winston).

Bandura, Albert, and Richard H. Walters
1963 *Social Learning and Personality Development* (New York: Holt, Rinehart and Winston).

Bullington, Bruce, John G. Manns and Gilbert Geis
1969 "Purchase of conformity: ex-narcotic addicts among the Bourgeois," *Social Problems* 16, 4 (Spring):456-463.

Cloward, Richard A., and Lloyd E. Ohlin
1960 *Delinquency and Opportunity: A Theory of Delinquent Gangs* (New York: The Free Press).

Cohen, Albert K.
1955 *Delinquent Boys: The Culture of the Gang* (Glencoe: Free Press).

Cressey, Donald R.
1955 "Changing the criminal: the application of theory to differential association," *American Journal of Sociology* 61 (July):116-120.
1965 "Theoretical foundations for using criminals in the rehabilitation of criminals," in *The Future of Imprisonment in a Free Society* (Chicago: St. Leonards House).

Empey, LaMar T.
1967 "Delinquency theory and recent research," *Journal of Research in Crime and Delinquency* 3 (January):28-41.

Empey, LaMar T., and Steven G. Lubeck
1968 "Conformity and deviance in the 'situation of company,' " *American Sociological Review* 33 (October):760-774.
1971 *The Silverlake Experiment: Testing Delinquency Theory and Community Intervention* (Chicago: Aldine-Atherton).

Glaser, Daniel
1964 *The Effectiveness of a Prison and Parole System* (New York: Bobbs-Merrill).

Jensen, Gary F.
1969 " 'Crime doesn't pay': correlates of a shared misunderstanding," *Social Problems* 17 (Fall):189-201.

Matza, David
1964 *Delinquency and Drift* (New York: John Wiley).

Miller, Walter B.
1958 "Lower-class culture as a generating milieu of gang delinquency," *Journal of Social Issues* 14 (Summer):5-19.

Reckless, Walter C.
1967 *The Crime Problem*, 4th Edition (New York: Appleton-Century-Crofts).

Short, James F., Jr., and Fred L. Strodtbeck
    1965   *Group Process and Gang Delinquency* (Chicago: University of Chicago Press).
Sykes, Gresham M., and David Matza
    1957   "Techniques of neutralization: a theory of delinquency," *American Sociological Review* 22 (December):664-670.
Tannenbaum, Frank
    1938   *Crime and the Community* (New York: Columbia University Press).
Tappan, Paul W.
    1960   *Crime, Justice, and Correction* (New York: McGraw-Hill).
Walker, Nigel
    1965   *Crime and Punishment in Britain* (Edinburgh: University of Edinburgh Press).
Wilkins, Leslie T.
    1969   *Evaluation of Penal Measures* (New York: Random House).
Yablonsky, Lewis
    1965   *The Tunnel Back: Synanon* (New York: Macmillan).
Zimring, Frank E.
    1971   *Perspectives on Deterrence.* Public Health Service Publication No. 2056, NIMH Center for Studies of Crime and Delinquency, U.S. Government Printing Office.

Chapter 5
Program Salience and the Short-Run Control
of Delinquency

Adams, Stuart
    1962   "The PICO project," in *The Sociology of Punishment and Correction*, N.B. Johnston, et al., eds. (New York: John Wiley), pp. 213-224.
Berelman, William C., and Thomas W. Steinburn
    1968   *Delinquency Prevention Experiments: A Reappraisal* (Seattle: Seattle Atlantic Street Center).
Cressey, Donald R.
    1958   "The nature and effectiveness of correctional techniques," *Law and Contemporary Problems* 23 (Autumn):754-771.
Empey, LaMar T., and Steven G. Lubeck
    1971   *The Silverlake Experiment: Testing Delinquency Theory and Community Intervention* (Chicago: Aldine Press).
Glaser, Daniel
    1970   "Correctional research: an elusive paradise," in *Probation and Parole*, Robert M. Carter and Leslie Wilkins, eds. (New York: John Wiley), pp. 531-544.

Klein,   Malcolm W.
  1971   *Street Gangs and Street Workers* (Englewood Cliffs: Prentice-Hall).
Lerman, Paul
  1970   *Delinquency and Social Policy* (New York: Praeger Publishers).
Miller, Walter B.
  1962   "The impact of a 'total-community' delinquency control project,"
          Social Problems 10 (Fall):168-191.
Pond, Esther M.
  1970   *The Los Angeles Community Delinquency Control Project* (Sacra-
          mento: California Youth Authority).
Rapoport, R.N., Rapoport, R., and I. Rosow
  1960   *Community as Doctor: New Perspectives on a Therapeutic Community*
          (London: Tavistock Publications).
Reckless, Walter C.
  1955   *The Crime Problem*, 2nd ed. (New York: Appleton-Century-Crofts).
Street, David, Robert O. Vinter, and Charles Perrow
  1966   *Organization for Treatment* (New York: Free Press).
Vasoli, Robert H.
  1970   "Some reflections on measuring probation outcomes," in *Probation
          and Parole*, Robert M. Carter and Leslie Wilkins, eds. (New York: John
          Wiley), pp. 327-341.

Chapter 6
Guidelines for Group Development

Cohen, Albert K.
  1959   "The study of social disorganization and deviant behavior," in *Sociol-
          ogy Today*, Robert K. Merton, Leonard Broom and Leonard Cottrell,
          Jr., eds. (New York: Harpers Torch).
Empey, LaMar T., and Steven G. Lubeck
  1971   *The Silverlake Experiment: Testing Delinquency Theory and Com-
          munity Intervention* (Chicago: Aldine-Atherton).
Gruner, LeRoy
  1972   "A Study of Group Development in Purposive Groups" (Diss. Los
          Angeles: University of Southern California).
Klein, Malcolm W., and Lois Y. Crawford
  1967   "Groups, gangs and cohesiveness," *Journal of Research in Crime and
          Delinquency* 3 (January):63-75.
Martin, E.A., and William F. Hill
  1957   "Toward a theory of group development," *International Journal of
          Group Psychotherapy* VIII:20-30.
Scott, Max L.
  1965   "Group   Development: An   Exploratory   Study   of   Small   Group

Growth Patterns," (Master's Thesis. Utah: Department of Sociology, Brigham Young University).

Short, James F., Jr., and Fred L. Strodtbeck
  1965 *Group Process and Gang Delinquency* (Chicago: University of Chicago Press).

Chapter 8
The Struggle for Survival

Empcy, LaMar T., and Steven G. Lubeck
  1971 *The Silverlake Experiment: Testing Delinquency Theory and Community Intervention* (Chicago: Aldine-Atherton).
Klein, Malcolm W.
  1971 *Street Gangs and Street Workers* (Englewood Cliffs: Prentice-Hall).
Miller, Walter B.
  1958 "Interinstitutional conflict as a major impediment to delinquency prevention," *Human Organization* 17, 3 (Fall):20-23.
  1962 "The impact of a 'total-community' delinquency control project," *Social Problems* 10 (Fall):168-91.
Miller, Walter B., Rainer C. Baum and Rosetta McNeil
  1968 "Delinquency prevention and organizational relations," Chapter in *Controlling Delinquents*, Stanton Wheeler, ed. (New York: John Wiley).
Smith, Robert L.
  1972 *A Quiet Revolution: Probation Subsidy* (Washington, D.C.: U.S. Government Printing Office).

Chapter 9
Program Salience and Long-Run Control of Delinquency

Adams, Stuart
  1970 *A Comparative Study of Recidivism Rates in Six Correctional Systems* (District of Columbia: Department of Corrections), Research Report No. 21.
California Legislature
  1969 "Analysis of the budget bill of the State of California for the fiscal year July 1, 1968 to June 30, 1969."
Campbell, Donald T., and Julian C. Stanley
  1963 *Experimental and Quasi-Experimental Designs for Research* (Chicago: Rand-McNally).
Costner, Herbert L.
  1968 "New approaches to the control of juvenile delinquency" (Paper

submitted to the National Commission on the Causes and Prevention of Violence).

Eichman, Charles J.
1969 *Issue on Youth Crime and Population* (Tallahassee: Florida Division of Corrections), Research Study 69-2.

Empey, LaMar T., and Steven G. Lubeck
1971 *The Silverlake Experiment: Testing Delinquency Theory and Community Intervention* (Chicago: Aldine-Atherton).

England, Ralph
1957 "What is responsible for satisfactory probation and post-probation outcome?" *Journal of Criminal Law, Criminology and Police Science* 47 (March-April):667-677.

Glaser, Daniel
1964 *The Effectiveness of a Prison and Parole System* (Indianapolis: Bobbs-Merrill).

Grunhut, Max
1948 *Penal Reform* (New York: Clarendon Press).

Hood, Roger and Richard Sparks
1970 *Key Issues in Criminology* (New York: McGraw-Hill).

Jesness, Carl F.
1970 "The Preston typology study," *Youth Authority Quarterly* 23 (Winter):26-38.

Kassebaum, Gene, David Ward and Dan Wilner
1971 *Prison Treatment and Its Outcome* (to be published by John Wiley).

Lerman, Paul
1968 "Evaluating the outcome of institutions for delinquents," *Social Work* (July).

Lerman, Paul (ed.)
1970 *Delinquency and Social Policy* (New York: Praeger).

Palmer, Theodore B., and Marguerite Q. Warren
1967 Community Treatment Project, CTP Research Report, No. 8, Part I (Sacramento: California Youth Authority).

Robison, James and Gerald Smith
1971 "The effectiveness of correctional programs," *Crime and Delinquency* 17 (January):67-80.

Seckel, Joachim M.
1965 "Experiments in group counseling at two youth authority institutions," (Sacramento: California Youth Authority), Research Report No. 46.

Stephenson, Richard M., and Frank Scarpitti
1967 *The Rehabilitation of Delinquent Boys* (New Jersey: Rutgers University).

Street, David
  1965 "The inmate group in custodial and treatment settings," *American Sociological Review* 30 (February):40-55.
Street, David, Robert D. Vinter and Charles Perrow
  1966 *Organization for Treatment: A Comparative Study of Institutions for Delinquents* (New York: Free Press).
Warren, Marguerite Q.
  1964 "An experiment in alternatives to incarceration for delinquent youth: recent findings in the community treatment project." Correction in the Community: Alternatives to Incarceration. (Sacramento: Board of Corrections) Monograph No. 4 (June):39-50.
  1968 "The case for differential treatment of delinquents," Mimeographed (Sacramento: Center for Training in Differential Treatment).
Warren, Marguerite, and Theodore B. Palmer
  1966 *The Community Treatment Project After Five Years* (Sacramento: California Youth Authority).
Weeks, H. Ashley
  1958 *Youthful Offenders at Highfields* (Ann Arbor: University of Michigan Press).
Wisconsin State Department of Public Welfare
  1966 *Testing Delinquency Classifications* (Madison: Bureau of Research Bulletin C-13).

Chapter 10
Relative Effectiveness: Before-and-After
Delinquency Rates

Campbell, Donald T., and Julian C. Stanley
  1963 *Experimental and Quasi-Experimental Design for Research* (Chicago: Rand-McNally).
Glaser, Daniel
  1964 *The Effectiveness of a Prison and Parole System* (Indianapolis: Bobbs-Merrill).
Wilkins, Leslie T.
  1969 *Evaluation of Penal Measures* (New York: Random House).

Chapter 11
Outcome Effects Attributable to Intervention

Baggaley, Andrew R.
  1964 *Intermediate Correlation Methods* (New York: John Wiley and Sons).

Blalock, Herbert M.
    1960   *Social Statistics* (New York: McGraw-Hill).
Blau, Peter, and Otis Duncan
    1967   *The American Occupational Structure* (New York: John Wiley and
            Sons).
Bryant, Edward C.
    1960   *Statistical Analysis* (New York: McGraw-Hill).
Curtis, R.F., D.M. Timbers, and E.F. Jackson
    1967   "Prejudice and urban social participation," *American Journal of Sociol-
            ogy* LXXIII, 2 (September):235-244.
Efroymson, M.A.
    1960   "Multiple regression analysis," in *Mathematical Methods for Digital
            Computers*, Anthony Ralston and Herbert Will, eds. (New York: John
            Wiley and Sons), pp. 191-203.
Empey, LaMar T.
    1956   "Social class and occupational aspiration: a comparison of absolute and
            relative measurement," *American Sociological Review* 21 (December):
            703-709.
Empey, LaMar T., and Steven G. Lubeck
    1971   *Explaining Delinquency: Construction, Test and Reformulation of a
            Sociological Theory* (Lexington, Mass.: D.C. Heath and Company).
Ezekiel, Mordecai
    1941   *Methods of Correlation Analysis* (New York: John Wiley and Sons).
Galle, O.R., and K.E. Taeuber
    1966   "Metropolitan migration and intervening opportunities," *American
            Sociological Review* XXXI, 1 (February):5-13.
Guilford, J.P.
    1956   *Fundamental Statistics in Psychology and Education* (New York:
            McGraw-Hill).
Gujarati, D.
    1970a   "Use of dummy variables in testing for equality between sets of
            coefficients in linear regressions: a generalization," *American Statisti-
            cian* 24, 5 (December):18-22.
    1970b   "Use of dummy variables in testing for equality between sets of
            coefficients in two linear regressions: a note," *American Statistician*
            24, 4 (February):50-52.
Hoel, Paul G.
    1962   *Introduction to Mathematical Statistics*, 3rd ed. (New York: John
            Wiley and Sons).
Kelley T.L.
    1924   *Statistical Methods* (New York: Macmillan).
Mandel, John
    1964   *The Statistical Analysis of Experimental Data* (New York: John Wiley
            and Sons).

McNemar, Quinn
    1962 *Psychological Statistics*, 3rd ed. (New York: John Wiley and Sons).
Morgan, David, and Brazer Choen
    1962 *Income and Welfare in the United States* (New York: McGraw-Hill).
Suits, D.B.
    1957 "Use of dummy variables in regression equations," *Journal of the American Statistical Association* LII (December):548-551.
Treiman, D.J.
    1966 "Status discrepancy and prejudice," *American Journal of Sociology* LXXI, 6 (May):651-664.
Walker, Helen M., and Joseph Lev
    1953 *Statistical Inference* (New York: Henry Holt and Company).

Chapter 12
Implications for Future Experimentation

Bordua, David J.
    1962 "Some comments on group theories of delinquency," *Sociological Inquiry* XXXII (Spring):245-260.
Call, Donald J.
    1965 "Frustration and noncommitment" (Ph.D. diss. Eugene, Ore.: Department of Sociology, University of Oregon).
Cohen, Albert K.
    1955 *Delinquent Boys: The culture of the gang* Glencoe: The Free Press.
Cohen, Harold L.
    1968 "Educational therapy: the design of learning environments," *Research in Psychotherapy* 3:21-53.
Cohen, Harold L., James A. Filipezak, et al.
    1968 "Case II: model project," *Research in Psychotherapy*, 3:42-53.
Cressey, Donald R.
    1964 *Delinquency, Crime and Differential Association* (The Hague: Martinus Nijhoff).
DeFleur, Lois B.
    1969 "Alternative strategies for the development of delinquency theories applicable to other cultures," *Social Problems* 17 (Summer):30-39.
Empey, LaMar T., and Steven G. Lubeck
    1971a *Explaining Delinquency* (Lexington, Mass.: Heath-Lexington Books).
    1971b *The Silverlake Experiment* (Chicago: Aldine-Atherton).
Etzioni, Amitai
    1961 *A Comparative Analysis of Complex Organizations* (New York: The Free Press).
Grusky, Oscar
    1959 "Role conflict in organization: a study of prison camp officials," *Administrative Science Quarterly* 3:452-472.

Hirschi, Travis
  1969   *Causes of Delinquency* (Berkeley: University of California Press).
Kobrin, Solomon
  1951   "The conflict of values in delinquency areas," *American Sociological Review* 16 (October):653-661.
Lindsay, A.D.
  1947   *The Democratic State* (London: Oxford University Press).
Matza, David
  1964   *Delinquency and Drift* (New York: John Wiley and Sons).
McKay, Henry D.
  1949   "The neighborhood and child conduct," *Annals of the American Academy of Political and Social Science* 261 (January).
Monahan, Thomas P.
  1957   "Family status and the delinquent child: a reappraisal and some new findings," *Social Forces* 35 (March):257.
Polk, Kenneth, and David S. Halferty
  1966   "Adolescence, commitment and delinquency," *Journal of Research in Crime and Delinquency* 4 (July):82-96.
Shafer, Walter E., Carol Olexa, and Kenneth Polk
  1970   "Programmed for social class: tracking in high school," *Transaction* 7 (October):39-46.
Short, James F., Jr.
  1963   "Street corner groups and patterns of delinquency: a progress report," *American Catholic Sociological Review* 24 (Spring):13-32.
Short, James F., Jr., and Fred L. Strodtbeck
  1965   *Group Process and Gang Delinquency* (Chicago: University of Chicago Press).
Sykes, Gresham M.
  1958   *The Society of Captives* (Princeton: Princeton University Press).
Thrasher, Frederic M.
  1963   *The Gang*, rev. ed. (Chicago: University of Chicago Press).
Toby, Jackson
  1957   "The differential impact of family disorganization," *American Sociological Review* 22 (October):505-515.
Whyte, William F.
  1955   *Street Corner Society* (Chicago: Chicago University Press).

Appendix
Comparability of Experimental and Control Groups

Bernard, Jesse
  1957   *Social Problems at Midcentury* (New York: Dryden).

Cloward, Richard A., and Lloyd E. Ohlin
   1960   *Delinquency and Opportunity: A Theory of Delinquent Gangs* (New York: Free Press).
Cohen, Albert K.
   1955   *Delinquent Boys: The Culture of the Gang* (Glencoe: Free Press).
Deutsch, Martin, and Associates
   1967   *The Disadvantaged Child* (New York: Basic Books).
Dunham, Warren H., and M.E. Knauer
   1954   "The juvenile court and its relationship to adult criminality," *Social Forces* 33 (March):290-296.
Empey, LaMar T.
   1956   "Social class and occupational aspiration: a comparison of absolute and relative measurement," *American Sociological Review* 21 (December): 703-709.
Glaser, Daniel
   1964   *The Effectiveness of a Prison and Parole System* (Indianapolis: Bobbs-Merrill).
Glaser, Daniel
   1970   "Correctional research; an elusive paradise," in *Probation and Parole*, Robert M. Carter and Leslie T. Wilkins, eds. (New York: John Wiley), pp. 531-544.
Goldman, Nathan
   1969   "The differential selection of juvenile offenders for court appearance," in *Crime and the Legal Process*, William J. Chambliss, ed. (New York: McGraw-Hill), pp. 264-290.
Labovitz, Sanford
   1968   "Criteria for selecting a significance level: a note on the sacredness of .05," *American Sociologist* 3 (August):220-222.
Lemert, Edwin M.
   1951   *Social Pathology* (New York: McGraw-Hill).
Matza, David
   1964   *Delinquency and Drift* (New York: John Wiley).
McCord, Joan, and William McCord
   1959   "A follow-up report on the Cambridge-Somerville youth study," *Annals of the American Academy of Political and Social Science* 336 (March):89-96.
McCord, William, Joan McCord and Irving Zola
   1959   *Origins of Crime* (New York: Columbia University Press).
McNemar, Quinn
   1962   *Psychological Statistics* (New York: John Wiley and Sons, Inc.).
Piliavin, Irving and Scott Briar
   1964   "Police encounters with juveniles," *American Journal of Sociology* 70 (September):206-214.

President's Commission on Law Enforcement and Administration of Justice.
  1967   *Task Force Report: Juvenile Delinquency* (Washington, D.C.: United States Government Printing Office).
Reckless, Walter C.
  1955   *The Crime Problem* (New York: Appleton-Century-Crofts).
Wilkins, Leslie T.
  1969   *Evaluation of Penal Measures* (New York: Random House).
Wilson, James Q.
  1970   "The police and the delinquent in two cities," in *Becoming Delinquent: Young Offenders and the Correctional System*, Peter G. Garabedian and Don C. Gibbons, eds. (Chicago: Aldine), pp. 111-117.

Author Index

317

Subject Index

About the Authors

LaMar T. Empey received his Ph.D. in sociology from Washington State University. He is a Professor and recent past Chairman of the Sociology Department at the University of Southern California. Dr. Empey is the Associate Director for Research at the Gerontology Center, USC; has been Director of the Youth Studies Center, University of Southern California; Director of the Provo Experiment; Director of the Silverlake Experiment; and visiting professor of criminology at the University of California, Berkeley. He has served as a consultant to the President's Commission on Law Enforcement and Administration of Justice, to the President's Committee on Juvenile Delinquency and Youth Crime and to other commissions of a similar nature. Professor Empey has contributed numerous articles to the scientific literature. His books include: *The Silverlake Experiment* and *Explaining Delinquency*, with Professor Steven G. Lubeck as coauthor; *Alternatives to Incarceration*; and (as coauthor) *The Time Game: Two Views of a Prison.*

Maynard L. Erickson received his Ph.D. from Washington State University. He is presently Associate Professor of Sociology at the University of Arizona, Tucson. He served as the Research Director at the Provo Experiment. Professor Erickson has published primarily on the topics of juvenile delinquency and criminology, particularly concerning the measurement of delinquency, but has also contributed to the growing literature on methodology in computer applications to sociological research.